' ibrai

Sacred Dialogues

Christianity and Native Religions in the Colonial Americas 1492-1700

By Nicholas Griffiths

ISBN 978-1-84753-171-1

Cover image: Codex Azcatitlan, Bibliothèque Nationale de France

Maps by Sue Grice.

Printed in Great Britain.

Acknowledgments: I would like to express my warmest thanks to
Fernando Cervantes, Trevor Dadson, Sabine MacCormack and Evelyn
Schlatter for their kind consideration of the manuscript, and for
suggesting many improvements. I would also like to thank John
Waddilove for many valuable suggestions for making the manuscript
more accessible to a broader readership. Finally, I would like to thank
David Brading for inspiring my interest and for providing the best
model of what a historian should be.

Note on publication: At the risk of perplexing colleagues, I have
published this book in this format in order to keep the cost relatively
low for the reader; in order to make the work accessible to readers who
might not come across it or consider buying it if it were published with
a more specialist press; in order to enable subsequent editions (perhaps
incorporating regions of the Americas not covered here yet) to be
produced without undue delay; and in order to keep the work in print.
Low-cost print-on-demand for serious, scholarly work is a vital new
venture, which I am confident will grow in future, and I wish to
express my commitment to this endeavour by publishing my work in
this format.

Contents

Introduction

A Spanish conquistador who posed as a sorcerer and cured native Americans as he trekked across an unknown wilderness; a French Jesuit who conjured rain clouds in order to impress his indigenous flock with the potency of Christian magic; a Puritan minister who healed a native chief in order to win him for God; a Mexican noble who was burned at the stake for resisting the gentle Franciscan friars; an Andean chief who was haunted by nightmares in which his native gods did battle with the Christian Father; a Huron magician who vied with French missionaries over spirits of the night in a shaking tent ceremony. These are a few of the individuals whose struggles are brought to life in the pages that follow. Their experiences, among others, reveal what happened when Christianity came into contact with Native American religions in three distinct regions of sixteenth- and seventeenth-century colonial America: Spanish, French and English.

Sacred Dialogues is intended to provide an accessible synthesis of the findings of a large number of quality specialist works on this subject, particularly (but not exclusively) those published in the last twenty to thirty years. It is not intended as an institutional history of the church or of missions in general, nor is it a comprehensive history of Christianity in the Americas, nor of the history of Native American religions. Rather it is a study of the interaction of religions when Europeans and indigenous peoples came into contact with each other. Drawing on material from both American continents in the early colonial era, its examples are intended to be representative, not exhaustive. The study does not attempt to provide a total (but unmanageable) history of the relations between Christianity and native religions in every region through two centuries. Much has been omitted. I apologise in advance to readers who might look, with disappointment, for coverage of Portuguese America, the Caribbean, Venezuela and Colombia, California, or British America outside New England. In his recent work *Empires of the Atlantic World: Britain and Spain in America, 1492-1830*, J.H. Elliott observes that hard choices are inevitable in a work that ranges so widely over time and space.

Although restricted to two centuries, the present work encompasses three regions, for which reason many omissions are necessary if it is not to become impossibly unwieldy. Perhaps the most glaring omission is Portuguese America, which I have excluded (except with reference to the Tupi-Guarani peoples) mainly because of a less extensive bibliography (especially in English) referring to the subject of my book. This has been my main criterion for omitting the other areas listed above. Although there have been publications on missionary work in these areas, not enough has yet been written on the specific issue of the interaction of Christianity and native religions there.

The greater attention devoted here to Spanish America in comparison with French or English America may be attributed to three factors: first, Spanish America's greater geographical extent, its larger number of ethnic groups and their greater social and cultural variety; second, the region's earlier and longer experience of Christian-native religious interaction, beginning a full century before similar sustained developments in French and English America; and third, the sheer quantity of research conducted on religious encounters in the region. The object of analysis is the formative years of Christian-native interactions, and so the time period is restricted to the sixteenth and seventeenth centuries. The eighteenth century is not covered in these pages since the mature years of religious interaction require a separate study. Since it is a work of synthesis, this book uses principally secondary sources, but also draws on primary sources, including mission reports, judicial trials, tracts and treatises, which are quoted in translation.

Part One is devoted to Spanish America, and Part Two to French and English America. Part One opens with Mesoamerica (Middle America). At the beginning of the sixteenth century, the hegemonic power was the Mexica who, from their capital city, Tenochtitlan (the site of present-day Mexico City), held sway over a domain (known to history as the Aztec Empire) which encompassed much of the south and southeast of present-day Mexico, and included not only fellow Nahuas (those who spoke the language Nahuatl), but also speakers of other languages, such as the Mixtec (or Ñudzahui) of the Oaxaca region, and the Mayas of Yucatán and Guatemala. These were the first peoples on the American mainland to be introduced to Christianity in a serious and sustained fashion by Europeans.

Part One continues with the peoples of the Andes, principally the Incas of Cusco but also their Quechua-speaking and Aymara-speaking subject peoples, such as the Lupaqa in the Lake Titicaca region; these peoples constituted the second principal arena for Christian-native religious interaction in Spanish America. The large number of ethnic kingdoms and tribal groupings within the Aztec and Inca domains came to constitute the core regions of the Spanish colonial realm – the Viceroyalties of New Spain (as Spaniards called Central Mexico) and Peru, respectively.

Part One also considers the many other ethnic groups that remained outside the confines of these indigenous empires and who similarly, under Spanish rule, remained on the frontier of expansion. They included, for example, in Mesoamerica, the Yaquis, the Tepehuanes, and the Tarahumaras, who inhabited the northwest of present-day Mexico (the states of Sinaloa and Sonora); and, in South America, the Mojos who inhabited the region near Santa Cruz de la Sierra, in present-day Bolivia, and the Guarani who inhabited present-day eastern Paraguay, north central Argentina, and southern Brazil. The social, economic, political, and religious conditions of these frontier regions differed significantly from those of the core regions of Spanish America, and therefore they will be treated separately. Constraints of space require many native peoples in Spanish America to be omitted from this survey – for example, those of the Caribbean, Venezuela and Colombia, California, New Mexico and Florida.

Part Two examines the interaction of religions in Francophone and Anglophone North America. Those who came into contact with Christianity through French and English missionaries include the Iroquois and the Hurons in the Great Lakes region, and the Massachusetts and Narragansetts on the coast.

The responsibility for evangelizing (proclaiming the gospel to those unfamiliar with it) the native inhabitants of the New World fell primarily, in regions of Catholic activity, to missionaries of three religious orders - the Franciscans, the Dominicans, the Augustinians - and to the Society of Jesus (Jesuits). Of these, the first three, whose members were known as friars, comprised the so-called mendicant orders, which is to say, those required to live off the alms of the faithful since they renounced all individual and collective property. (Borges 1992, 1:214) They established their primacy in the Americas as a consequence of their early arrival (the Franciscans in 1493; the Dominicans in 1510; the Augustinians in 1533) and the absence of a secular ecclesiastical hierarchy. It should be explained that the Catholic clergy was divided into two branches, secular and regular. The secular branch lived in the world (*saeculum*); it was composed of those priests who took vows of ordination, normally administered a parish, were under the authority of the archbishop and bishops, but were not bound by vows or rules. Members of the regular branch lived by the rule (*regula*); they followed strict regulations governing their lives and conduct, often lived in cloistered communities, and took perpetual vows, the most important of which was obedience to one's superiors. "Virtually the whole education of a regular priest or nun consisted of learning to annihilate one's self - one's pride, vanity, independence - in order to be subsumed completely by God's will, for a soul filled with the natural self had no room for the infusion of the Holy Spirit. Because of its inherent difficulty, self-abasement before God was learned in stages, before one's religious superiors. To renounce one's own judgment and to blindly obey the church and its representatives was considered the most appropriate and most efficacious training for the spiritual life." (Axtell 1985: 54) The regular clergy included both monks and friars, but whereas the former withdrew from the world and dedicated themselves to prayer and contemplation, the latter went out into the world, ministered to the laity, and developed a special vocation for missionary work. The unprecedented challenge of the evangelization of the Americas led the Papacy to confer upon the friars there all the prerogatives normally reserved to the secular clergy, including the power to act as parish priests, administer sacraments, tend congregations, and even act as inquisitors. (Duverger 1993: 26; Burkhart 1989: 15) The fourth key player, the Jesuits, whose members were known as Fathers, were latecomers, who did not arrive in America before 1566; hence their endeavors belonged to a second, later phase of evangelization. In the beginning, the Franciscans played the major role in Spanish America, but, once deployed, the Jesuits surpassed them, and from the beginning took the lead in French America. The Franciscans and the Jesuits provide most of the material in this survey. In Protestant regions of North America, responsibility for spreading the gospel to natives was more diffuse and fell to lay societies and individual pastors.

Europeans did not approach native societies and cultures with an open mind, but interpreted them in terms of their own pre-existing philosophical, cultural, and religious concepts. One of the most important preconceptions that Europeans took to the New World was the figure of the devil. American religion was interpreted in a form compatible with the Christian understanding of the world, and since the native deities were not God, they were cast as devils. This was in accord with I Corinthians 10: 19-21, which stated: "But the sacrifices the heathens offer are offered (in the words of Scripture) 'to demons and to that which is not God.' And I will not have you become partners with demons. You cannot drink the cup of the Lord and the cup of demons. You cannot partake of the Lord's table and the table of demons." (*New English Bible* 1970: 218)

There remained much disagreement, however, over whether diabolical intervention in the Americas had entirely invalidated native religion, or, conversely, whether indigenous religion could provide a suitable foundation for evangelization. It has been customary to attribute to virtually all evangelists, except the Jesuits, a determination to reject native religion in its entirety and to start from scratch, a policy to which contemporaries gave the name *tabula rasa*, literally "scraped board," although we might call it a "blank slate," upon which they intended to inscribe a pure form of Christianity, unadulterated by the influence of indigenous beliefs. Traditionally, the Franciscans, in particular, have been closely associated with this policy. The Jesuits' missionary work, by contrast, rested on the premise that a revelation of divine truth had been vouchsafed to all humanity before dispersal across the globe; therefore, even if the devil had intervened to frustrate God's purpose, traces of the divine word persisted and provided a basis for indigenous reception of the Christian message after the conquest. (Aburto Cotrina 1999: 81) For the Fathers, espousing an approach which was the opposite pole of *tabula rasa*, the role of missionaries was to look amongst native beliefs for precursors of Christianity in order to make easier the assimilation of the new religion and to develop that innate seed of recognition of the true God which was to be found in every people of the world. (Lafaye 1997: 60-61)

But the contrast between Jesuits and Franciscans has been overdrawn. All missionary orders, whatever their theoretical position, showed a willingness, in practice, to use native religion as a starting point for evangelization; the Jesuits may have embraced the policy the most explicitly but it was not unique to them. Although every missionary's proclaimed aim was to disseminate new ideas which were intended to replace or transform what was there before, in a one-way transmission, in reality evangelization entailed a religious dialogue, a deliberate negotiation between two sides. If genuine communication was to occur across the cultural gap, common ground had to be found between natives and missionaries, and the Christian message would find a readier reception if it was presented not as something foreign but as the fulfillment of the recipients' own highest hopes and expectations. Therefore, evangelists made a conscious effort to translate the universal message of the gospel into the religious terms and categories of the target society. Any translation into another language and cultural tradition involves a measure of assimilation, and the difficulty for missionaries was to assess at what point this becomes a deformation of the gospel. Christianity is a revealed religion, and there can be no tampering with its body of dogmatic and moral truths, but the universal, absolute and immutable in Christianity could be distinguished from the particular, the relative, and the adaptable (cultural forms, social customs, language, thought). Christ's message could be expressed in terms that made sense within the cultural references of Native Americans without betraying its universal truths.

The strategy of inserting Christianity, without compromising its principles, into the host culture is given the name *inculturation*. (Marzal et. al.1996: 18; Neill 1971: 4; Dunne 1962: 227-28; Murray 1999: 1; Morrison 1985: 366)

Thus, far from being unyielding in their determination to teach a pure form of Christianity, Europeans presented their faith in such a way that it made sense to indigenous peoples on their own terms, even if this meant adapting the new religion to native ways of thinking, for example by translating the Christian message into American languages, or by imitating the behavior of indigenous shamans (inspired intermediaries with the supernatural world) in order to win the natives' allegiance. Thus the reader will find within these pages a Spanish conquistador who, under native pressure, took on the role of a sorcerer/healer and cured indigenous peoples as he trekked across an unknown North American wilderness; a French Jesuit who conjured rain clouds in order to impress his indigenous flock with the potency of Christian magic; and a Puritan minister who healed a native chief in order to win him for God.

The reader will also encounter, among Native Americans, a Mexican noble, one of the earliest and highest-ranking converts of the Franciscans and an exemplary student of Christian doctrine, who was burned at the stake by the gentle friars for sophisticated denigration of their message, and for inciting rebellion; an Andean native lord who assisted his local Christian priest in destroying ancient deities with a zeal and ferociousness which went well beyond the call of duty, all the while haunted by nightmares in which his native gods did battle with the Christian Father; and a Huron sorcerer who first vied with French missionaries for control over spirits of the night in a shaking tent ceremony, before abandoning his ancestors' ceremonies in favor of superior Christian magic.

These cases illustrate that, for their part, indigenous peoples acknowledged Christianity, but they did not necessarily accept it in its entirety. Whereas it has often been assumed that native peoples either embraced Christianity as if they had been longing for it, or else fiercely resisted it, in fact they made the new religion their own by interpreting it according to their own spiritual worldview, by accepting what they could use and by rejecting what they could not. They reacted favorably to missionaries to the extent that the latter shared attributes that characterized their own native religious leaders, and they evaluated the Christian message according to its relevance for their pre-existing religion and culture. They borrowed Christian ideas and ritual practices selectively, for purposes of their own, often modifying the ideological message of the new religion. Although Christianity was the cause of great turmoil in native communities, and despite the fact that missionaries brought an alien culture, subordination to newcomers and killer diseases in their wake, the new religion functioned among some native peoples as the vehicle for a revitalization of their society, and paradoxically provided a means whereby native peoples could adopt Christianity in order to preserve their indigenous identity.

Native response to Christianity took a variety of forms, ranging from the acceptance of new rites and values, to the integration of certain Christian elements while rejecting the essence of the new message, to active resistance to all missionary work. (Ronda 1979: 2; Morrison 1985: 365; Brenner 1980: 139) The type of response varied according to ethnic group, differences in the pre-existing native culture and society, and differences in the circumstances of contact between missionaries and indigenous peoples. European missionary will was not sufficient for the process of change; a response by natives to the action of the religious was necessary. And native realities played a greater role in determining the outcome of the interaction than did the intentions of missionaries, or differences between missionary orders. Native peoples were actors in this spiritual drama, on a par with Europeans; indeed in many instances they took the lead. Hence, the interaction of religions is a two-sided story, with two principal players - natives and Europeans.

To reconstruct empathetically the worldview of both groups is not, however, a straightforward task. From the perspective of the early twenty-first century, both European missionaries and indigenous

INTRODUCTION

American peoples of four or five hundred years ago can seem alien, but each requires sensitive treatment on its own terms. Since Europeans produced most of the written documents that we have from the period, it is not easy to achieve an understanding of the interaction of native and Christian religions that is rooted in indigenous as well as European worldviews. But a history that does justice to the creativity, as well as the suffering, of this interaction must uncover native thought and actions, and must try to explain native and missionary responses to each other.

For a long time, native peoples remained largely invisible to the historian's eye, or served as a foil for the glorious triumph of white man's civilization. Through much of the twentieth century, historical accounts reproduced the missionaries' view that their own determined and selfless endeavors overcame the resistance of uncomprehending "primitive" peoples. The evangelizers' self-evident success (except where native peoples obstinately clung to ancient ways) rendered unnecessary, even distasteful, questions regarding the morality of the enterprise. In more recent times, however, influenced by the insights of anthropology and ethnohistory, a growing number of historians began to question the traditional account and to insist on the restoration of historical agency to indigenous Americans in order to reconstruct the native perspective. Whereas traditional history viewed the missionaries as the decision-makers - the active and dynamic individuals who "do things to" native groups - and the Indians[1] as passive victims "having things done to them," the new approach presented native peoples as agents in their own right, full participants in the interaction of their religions with those of whites, rather than simply docile recipients of superior European ideas. To recognize native agency is not to succumb to political correctness but to gain a richer perspective by including the complete cast on the stage of cross-cultural relations.

The restoration of protagonism to indigenous peoples has sometimes carried the danger of creating two-dimensional villains out of the missionaries, who have often been attributed with sinister motives or ascribed responsibility for all the tragedies that struck native societies with the advent of the Europeans. One historian has observed the irony that those who take great pains to understand the thoughts and motives of non-western peoples are often the least willing to understand people of their own culture who happen to hold views different from their own. (Trigger 1965: 51) The primary aim of the missionaries, whether Spanish friars, French Jesuits or English Puritans, was not to promote European colonial interests, or even their own financial interest, but to convert native peoples to Christianity. That we may not agree with or approve of their goals does not mean that we should question their sincerity. To judge the missionaries *only* by the standards of their day, as some historians would urge us to do, may not seem acceptable given the appalling consequences of their contact with Native Americans, consequences which have reached into the present time; but, equally, to judge them *only* by the standards of *our* day is to restrict our perspective on, and hence our understanding of, those same consequences. Neither missionaries nor natives adhered to moral principles that were identical to our own.

At the same time, it should not be forgotten that indigenous peoples did not invite the Europeans to impose Christianity upon them. If, out of courtesy to the missionaries, we try not to distort their motives, equally, out of respect for the Native Americans, we can recognize that evangelization entailed intrusion into the most intimate reaches of native spiritual life, as well as the (generally unintended) physical destruction of indigenous populations. The tendency to portray the interaction of natives and missionaries as one between heroes and villains, on one side or the other, is excessively simplistic. No side had a monopoly on heroism or villainy. At the same time, the sincerity of the missionaries' motives does not obviate their harmful impact on native communities. Native peoples endured immeasurable pain and suffering as a result of the coming of the white man in general, and of the militancy of the standard-bearers of Christianity, in particular. But out of this suffering arose a creativity that both molded the new religion to the old, and refashioned the traditional religion to meet the challenge of the invading faith. That creativity is one of the principal subjects of this book.

INTRODUCTION

The change in religious allegiance in the New World is often discussed in terms of *conversion*, even though sixteenth-century Europeans and natives rarely employed this concept. Conversion involves not only an exterior process of baptism, instruction, and formal inclusion within the fold (which we might term *Christianization*) but also an interior process whereby the new Christian becomes immersed in the meaning and values of the religion (which we might term *Evangelization*). (Meiklejohn 1988: 248-50) Clearly the interior process is much harder to evaluate than the exterior process. Sixteenth-century missionaries could broadly agree on what constituted the core of the faith that must be understood and believed in order for an Indian to be considered a Christian: God's creation of the world, His sovereignty and omnipotence, the Fall and Original Sin, the divine incarnation in Christ, his crucifixion for human sins, his triumph over death in the resurrection, and salvation through apprehending the Redeemer by faith. (Cohen 1993: 237) Instruction could be measured, but the interior acceptance of the Lord was harder to fathom.

The reaction of native peoples to Christianity has often been understood in terms of the concept of *syncretism*, which may be defined in two ways: more broadly as the amalgam or blending of religions, or of different elements of religions; and more specifically, as the reinterpretation of elements of the Christian religion in terms of the pre-existing native religion. In either case, by the process of syncretism, a third kind of religion or religious trait comes into being, shared by members of the two contacting religions, but different from what either side had before the meeting. (Neill 1971: 4-5) For example, an image of a Christian Virgin Mary is accepted by natives because it is understood to be a deity in its own right, capable of talking with Indians and curing them of disease. In this case, the Christian concept of the Virgin Mary and the native concept of a deity are amalgamated to form a native Virgin Mary, different from the original two. The concept of the Virgin has been accepted but reinterpreted as a new form of native god. The motive behind syncretism is an attempt by the evangelized to retain vestiges of their own religion, not so much in opposition to the Christians as in re-clothing the accepted tokens of Christianity in the appropriate aboriginal religious forms. (Marzal 1996: 18) This does not mean that syncretism implies confusion; the native may be as clear about the purpose and function of the new Christian Virgin as a European Catholic. Nor does it necessarily involve deceit. It may be the case that the Indian worships the old god under the guise of the Christian image. But more commonly, he may sincerely accept the Christian supernatural as a new expression of a familiar deity. In syncretism, local religious practices and concepts may be "taken possession of" by Christ, given a new or transposed meaning, and so be baptized into the church to enrich its life, and plant it more firmly in local soil. (Neill 1971: 580) In all this, as one historian has observed, there is more "conversation" than "conversion." (Sweet 1995: 9) One of the most important of these conversations was that between the missionary – the Christian man of power – and the native shaman – the native man of power.

Shamanism, which is to say, a visionary tradition, an ancient practice of utilizing altered states of consciousness to contact the gods and spirits of the natural world, was one religious characteristic shared to a greater or lesser degree by all Native Americans (North, Middle and South). The shaman was an inspired intermediary: inspired, because the spirits inhered in him, and intermediary because he acted as a bridge between his community and the supernatural world, and served as the vehicle whereby the spiritual realm manifested its presence. His specialist techniques were clairvoyance and the trance state, which he employed to cure the sick and reveal things hidden in time and space (divination). His expertise in the field of magic was applied in order to secure the success of the community's economy. He was typically a conjuror of rains and supervisor of hunting and harvest ceremonies. He also functioned as a priest and wise man, leading group ceremonies and rites, and was often the foremost authority on the communal traditions. (Hultkrantz 1979: 102) It is not accurate to say that the religion of the Americas was shamanism; shamanism was not a religion, but a collection of practices typical of the shaman.

The term shaman is used here, according to scholarly custom, even though it is foreign to the Americas. It applies, in origin, to inspired intermediaries in Siberia, and has been adopted to refer to his counterparts elsewhere in the world. Native American peoples had a plethora of terms for their inspired intermediaries, most of which signified "power men" or "mysterious men." Europeans tended to translate these native terms as "medicine men" (or more pejoratively, "witch doctors"), since one of their principal functions was healing, but, in the Indian view, medical skill was only one of the symptoms of the supernatural capacity of their inspired intermediaries, and the concept of "medicine" comprised every manifestation of supernatural power.

In fact, the "shaman" may be distinguished from the "medicine man." The defining characteristic of the shaman is the ecstatic experience, which is to say, the condition of literally "standing outside oneself," departing from one's own body in a deep trance, akin to an "intensively clear, conscious and realistic visionary state of dream," in some cases characterized by an "almost dazzling inner clairvoyance or illumination" with "actual perceptions of light of a purely hallucinatory or physically sensuous nature." (Arbman 1963: xv, 297; Hultkrantz 1981: 81) Automatic speech (messages from the spirits, delivered either in a normal or abnormal voice, sometimes in intelligible language, sometimes not), like light visions, is a classic characteristic of the ecstatic trance. The power to enter such a trance is acquired by experiencing a real or imagined illness that gives the shaman the conviction of having died and been reborn. During the trance state, the guardian spirits can enter his body and speak through his mouth, and his free soul (sometimes in the figure of these guardian spirits) can be guided on long journeys to the sky or the underworld; it is this soul-flight or soul-journey that is the distinguishing characteristic of the classic Siberian shaman.

Like the shaman, the medicine man is a visionary and clairvoyant who heals by means of helping spirits but he does not necessarily enter an ecstatic state. He may have attained his profession through an ecstatic experience in which the guardian spirits have appeared and delegated their power to him, but in his healing activity he can operate without falling into a trance. If he does enter the trace state, it is reserved for the summoning of his assistant spirits for consultation or active intervention in healing or finding lost articles. He does not undertake soul-flights to the realms of the gods or of the dead (though he may on occasion send his free soul to overtake the soul of his patient).

Both shaman and medicine man share the characteristic that they remove disease by supernatural means. Whereas the shaman of the soul-flight appears in much of Asia, his presence is rare in the Americas, and is confined to the Northwest Coast area and the Arctic regions of North America (the Inuit are almost the only people whose shamans perform the soul-flight so important in Asia), and to the north of the South American continent. The majority of contemporary American inspired intermediaries perform without the deep ecstasy characteristic of their Siberian counterparts; this may have been the case in pre-contact times too, though it is impossible to say for sure. Since the medicine man practices shamanistic activity, albeit not soul-flight, henceforth he will be referred to as a shaman. In any case, the use of the term shaman to refer to the inspired intermediary of the Americas has become so commonplace that it would be futile not to follow the practice. (Hultkrantz 1979: 83; Hultkrantz 1981: 64; Hultkrantz 1992: 18-19; Underhill 1965: 85-86, 88)

Both shaman and medicine man may also be distinguished from the wise man - a non-inspirational person who uses experience and tradition, such as healing herbs or surgical incision, but not necessarily supernatural power, to treat aches and wounds, set bones and generally cure the sick; and equally they may be distinguished from the priest, a leader of religious ceremonies and a repository of sacred knowledge, whose source of wisdom is other human beings. Shamans, by contrast, acquire special knowledge from supernatural beings through a vision or dream. But the distinction is often theoretical only, since the inspired intermediary fulfilled both roles. It was not so much that he had knowledge that others did not, but that he had more of it than others. Nor was the source of knowledge so important, since shamans learned from other humans as well as from supernatural entities. (Tooker 1979: 94-95)

INTRODUCTION

The healing skills of the inspired intermediary were brought into play when the cause of disease was believed to be either soul loss (the common diagnosis for mental disorders and disabilities) or the penetration of the body of the patient by a foreign object, usually transmitted by a spirit or a sorcerer (the normal diagnosis for bodily pains and injuries). In the case of penetration, a shaman who acted as a medicine man (without trance or ecstasy) was consulted. The intruding object's position was determined by clairvoyance, and it was then extracted from the patient's body either by sucking it out (with a straw or with the mouth directly on the sick man's skin), or by blowing it away, or by massaging it away. In some cases the extracted disease object was displayed as proof of the success of the ritual. In the case of soul loss, recourse was made to a shaman who in a trance state would send his own soul, or possibly one of his guardian spirits, to retrieve the runaway soul, often from the land of the dead. In some regions, for example northern South America, the trance state was more widely used, for example to seek the advice of spirits on cures or summon them to determine the diagnosis or expel the disease through their assistance. Through a vision or other inspiration, the spirit communicated the nature of the disease and how to remove it. The trance constituted a means to a deeper contact, whether to summon the spirit for information about disease, or to dispatch the spirit to seek the departed soul. Thus, the diagnosis of cause of disease called for the healing skills of different types of shaman. (Hultkrantz 1979: 88-90, 99)

There were four principal means of becoming a shaman: natural predisposition, family heritage, a calling from the spirits, and voluntary pursuit of the powers. Some individuals were considered predisposed for the role, on account of their nervous disposition, special bodily features or other distinctive traits, and at an early age, sometimes as young as ten, came to the attention of their elders. Others learnt the profession from their fathers or were favored by a call from the spirits. Yet others, as in the forest regions of South America, established direct contact with the spirits through asceticism, intensive training, swallowing tobacco smoke, and consumption of narcotic plants.

SACRED DIALOGUES

In all cases, the shaman established a relationship with his guardian spirit(s) - the number could vary considerably and corresponded to the individual's qualitative ability - who enabled him to cure and often imparted the right technique. In South America, they were often spirits of the dead, particularly those of dead shamans, or animal spirits. There was a close correlation between what the shaman learned through his internal life - visions and dreams - and what he learned from human masters (socially approved observations and experiences). (Hultkrantz 1979: 101) Guardian spirits were generally summoned in a dark place, sometimes in a form of tent erected for the purpose, which was located outdoors or in a large lodge or house, and which would shake when the spirits were present. An important aid for establishing contact with the other world was the gourd rattle, a sacred instrument enclosing stones in which the spirits hid; the sound of the rattle was interpreted as the voices of the spirits. Most shamans on both continents were male, although nearly everywhere there were small numbers of females, usually women past menopause. (Hultkrantz 1979: 101)

It is important to understand that the inspired intermediary was (and is) a positive figure in native society who uses his supernatural power for its benefit. The shaman who can journey to other worlds and return with revelations from the gods universally commands awe and respect. (Drury 1989: 1) Healing often requires the highest mobilization of all physical and psychic resources, visionary insight (clairvoyance), ecstatic disposition, ventriloquism, dexterity, and gymnastic fitness. (Hultkrantz 1979: 85-98) These are skills of an exceptional individual. It has been suggested that shamanism may be seen as a performance that, by means of apparent communications with spirits, dramatizes and resolves social tensions, between both individuals and groups. By this interpretation, the shaman is a form of therapist, giving expression to people's desires and feelings, and finding a satisfactory resolution to the conflicts that they provoke. Sometimes the shaman has been portrayed as a wounded or flawed individual, even an outsider, but he is most emphatically not a psychotic. His relationship with his guardian spirit is very rarely a question of true possession, that is to say when the man's own personality is totally suppressed by or in alternation with that of the spirit by whom he is occupied. The shaman is not insane, but an integral part of the physical and mental health of his community. His was to be a pivotal role in the response of native societies and religions to the advent of Europeans and the unprecedented spiritual challenge posed by Christianity. Let us now turn to the "sacred dialogues" that occurred when native religions met Christianity.

PART ONE

Spanish America

1 Preserving the Cosmic Order

Although the peoples of Mesoamerica shared a religious heritage, there were also local aspects or variants. We know more about the Nahuas (and especially the Mexica) than other ethnic groups so analysis should concentrate on them, but in fact, most of the characteristics of Nahua religion were common to other Mesoamericans. Nahua religion was very different from European religion, and is misunderstood if one tries to interpret it using purely European concepts and categories. Deities represented, or more accurately simply were, all the basic elements of Mesoamerican existence: the physical world (sun, moon, stars, Milky Way, earth, water and mountains), the elements (rain, lightning, clouds, wind), flora and fauna (maize, tobacco, maguey, peyote, deer, eagles, snakes, jaguars, pumas) and major cultural functions (fishing, hunting, war, sex, death) as well as evil forces. Maize was both a material (called *centli* in Nahuatl) and also at the same time, a god (Centeotl) and the name of a day, Chicome-Coatl (Seven-Snake), without the Nahuas perceiving any conceptual difference or dividing line between these different aspects.

Another characteristic that distinguishes Nahua religion was that it was both monistic (believing in the oneness of God) and dualistic (believing that God had a dual nature). Lest this seem contradictory, let us not forget that a central tenet of Christianity was that Jehovah was one god but three persons (the Trinity). For the Nahuas, the originator of the universe was one god, Ometeotl, but this was also a "dual god" who had both a male and a female manifestation, Ometecuhtli "Two Lord" and Omecihuatl "Two Lady." Through their union, four sons were born - white, black, red and blue Tezcatlipoca (Smoking Mirror) - each of whom was responsible for the creation of particular worlds and all the creatures that lived in them. But these four creator-gods were simultaneously different aspects of a single all-seeing and all-powerful deity, Tezcatlipoca. Thus, Nahua deities had dual and quadruple natures at the same time, the former associated with the concept of opposites (male/female, night/day) and the latter

1

with the cardinal directions (north, south, east, west). Nahua deities represented qualities that in western thought have been understood as opposites. The goddess Tlazolteotl was the agent of both temptation and redemption; Coatlicue was goddess both of birth and death, destruction and creation. Thus, Mesoamerican gods lacked fixed identities, in the Judeo-Christian and Greco-Roman sense. Jehovah was god of justice, not injustice; Mars was god of war, not of peace. But in Mesoamerica opposite attributes could be given to the same deity, or a quality associated with one god might be assumed by another. (Ruiz de Alarcón 1984: 14; Williamson 1992: 45; Ortiz de Montellano 1989: 375; Katz 1972: 160)

The status of gods could change too. Huitzilopochtli ("Hummingbird on the Left" or "of the South"), the tribal or patron god of the Mexica, was not considered significant by other ethnic groups before the birth of the Aztec Empire; but as the Mexica rose to dominance, Huitzilopochtli spread, and subjugated groups were required to recognize him as the lord of gods, synonymous with a much older and more important deity, Tonatiuh, the Sun God. Although Huitzilopochtli came to occupy the highest rank among Mesoamerican deities, he was an addition to, not a replacement of, the local gods of conquered regions. In addition to the principal deities already mentioned, there were also gods that corresponded to particular socio-political groups; towns, trades, professions, and social classes had their own special tutelary deities. Domestic households and even individuals also had their own family and personal gods.

Mesoamerican religion was far less concerned with the after life than it was with the present life. Whereas in Christianity, the major emphasis is put on the salvation of the soul and thus on the welfare of the individual in the after life, in pre-Hispanic religion, the emphasis was put on preserving the cosmic order, and the individual, as such, had almost no value in isolation except to the extent that he contributed to collective activities that had the conservation of that order as a goal. (Ortiz de Montellano 1989: 366) The fulfillment or neglect of religious duties and obligations was considered to have real effects in the here and now. By delivering blood, hearts, fire, incense, and quail sacrifices

2

to the gods, human beings obtained crops and water and were freed from illness and plagues. The relationship between man and gods was fundamentally commercial; the word for sacrifice to the gods meant "the act of payment." One of the purposes of warfare was to gain captives, whose sacrificed hearts and blood would nourish the sun and maintain its continuous motion across the sky. Only in this way could the end of the world be forestalled. (Ortiz de Montellano 1989: 362)

Violations of ritual or offenses against particular gods were believed to bring punishment in the form of diseases particularly associated with that deity. If a couple had sexual intercourse during periods of ritual abstinence, Xochipilli, god of sex and love, would afflict them with venereal diseases and hemorrhoids. Tlaloc, the rain god, expressed his anger through gout, dropsy, rheumatism, and other ailments associated with dampness. Xipe Totec, the god of spring and renewal, caused and cured skin infections and ailments. Tezcatlipoca punished violations of religious vows or of ritual fasting by contagious or incurable diseases. Deities not only inflicted but also cured disease, so those stricken by ailments due to the gods could seek cure by offerings. Tlaloc could be propitiated by offering dough images of the gods at shrines on the appropriate hill or mountain. Thus, much of Nahua religion was aimed at retaining or regaining the favor of gods so that disease would be prevented or cured. The Mexica had a complex understanding of human anatomy, and they possessed considerable empirical knowledge of the pharmacological properties of plants, based on lengthy observation and practice. (Ortiz de Montellano 1989: 365, 388) Mesoamericans were not ignorant, then, about scientific medicine, but their approach to the subject derived from religious assumptions about the relation of the self to others, to social norms and to the gods. Physical and psychological health were intrinsically linked to the social and spiritual life of the world in which one lived. Symptoms of illness were an expression of the disturbance of the relationships surrounding the individual. The rupture of social norms could lead to disease in the community, as a reflection of the imbalance that the individual's behavior had brought into the relationship between man and gods. Theirs was primarily spiritual medicine, based on diseases of the soul, since bodily diseases were

3

considered symptoms of soul diseases. Diagnosis entailed not only identifying the symptoms of disease, but also determining the underlying supernatural influences. Psychoactive herbs, such as *ololiuhqui* (morning glory seeds), and peyote (*Peyote tlapatl*, a small spineless cactus) were consulted to determine whether a sorcerer had caused the ailment, and, if so, his identity. If, on the other hand, a god was considered the cause of the ailment, he was appeased by offerings, pilgrimage, and auto-sacrifice. Thus, the supernatural causes were identified and appeased while medical remedies and treatments were simultaneously applied. (Ruiz de Alarcón 1984: 29-35)

2 Shock Troops of Conquest

As if unleashed by wrathful gods and ancestors, in the form of an invisible tsunami, deadly disease accompanied or preceded Europeans across the Americas, wreaking probably the greatest demographic catastrophe in recorded human history. Smallpox, plague, typhus, measles, mumps and influenza – these were the shock troops of conquest, sweeping all before them, either singly, or immeasurably more deadly, in sequence and combination. Whereas inhabitants of the Old World (Europe, Africa and Asia) had become resistant through centuries of inheritance, native peoples lacked immunity to these new diseases. The dense populations of Central Mexico and the Andes were ravaged, and Aztec and Inca imperial military resistance to the Spaniards was broken. Native peoples did not submit without a fight, but the decimation of their population by disease both eliminated irreplaceable warriors and military leaders, and undermined the fighting strength and morale of those who remained. In most regions Spaniards were faced only with the sickly survivors of an epidemic holocaust.

There is little agreement on the exact extent of early population decrease. Most of the depopulation had already taken place by the time early Europeans began to assess population numbers. Estimates are further complicated by the fact that there was no one 'moment of discovery', but many individual ones as European contact with Native American peoples gradually moved from east to west. In many cases, the mortality impact of epidemics long preceded actual contact or at least historical documentation, and thus Native American population dramatically reduced in size prior to the first accounts recorded by Europeans. This is even more likely to be the case for the frontier regions of the Mexican northwest than for the core regions of Central Mexico or the Andes, for which historical records (though not population counts) began at the moment of contact. (Reff 1992: 265)

Despite all the difficulties, it has been estimated that, across Spanish America as a whole, the loss of at least three quarters of the pre-contact native population seems to have been the rule by the end of the sixteenth century; in areas of dense population, such as Central Mexico, the figure was closer to ninety percent. In Mexico, disease spread from the capital in widening concentric circles; in the Andes, disease spread along river valleys and down from the highlands. As a result, the infection rate would be more than three times higher in Mexico, and so the mortality rates in Mexico would be correspondingly higher than in the Andes. In both regions the onslaught was relentless. Epidemics came in waves every ten years or so until the end of the sixteenth century, and continued to ravage the population periodically after that. (Baker and Kealhofer 1996: 4; Bakewell 1997: 151-53; Cook 1981: 436; Cook 1992: 207, 210; Cook 1998: 137; Dobyns 1963: 494, 509-10; Lovell 1992: 429, 435; Spalding 1999: 932; Thornton 1987: 44-46; Williamson 1992: 87)

It is much more difficult to estimate the impact of the ravages of disease upon the receptiveness of native Americans to Christianity, and it is particularly difficult to correlate the incidence of disease with attitudes to Christianity. Since disease-induced reductions frequently began before sustained contact with Spaniards (Cook 1998: 206), there arose a widespread belief that the native world was collapsing and that the gods had departed; Christianity might therefore be accepted as a new world view which made sense of catastrophic unprecedented events. There is little doubt that European epidemic diseases were the force that did most to undermine the natives' faith in their shamans and healers. (Axtell 1988: 113) European missionaries were quick to take advantage of this fact.

Missionaries – Men of Power

The evangelization of the Americas was first and foremost an enterprise of the Spanish state. By the *Patronato Real* (royal patronage) of 1508, the papacy had bestowed on the Castilian Crown sole responsibility for the provision of missionaries. Members of religious orders were preferred to secular clergy, because they were experienced in missionary activity, because their own vow of poverty

6

and their varied sources of support made it easier to provide for them, and because they were easier to supervise, since protests or requests by the Crown could be made to one central head instead of to bishops of many dioceses. The Crown contributed to the financing of evangelization not only by providing the friars with an annual subsidy, but also by exempting the mission populations from taxation until their conversion was complete. Once the natives could be considered full Christians (originally expected within ten years from their introduction to the new religion), the role of the mendicants would lapse, the friars would be replaced by secular priests and would move on to new areas of unevangelized Indians, and the former mission communities, now considered as regular parishes, would become liable for tribute payment to the Crown.[1] In reality, this transformation was postponed for several decades since the mendicants did not trust the secular priests to maintain the high standards of Christian devotion that they believed the Indians had attained under their tutelage. As a result the mendicants became far more than a transitory phenomenon.

Of the three mendicant orders, the Franciscans were the first to set foot not only in America but also in New Spain (as Central Mexico was called by its Spanish rulers), a fact which enabled them to establish a pre-eminence that they never relinquished. Before arriving in America in 1493, the Franciscans already had expertise in missionary activity, having converted pagans in central Asia and China. Members of the order, founded in 1209 by the Italian Francis Bernardone of Assisi, emulated the humble and frugal life of a medieval Italian peasant. They traveled on foot rather than on horseback, wore sandals rather than shoes, and dressed in robe and cowl. Since their vows forbade them to possess private or community property, they lived on alms, for which they begged or which the king or other patrons bestowed upon them. Within the Franciscan Order, there existed a tension between those who adhered strictly to an original rule of austerity, simplicity, and renunciation of property (Observants) and those who led more material lives as a way to exert greater influence in the world (Conventuals). In 1517, the division was formalized by the creation within the Order of two independent bodies; the Observants, who had been the principal part of the order in reality, now became so

7

officially. One of the strictest of the Observant groups in early-sixteenth century Spain, known as the Minorites of the Blessed Juan de Puebla and the Minorites of the Holy Gospel, with their own province of San Gabriel, founded in 1518, supplied many of the early Franciscans in Mexico, including members of the original twelve friars who came to New Spain in 1524; they practiced extreme poverty, a rigorous regimen of flagellation, and silent spiritual retreats. The Observant Franciscans maintained that the example of a holy and moral spiritual life offered the most powerful incentive in the conversion of others. This point distinguished them from the Dominican Order, which favored programs of doctrinal preaching and philosophical arguments with religious opponents as the most effective means of conversion. (Weber 1992: 93)

The Jesuits were founded as a missionary and teaching Society by Ignatius Loyola in 1534, and formally recognized by the Papacy in 1540, explicitly for the purpose of converting heathens outside Europe. Their earliest evangelizing endeavors were those of St. Francis Xavier in India and the Far East (1542). (McNaspy 1982: 9) The first Jesuit missionaries in the New World were Manuel da Nóbrega and his five companions, who arrived in Brazil in 1549. The establishment of the Jesuits in Spanish America was slower because the Crown preferred the older orders. The first Jesuits in Spain's territories were Pedro Martínez and six fellows who arrived in Florida in 1566, but the mission was soon abandoned in the face of Indian hostility. The true beginning of Jesuit missionary work in Spanish America was their arrival in Peru in 1568 and in Mexico in 1572. (Marzal 1992: 18) Far from impeding the young Society's subsequent success, the Jesuits' late entrance in New Spain worked in their favor, enabling them to expand into frontier areas. It is true, though, that they never attained in Spanish America the overwhelmingly preponderant role that they did in Portuguese Asia and Brazil. They were markedly different from the three major mendicant orders already in New Spain. As a religious body, they were better trained than the friars, and were equally qualified to serve as priests, teachers, or missionaries: "The Jesuits were meant to excel. They were chosen on the basis of mental and physical fitness, good appearance and family background, and above all suitability for a life of rigorous discipline, complete obedience and unswerving devotion, trained long and honed on Spiritual Exercises to a fervent edge, full members of the Society of Jesus emerged as superbly confident soldiers of God." (Kessell 1970: 8) They arrived with conquering momentum at a time when the friars were beginning to rest on their laurels. Unlike the mendicants, the Jesuits were not subject to the Patronato Real but answered only to their superiors in Rome and to the Pope. (Hu-Duhart 1981: 23) It was the Jesuit Father General in Rome, not the Spanish Crown, who chose missionaries and organized expeditions, which protected the order from the centralizing attempts of the Crown, and so allowed more independent action than was possible for other orders. (Malaga 1992: 33)

The challenge of preaching to an entire continent was an unprecedented undertaking. By 1540, there was a territory of about two million square kilometers to be evangelized; by 1600 this had increased to two and a half million. This vast territory was to be covered by a few thousand men.[2] The majority were Franciscans who contributed fifty-six percent of all missionaries who went to the New World between 1493 and 1822 (eight thousand four hundred and forty-one out of a total of fifteen thousand and ninety-five). (Gómez Canedo 1993: 137) The number of Dominicans and Augustinians greatly decreased after their initial arrivals. (Borges 1977: 481-535)

3 Franciscan Triumph: Converts Without Number

The Franciscan order, the first to set foot in New Spain, dated its beginnings symbolically from the moment on 13 May 1524 when Fray Martín de Valencia led his eleven brethren off the ship at San Juan de Ulúa, their number (twelve) self-consciously evoking the memory of the first apostles of the primitive church, since to these latter-day apostles fell the task of preaching the faith to the last peoples (they supposed) not yet reached by the Word. From there they traveled barefoot the great distance to Mexico City, where Hernán Cortés himself welcomed them in person, kneeling to kiss Valencia's hand, and thus conferring on the twelve gentle holy men the full political authority of the conquering warriors. From the outset, the evangelizing mission was represented to the native peoples as the spiritual purpose of the conquest, and the gentle message of Christ was thrust under their noses on the tip of a sword. Such was the auspicious start for the first systematic attempt at evangelization on the American mainland. (Lafaye 1976: 34; Klor de Alva 1993: 173)

The Franciscans were able to establish an early, uncontested dominance in certain areas - Mexico, Michoacán, Yucatán, Guatemala, and Nicaragua - as the privilege of the first to arrive. They rapidly occupied the principal Nahua regions of Central Mexico, including Nueva Galicia (Jalisco and Nayarit), the Puebla-Tlaxcala region, and, most important of all, the Valley of Mexico, concentrating their first efforts on the four principal cities of Mexico, Texcoco, Tlaxcala and Huejotzingo. (Duverger 1993: 111, 113) They expanded into the territories of Tula and the Tarascans of Michoacán, penetrated the regions of the Huaxtecs and the Totonacs and were the only missionaries to attempt missions among the Chichimecs, the non-sedentary Indians to the north of the Valley of Mexico. For the rest of the sixteenth century, they surpassed their mendicant rivals in terms of numbers of missionaries. The Twelve were soon joined by a flurry of enthusiastic brothers, taking their numbers to sixty in just over ten years. Another quarter of a century later, by 1559, their number had expanded to three hundred and eighty friars, and they had founded eighty friaries. The other two mendicant orders, by comparison, were represented by only forty friaries apiece and just over two hundred religious each. (Ricard 1966: 23) By the end of the century there were possibly one thousand Franciscan friars and two hundred Franciscan friaries in New Spain. It has also been suggested that the caliber of their missionaries - men such as Bernardino de Sahagún, Toribio de Benavente (better known as Motolonía), Andrés de Olmos, Pedro de Gante (Peter of Ghent), and other notable figures - also put their rivals to shame. The majority of Franciscans devoted their lives to New Spain and never returned to the homeland. Mexico was not a transitory career but a vocation for life. (Duverger 1993: 132)

The Dominicans, who followed the Franciscans to New Spain in 1526, put down roots and founded friaries in Mexico and Puebla-Tlaxcala but found themselves playing second fiddle in these areas, where the Friars Minor had already embedded themselves. They established a more significant presence in the south, in Morelos, and were able to enjoy an almost absolute monopoly in Oaxaca, in the Mixtec and Zapotec territories abandoned by the Franciscans, where they showed an interest in minority groups such as the Mixes, Chintales and Chochos. In the more distant regions of Guatemala, Chiapas and Yucatán, the Dominicans' missionary activity was severely limited by the pre-eminence of the Friars Minor. (Duverger 1993: 115) The first seven Augustinians arrived in 1533, and eased themselves into the gaps left by the others, to the northeast, south and west of Mexico, among the Nahuas, Otomíes, Tarascans and Huaxtecs. (Azoulai 1983: 130; Duverger 1993: 116-117) The Jesuits did not arrive in New Spain until the 1570s, long after the mendicants had established themselves. For this reason their major contribution was to be in frontier areas.

The creation of a "visible church" - the division into parishes, the building of churches, the introduction of ceremonies - was the most pressing task and was carried out with breathtaking rapidity. The Franciscans took the lion's share of the parishes into which the Nahua regions of Central Mexico were divided, between the 1520s and the 1540s. (Lockhart 1992: 206) In this most densely populated territory of the Americas, the friars were able to welcome millions of Indians into the church through baptism in the ten to fifteen years after their arrival. The most effective method was that of a good example - the Indians' own native lords - whose embrace of Christianity would lead their people to flock to the Cross. Missionaries made an early priority of winning the allegiance of the native rulers of Mexico, Texcoco and Michoacán, among others. (Duverger 1993: 105) The reward was their assistance in organizing church services and in calling on native labor to construct churches, as well as a flood of conversions en masse. The bishop (later archbishop) of Mexico (1528-48), Fray Juan de Zumárraga, wrote in 1531 that more than one million Indians had been baptized by that time (the same figure appeared in a letter of Martín de Valencia in the same period). Motolonía, himself said to have baptized more than four hundred thousand people in his lifetime, wrote in his *History of the Indians of New Spain* (1541) that between 1521 and 1536 more than four million people had received the sacrament; in the same work, using alternative methods of calculation, he estimated more than five million, and more than nine million. (Motolinía 1951:179, 182-83; see also León-Portilla 1974: 13; Duverger 1993: 106) Although it is probable that the numbers of conversions have been inflated to some extent in order to demonstrate that the Indian church was a worthy successor to, if not an actual rebirth of, the primitive apostolic church, it is also likely that the figures are not wildly inaccurate, since baptisms were usually conducted en masse, with natives gathered by residential quarter, or even by entire communities. It was reported that, around 1530, two priests baptized, in one day, more than fifteen thousand inhabitants of Xochimilco. Ghent claimed that he had baptized as many as fourteen thousand, in one day (and more than two hundred thousand over the course of his career). (León-Portilla 1974: 12)

These impressive statistics were made possible by the use of a simplified ritual on each Indian. Although these were not forced baptisms, they were not much more than formal conversions. (Duverger 1993: 107-108) It was standard practice to limit pre-baptismal preparation to short preaching, and to teach the catechism after administering the sacrament. Thus the Indians generally remained unenlightened with regard to what they had given their assent in the ceremony of baptism. Indeed, the most likely motive for submission was as a sign of political allegiance to the new sovereign, as was the norm in Mesoamerican society when one group conquered another. Still, although doubt remains regarding the meaning to be attributed to these conversions, their vast number is a fact. If the figures are to be trusted, then by 1540 about one third of the population of central Mexico had been baptized, almost exclusively the result of Franciscan efforts; and by 1609 more than sixteen million Indians in New Spain had received the sacrament from the Franciscans alone. Although the Friars Minor were the principal contributors, the other orders reported similar successes. The Dominicans also related large numbers of baptisms, and were happy to boast of entire provinces of more than twenty thousand or fifty thousand Indians baptized. (Borges 1992, 2:595)

But baptism was only a start. How were native peoples to be encouraged to participate directly and actively in Christian worship thereafter? One approach was to evoke a strong emotional commitment through the liberal use of music and dance, chants and song. Indians poured into the courtyards of churches singing and reciting prayers in Nahuatl set to music, and willingly joined in processions for images of their favorite saint. The friars' breathless, exultant wonder at the boundless enthusiasm that the celebration of the Catholic liturgy evoked among the Indians has prompted historians to comment on the "sunlit, euphoric quality about the spiritual conquest in central Mexico." (Brading 1991: 103) But Christianity was a religion not only of the heart but also of the head, and the friars sought to elicit an intellectual commitment on the part of those who were capable of making it. Some insuperable obstacles would remain to the genuine conversion of those who grew to adulthood in the old religion, but young minds were more pliant, and it was for the young sons of the native lords that the friars reserved their greatest endeavors.

The first step was isolation of these boys in special schools built alongside friaries, and their education in Christian doctrine. The first school was set up by Peter of Ghent in Texcoco in 1523, and his example was followed by the Twelve; within a year of their arrival, there were around one thousand children in Franciscan schools in Mexico City, Texcoco, Tlaxcala and Huejotzingo. By 1531, Ghent alone had in his charge six hundred pupils in the school of San José de los Naturales in Mexico City (where he had moved in 1527) and there was possibly a similar number at the school in Tlaxcala. (Duverger 1993: 103; Osorio 1990: xvii) In these friary schools, the boys were instructed in reading and writing (in Latin and Spanish), singing, and the essentials of the Christian faith. The boys were expected to understand the existence of a single god who created everything, the joys of Paradise and the miseries of Hell, the mystery of the Incarnation, the Virgin Mary as mother of God and intercessor for Man before God, and other important Christian concepts. (Kobayashi 1974: 252) They also had to learn how to make the sign of the cross. Throughout the remainder of the sixteenth century, each Franciscan friary maintained its own school for the sons of native chiefs, the purpose of which was not only to provide a complete education in Christian religion and culture, but also to govern every aspect of the boys' lives, including future marriage partners and inheritance of family goods and property.

The interns served several purposes. First, they were an elite cadre for evangelization, employed by the friars to educate their fellow young Indians, including the sons of non-nobles, who lived at home and visited the church patios each morning to be instructed in doctrine (although not reading and writing). Second, they served as hostages for their pagan fathers in that they remained in the friaries until their fathers converted (or alternatively the boys married). Finally, in a conscious strategy to pit the young against their fathers, they were used as agents of direct penetration into their own families. Instructed that all their ancestors had gone to Hell and that they would be the first to attain Heaven, where they would intercede for their living elders' accession, interns were encouraged to reveal parental sins to the friars, to denounce relatives who worshipped native gods, and to target for conversion servants, family members and even their own mothers in order to isolate their fathers in their own home. Some were sent on missions in order to preach, smash pagan images and even break into houses to seek out and destroy idols. By granting paternal approval in the measure that the boys succeeded in reforming their families, the friars sought gradually to achieve a transfer of filial loyalty from their charges' real fathers to themselves; in this way, the Indian young were carried over ethnic borders and found new fathers among the priests.

This strategy held potential dangers as well as benefits. Even if the friars secured the genuine devotion of the boys by providing for their welfare, at the same time, by alienating them from their past culture, they made them outsiders to the world they had now to convert. A few were even killed by their fathers and became martyrs to future interns. A famous example was Cristóbal, son of Cristóbal Axotecatl, lord of the village of Atlihuetza (Tlaxcala). Educated in the friary in Tlaxcala, young Cristóbal learnt his lessons so well that he preached doctrine to his father, contradicting him, and reproaching him for his idolatry, and exhorted him to devote himself to God. When he called on his mother to intervene, the father became so angry that he had her killed. Not to be discouraged, young Cristóbal told his father that he risked losing the obedience and respect of his son and that he would seize his idols from him if he did not give them up. Finally the father berated his son for contravening his will, and, denouncing his ingratitude for his upbringing, struck him on the head and killed him. When the friars missed the boy, they investigated, denounced the lord and had him tried and hanged. The bodies of the wife and boy were dug up and transferred to the friary in Tlaxcala as martyrs to the faith. Similar events occurred in the village of Santiago Tecalpan, where some religious from Tlaxcala went to preach and took with them some boys to look for idols. The lords of the village, feeling hounded by the boys, invited three of them to dinner, intending to kill them. Two escaped but one died while still preaching.

If some of the interns met a martyr's death, many others were accepted by their families and communities, and were able to exercise, within adult society, the authority conferred on them by carrying the sacred objects - rosaries and images - of the holy men of the new religion. Thus, hundreds of young boys succeeded in serving as mediators between the friars and adult Indian society. Although, in general, the methods of evangelization among the orders displayed only minor differences, the Franciscan contribution to the education and formation of a new Christianized native elite went well beyond what any other order attempted. (Duverger 1993: 120; Trexler 1982: 115-25, 130-33)

4 Christianity in a Native Context

An important premise of the friars' approach was that Christianity would not flourish if it was perceived by native peoples as entirely alien, and therefore it must be made more familiar by seeking connections between the new religion and the old, and by establishing a certain continuity between the European and pre-Columbian faiths. (Burkhart 1989: 16; Duverger 1993: 20) One approach was to look for similarities between Christianity and native religion, and in reality there was a close parallel between many aspects of Spanish and pre-conquest Nahua religions. Both religions were institutionalized; both had a professional priesthood distinguished from the laity by distinctive dress, sexual abstinence and severe self-mortification, by access to special knowledge and by their role as intermediaries between ordinary people and gods; both were populated by a plethora of divine beings, whether Mesoamerican deities or Catholic saints, who specialized in particular human needs.(Clendinnen 1987b) Furthermore, some Nahua religious practices and ceremonies could easily be interpreted as parallels, if not prototypes, for Christian practices, for example, the native bathing ceremony for infants several days after birth (baptism); a ritual in honor of the goddess Tlazolteotl, known as "straightening one's heart," which restored internal order (penance); the practice of eating representations of Huitzilopochtli, Omacatl or Tezcatlipoca in amaranth dough (eucharist). (Hassig 2001: 160-61) The parallel between this last practice and the Mass was much noted:

"There was one form which more closely resembled Communion. Namely, about the month of November, after harvesting their corns and other grains, they made tamales, that is, round cakes, from the seed of a certain plant which they call *xenixos* mixed with corn dough. These *tamales* they boiled in water. While the *tamales* were boiling, children played on a sort of drum, constructed entirely of wood and having neither hide nor parchment, thus proclaiming in song that those loaves were changing into the flesh of Tezcatlipoca, the god or demon whom they held in special veneration and to whom they attributed greater dignity. Only the afore-mentioned children ate those loaves, as if they were thereby communing with that demon and partaking of his flesh." (Motolinía 1951: 97)

The appeal to similarities between Christianity and indigenous religions had ample precedent in the history of the early church, whose theologians argued that pagan religion and philosophy were a kind of Christianity in the rough that could be tapped to facilitate conversion. (MacCormack 1985: 443) There was disagreement among missionaries in the New World as to whether the similarities between the two religions should be attributed to providential preparation (God had planted them in order to make the friars' task easier) or to diabolical intervention (the devil made fun of God by parodying Christian practices). But those (later) churchmen, such as the Jesuit José de Acosta, who saw these similarities as a hindrance on account of their demonic inspiration tended to be in a minority. In the early days of evangelization in New Spain, the friars believed that these similarities created a bridge between the two religions. It was only a short step to the conclusion that Christianity could be inserted into a native context, which, once stripped of its religious errors, should provide a fertile soil in which to plant the true faith. Ghent and Motolinía consciously built on native culture as a vehicle for Christianity and expected that the old would mingle with the new.

This approach is well illustrated by the friars' use of native pictographs, native dance and music, and native theatre. In the early stages of evangelization, the Indians knew no Spanish and the friars had only a rudimentary knowledge of native tongues, so the missionaries attempted to convey Christian teaching through pictographic catechisms, or books of instruction which used native glyphs or picture writing in order to represent Christian concepts, such as Hell or different sins. (Clendinnen 1987b) Not only was transcription of the teachings of the church in ancient glyphs a highly practical way of overcoming the language barrier, but it was also an excellent way of conferring sacred authority on Christianity in the eyes of the Nahuas. (Duverger 1993: 171) The importance that the friars gave to the role of music in Indian Christian ceremony reflected the emotional and sensual character of pre-Hispanic religious life. Since chants and dance had played such a large part in native religion, Ghent readily adopted dances and pagan songs to communicate Christian doctrine. The result was that pagan ceremonies that did not overtly contradict Catholicism were accepted and encouraged. Friars composed songs in the native language about the Virgin Mary and the birth of Jesus and allowed Indians to make special costumes for performances, in the expectation that the sacred associations of the traditional dances would rub off on the ceremonies of the new religion. (Duverger 1993: 164) Ignoring official prohibitions, the friars even allowed native dances inside the church during Christian feasts. This tolerance for the coexistence of ceremonies and allowance for specific local practices was not an aberrant departure from usual practice, but was also common in Europe before the Council of Trent (1545-63) redefined what was acceptable and what was not. Evangelizing theatre, which began in the 1530s, took the form of *autos*, which is to say, dramatized scenes designed to illustrate stories from Scripture or central doctrines of Christian faith (corresponding to the stage plays of medieval England, the so-called mystery, miracle and morality plays). These were written in Nahuatl by specialists of the order, such as Olmos and Motolinía, and were conceived for a native public, employing not only Indian language, but also Indian scenery, actors and costume. (Duverger 1993: 165)

From the moment he set foot in Mexico, Hernán Cortés planted crosses atop pagan temples (Duverger 1993: 15-16; Díaz 1975). His companion, Mercedarian Fray Bartolomé de Olmedo, wary of the significance natives would attribute to this act, opposed raising the cross in Indian villages until the natives had a more thorough knowledge of Christianity. The friars ignored the cautious precedent of their fellow religious and instead eagerly adopted Cortés's strategy, which allowed the new cult to become rooted in historical continuity and so benefit from legitimacy conferred by the pre-existing sacred landscape. (Duverger 1993: 20) One of the most famous instances is the shrine to the Virgin Mary erected at the site apparently dedicated to the pre-Hispanic goddess Tonantzin. According to the Franciscan chronicler, Juan de Torquemada, the decision to plant a Christian shrine at this site was that of the Franciscans of Tlatelolco. (Duverger 1993: 199-200)

Nor was this an isolated example; there were four further instances in the Puebla-Tlaxcala valley. In the village of Chiautempan, near Tlaxcala, the Franciscans founded a friary on a site formerly dedicated to the native god Toci - whose name means "our grandmother," since she was the mother of gods - and consecrated its church to Saint Anne, the maternal grandmother of Jesus, and hence of all Christians. The saint rapidly became known as Santa Ana Toci, a development that apparently was not resisted by the Franciscans, since it helped to retain for the saint's cult the former pilgrims to the native shrine. Similarly, in Tianguismanalco, west of Puebla, a church erected on the site of a temple to Telpochtli, an aspect of Tezcatlipoca, meaning "young man," especially with the connotation of "young virgin male," was dedicated to Saint John the Apostle, who was reputed to have been a virgin; the saint at this site became known as San Juan Telpochtli, and the village San Juan Tianguismanalco. In Contla, a pre-conquest temple to Camaxtli was reconsecrated as a church for the patron saint San Bernardino, who, uniquely in the world, was depicted here, like Camaxtli, holding a solar disk against his chest with both hands. Just as Camaxtli was represented as the lover of Xochiquetzalli (goddess of love and beauty, arts, flowers and games), the original owner of the mountain where the shrine was located, so now San Bernardino was depicted as the lover of La Malinche, the new name of the mountain, clinching the identification of Catholic saint and native deity. Finally, an important temple for Xochiquetzalli, also known in the Tlaxcala valley as "mother of gods," became the site for a shrine to the Virgin of Ocotlán, the patron saint of Tlaxcala. The establishment of a Catholic shrine at this place was not simply the initiation of a new cult to the Virgin, nor merely a continuation of the cult of Xochiquetzalli under a Christian guise. Rather, the Virgin of Ocotlán is a new supernatural entity partaking of the interacting natures of both Xochiquetzalli and the Virgin Mary. (Durán 1967, 2:1151-58) The friars regarded the Virgin of Ocotlán as a Christian triumph because the Catholic element seemed to predominate. (Graziano 1999: 100) For the Franciscan Martín Sarmiento de Hojacastro, it mattered little whether the Indians saw the Virgin or the indigenous goddess, as long as the ultimate effect was the veneration of the mother of God. (Cervantes 1991: 54) The readiness to make use of the ruins of the old religion in order to construct the new even led to the recycling of building materials. In Tlatelolco, a church was built for Santiago out of the stones from a wrecked temple to Huitzilopochtli.

The strategy was not exclusive to the Franciscans, but was used by the other orders. (Duverger 1993: 200) In 1533 the Augustinians replaced a statue of the god Oztoteotl in the caves at Chalma, a famous pre-Columbian shrine, with a miraculous crucifix. It became standard practice, in naming villages, for the friars to join the pre-Hispanic name to the Christian saint's name, for example, San Miguel Tuxpán, San Andrés Tuxtla (according to Spanish medieval practice, every community had a patron saint associated with it). Although the patron saint was often chosen at random, on many other occasions it bore a direct relation to the local tutelary god. Saint James (Santiago) and Saint Michael often replaced warrior gods, Saint Lucy replaced erotic goddesses, and the Virgin Mary replaced mother-goddesses. (Duverger 1993: 201) Saint Thomas whose name Dídimo means "the twin" stood in for Quetzalcoatl, (Plumed Serpent), known to the Aztecs as "precious twin." The goddess, Xilonen, whose fate was to be beheaded, was associated with Saint Prisca, who died by decapitation. (Duverger 1993: 206) This policy of substitution was wittingly executed by the Franciscans and others in the early days as a bridge to the native world, since the Christian message would be rejected if it was not rooted in the ancient religion. (Duverger 1993: 21 and 162)

The insertion of Christianity into a native context was not limited to the construction of churches on pagan temples. The assignment of Indian communities to parishes conformed to indigenous ethnic divisions (parish boundaries followed those of *encomiendas*, grants of Indian labour to privileged conquistadors, themselves reflecting discrete ethnic groups), making the Christian church, like the native temple, a central symbol of the ethnic community. Secondary churches or chapels sprung up, corresponding to the different residential quarters (*calpulli*), just as temples had done in pre-conquest times.

(Lockhart 1992: 206) The division of friary schools into those for nobles and those for non-nobles, as well as the content of their curriculum, derived from the Aztec model of the elite school (*calmecac*) and the non-noble school (*telpochcalli*). (Kobayashi 1974: 249) The elite school struck the friars as a providential forerunner of friary schools in the Franciscan fashion, run by priests, with similar activities such as fasts and prayer and self-flagellation, and similar characteristics such as abstinence, asceticism, obedience, and self-sacrifice. The Franciscan College of Santa Cruz Tlatelolco, founded in 1536 for the sons of native lords, was inspired by Olmos's research into the teaching methods of the Aztecs (Baudot 1995: 106-07), an excellent example of how the friars were prepared to make use of native cultural elements where they did not conflict with Christian principles. The use of the open chapel for evangelization by the middle years of the sixteenth century was peculiar to New Spain and owed much to native tradition. This unusual outdoor approach to Christian worship, consisting of a large walled courtyard, a chapel facing the courtyard so that the outdoor congregation might witness the mass, secondary smaller chapels (*posas*) in each corner and a large cross near the center of the court, was characteristic of both pre-conquest temple structures and Christian church architecture. (Lockhart 1999a: 117)

A further example of the willingness to insert Christianity into a native context was the ancillary role that Indians were allowed to fill as lay assistants to the priest. The day-to-day running of the church and even some of the priest's non-sacramental duties were usually left to Indian officials, selected from among the children of nobles, who served as mediators between priest and congregation. The priest's chief assistant was the *fiscal*, a general steward and manager of the church. (Lockhart 1992: 210) Below him were lesser officials who, in a clear sign of continuity with native culture, retained pre-Hispanic names. There was the *tepixque*, whose prime function was to act as guarantor of regular and properly Christian religious practice, for example, by ensuring that the newborn were baptized, by verifying the identity of couples to be married, by establishing that the traditional native marriage ceremony took place after, and not before, the Christian ceremony, and by indicating witches and drunks to the priest. Then there was the *tlapixque* who was responsible for the church and the accessories of worship, maintaining the archives, keeping accounts for offerings and alms, indicating fiestas to be kept, directing funerals, teaching the catechism if the village was too far from the friary, and even baptizing children in danger. The priest came to depend on these officials, and in many instances the education of the Indian congregation in the faith fell into their hands. The nomination of two *tlapixque* to exercise their functions in turns each week conformed to native tradition since pre-Hispanic priests had acted in pairs. (Duverger 1993: 182-83)

The context of native religion even determined which aspects of the Christian message were emphasized or downplayed. Discussion of the Trinity was avoided since it might encourage polytheism, as was the death of Christ which might suggest human sacrifice. However, Mary could be emphasized, since as the Virgin and mother of God she found an echo in Coatlicue (native earth goddess and mother of gods), who miraculously conceived Huitzilopochtli. (Duverger 1993: 162)

5 Choosing the Right Word for the Word of God

Probably the most significant aspect of the decision to insert Christianity in a native context was the systematic use of native languages to convey the Christian message. By 1540 Nahuatl had been designated as the language of conversion, in preference to Spanish. (Dibble 1974: 226) But where Nahuatl was not widely spoken, the friars ensured that they became proficient in local tongues as well. The specialization of religious orders in particular indigenous languages derived from the division of territories during the conquest. As the most numerous missionaries, and also those that had the most extensive and varied territories, the Franciscans developed a particularly large group of linguists, proficient in two, or even three, native tongues as varied as Nahuatl, Tarascan, and the Mayan languages of Yucatán and Guatemala. Olmos was reputed to be able to preach in more than ten different languages. The Augustinians also faced considerable linguistic variation in their territories. At least twelve Indian languages were spoken in Augustinian missions: Nahuatl, Otomí, Tarascan, Huaxtec, Matlalzinco, Totonac, Mixtec, Chichimec, Tepehuan, Serrana, Tlapanec and Ocuiltec. Dominican missionaries had less extensive and varied territories but they usually knew two languages - the general tongue (ie Mixtec, Zapotec or Nahuatl) of the area, and the local one (Mixe, Chontal, Chochona, Zoque). (Pita Moreda 1991: 222) All in all, the friars managed to master about twenty languages between them (only among sedentary Indians - northern nomads were to be instructed in Nahuatl, in order to civilize them). There was an urgent need for missionaries to learn indigenous languages since it would take too long to bring natives to a level of Spanish sufficient for their evangelization to be conducted in that language. The friars were fewer and more able at languages, and had the incentive to learn.

This was not merely a pragmatic decision based on necessity but also represented an important aspect of their philosophy. The friars chose to present themselves not as agents of a colonizing power but rather as agents of an autonomous religion. And all Indians were to be converted within the context of their ethnic diversity. (Duverger 1993: 135)

The command of native tongues allowed priests to baptize, confess, and lead prayers in Nahuatl and other languages. But written sources of Christian knowledge had also to be produced in indigenous languages. Nahuatl, like other native tongues, had been recorded on bark paper by means of glyphs. Before religious writings could be produced in Nahuatl, the friars had to devise a means of transcribing native languages in the Latin alphabet. From the early 1530s, a system that used sixteen letters of the Latin alphabet to represent the sounds of Nahuatl was taught in schools for young Indians. Other languages were also transcribed, and by 1550 all the major languages had been alphabetized. This allowed the emergence of an extensive corpus of religious writings, principally but not exclusively in Nahuatl, including confessionals (which contained questions to be asked and likely responses, together with Spanish translations), catechisms (and other compendia of the basic tenets of Christianity), psalms, sermons, and religious plays. Talented linguists such as Olmos and Sahagún wrote sermons in Nahuatl in the 1530s for use by less gifted fellow Franciscans. From mid-century, native language catechisms, not only in Nahuatl but also in other languages such as Otomí and Huaxtec, were used systematically to provide translations of the Creed, the principal prayers, the articles of the faith, the commandments of God and the church, and a list of sins and virtues. Indeed, the first book printed in New Spain was probably the Nahuatl *Christian Doctrine* (1539), of which no copy has survived. Franciscans and Dominicans excelled as authors of confession manuals. The earliest known bilingual (Nahuatl-Spanish) confessional handbook by Fray Alonso de Molina was published in 1565, but informal bilingual confessional guides, in abbreviated manuscript form, circulated widely before this time. The friars even undertook translations of the New Testament, in the early days before the spread of Protestantism in Europe made such things anathema. Between 1524 and 1572, the mendicant orders in Mexico printed one hundred and nine books pertaining to evangelization in various Indian languages. (Verastique 2000: 106; Klor de Alva 1991: 92; Duverger 1993: 136-43)

The decision to evangelize in native languages entailed finding the right words. There was considerable debate among missionaries about whether the potential dangers of translation outweighed the potential benefits of Indians learning in their own language. The issue posed something of a dilemma: on the one hand, concepts expressed in an alien language (Spanish, even more so Latin) risked the failure of native peoples to grasp them; on the other, the use of native words to translate Christian concepts might distort, even betray, their true meaning. The Christian God and his message might be Indianized if they were presented through a filter of native concepts. (Duverger 1993: 146)

After initial doubts, the friars considered that in most cases Nahuatl offered sufficient semantic range to allow translation. In some cases, the friars felt that the native tongue provided a more or less direct translation. "Lord" could be translated as *temaquixtiani* ("saviour") or *tetlaocoliani* ("merciful"). In other cases, the friars decided that a native word could be used to mean what they decided it would mean. The words *teoyotl* (as a noun) and *teoyotica* (as an adjective) designated the divine, sacred, saintly, and spiritual. The Franciscans hit on the idea of using these words to mean "Christian." Thus, whereas the pre-Hispanic marriage rite was called *nenamictiliztli*, the Catholic sacrament was to be called *teoyotica nenamictiliztli*; in the same spirit, Christian confirmation was called *teoyotica techicaualiztli*, since *techicaualiztli* was the Nahuatl word for a Nahua ceremony of "spiritual affirmation," the closest analogy the friars could find to the Christian ceremony. The expression "to convert" was translated as *teotia tlatocatia*, literally "to recognize as god and as sovereign," which the Franciscans thought adequately embodied the meaning. In yet other cases, neologisms (new words) in Nahuatl could be invented by the friars; for example "rosary" was called *teocuitlaxochicozcatl* or "necklace of flowers of gold," since "flower of gold" was the name that the Indians gave to the rose of Castile. In order to translate "Christian priest," the friars had to coin a new term, since they were not prepared to use one of the Nahuatl words for native priest. They chose to invent the word *teopixqui*, or "guardian of God," inspired by the title of the administrative official, *calpixqui*, or tribute collector. (Duverger 1993: 101, 147)

The greatest difficulty lay in choosing a translation for God; here there were two schools of thought. For some, God was untranslatable and should be left as *Dios*, or, alternatively, might at a pinch be rendered *iceltzin nelli teotl* ("the only true God") or *teotl tlatoani* ("sovereign god/lord"), which were terms not used by the pre-Columbian Nahuas, in order to distinguish Him from Mexican deities. The second school of thought went further in allowing the use of Nahuatl terms to designate God and considered it acceptable to apply epithets used by the Nahuas for certain deities, which in their (the Franciscan) view could only belong to the Christian God. For example the pre-conquest Nahuas had referred to the god Tezcatlipoca as *teyocoyani* "creator," *ipalnemoani* "he for whom things live," or *moyocoyatzin* "he who creates himself." Now the native god was stripped of these epithets, which were only to apply to the Christian God. The epithet "he for whom things live" may have been the origin of the expression "he who gives life to all things," used by Franciscans to designate the Christian God. Another invocation of Tezcatlipoca, Tloque Nahuaque, not opposed by the friars, gradually supplanted other terms until it became the indigenous name for God. Despite the best of the friars' efforts, Indians continued to recite the Lord's Prayer to God under the name of Totatzin, an invocation of the Sun God. (Duverger 1993: 76, 99-100, 202)

Some Christian terms and concepts - including "church," "spirit," "cross," "paradise," "purgatory," and "Last Judgment" - were normally not translated. Evidently the friars believed that here the limits of translation were reached, since the risk of confusion appeared too great. The cross (*nepaniuhtoc*) was known by the Nahuas, but its symbolism was entirely different from the Christian. The Nahua cross represented the intersection of cosmic axes, the center of annihilation of opposite forces, a place of inertia and instability and of forces which destabilize life. (Duverger 1993: 149) This was why all manifestations of the center, for example crossroads, were feared. The Franciscans wished to avoid conserving these ideas and so rejected translation. The Nahuatl word *yolia* referred to a life force located in the heart, which survived death and went on to an afterlife, and was widely accepted as a parallel for the concept of "soul." It was not entirely trusted, however, and the Spanish loanword *ánima* was frequently used, as a basic part of Nahua vocabulary by the end of the sixteenth century, both alone and paired with *yolia*. Such pairing of a Christian religious term and the native term selected as its closest equivalent served to support the fiction that native and European ideas were in fact cognate. The friars could take comfort in the fact that the "right" word was there, while native people could focus on the familiar term. (Burkhart 1996: 174, 181; Lockhart 1992: 253-254) There was, however, no consistent policy, and much remained at the discretion of the individual. Sahagún favored the use of the Spanish term *Dios*, but on other occasions the word was rendered in Nahuatl. Although Sahagún opposed the use of the term Tonantzin for the Virgin Mary, it was widely used in doctrinal texts prepared by him and his students. (Dibble 1974: 226) Most Franciscans favored translation despite the risks. As one historian has noted, "Systematic non-translation would make Christian teachings superficial and unassimilated in native mentality and would have substituted the risk of incomprehension for that of error." (Dibble 1974: 227). In the end, the room for error was tolerated as a lesser evil than total incomprehension. The upshot was that the friars, by inserting Christianity in a native context, had inadvertently allowed the Christian message to be adapted and Christian doctrine to be assimilated to pre-Hispanic beliefs.

There were some Christian concepts, such as sin, good and evil and the figure of the devil, which were wholly alien to the Nahua mind, leaving the friars no choice but to grasp the closest parallels they could find. For sin they substituted the native concept of *tlatlacolli*. The most literal meaning of *tlatlacolli* is "something damaged"; the word could describe any sort of error or misdeed, from moral transgressions to judicially defined crimes to accidental or unintentional damage. Thus

31

the concepts of sin and *tlatlacolli* overlap but are not synonyms (most significantly, the concept of *tlatlacolli* did not contain the Christian notion of individual moral responsibility). *Tlatlacolli* assumed the intervention of supernatural entities to impose sanctions in this life but not in the afterlife. Thus natives who heard that envy of their neighbors was *tlatlacolli* were more likely to think in terms of punishment in this life that affected native society collectively (e.g. through disease) than penalties after death, which involved the suffering of the soul of the individual (a concept which did not exist in pre-conquest religion). So even though the acts classified as *tlatlacolli* were different under Christianity (for example, they included bad thoughts as well as bad actions), the nature of sin itself was made continuous with native thought, and hence was Nahuatlized, or Indianized. (Burkhart 1989: 28, 31; Burkhart 1996: 183)

This was not an isolated instance. In the translation of the Lord's Prayer, the Franciscans used not only *tlatlacolli* to translate sin, but also *popolhuia* for pardon and *yeyecoltiliztli* for temptation; resort to these words placed Christian concepts within a native moral framework. (Duverger 1993: 148) Similarly, the friars' use of the Nahuatl term for the ritual of "straightening out the heart" in order to designate Christian penance made the sacrament more familiar in native frames of reference, but it also predisposed its adaptation and the survival under cover of its prehistoric parallel. (Burkhart 1989: 181-83; Graziano 1999: 97) The words used in Nahuatl for Christ's resurrection derived from the verb *izcalia*, which meant "reviving," or "resuscitating," but since it did not necessarily refer to a return from death, it imparted less of a sense of the miraculous than does the idea of resurrection as used in Christian contexts. (Burkhart 1996: 244)

The Christian concepts of good and evil had no equivalents in Nahua thought; there was no native word for good or for evil, in the abstract sense. The fundamental cosmic conflict for pre-conquest Mesoamericans was not between the forces of good and the forces of evil, which were different facets of the same reality, but between the principle of order and the principle of chaos. Nahua gods were never exclusively good or exclusively evil. They were ambivalent beings that

32

could be both benevolent and malevolent, depending on how people treated them and fulfilled their obligations to them. Some could even express opposing principles in their different manifestations. The problem was not how to align oneself with good and not evil, but to discover the proper balance between order and chaos. In order to refer to the concepts of good and evil in the abstract, the friars chose terms that derived from this dualism of order and chaos. To refer to evil, the friars used *tlahuelilocayotl*, which meant frenzy or raving madness, an uncontrolled state of emotion rather than badness itself. Thus, although the friars insisted on maintaining the Christian categories of good and evil, they ended up expressing them in terms of the order-disorder dialectic. This was the only way of making their value judgments meaningful to the Nahuas, yet it effectively Nahuatlized what they were trying to say. (Burkhart 1989: 37-38)

The concept of the devil was also Indianized by the use of Nahuatl terms. Some friars, such as Olmos, preferred to use the Spanish terms (Olmos 1990: xxv), and the words *diablo* (with a Nahuatl plural form *diablome*) and *demonio*, and the names Lucifer and Satan were introduced. Others employed Nahuatl translations. Molina translated devil as *tlacatecolotl*, which meant literally "human owl," and referred to a malevolent type of *nahualli* or shape-changing shaman who took the form of an animal alter-ego in trances, and inflicted sickness and death. Like the devil, the "human owl" was associated with night, underworld, sorcery, ghosts, and even horns, but he was a human being, not a cosmic entity. There was no intermediate category in Nahua thought between god and human, as there was in Christianity (angels were in a separate category, and Lucifer was a fallen angel) so friars had to choose either a divine or human being to represent the devil. Sahagún objected to the use of the word *tlacatecolotl* for the devil, since it effectively elevated a category of indigenous sorcerer to the role of God's adversary. Even so, the word was widely used in doctrinal texts prepared by him and his students. The Nahuas accepted the word *tlacatecolotl* and used it, as well as *diablo* and *demonio*, to refer to native deities, including Tezcatlipoca, Quetzalcoatl and Huitzilopochtli. Another native term, *tzitzimime*, monstrous female lesser deities associated with twilight and the end of the world, was also used to mean devils or demons, again Nahuatlizing the Christian concept. (Burkhart 1989: 40-42; Burkhart 1996 183; Duverger 1993: 78) The use of the Nahuatl Mictlan "place of the dead" (a northern subterranean place where most men went after death) for Hell also appealed to Nahua cultural references. The journey to Mictlan was a return to the tribal land of origin, an inverse migration to the great plains of the north (from where the Nahuas had migrated south). In the friars' translation of the Christian Creed, the descent of Christ after death to Hell was rendered as the descent of Mictlantecuhtli ("Lord of Mictlan," a pre-Hispanic deity) to Mictlan, and effectively assimilated him to a Mexican god. (Duverger 1993: 151)

The decision to evangelize in native tongues opened the way for indigenous concepts to be carried over into the most fundamental aspects of Christian moral teaching. (Burkhart 1989: 28) In their efforts to seek the closest parallels for Christian concepts in order the more readily to slip them into the native spiritual consciousness, the Franciscan friars were obliged to accommodate their teachings to native thought categories, as one historian has observed, "to a greater degree than they or their apologists dared to admit, and even greater than they may have realized." "The most original and at the same time the most ambiguous aspect of the apostolate of the Franciscans was that Catholicism could only be imposed in so far as it was inserted into pre-existing religious sentiment, but this fact was inadmissible. The friars never openly admitted such a policy but it can be read in their acts." (Burkhart 1989: 184)

The premise on which the Franciscans based their approach is illustrated by a story told by Jerónimo de Mendieta. In the early days, before the natives could write Nahuatl in the Latin alphabet, the Franciscans tried to teach Indian children the Lord's Prayer in Latin, partly from fear of corrupting the words' meaning, and partly because they believed those particular Latin syllables could open the way to God's grace, even if spoken with little understanding. Some children were quick to pick it up through rote repetition, but others, especially those who were slightly older, and those with less mental agility, had to find alternative methods. Some moved little stones or grains of

34

maize to count off phrases as they recited the prayer, until they were able to recite it by heart. Others jogged their memories by drawing glyphs for Nahuatl words whose pronunciation resembled the Latin words of the prayer, hoping that by reciting them in the correct order they would arrive at an approximation of the original Latin. For example, the word that was closest in pronunciation to *pater* was *pantli*, which was the Nahuatl for a little white flag symbolizing the number twenty. Thus they drew the glyph for *pantli* in order to remember to recite *pater*. For *noster*, they used the Nahuatl *nochtli*, which meant the fruit of the prickly pear cactus, and so after *pantli* they drew *nochtli*, and so on, until the entire prayer was represented in glyphs. (Mendieta 1971: 246; Duverger 1993: 168) Mendieta observed that this method seemed difficult, but he missed a far more important drawback. *Pantli*, as well as meaning flag, also meant white banners of human sacrifice; *nochtli* was for the Aztecs a symbol of the excised human heart, the "precious eagle cactus fruit" upon which the gods fed. As one historian comments, "clearly when the Indians muttered *pantli nochtli*, something other than what the friars intended passed through their minds" (Clendinnen 1987b). The friars disregarded the fact that words like *pantli* and *nochtli* conveyed their own meanings, from which they could not be detached in order to make them serve as mere sounds that happened to resemble Latin words.

A similar disregard was evident in the more complex task of using Nahuatl words, not for their resemblance to the sounds of Latin words, but as vehicles for a Christian message. They forgot, or chose to ignore, that words cannot be so easily emptied of their former meaning and "filled" with a new Christian one. The Franciscans assumed that elements in native religion could provide a foothold for their own replacement by roughly equivalent "correct" beliefs and understandings from the new religion until with the insertion of enough pieces conversion was effected by a process of incremental substitution. (Clendinnen 1987b) This derived from a view of native religion as a "bundle of discrete beliefs and bits of behavior" rather than as "a distinctive imaginative universe, another coherent way of making sense of world." Convinced of the transforming truth of their own doctrines, they neglected the possibility that the belief system of

35

the majority of Nahuas, rather than being smashed by Christianity into lots of little bits which could then be used to construct a new religion, might instead re-emerge by absorbing many Christian elements while maintaining its essential principles. (Burkhart 1989: 192)

The irony is that the strategy of rooting the new cult in the old made it easier for Christianity to gain acceptance but also more difficult for native religion to be abandoned. (Duverger 1993: 21) By establishing continuities, whether intended or unintended, the friars ensured that Christianity in some form would be adopted, but at the same time, they made it more likely that Indians would interpret it in their own terms. The result was that the Nahuas were able to become just Christian enough to get by without compromising their basic ideological and moral orientation. (Burkhart 1989: 184, 191) For their part, the friars contented themselves with an Indian Christianity of questionable orthodoxy, the result of unwitting doctrinal flexibility and unacknowledged molding of Christianity to the contours of Nahua religiosity. Christianity as presented in Nahuatl was not quite the same thing as orthodox Christian doctrine. These subtle changes helped the Nahuas to align Christian teaching with their own religious and moral outlook; the end result was a Nahua version of Christianity that appeared satisfactorily orthodox to all but the most perspicacious observers. (Burkhart 1988: 65-66)

It is relatively recently that historians have come to realize that the Nahuas saw the religion of the missionaries as a continuation of their own rather than as a sharp break, and that Christianity continued to be experienced more within the continuum of the familiar than as a break with it. (Klor de Alva 1993: 175, 180) The traditional view, taking at face value the account that the missionaries gave of their own activities, denied that the first missionaries were interested in understanding native religion or that they tolerated any aspects of native religion (since that would only preserve it) and insisted that they introduced Christianity as something entirely new, a complete rupture with the past. (Ricard 1966: 36) This view overlooked the missionary strategy of the Franciscans, the adoption not of a model of exclusion of all elements of native religion, but instead of a model of cultural

36

osmosis. (Duverger 1993: 209) This is not to say, as some historians have argued (for example, Nutini and Bell 1980), that the friars deliberately intended to promote the blending of the two religions. But, by allowing Christian doctrine to be shaped by Nahuatl terminology, the friars inadvertently fostered the retention of much indigenous belief within a colonial Nahuatl interpretation of Christianity. (Burkhart 1989: 39) Hence, evangelization occurred within "an essentially Mesoamerican universe." This was the outcome of a method of conversion that had turned Indians into Christians while letting them remain Indians; and, paradoxically, many natives converted in order to *continue to be Indians*. This was not unknown to the friars but was accepted as a lesser evil compared to rejection en masse or the failure of the religion to take root. (Duverger 1993: 202)

6 "Gentle, Holy Men, with Long Claws and Great Fangs"

In the sixteenth century, becoming a Christian involved an act of assent on the part of the convert, but this did not mean that the process was entirely voluntary. Assent to Christian teaching was based, on the one hand, on reason and argument, which entailed persuasion, and, on the other, on faith, which entailed unquestioning submission to the institution of the church and the immutable authority of scripture, which could brook no opposition or deviation. Here lay the roots of an unresolved tension between persuasion and coercion. (MacCormack 1985: 444)

There was considerable debate among Spanish theologians and jurists regarding the role of coercion in evangelization. In *The Only True Way* (1538-40), Dominican Friar Bartolomé de Las Casas repudiated the use of force and insisted that the church must follow the missionary methods of Christ. Since all peoples in the world possessed the same range of qualities, and in all nations God had predestined a certain, albeit unknown, number of souls for eternal salvation, so the gospel should be universally preached in the same way to all men, with love and by means of rational persuasion. (Brading 1991: 64) His opponent, Juan Ginés de Sepúlveda, argued that, although the primitive apostolic church had not used coercion, the emergence of one unified Christian society during the reign of Emperor Constantine meant that the church had acquired a secular arm which, under the legitimate authority of the spiritual power, could employ force to convert the heathen.

The position of Franciscan missionaries was closer to that of Sepúlveda than to that of Las Casas. The Franciscan chronicler Jerónimo de Mendieta implicitly repudiated Las Casas' premise that there was an "only method" of converting all races of mankind in all times and places. If Spain had been chosen by God to undertake the conversion of the Indians, then the act of conquest that had allowed the entire enterprise to begin could not be against His wishes. Although, technically, no one could be forced to convert to Christianity, which was an act of internal assent, most missionaries, following the principles which the great scholar Francisco de Vitoria considered to be enshrined in natural law, accepted that it was legitimate to use force in three cases: first, to suppress idolatry and false religion; second, to hold newly baptized Indians to the faith to which they had committed; third, to prevent those who had not yet been baptized from drawing the converted back to the old religion. With force justified in all these cases, which covered almost every eventuality likely to face evangelizers, it was in practice impossible to distinguish activity designed to secure conversion from activity designed to root out the old religion or hang on to new converts. In the overwhelming majority of cases, conversions followed the use of force. In any case, the day-to-day reality of evangelization was never likely to bear much resemblance to the theory. Leading the Indians to the faith by means of preaching, education and good example was the preferred method among all missionaries, but in practice, many were prepared to resort to force when persuasion failed to work quickly enough, and when faced with recalcitrance or back-sliding.

The resolve to punish recalcitrant Indians corporally was formalized when, in 1539, the bishop of Mexico and the heads of the three orders in New Spain laid down that missionaries could impose "light punishments" on Indians, as appropriate to "the master with his apprentice, or the teacher with the person in his charge." Thus force became integrated into the standard repertoire of missionary strategies used not only by Franciscans, but also by members of other orders and by secular clerics. Nor would it be true to say that the friars only had recourse to coercion as a last resort, after many years of exhaustive techniques of persuasion. The use of force to maintain the orthodoxy of baptized Indians was tolerated by the friars from the very beginning of evangelization. The first Franciscan friar, Martín de Valencia, began to persecute recently baptized Indians (in his capacity as commissary of the Inquisition) shortly after his arrival in 1524. He had no qualms about employing the death penalty, and by 1527 he had had four Tlaxcalan leaders executed as idolaters.

The power to try and punish offenders against the faith was a complicated business, and a brief digression to consider it will put Valencia's actions in perspective. The original historic authority for the exercise of inquisition (which originally meant simply inquiry) lay in the hands of the bishop, under whose jurisdiction matters of heresy (or deviation from Christian orthodoxy) fell. But in Spain, as in some other countries, a separate institution, not subject to the secular ecclesiastical hierarchy, had grown up whose exclusive purpose was investigation of the orthodoxy of Christians: the infamous Spanish Inquisition. Although staffed by men of the church, the Inquisition (in its re-founded form after 1478, as opposed to its earlier incarnation in the thirteenth century) was an institution of the state, not of the church, and was therefore under the power of the Crown. Furthermore, it had been re-founded in order to investigate converted Jews in Spain, and did not acquire a role in America until the later sixteenth century; there was no Spanish Inquisition in America before 1571, and even then its jurisdiction was limited to Spaniards, mestizos and Africans and did not include Indians. The power to investigate Indian religious orthodoxy in America, then, always lay in the hands of the bishops' or Episcopal inquisition. But in the early days there were not even bishops. In their absence, under the authority of Pope Adrian VI's bull *Exponi nobis* (May 1522), known in the Spanish world as the *Omnímoda*, the prelates of monastic orders were authorized to exercise almost all Episcopal powers (except ordination) in a territory where there was no resident bishop or where the Episcopal see was two days distant; thus jurisdiction over heresy was conferred on them together with the right to exercise the powers of inquisitors. So Valencia had the power to act as he did. But it is the alacrity with which he, like many of his Franciscan fellows, took to the task that is most notable. The willingness to commit violence on recalcitrant Indian bodies sits uneasily with the commitment to Christian love. But then sixteenth-century Christian love was tough love.

As bishops were appointed to sees, they assumed the inquisitorial function in their dioceses and the monastic inquisition (headed by friars) ceased to operate except in geographically isolated areas, such

41

as the Yucatán. Juan de Zumárraga launched an (Episcopal) Indian Inquisition in Central Mexico between 1536 and 1543, under which at least nineteen different trials involving seventy-five Indians were conducted (the most famous being that of Don Carlos of Texcoco, recounted below). The major concern was with native dogmatizers (who preached against the teachings of the missionary friars and urged Indians to return to paganism), and the native lords who supported them, or who encouraged idolatries and ceremonies of the old religion. Most of the investigations took place in Central Mexico, though Zumárraga did send Friar Andrés de Olmos to the Yucatán where, for example, he punished a native lord who practiced idolatry and made sacrifices. (Greenleaf 1962: 63-64)

One of the first to be tried in Central Mexico, in 1536, was Martín Ocelotl of Texcoco, baptized by the Twelve in 1525, but who nevertheless preached against Christianity and practiced as a native sorcerer. He was greatly respected by the native population in the Texcoco area, and the (present-day) states of Hidalgo and Tlaxcala, and worshipped as a god since he reputedly could foresee the future, predict famines and droughts, control rains, cure illness and transform himself into an old man or a child, to outsmart time, and even into animals such as jaguars, lions and dogs. Many pre-Hispanic sorcerers were renowned both for causing rain and for being able to project their souls into their animal alter ego, the jaguar, a creature whose association with rain goes far back into Mesoamerican prehistory. (Musgrave-Portilla 1982: 41) He claimed to be one of those prophets who warned Moctezuma of the coming of the Europeans. The Emperor was reputed to have put him and his fellow sorcerers in a cage, from which only Ocelotl escaped. Another version told how Ocelotl had been put to death, his body pulled to pieces, and his bones pulverized, only for him to come back to life. He knew enough Christianity for one Franciscan friar to be able to pay tribute to his repartee as worthy of a theologian. (Gruzinski 1989: 42) As if envisaging himself as a counterpart to the friars, he practiced a kind of missionary activity in reverse in the footsteps of Franciscan preachers; whenever he saw a friar going to preach he bade him go ahead and promised to catch up with him later. He went into villages to attack

42

Christianity, sometimes by rekindling old apocalyptic cyclical terrors to interpret the coming of the missionaries. "There had just arrived two apostles sent by God, with very long nails, with recognizable teeth and markings, who sowed terror, and the friars would change into *chichimicli*," and eat people and provoke the end of the world, unless the natives returned to the old religion. *Chichimicli*, or *tzitzimime*, were foul cannibalistic beings, "women with neither flesh nor bones," who lived in the air, and came down to earth to plunge the world into darkness and annihilate humanity at the end of each sun or era. Thus, in a very early reinterpretation of the Christian tradition, the friars were assimilated to devouring monsters, and the apostles of Christ, with whom the Franciscan religious had identified themselves, were transformed into beings with long claws and great fangs, just like the ancient jaguar-god recalled in Martín's own totemic name, Ocelotl. (Lafaye 1976: 21-23; León-Portilla 1974: 26) The friars considered the prophet to be a danger to the missionary effort, and recommended that he be banished from New Spain, and Zumárraga sentenced him to be transported to Spain in 1537 (and possibly he was lost at sea). Even so tales from his region persisted that he was still at large. (Gruzinski 1989: 43)

Another sorcerer, Andrés Mixcoatl (Cloud Serpent), tried in 1537, and also a baptized Christian, claimed to be Ocelotl's messenger or brother, presumably in order to assume his prestige and magical powers, even though there were no known connections between the two men. Subsequently he insisted he was Ocelotl, and that only one of his messengers had been sent to Spain by Zumárraga. One of the prophet's servants recognized Mixcoatl as Ocelotl and claimed that his master had reappeared. This should not be dismissed as mere bluff or deception. Mixcoatl was a "man-god," which is to say an individual who communicated directly with the tutelary deity and in a state of ecstasy was transformed into a faithful replica of that god. Thus, Mixcoatl could begin as the brother of Tlaloc, the rain god, and the brother of Ocelotl, and end up becoming Ocelotl, without ceasing the whole time to be Telpochtli Tezcatlipoca, the omniscient god of the night sky, of winter and of the north, in his aspect of "the young man." Humans and gods were superimposed on one another in Nahua culture, and individuals like Ocelotl or Mixcoatl were seen as "the covering, the bark, the skin" of the protective divine force. While in the West we would say that such a man was possessed by the god or spirit, the Nahuas understood that the man-god *became* the very authority that he worshipped. There was nothing contradictory for the Nahuas in the merging of Ocelotl and Mixcoatl into a single identical man-god. (Gruzinski 1989: 22, 43)

Mixcoatl acted as a shaman and followed an itinerant life, which took him northeast from the Valley of Mexico to the Sierra de Puebla, more than one hundred and eighty kilometres from Texcoco, as the crow flies. He passed through villages asking Indians for incense and paper to prepare sacrifices and rites of sorcery, and preached to the people, telling them not to fear, their maize would not frost. (Lafaye 1976: 22) He was given tribute of mantles and hallucinogenic mushrooms whose ingestion induced in him prophetic visions. He practiced divination with grains of corn, and performed sacrificial rites to "his brother" Tlaloc, and claimed to be able to make it rain and change the direction of the clouds. His followers reportedly regarded him as a rain god (or alternatively Tezcatlipoca) and made sacrifices to him. Mixcoatl promised death to the lukewarm and those who resisted his demands. He foretold the ruin of the corn and cotton harvests, an avenging frost, a drought. "If you had not given me mantles, I know what I would have done: I would have spoken to the god of fire and told him to get angry." (Lafaye 1976: 47)

He showed both accommodation of and resistance to Christianity. On the one hand, he maintained bands of disciples who, in imitation of Christ, he told to "follow him." On the other, he preached against the friars, deriding their inability to bring rain, urged the natives to resist baptism and to refuse to learn the articles of faith, and boasted that he had been charged by Ocelotl to collect three thousand six hundred arrow heads to fight the Christians. Perhaps because he had been baptized much later, Mixcoatl had not grasped the subtleties of Christianity to the point where he could become a virtual theologian, like Ocelotl, but his mastery was enough to work out a blasphemous parody of the Creed in which he told his followers that just as

Christians recite in the first article "I believe in One Almighty God," so they should recite a first article "I throw God in the fire," a second article "I drive him away with a stick," and so on. (Gruzinski 1989: 54, 56) He urged the people to return to the ancient gods on whom they could rely and not to trust the friars:

Why are you forsaking the things of the past and forgetting them if the gods that you adored in the olden days helped you and gave you what you needed? Don't you realize that all that the friars say is only lies and falsehood? They have brought nothing to help you; they do not know us, nor do we know them. Our fathers, our grandfathers - did they know these monks? Did they see what they preach, the God they talk about? They did not. On the contrary, they are deceiving us. We, we are eating what the gods give us; it is they who are feeding us, are teaching us and giving us strength. Do we in any way know the friars? I intend to make these sacrifices, and it will not be on their account that I give them up." (Gruzinski 1989: 54)

Mixcoatl worked at a time - 1537 - when Christianity was still in nascent state in the Sierra de Puebla, and so he may have exercised considerable influence over the religious consciousness of those to whom he preached. But at the same time, he was not simply a traditional pagan priest of old. Disassociating himself from the pre-Hispanic native priests, he refused to take with him indigenous gods or wear the fine costumes of pagan priests, but instead concentrated in his person sufficient sacred force to be able to do without accessories, to the point that his style ended by mimicking that of his Franciscan enemy, who, also equipped with meager means, traveled throughout the country disseminating the word of God. It is almost as if anti-Christian action had already come under the influence of what it strove to drive out, as if the religious strategies were exact copies of each other. (Gruzinski 1989: 55, 61)

The inquisition knew enough of his reputed powers to caution him ironically when he was arrested: "Listen, do not change into a lizard or anything, let yourself be taken away, simple man that you are, to the Emperor." Unlike Ocelotl, who maintained a dignified and obstinate silence under questioning, Mixcoatl cracked, forced some of his followers to confess, and attributed his deviation from Christianity to the devil, and declared a wish to return to the fold and believe what the friars preached. He was whipped, returned to the villages where he had preached and forced to abjure his sins, and was incarcerated for a year. It is important to remember that it was native lords and neophyte Christian Indians who initiated proceedings against him. There was considerable diversity of behavior in the indigenous world from the earliest days of Spanish domination. Some collaborated early on and became skilled tacticians in turning to their advantage the standards of the victors; others learned to hide behind a Christian mask and to use doublespeak; still others - such as Mixcoatl - resisted. (Gruzinski 1989: 57-60)

The most famous Indian tried by Zumárraga's Inquisition was Don Carlos Chichimecatecuhtli or Ometochtzin, grandson of Netzahualcoyotl and son of Netzahualpilli, rulers of Texcoco. Carlos was one of the first Indians to be baptized in around 1524, had been reared in the household of Cortés and educated at the College of Santa Cruz Tlatelolco, which he entered in 1536. Having succeeded his brother Hernando Ixtlilxochitl as *cacique*, or lord, of Texcoco in around 1531, he was a major figure of the Hispanized Indian establishment. Despite his elite status in the post-conquest world, he was a declared anti-Christian, articulated a thoughtful critique of the friars, and put his European culture at the service of native values. He was denounced as a dogmatizer in June 1539 by an Indian of the village of Chiconautla, where, finding the area beset by plague and drought, and the Indians encouraged by the priest to pray and make processions, he had publicly ridiculed the activities and teachings of the friars, who, he said, in statements which recall those of Mixcoatl, deceived the people. (Greenleaf 1962: 87) One of his most interesting observations was that since each one of the three religious orders observed a different rule, each one good in itself, then it was perfectly correct that the natives should have their own way of living and making worship. (Duverger 1993: 189-90) He told his supporters that they should not give up their own beliefs for something they did not understand; since their ancestors Nezahualcoyotl and Nezahualpilli,

46

who were prophets, had said nothing about a new law or god, then there was no reason to change their way of thinking. (León-Portilla 1974: 28-29) He ridiculed the sacrament of confession as a device whereby the friars satisfied their curiosity about other people's sins. He accused the Franciscans of sexual immorality, but defended concubinage among the Indians as an ancient custom which should continue, suggesting that the only reason that Indians were punished for this practice was that Spaniards wished to reserve the privilege for themselves. He caused public scandal by proclaiming that he slept with his niece, Inés, whenever he wished, a boast that was confirmed by Zumárraga's discovery that the woman had given birth to Carlos's child. His sister-in-law testified that he had tried to make her his concubine shortly after her husband died, and while she was still in mourning. But Carlos's most serious offence was to attack the political power of the church and the Spanish regime:

"Who are these people who disrupt and molest us, and live off us, and who we cannot get off our backs? Here am I, and there is the lord of Mexico, Yoanizi, and over there is my nephew Tezapili, the lord of Tacuba, and over there is Tlacahuepantli, the lord of Tula, we are all one in our positions and agreed that this is our land, our possession, our jewel wherein no one shall equal us. Sovereignty is ours and belongs to us alone, who are they to come here and subjugate us, they are not our relatives nor of our blood, yet they make themselves our equals, well we are here and nobody is going to make fools of us..." (Greenleaf 1962: 88; Padden 1967: 261)

There were enough witnesses to this speech to convince Zumárraga of its reality. However, the further charge of idolatry was not substantiated. Carlos had been heard to claim that his father and grandfather maintained contact with him and advised him on how to govern his peoples, and to follow the instructions of the ancient gods of Aztec religion, but nowhere in the testimony was Carlos accused of making sacrifices. He testified that he knew nothing of the idols, including Quetzalcoatl, Xipe, Tlaloc and Coatlicue, which had been found in one of his palaces after Zumárraga himself conducted a search, and that the palace, formerly a pagan temple, had been the residence of his late uncle, and had been closed since the man's death. Carlos' wife and child knew nothing of the palace and idols, and other witnesses gave no testimony of the lord's idolatry. After finding the idols in Carlos' house, Zumárraga ordered a hunt throughout the region of Texcoco, which was supervised by the governor, Lorenzo de Luna, illegitimate brother of Carlos. The hunt uncovered a cult of the god Tlaloc, which had been revived with the drought of 1539. As in pre-conquest times, natives came from Tlaxcala, Cholula, and Chalco, to a mountain near Texcoco, where Tlaloc was believed to reside. But this activity was not connected to the case of Carlos. It was considered proven, on the other hand, that the lord was a poor Christian; his small son, whom he had forbidden to go to church, did not know how to cross himself, nor could he recite any prayers or Christian doctrine.

When Carlos was formally interrogated in Mexico City by Zumárraga, he denied the charges of dogmatizing and criticizing the clergy and Christianity, though he confessed he had a concubine. Carlos was given thirty days to provide witnesses to support his assertion that he was a good Christian, but he was unable to do so. At the very last minute he alleged that the testimony against him was the result of an attempt on the part of a disgruntled group whom he had punished to remove him from the lordship and replace him. It is impossible to say if there was any truth in this defense. We know, though, that his half-brother, Lorenzo de Luna, succeeded Carlos as governor and testified against him in this case. We do not know what happened to his wife and son, nor what became of all his property that was confiscated. Zumárraga found him guilty of being a dogmatizer and, probably on account of his refusal to confess or to plead for mercy, and on account of the seriousness of his disloyal speech about the Spanish government of Mexico, the bishop recommended that he be relaxed to the secular arm; no mention was made of concubinage and he was exonerated of the charge of idolatry. The Viceroy and the *Audiencia* (supreme judicial and administrative authority) supported the sentence, which was carried out in public on 30 November 1539. Repenting at the last moment, Carlos asked permission to make a speech to the Indians gathered, telling them to renounce idolatries and follow the true faith. He did not escape the death sentence since his repentance was so late but it is possible that he was strangled before his corpse was burned, a common practice with those obstinate heretics who repented at the last moment. The burning of Carlos aroused a storm of protest in Spain, since many believed there was insufficient evidence to merit such a severe sentence, and Zumárraga was reprimanded for excessive use of force and instructed to desist from investigations of Indian orthodoxy. A few years, later he was relieved of his duties as Apostolic Inquisitor. This affair gave great impetus to the movement for the exemption of Indians from inquisitorial jurisdiction.

Even so, an independent inquisitor continued to investigate idolatries under Zumárraga between 1544 and 1547, not only among the Nahuas but also further south among the Mixtecs, and persecution was revived under the next Archbishop of Mexico, Alonso de Montúfar. The use of force on Indian bodies, then, did not subside. For their part, the Dominicans in the Mixtec and Zapotec provinces embarked, from 1558, on idolatry prosecutions, in which the methods were so harsh that they provoked furious protest to the authorities. Not only had the friars publicly accused supposed idolaters from the pulpits and had them whipped and imprisoned, they had also employed torture and broken canon law by keeping Indians prisoner in a friary. One woman miscarried and one native lord hanged himself for fear of the friars. Even though these activities were considered so harsh that the Audiencia felt obliged to intervene, and even though the principal initiators were removed from office, the campaign not only continued with the same rigor, but also spread to areas inhabited by the Mixes, Chochones, and Chinantecos. Coercion was not easily abandoned.

7 Franciscan Inquisition Among the Maya

The most infamous prosecutions of Indian idolatry in the entire sixteenth century are those of Friar Diego de Landa, Franciscan Provincial of Yucatán. In 1562, the friars at Mani (Mérida) were confronted by evidence that large numbers, possibly the majority, of Christian Indians in the heartland of their mission enterprise, many of whom had been the first to receive the faith, had continued to worship native gods in secret in order to secure adequate rain and abundant corn and deer. Even before the basic facts were established, groups of Indians were flogged, hung with stones attached to their feet and had burning wax poured on their bodies until they revealed the idols they had owned; the confession of small numbers of idols would provoke further torture until satisfyingly large numbers were confessed. These Indians were then ordered to surrender the precise number that they had admitted to owning, and were returned to jail to await formal punishment. Although the first victims were non-nobles in the area of Mani, Landa subsequently extended the enquiry into the ranks of native chiefs and lords, and spread his net to include the adjacent provinces of Sotuta and Hocaba-Homun. All in all, more than four thousand five hundred Indians were put to torture during three months of inquisition, and an official enquiry later established that one hundred and fifty eight had died during or as a direct result of the interrogations, at least thirteen people had committed suicide to escape torture, another eighteen had disappeared, and many more had been left crippled. Not only were these actions brutal, they were also illegal. Torture was applied without any of the safeguards which regulated its use in Spanish ecclesiastical and civil courts, no records of any kind were kept, and the penalties imposed - floggings, heavy fines, and periods of forced labor of up to ten years' duration - were well in excess of officially approved limits. Landa later justified his disregard of legal formalities, arguing that it was not possible to proceed strictly according to law because the province of Mani alone would have required twenty years of effort and meanwhile the Indians would all become idolaters and go to Hell. He pointed to the testimony which he had extracted regarding human sacrifices by some chiefs and schoolmasters in Sotuta, sometimes in the blasphemous form of human crucifixion, and idolatrous acts carried out in Christian churches, as sufficient justification for his methods, but the fact was that these were only confessed several months after the investigations began; the friars had responded with swift ruthlessness and startling violence long before there was any hint of such horrors. Some Spanish settlers, having seen Indians combing ruins looking for idols, doubted the authenticity of those handed in (especially those that were suspiciously dilapidated, or remarkably new), but Landa, with his characteristic high-handedness, banned any discussion of the legitimacy of his investigations under threat of excommunication.

The investigations were only halted by the arrival of the newly appointed Franciscan bishop of Yucatán (1560-71), Friar Francisco de Toral. Agreeing with those Franciscans who opposed Landa's actions, for there was already internal dissent in the order, Toral was convinced that Landa and his associates had grossly over-reacted to minor delinquencies, themselves more the result of Indian indolence and the inadequacy of the friars' teachings rather than full-blown apostasy, and that they had been moved by anger, arrogance and cruelty. After reading the confessions, he confirmed Landa's inquisitorial authority but prohibited any further use of torture, which clearly implied a degree of scepticism as to the veracity of the confessions. He was impressed by the Indians' testimony that, although the confessions of idolatries were true, they had invented the stories about human sacrifices when they had been tortured, and since they had been kept in a common prison, had conferred with their fellows in order to produce a mutually agreed fabrication. Toral imposed light penances on the chiefs and lords for the confessed idolatries and returned them to their villages and offices. Leading Spanish citizens, who loathed Landa, testified to his lust for power and intolerance of opposition. Summoned by the Council of the Indies to give an account of his actions, Landa was forced to return to Spain to defend himself. There he was fully exonerated. The Provincial of the Order in Spain concluded in 1565 that Landa had been justified in his assumption of Episcopal authority and in his procedures, given the nature of the crimes; that the Indians had not lied when they made their confessions;

and that it had been the bishop, not Landa, who had erred. When Toral died in 1571, Landa was appointed as his successor, a post he held until his death in 1579. Shortly after his return to Yucatán, Landa mounted a new enquiry into backsliding among Indians in the Campeche region. The governor of the province, with the support of leading Indians, complained to the Audiencia in Mexico that once again the punishments had been excessive, that ecclesiastical authorities had no right to administer them and that the Indians dreaded a repeat of the excesses of 1562. The Audiencia instructed Landa to abide by a regulation of 1570 that forbade imprisonment, flogging or shearing of Indians by ecclesiastics, and the governor of Yucatán was required to ensure enforcement. Thus, although his freedom was curtailed to some extent, Landa was returned to a position of power and authority, which he was able to exploit to revive his inquisition. For Landa there was no question of his having committed an error.

At first sight, such cruelties by the friars appear aberrant and uncharacteristic. It is true that, to some extent, Yucatán was a special case. The type of conquest carried out there made evangelization very difficult. Subjugation of the region took twenty years (1527-47) and was marked by continual rebellions and bloody pacifications. The first Franciscan entry in 1537 lasted no more than two years, and permanent missions were only established in 1544-45. The population was small (around two hundred and sixty thousand inhabitants in 1545) and very widely dispersed in a territory that was one quarter of the size of Spain, with a density of about two people per square kilometer, a situation not greatly altered by attempts at resettlement from 1552. The Franciscans had insufficient numbers to conduct a profound evangelization. In 1562, there were no more than twenty friars in Yucatán when in New Spain there were around four hundred, if all three orders are taken into account. Landa estimated in 1563 that the friars attended to two hundred villages; a more precise figure for 1580 reveals thirteen Franciscan friaries looking after one hundred and seven villages, with a population of ninety-two thousand natives, or about seventy percent of the Maya population of that time. Nor were there friars from other orders to assist them, since in Yucatán the

Franciscans enjoyed a monopoly of the mission field throughout the sixteenth century. This privileged status was a major factor in allowing their domination of the Indians to go unchecked. The friars were also a very different breed from those who had evangelized New Spain. Although some of the friars had moved to the Yucatán from Central Mexico, the majority came direct from Spain, where the environment had changed considerably from that of thirty years before. The dreams of reestablishing the primitive apostolic church had given way to the harsher realism of the Council of Trent, and as a result, the attitude of the Franciscans in Yucatán was less idealistic, more demanding, and rigid. Frustration at the failure to eradicate native religious rites led to punitive force becoming, within a decade of the start of serious evangelization in Yucatán, a standard part of evangelical strategy, in stark contrast to the instructions given to the early friars to "convert by word and example." (Borges 1992, 2:199-205; Clendinnen 1982: 29)

But Landa's activities were not principally due to the particular circumstances of the Yucatán since the resolve to employ coercion derived from the ideology at the heart of the Order: the paternalist ethos which saw Indians as fickle and wayward children, in need of a loving but firm hand, and chastisement for their own good. Furthermore, the Indians' childlike need for tutelage was not a temporary stage, but a long-term, even permanent state, necessitated by their character, not just their ignorance of Christianity. For the friars, Indians were like soft wax, quick to take an impression and equally quick to lose it, unless the impress were repeated again and again, most effectively through the whip. It should be remembered that corporal punishment was the norm for this time; the flogging of schoolboys, for example, was routine in Spain. But something more is required to explain the Franciscans' violence towards their charges: a sense of filial betrayal. The friars' paternalism had its benevolent side, a protective, nurturing urge, but it also had its counterpart, a dark side that would countenance no defiance from disobedient children. If the Franciscans were so affronted by the Indian treachery, it was because they had fought battles for the Maya, such as forcing reductions of tribute, and now found themselves treated, so they felt, with ingratitude and deceit. Landa painfully reflected how his initial patience and gentleness in rebuking them had been rewarded with intent to deceive him further. He argued in his *Relation* that only through punishment could such a people be improved, and, indeed, afterwards that they had shown great repentance and readiness to become good Christians. Although Toral and some other veteran friars dissented, Landa and his colleagues (maybe fifteen to twenty friars) were passionately persuaded of the appropriateness of their conduct, and of the continuity of their behavior with the ideology of their order. As a principal historian of the Landa trials concludes, "violence and cruelty [were] threaded too deeply into missionary Franciscan performance to be diagnosed as aberrant." (Clendinnen 1982: 32)

The paradox is that it should have been Landa who unleashed such destructiveness when there was no missionary who had taken a greater interest in Maya culture nor had succeeded as well in earning the trust of the Indians. As a young friar, he learnt Mayan to perfection and translated an approved catechism and some sermons into the language for his fellow missionaries. Not satisfied with confining himself to the regions settled by conquest, he traveled alone to more remote areas in order to spread the faith among the Indians of the interior, and persuade them to smash their idols and convert. The detailed knowledge of all aspects of native culture revealed in his *Relation* suggests that the Maya accepted him with an exceptional degree of trust. He learnt some of the secrets of the elders, including Maya systems for measuring time, and was privileged to see the sacred writings of the Cocom ruling lineage preserved in folding deerskin books. "The revelation of that treasure - especially to a Spanish outsider - can only be explained as the expression of a confidence and attraction so powerful as to override traditional prescriptions and even conventional caution." (Clendinnen 1987a: 69-70) He developed an unusually warm relationship with Nachi Cocom, head chief of Sotuta and long an enemy of the Spaniards, who became his friend and benefactor. How painful it must have been, then, to learn in 1562 that it was precisely this friend and his family who had initiated the practice of human sacrifice by crucifixion in Sotuta. How wounding to discover that the very people with whom he had shared experiences and learnt so much in their huts and yards, the very people whose

Christianity he was most personally responsible for, who had recognized him and the truth of his message, as he thought, had been among the first to revert to pagan ways, and to mix devilish rites with symbols and ceremonies of the True Faith. How startling, too, that Landa's *Relation*, so much of which is devoted to the reconstruction of the religious rituals of the pre-contact Maya (to such an extent that it constitutes the principal source for the pre-Hispanic Yucatán), not only reveals nothing of Landa's feelings about the events of 1562, but does not even contain any explicit statement of the precise nature of the Indians' crimes in that year. Instead Landa writes: "they returned to the worship of their idols and to offer them sacrifices not only of incense but also human blood," an extremely ambiguous phrase since elsewhere Landa gave descriptions of self-laceration and drawing of blood from different parts of the body as an offering to gods. Nowhere does he say that they performed human sacrifice. Why is he so bafflingly silent on this one matter on which it was in his interest to provide irrefutable proof?

Most historians have taken the accounts of human sacrifice at face value, but one historian has doubted them. In the suspiciously opportune appearance of confessions to human sacrifice and murderous crucifixions may lie an alternative, more disturbing answer. Landa was the first of the friars to extract confessions to human sacrifice; this abominable crime was not mentioned before an indictment of 11 August 1562. Is it merely coincidence that this was the very day that everybody expected the arrival of the bishop, the only man who had the power to end Landa's trials? Landa was the only friar ever to extract confessions of blasphemous crucifixions. These stories appeared for the first time three or four days after the arrival of the bishop, from the mouths of witnesses whose villages had already been investigated, without any reference to such horrors. Could this be because Landa needed proof of inexcusable horrors in order to convince a sceptical bishop? Only Landa, with his intimate and personal experience of pre-contact and contemporary native religion and culture, had the wide knowledge of traditional Maya rituals necessary to shape his questions and the Indians' responses into accounts that could prove the true extent of their treachery. Nobody had been closer than Landa to the Indians of Yucatán, nobody could feel more personally the pain of their bitter betrayal. Could it be, as one historian has suggested, that the confessions as we have them reveal more about the shaping power of Landa's imagination than the actual behavior of the Indians? The circumstances of the confessions - Spanish assumptions of Maya guilt, the framing of questions in a way that proposed the answers, the continual threat or application of pain until a confession was extracted, the correlation between Maya confessions and fifteenth-century tales of Jewish ritual murders in Spain - all these suggest that such testimony may tell us more about Spanish fears than about Maya deeds. (Restall 1997: 148) This is to suggest nothing as crude as invention on Landa's part, rather that the hints of a very small number of human sacrifices, which maybe only Landa knew enough to elicit, were blown out of proportion by a man whose self-righteous rectitude convinced him that his treacherous former charges had descended to the very worst forms of paganism, and deserved to be severely punished in order to wrench the last root of opposition out of them. (Clendinnen 1987a)

The Landa affair illustrates how the corruption of the ideal of conversion by word and example jeopardized the entire missionary project. The violent outcome of the Landa trials may have been the major factor in wrecking the chances of a deep evangelization of the Yucatán. The events of 1562 probably marked a major shift in Maya evaluation of the status of Spanish religion. Until that point, Christian teachings were probably seen as little more than interesting novelties to be scanned for useful notions. That attitude changed with the trials. The books of Chilam Balam (or books of the Spokesmen of the Jaguar Lords) of Chumayel characterize 9 Ahau as the *katun* (twenty-year period) when Christianity began. From that time, the rule of the Lord *Dios* was accepted by the Maya in response to the experiences of that year, the three-month reign of terror of the friars. But the Indians remained recalcitrant. Pedro Sánchez de Aguilar complained in the seventeenth century that they failed to learn the basic Christian doctrines. In Yucatán, there was an almost complete lack of the apparatus of popular piety - the rosaries, the shrines, the images - so abundant in Mexico. Yet at the same time they lavished care on the village churches, filled them with flowers, and sang songs and hymns in their own tongue. (Clendinnen 1987a: 191) The trials may have been a major determinant of the sort of Indian Christianity that was to emerge in Yucatán.

The Landa trials were a powerful impetus both for the establishment in the Americas of the Holy Office of the Inquisition on the same pattern as in Spain, and for the permanent exclusion of the Indians from its jurisdiction; the first because the abuse of power by the Episcopal and monastic inquisition, of which the events in Yucatán were the prime example, highlighted the need for a centralized and more accountable authority, staffed by personnel trained for the pursuit of heresy, and the second because the Crown wished to avoid repetition of such brute force being employed with Indian neophytes. Henceforth, control of Indian orthodoxy was placed under the direct control of the bishops, and the power to try and punish was vested in the Provisorato (office of the vicar general), which contrived an entire bureaucracy of officials to cope with the new function and appointed delegates and commissaries in provincial areas. The co-existence of two jurisdictions, the *Provisorato* and the Holy Office, created confusion over functions, titles and procedures for several decades, especially since the latter continued to act as a fact-finding agency in uncovering and disciplining Indian transgressions against orthodoxy, and continued to investigate, though not to try, Indian cases.

Despite the suspension of their official inquisitorial role, the use of force and judicial process by the missionaries continued. Around 1575, idolatry investigations were renewed in the Dominican territories in Oaxaca, with the same harsh methods employed as a decade before. The Audiencia responded to protests by issuing a request that all materials regarding the cases be handed over to them, which was refused by the Dominicans, who claimed a commission as inquisitors, despite the fact that these powers had been revoked. (Spores 1984: 150-52; Pita Moreda 1991: 231- 233) Even at this stage, the mendicants refused to accept accountability to anyone except their own superiors and the Pope. Nor was this an isolated instance. Around 1580, Dominican missionaries in the Tzendal area of Chiapas resumed extirpation, or uprooting, of idolatry and a general visitation of the district took place in 1584 under Pedro de Feria. It is noteworthy that those areas that had seen persecution do not seem to have become paragons of Christian virtue thereafter, but on the contrary needed revisiting in order to continue attempts to eradicate what had simply survived. Persecution seems to have reinvigorated native religion rather than to have eliminated it.

8 Nahuatlized Christianity

The preoccupation with idolatry, understood to be incompatible with and diametrically opposed to Christianity, meant that Spaniards underestimated the potential for overlap between the religions and overlooked the gradual native appropriation of Christianity, whereby Indians accepted the new religion on indigenous terms and incorporated elements of it into their own religion. The Nahuas' complex but flexible pantheon could include new deities, transform the significance of old ones, and reject those that had lost their efficacy. In pre-Columbian times, victors had traditionally burned the temples of the vanquished, frequently replacing the defeated gods with their own. Thus the Nahuas were prepared to accept into their religion the gods of the Christians and the rites that came with them. Friar Bernardino de Sahagún's account of the dialogues in 1524 between the first friars and the native lords and priests reveals that a principal reason for the latter's acquiescence in the new religion was the conviction that their gods had not been powerful enough to save them from the Spaniards. For their part, the missionaries, albeit insisting that Christianity was completely different from and exclusive of the beliefs and practices of the natives, at the same time linked the two religions since the Christian Satan was understood to be the origin of indigenous religion. By placing the native deities within the Christian concepts of the supernatural, a certain power, even if a subordinate one, was thereby attributed to indigenous gods. Their ability to cause evil in the world was accepted by the missionaries no less than the Indians, and therefore to this extent their reality was not challenged. (Ruiz de Alarcón 1984 19-20; Lockhart 1999a: 112) This idea complemented the native notion of religious continuity and ended up erecting bridges between the two religions that permitted each side to see the other's faith as intelligible, even if not wholly acceptable. (Klor de Alva 1993: 175, 179) These bridges allowed natives to adopt Christianity because it made sense in terms of native ways of thinking about the sacred and supernatural world.

A great deal of what we know about native adoption and adaptation of Christianity in Central Mexico has been discovered as a result of the work of a group of historians who have translated and analyzed colonial documents in native languages, written in the Roman alphabet, as opposed to sources in the Spanish language.[1] Native-language documents indicate that the Nahuas reacted or adapted to the Spanish colonial presence in general, and to Christianity in particular, in a semi-autonomous process (not imposed by Spaniards) in which the Nahua component was as important as the Hispanic component. In religious interaction, as in other spheres of life, there were three broad stages. During the first stage (1519- ca. 1550), native peoples accepted God and baptism, but almost entirely on their own terms; at the level of the mass of the native population (as opposed to shamans such as Ocelotl or Mixcoatl) there was relatively little genuine religious interaction or religious change for about a generation. During the second stage (ca. 1550- ca. 1650), which occupies most of the time period of this study, religious interaction and change occurred largely at the level of the corporate community, with the adoption of patron saints that took on attributes of native deities, and Hispanic religious elements entered the framework of the Nahua supernatural as discrete items, without radically altering the structure of that framework. During the third stage, from 1650 to the present day, there was more interpenetration of the two religions at the level of individuals, and more structural change in the native religious framework. (for the "three stages" concept, see Lockhart 1992; Lockhart 1999b 207-09)

The most important element of the second stage of interaction was the introduction of the Christian church building and its patron saint to individual native communities. The founding of Christian churches on native temples and sacred sites opened the door for Indians to identify Christian saints with pre-Hispanic native gods. The definitive word for "church" in Nahuatl became *teopan*, one of the names for a pre-conquest temple precinct, and the personnel were called *teopantlaca*, or "church people," just like the staff of the old temples. (Lockhart 1999a: 116) Effectively, the village patron saint simply replaced the old district deity or tutelary god of the community (*calpulteotl*). Numerous parallels may be drawn between their roles. Just as pre-conquest temples were the houses of gods honored there, so churches became the home of the saint to which they were dedicated. (Lockhart 1992: 236) Feasts for the saints were timed in order to coincide with traditional sacred celebrations for communal gods. Saints' images were supplied with candles, flowers, and *copal* incense, in acts of devotion that drew on native traditions (especially the flowers) as much as Spanish practice. Ceremonial packets (*tlaquimilolli*), containing relics of the pre-Hispanic communal god (understood to be a channel through which sacred forces flowed), were placed inside the statues of saints. Just as the pre-Hispanic gods had inhabited their wood and stone representations, so images of saints became a living supernatural presence, rather than an inanimate object serving to remind the devotee of the saint now located in Heaven. For the Indians, the saint and the image were one and the same. Like native deities before them, saints were regarded as the parents of the people and the true owners of their land. The enthusiastic participation of Indians in religious lay brotherhoods or confraternities (*cofradías*), which emerged in earnest in the later-sixteenth century, also owed much to the identification of saints with pre-conquest group symbols. In the Spanish medieval tradition, confraternities were local associations of lay people dedicated to a particular Christian saint or advocation and celebration of its annual feast. Their original purpose was to allow the faithful to pursue personal salvation through individual contributions, but natives turned them into institutions dedicated to promoting the welfare of the whole community. Thus Indians accepted from their Spanish overlords an institution that they made a new expression of ancient communal religious life, and a means to meet their own social needs in the colonial era. (Farriss 1984: 329) Even the manner of selection of the patron saint also echoed pre-conquest patterns. Many were chosen as patrons because, in pre-Hispanic native style, they appeared to native elders and wise men in dreams, just as former communal gods had done. It could almost be said that the new patron saint picked the village rather than the other way round. (Duverger 1993: 207) In these important respects, saints assumed the role of the immediate, familiar gods of pre-Hispanic times and became the primary symbol identifying and unifying each residential district. Just as communal gods gave way to patron saints that embodied their functions, so household deities were replaced by personal images of saints in individual homes. (Lockhart 1992: 237) The great importance that Indian Christianity accorded to the saints contrasts with the minimal attention paid to the Trinity, Jesus, and even God. The native cult of saints was not simply imposed by Spanish churchmen but was also motivated by the deep-seated native belief that the most powerful gods were beyond the reach of human supplications, and that supernatural support was most effectively sought from these highly personalized Christian "gods." (Klor de Alva 1993: 179-80)

This new relationship with Christian supernatural beings is illustrated very clearly in the native cult of the Virgin Mary. The phenomenon of Christian Virgins acquiring the characteristics of native deities, and in the process becoming effectively Indianized, was widespread, as the example of the Virgin of Ocotlán, mentioned earlier, indicates. This is an example of the syncretism of native religion and Christianity for which Mexico is so famous, whereby elements of the alien religion (Virgins) were understood in terms of some indigenous counterpart (native deities). According to tradition, Our Lady of Ocotlán appeared in 1541 to an Indian named Juan Bernardino at the very spot where there had stood a sanctuary dedicated to the goddess Xochiquetzalli, who was regarded in the region of Tlaxcala as the mother of gods and who wore a blue shift, like the Lady of Juan Bernardino. (Gruzinski 1989: 97) Like native deities before them, the Christian Virgins were believed to exercise power over the rains. The Virgin of Ocotlán was invoked against drought; the Virgin of Remedios was revered by Indians as a bearer of rain (and hence a replacement for Tlaloc, and a Christian response to the accusations of those like Mixcoatl who derided the friars for their inability to bring rain), and the Virgin of Guadalupe was seen as a protector against floods. The most frequently cited example of native appropriation of a Christian symbol is the shrine to Our Lady of Guadalupe at Tepeyacac, now part of Mexico City. According to the traditional view, the cult of the Virgin of Guadalupe has been, since the mid-sixteenth century, the most important focus for Christian Indian piety, and a unique contributor to the successful evangelization of Central Mexico. Her role in demonstrating to whites and mestizos their land's favored status in God's eyes and in serving them as a powerful symbol of nationhood ever since the independence era is well known; but, more important still, she was the first Indian Virgin Mary (the image of her at Tepeyacac shows a "dark Virgin"), the first Christian supernatural to belong to Indians as their own, and the most powerful expression of the blending of Spanish and Central Mexican spirituality which produced colonial Indian Christianity. The potency of Guadalupe is based on a famous legend:

"Early on the morning of 9 December 1531, a poor commoner named Juan Diego, from the town of Cuauhtitlan, was on his way to the Franciscan church at Tlatelolco for religious instruction. Passing the hill of Tepeyacac just as the sun was rising, he heard singing on the hilltop, as of various precious birds, and it was as if the hill answered them. Juan Diego wondered why he deserved to hear such music, whether he was dreaming and where he was, whether he was in the place his grandfathers spoke of, the flower land, the sunshine land. Or perhaps it was Heaven? He went looking on the hilltop where the heavenly song was coming from, and then the song suddenly stopped and he heard someone calling him by name. When he reached the hilltop he saw a noblewoman standing there. She called to him to come near her, and as he approached he marveled at how splendid she was. Her garments were beaming and shimmering like the sun, and the rocks she stood on were shot through by her radiance as if they were precious jades or bracelets. The ground was glistening like a rainbow, and the cactus and other plants that grew there were like quetzal-green jades and turquoises, the way their leaves appeared, and their stalks and thorns shimmered like gold. He knelt before her and when he told her where he had been going, she revealed to him her identity as the 'always maiden Saint Mary, the mother of the very true deity God.' She told him she wished a temple of hers to be built there so she could show her love and mercy to those who invoke her and confide in her. She ordered him to go to the bishop and tell him her desire, relating all that he had seen and heard, and promised him ample reward. Juan Diego went directly to the palace of the newly arrived bishop and told his story. But the bishop did not take him seriously and told him to

return another day. Juan Diego returned to the hilltop and told the
heavenly noblewoman what had happened, suggesting that she find
some well-known honored noble person to carry her message. But she
insisted that it was he she wanted as a messenger and bade him go
once again to the bishop. The bishop questioned him closely this time
and was impressed by the description of the noblewoman but told Juan
Diego he must bring a sign. Juan Diego was delayed from returning to
the hilltop by the illness of his uncle but when he was on the road to
get a priest, the Virgin appeared to him and told him his uncle was
already cured. When Juan Diego asked for sign to take to the bishop,
the Virgin Mary told him to go to the hilltop and to cut various flowers
there. The hilltop was a place where no flowers grew because it was so
rocky and full of thistles and thorns, but on his arrival Juan Diego
found various precious roses blooming and blossoming even though it
was not yet their season and the frosts should have destroyed them.
They were fragrant and full of the night's dew, which was like
precious pearls. He cut them and gathered them up in his cloak and
took them to the Virgin. She told him to go to the bishop and unfold
his cloak and reveal what he carried. When he did unfold his cloak in
the bishop's presence, the flowers scattered and the image of Saint
Mary appeared emblazoned there, as it is kept today in church at
Tepeyacac. All knelt before the image praying and the bishop
repented, took the cloak from around Juan Diego's neck and hung it in
his oratory. Since the Virgin had told Juan Diego she was called
'always maiden Saint Mary of Guadalupe', the bishop decided to so
name her image. A church was erected on the spot to house her image,
and its devotees began to be blessed with miraculous cures and
escapes." (Burkhart 1993: 201-03)

The transformation of a Virgin Mary of European origin into an
indigenous one has traditionally been taken as an early sign of the
appropriation of the Catholic religion by Indians. (Duverger 1993:
110) However, recent research has thrown doubt on many of the key
assumptions of the traditional interpretation of this cult. It has never
been easy to determine to what extent and at what point the Virgin
genuinely became a focus of devotion for Indians rather than for
Spaniards, Creoles (white Spaniards born in the Americas) and

mestizos. Not only is the written evidence for Indian devotion in the sixteenth century extremely slim, but also its authorship is in doubt, and in any case, it was not set down until the mid 1550s, supposedly a quarter of a century after the events it describes. Furthermore, the apparition legends may have originated in native oral tradition in the late-sixteenth century, or more likely the early- to mid-seventeenth century, but were not widely known until two Creole priests published versions of the legend in the 1640s, long after the initial founding of the shrine (which probably took place around 1556, rather than in or just after 1531). This makes it likely that the cult took off in the mid-seventeenth century, and then largely among Creoles rather than Indians. According to this interpretation, Guadalupe was never the object of an important Indian cult, and least of all in the early colonial period; rather natives did not begin to share the cult until the second half of the eighteenth century (for which there is clear unambiguous written testimony). Several historians have concluded that the apparition legend has no basis in the actual events of early post-conquest Mexico, and attempts to authenticate the apparition and its early date should be seen as expressions of piety rather than historical scholarship. (Burkhart 1993: 200; Burkhart 2001: 1; Poole 1995) Another historian has suggested that there was an Indian cult of Guadalupe but that it was much more narrowly circumscribed than the traditional view has assumed, probably being confined to the Indians who lived near the sanctuary and in the district of Cuauhtitlan (where testimonials to the apparition were taken from local Indians in 1666 as part of the official church authentication). He also speculates that the Indian cult may have corresponded roughly to the territory of the pilgrimage and worship of the pre-Hispanic goddess Tonantzin at Tepeyacac (whatever that territory may have been). (Taylor 1987: 15)

The assumption that the shrine was founded on a pagan temple raises another complication. As we have already seen above, Sahagún, writing in the second half of the sixteenth century, expressed concern that the cult of Guadalupe grew from idolatrous roots since it had substituted the Aztec cult of the goddess Tonantzin at the same site, merely Christianizing in appearance a native shrine which had existed there in pre-Columbian times (Sahagún 1975: 704-05) Unfortunately, although Sahagún reported that Indians came to worship at Tepeyacac from distant places as in former times, he said little more about who the pilgrims were, where they came from, or what they believed. Even so, the fact that contemporary Spaniards were alarmed at the growth of the Guadalupan cult in the mid-sixteenth century testifies to the antiquity and popularity of the cult among natives, and has not been satisfactorily explained by those who argue for a late-colonial origin. On the other hand, if the Indian cult was as extensive and significant as Sahagún feared, it is surprising that there are no other references to it by contemporary chroniclers. Motolonía, who had every reason to refer to proof of Indian devotion, makes no reference to the cult in his *History*. It has even been questioned whether Tonantzin actually was the name of a pre-Columbian goddess. The literal meaning of the word is "our revered mother," and may simply have been a form of respectful address. The title "Tonantzin" is used by Sahagún's informants with reference to various indigenous mother goddesses, including Cihuacoatl. Nowhere do these informants mention a shrine at Tepeyacac in the pre-Columbian period. "Tonantzin" was also promoted as a title for the Virgin Mary by preachers, including Sahagún himself in the 1540s, but with no particular connection to Guadalupe, contrary to what one would expect if it were linked to ancient devotion at that particular shrine. It was also widely used in the expression "Tonantzin Holy Church" for "Our Revered Holy Mother Church," which seems unlikely if it was the name of a pagan goddess, rather than a form of reverential address. In any case, other reports give Ichpochtli, not Tonantzin, as the name of the idol formerly worshipped at Tepeyacac. Ichpochtli is a term for "young woman," which was appropriated by the friars as a synonym for "virgin" and so was constantly associated with Mary. But the old mother goddesses called Tonantzin by Sahagún's informants would not have been addressed as "maiden." Thus, one revisionist historian concludes that Indians used Tonantzin as a title for Mary because she was a maternal figure personally connected with them, the title had little if any connection to pre-Columbian deities, and Indians who used this title in the later-sixteenth century were not thinking of any sacred figure other than the Virgin Mary. She concludes that Indians were not perpetuating memories of a pagan goddess but were projecting elements of their Christian worship into their pre-Christian past, reinterpreting their ancient worship in terms of Mary. Thus the link between Our Lady of Guadalupe and any pre-Columbian goddess is at best tenuous. The historian also concludes that only after the mid-seventeenth century did the cult spread significantly beyond the Mexico City area, and at no point did it spread spontaneously among Indians at grass-roots level. (Burkhart 1993: 208-09, 218; Burkhart 2001; Poole 1995)

The recent revisionist historians have succeeded in placing a question mark over all of the key assumptions of the traditional Guadalupe legend, including that a pre-Columbian goddess Tonantzin was worshipped at Tepeyacac, that she was deliberately associated with the Virgin Mary by early Christian evangelizers, and that Indian devotion to the Virgin of Guadalupe was an early colonial phenomenon and the first important example of the fusion of the pre-Columbian and Christian religious traditions. But revisionists still debate whether the Indian cult was virtually non-existent (in which case what are we to make of Sahagún's reference to it?), or was found only in the Mexico City area, or extended the length of the old pilgrim route to Tonantzin; and are still divided as to whether Tonantzin was the name of a goddess or a reverential form of address. Furthermore, there are many who still support the traditional interpretation. One historian has observed that the new Indian enthusiasm for the faith, which only emerged some ten years after the conquest, should be attributed to the Virgin's apparition in 1531. Since Motolinía himself referred to this phenomenon, his writings may be said to testify indirectly to the apparitions. If the friars barely took notice of her intervention it was because many Indians at this time claimed to have seen visions of Mary. He reaffirms that in the early decades devotion to Guadalupe was primarily an Indian affair. (Brading 2001: 355) The dispute was further complicated, and the traditional view reinforced, by the canonization of Juan Diego by Pope John Paul II in 2002. I have referred to these disputes not in order to try and arbitrate between them and find a definitive, authoritative solution, but in order to show the complexities of the issues and that the evidence may not admit of any certainties. But, whatever the relative merits of the arguments outlined above, and even if, as seems possible, the identification of the Virgin of Guadalupe with a particular pre-Columbian goddess, and her role in nascent Indian Christianity has been overplayed, this does not diminish the fact that Christian Virgins, including the Guadalupe, were appropriated by natives and interpreted in terms of their own religious world view.

The account of the Guadalupe apparition quoted above conforms to native religious paradigms. When Juan Diego hears delightful singing on the hilltop "as of various precious birds," he asks himself whether perchance he had entered the "flower land" or "sunshine land" of which his forefathers spoke. For pre-conquest Nahuas, the "flower world" was a sunny garden of light and heat, filled with flowers and their fragrant aromas, brightly colored tropical birds, precious stones like jade and turquoise, and accompanied by beautiful music. The hilltop of Tepeyacac is transformed into such a world by the Virgin's presence: "the rocks she stood on were shot through by her radiance as if they were precious jades or bracelets. The ground was glistening like a rainbow, and the cactus and other plants that grew there were like quetzal-green jades and turquoises." The Virgin's appearance to Juan Diego on a hilltop, just as the sun was rising, recalls the traditional location of the flower world, and its identification with Sunshine Mountain, the mythological source of food crops for pre-conquest Nahuas. The Indian asks himself whether this might not also be the heavenly land, in other words the Christian paradise. It was commonplace for the colonial Nahuas to interpret the Christian concepts of Heaven and paradise invariably described as a garden filled with flowers and tropical birds, in terms of their own sacred "flower world." Christian songs and prayers composed by Nahuas often invoked the image of a sacred garden. A song to Saint Clare described Christ's home: "There our lord's flowery world lies visible, lies giving off warmth, lies dawning...The roses, dark red ones, pale ones, the red feather flowers, the golden flowers lie there waving like precious bracelets, lie bending with quetzal feather dew" (Burkhart 1993: 210) The imagery is strikingly reminiscent of that of the Guadalupe legend. But an interesting transformation has taken place, since the pre-conquest native flower world was not the same as the afterlife, which was a shadowy underworld called Mictlan. The flower world, the ultimate reality for Nahuas, was a sacred idealized version of this earthly world. It was related to earthly existence, unlike the Christian paradise, which was located on a transcendent spiritual plane separate from the material realm. The blending of these separate notions of flower world, Sunshine Mountain, afterlife, Christian Heaven and paradise, produced a new post-conquest flowery Heaven that was the destiny of souls. The sacred flower world remained essentially the same as the pre-conquest one, except that now access to it was limited to Christians of good life, and Christian figures such as the Virgin Mary and Jesus Christ were absorbed into it. Christian symbolism linked Mary with the lily and the rose, and depicted angels as her frequent companions. To Nahuas, these associations placed her in the flower world, in which angels merged with tropical birds. Christ, referred to by the friars as the "sun of righteousness," came to be seen by Nahuas as the sun that animated the flower world, and Mary, as mother of Christ, was therefore invoked as the dawn (hence the hour of her appearance on the hilltop in the legend). (Burkhart 1993: 211)

Mary was revered by Indians because of what she meant to them, and not just because Spanish priests told them to do so. The constant association of the term Ichpochtli with Mary and references to her sexual innocence suggest a being eternally young as well as eternally virgin. In pre-conquest times, young noblewomen often spent a year in temple service prior to marriage, for which chastity was a strict requirement. It is in this context that Mary's youth, purity, and virginity "made sense" in Nahua terms; Mary remains pure to serve Christ in his temple in Heaven. The wearing of rosary beads and the recitation of associated prayers was popular among Nahuas who were taught that these practices would result not only in rewards after death but also (as fitted the native world view) in favors during life as well. One story tells of five Indians from Tepoztlan who took shelter under a rock outcrop during a storm; when lightning struck, two were killed but the three wearing rosaries were spared. The rosary represented a garland of flowers that the worshiper presented to Mary, thus fitting very well with the Nahuas' practice of offering such ornaments to their sacred beings. The term "miracle," often associated with advocations of Mary revered by Nahuas, was translated into Nahuatl as *tlamahuizolli* or "something to be marveled at." Unlike the Christian concept, this term does not indicate that the event violates the natural course of events or has a divine cause. Rather, it preserves the Nahua sense of reality for which the normal course of events is already, by its very nature, infused with sacred power, observable manifestations of which are worth noticing, but are not "miraculous" in the Christian sense. Thus Christian miracles were understood by Nahuas and became meaningful to them in terms of the native religious worldview. For the rest, Marian devotion offered the Nahuas active participation in religious life, which was otherwise dominated by the friars. Mary offered not judgment and punishment, as God did, but sympathy and mercy. She intervened at the moment of death to ensure that the souls of her devotees would be admitted to Heaven; she also intervened in affairs of the living, saving her devotees from peril. She served the Nahuas as a divine protector and advocate. (Burkhart 1993: 212-14) Indeed, invoked as Tonantzin or "our precious mother," she came, contrary to orthodox Christianity, to occupy the role of a mother goddess to humanity parallel to the Father God. (Lockhart 1992; Burkhart 2001: 11)

The figure of Christ featured much less significantly in Indian Christianity than saints and virgins, but insofar as he did play a role, he too was assimilated to native religious expectations. The most common interpretation of Christ was as a new embodiment of the solar deity. To a certain extent, the friars encouraged the association of Christ and sun, since orthodox Christianity often referred to the Son of God as the sun, the Bearer of Light in darkness, and they assumed that this reference would be understood symbolically by the Nahuas, as it was by Europeans, as long as the words were translated accurately into Nahuatl (once again underestimating the difficulties entailed in conveying such complex concepts). But the natives appropriated this image in ways that were not intended, or even understood, by the friars. Christ was seen as a deity who had taken the place of the sun, thus becoming a new sun presiding over a new segment of history. The pre-conquest Mexica believed that they were living in the age of the fifth sun, the world having already been born and destroyed four times previously, each era being presided over by a new sun. Since they believed in cyclical repetition of ancient patterns, by which the present was brought into line with the past, it made sense for a new epoch to have a new sun. Whereas for the friars, Christ's light represented spiritual enlightenment, for the Nahuas their new sun stood for cosmic order; and his beneficence related to living people and their crops, and the material conditions of earthly life, rather than to immaterial souls, and the spiritual, metaphysical level of reality. Thus, an identification came about of whose existence the friars were aware, but whose meaning was probably not familiar to them. This is one of many examples where each side of the cultural and linguistic divide interpreted the same phenomenon in different ways, but both assumed that their interpretation was the one shared by the other. (Burkhart 1988: 235, 240, 252) One historian has called this process "Double Mistaken Identity." Each imagined the other to be more similar to itself than it actually was, and assumed that ideas that were in fact quite different bore analogous meanings in both cultures. These mutual misunderstandings allowed conqueror and conquered to coexist within a single, hierarchical order. (Lockhart 1999a: 99; Burkhart 1996: 41)

A similar process was at work in Indian adoption of the Spanish national saint, Saint James or Santiago. Despite, or perhaps because of, the association of Santiago, the Spaniards' patron saint of war, with Spanish conquest, this powerful symbol of divine favor was rapidly appropriated by natives. He became patron saint to some communities, and in others he was enlisted to heal, protect and fertilize. A common function was as a protector of Indian villagers in the colonial period against wild, heathen Chichimecs, especially in western and north Central Mexico, reflecting a belief that Santiago's power could be acquired and turned against enemies. In 1624 at Ixmiquilpan in central Hidalgo, where nomad Chichimecs still threatened colonial peace, an Indian woman named María reportedly claimed that her renowned curing powers resulted from having had intercourse with an invisible Spaniard who came, like Santiago, on a white horse. The Spanish saint was no longer a symbol of Indian subjugation; on the contrary, by union with the phantom Spaniard, María was magically empowered. More commonly, Santiago was invoked for help with the weather, since, from the earliest days of the conquest, probably on account of the Spanish habit of shouting the saint's name when they fired their cannon, he had become identified as a new manifestation of the god of thunder and lightning. According to the priest Jacinto de la Serna, an Indian shaman in Tenango del Valle district tried to alter the direction of clouds and storms as the corn harvest approached by appealing to Christ, the Blessed Virgin and Santiago. In the later colonial period, attention was increasingly focused on the saint's horse. Possibly drawing on Aztec traditions associated with eagles and jaguars, horses in post-conquest times were seen as powerful, independent agents of divine power, perhaps even as gods in their own right. By the eighteenth century, Santiago's horse was increasingly treated as if it had become the saint; pregnant Indians, unable to give birth, made offerings to the creature. Thus Santiago's significance to Indians of Central Mexico was rooted not only in official Spanish messages about conquest and conversion, but also in native understandings of animals and the sacred, and in adjustments to colonial rule at local level. (Taylor 1994: 37-45)

Hence, native religious identity could be consciously Christian without simply reflecting the expectations of parish priests and other Spaniards; instead it creatively adapted official Christian symbols like Santiago in order to make them meaningful for natives in their everyday lives. Indian understandings were far from carbon copies of Spanish intentions. Another good example is the *cristos de caña*, that is to say crucifixes made from sugar cane, which still today make a close association between Christ and maize, the divine and the fruits of the land. These figures of Christ are not simply Christian on the outside and pagan on the inside, but rather present the Son of God in Christianized native terms. One historian has seen them less as a sign of disrespect for official Catholic tradition than as a means of enlarging upon that tradition. (Taylor 1994: 35, 47)

A fine illustration of how native Christianity emerged independently of missionaries and churchmen is provided by the only known extant manuscript of a Nahuatl-language play, entitled Holy Wednesday, which was composed around 1592 by an anonymous Nahua pupil of the Franciscan friars. Taking as his source a Spanish play on the subject of Jesus Christ's conversation with the Virgin Mary prior to his arrest and crucifixion, the author produced a drama for performance in Nahuatl, which not only translated the original, but also adapted its content to Nahua expectations and sensitivities. For example, the Mary in the Nahuatl drama is invested with more authority and more knowledge than her counterpart in the Spanish play. Christ is represented as a dutiful and obedient Nahua son, less inclined to contradict his mother. Furthermore, he is less responsible for his own actions than is his Spanish model. He does not freely sacrifice himself but is a victim of forces that he does not control. Contrary to the Christian emphasis on free will, the Christ in the Nahuatl drama has no choice; his actions follow a pre-established pattern announced by the voices of ancestral authorities, from which he feels no temptation to diverge. In presenting a Christ who allows his behavior to be wholly determined by the demands of his parents and the prophecies of his ancestors, the Nahua playwright contradicts Christian doctrine - especially the notion of free will and the autonomy of the moral agent - in a manner that may be seen as an assertion of Nahua moral values. The author's recasting of the Spanish text reveals how distant from European conceptions even the most Christianizing Nahua mind could be.

The content of the Nahuatl play also reveals the aspects of native religion through which Christianity was perceived. The prophets and patriarchs of Christianity's ancient past, easily identified with the Nahua elders and ancestors, lent the new religion an aura of ancestral authority. Christ's participation in acts such as bloodletting, fasting and other penitential practices, which had already been present in pre-conquest native religion, helped indigenous people accept him as their own. And teachings about the mystical power of Christ's blood fitted well with Nahuas' traditional attitudes; according to one ancient myth, Quetzalcoatl contributed blood to the dough of ground bones from which humans were formed. Christian Nahuas were taught not to pierce their flesh directly in order to offer blood, but they could do it indirectly by flogging themselves. Christianity was Nahuatlized too through the participation of Nahua actors in the roles of Christ and

Mary, who delivered their sacred dialogue in the native tongue. Even if the actors followed the script word for word, the friars were unable to recognize and understand, let alone control, the manner in which actors interpreted their roles. The sacred beings of Christianity appeared in Nahua guise and spoke directly to their fellow Nahuas, and Christian narratives were accommodated to the Nahuatl language and given local nuances via word, costume and gesture. (Burkhart 1996: 1-6, 47-48, 89-92, 97-98, 177, 197)

By the end of the sixteenth century, a hybrid Nahua-Christian religion had emerged, in which, on the one hand, Christian preaching began to influence the meanings of Nahuatl terms, and indigenous religious life gradually became expressed in Christianized form; and, on the other hand, Christian concepts picked up new meanings and symbolic associations as they were translated into Nahuatl, and Christian terms of reference became transformed in native hands. Not only were elements of native belief carried over into what was effectively an indigenous interpretation of Christianity, but Christian doctrine was also Nahuatlized in the process of adaptation. In most instances, colonial Nahuas felt no particular need to make sharp distinctions between Christian and non-Christian aspects of their religion. However, this does not mean that the interaction took place on equal terms. The Nahua-Christian religion tended to combine the two cultures in such a way that native structures and functions imposed themselves upon Christian content. The indigenous organization of the cosmos, time and space, order and disorder - everything that was fundamental - were maintained. Indigenous peoples adjusted to aspects of Christianity that accorded with their own vision of the cosmos, and adapted the remaining elements to suit their own purpose. Acceptance of Christian forms took a distinctively native character, and maintained independence from Hispanic religious norms. For example, the institution of the religious confraternity was adopted by Indians not merely for the purposes that missionaries desired, but in order to consolidate what was left of Indian beliefs and weld them into a form sufficiently coherent to recreate local identity within the changed circumstances of the later-sixteenth century. The Nahuas merely adopted the Spanish religious form (the confraternity) without abandoning the essence of their own religion (the communal spiritual identity).

These tendencies were exacerbated by the fact that Christianity as presented by the friars was not a coherent, internally consistent system. Its presentation varied from friar to friar, and even from one sermon to the next. The result was "a hodgepodge of concepts - shreds of Christian orthodoxy and patches of Nahuatl meaning." From the Christianity introduced, the friars were unable to weave a whole cloth; the Nahuas could take from it only threads with which to mend the fabric of their own belief system. (Burkhart 1989: 187-88) The differences between the two worldviews were not consistently stated and stressed in terms that would have made them clear to the Nahuas. They did not view their conversion as ushering in a new spiritual order of reality that superseded all preceding history. The moral dualism that placed Christ's significance far beyond that of any earthly phenomenon was alien to indigenous thought. Although some Nahuas adopted a Christian worldview, for the population as a whole, the friars were too few and the level of indoctrination too rudimentary for a fundamental shift in world view to be effected. (Burkhart 1989: 185-90; Burkhart 1988: 235) If the interaction of the two religions had this result in Central Mexico, where Christianization and evangelization had been most intense, how much more compromised must Christianity have been in other areas. (Lockhart 1992: 203, 243, 260; Hamnett 1999: 65-68)

9 Mixtec and Maya Appropriation of Christianity

Native acceptance of Christianity on indigenous terms characterized other peoples of Mesoamerica. The Mixtecs (as the Nahuas and Spaniards called them) or Ñudzahui (as they called themselves) inhabited an area (the Mixteca) that stretches west to east from the border area of the modern state of Guerrero to the Valley of Oaxaca, and north to south from southern Puebla to the Pacific Ocean. Native-language writings from this area reveal how Christianity was accommodated to native traditions, language, and worldview. The use of the term *huahi ñuhu* "sacred house" in reference to the edifice of the church, rather than the borrowing of the Spanish word *iglesia*, suggests how natives identified the new structure with a pre-conquest temple. Native-language writings never incorporated the Spanish loanword for the church during the colonial period. Furthermore, in sixteenth-century maps, ruling couples were seated near or in front of the church, in the same manner as they appeared before temples in the pre-conquest codices. Native-language wills reveal the terminology employed to refer to Christian concepts such as the saints, Virgin Mary, Purgatory, and Heaven, and indicate how ordinary people understood these concepts. The preferred term for God was *stoho Dios* meaning "high lord God," but He was also referred to as *ñuhu* ("deity") or *yya toniñe* ("male ruler"). Jesus too was called by this latter title, or simply *yya* (lord). Saints as well were interpreted as *yya* who suffered on earth and joined God in Heaven. The Virgin Mary was variously referred to as a "female ruler," "noble woman" or even as a goddess, for example *ñuhu Santa María*, using the same word for "deity" (*ñuhu*) usually applied to God. For contemporary Spaniards, Mary was more of a mediatrix than a ruler, and she was certainly not a goddess. Her equal status with God was also implied in native translations for the Christian "Kingdom of Heaven" which was rendered as *yuhuitayu andehui gloria*. This term employed native vocabulary for the largest political entity (*yuhuitayu*) and the sky (*andehui*), modified by a Spanish loanword (*gloria*) in reference to its everlasting glory. But the word *yuhuitayu* referred to a community where male and female lords ruled jointly; furthermore, native Mixtec origin legends spoke of a sacred male-female creator couple who constituted the first *yuhuitayu*. Therefore, the native "Kingdom of Heaven " envisaged Mary and God as co-divinities and co-rulers. This is further demonstrated by native-language wills that associated the Virgin Mary directly with the *yuhuitayu andehui*, in a manner that was quite at variance with orthodox Christianity. Finally, the complex concept of the Holy Trinity was referred to as *dzutu Dios, dzaya Dios, espiritu santo Dios*, or "Father God, Son God and Holy Ghost God," but then qualified by acknowledging three persons and only one true God. However, it was not unusual for testaments to get this part confused. The language of these testaments, which was not selected or edited by the friars, reveals how native beliefs influenced popular Christianity. The most recent historian of Mixtec Christianity concludes that, in most cases, native terminology, conventions, and ideological constructs were employed to describe and understand Christian phenomena throughout much of the colonial period. In other words, Mixtecs understood Christianity in their own terms. (Terraciano 1998: 116, 120, 126-31, 134; Terraciano 2001: 287, 306)

By contrast with the Nahuas, among whom a new religion was created by means of aspects of the old and the new religions, among the Maya Christian elements were incorporated into the structure of indigenous religion which, broadly speaking, was maintained. Paradoxically, innovation was often the most effective way to preserve Maya culture. The very need to make sense of the colonial world and the advent of Christianity encouraged the revival and reinvigoration of ancient Maya wisdom. Although the great painted collections of hieroglyphs which served the Maya as repositories of sacred knowledge were systematically destroyed by the friars (only three of the pre-conquest books have survived), their contents were transcribed by native chiefs and priests into books of the European kind and were thus preserved in Mayan but using the Spanish alphabet; by the end of the sixteenth century, most villages had their sacred writings secreted away in this new form. By means of these books of Chilam Balam, the Maya jaguar priests were able to continue into the colonial period their tradition of prophecy, based on the cyclical sequence of *katuns*, whereby the secrets of the future were revealed through the study of the past. The considerable knowledge of Catholic doctrine possessed by the authors of these anthologies, who must all have been masters of ceremonies in the parish church (or their scribes), facilitated the blending of Christian concepts and biblical lore (learned from the friars) into the esoteric learning of traditional Maya cosmology. Hence, the Maya count of years was correlated with Christian chronology, and the liberation of the Mayas from their hardships was prophesied as the outcome of the second coming of Christ. The books suggest a response to Christian dogma at a highly sophisticated level of interpretation. Even the Spanish conquest itself, interpreted as one further invasion of the peninsula, comparable to the arrival of the Itza some eight hundred years before, was incorporated into the flow of Maya history. Thus, the Chilam Balam preserved the basic continuity of Indian history and of the Indian worldview, with the conquest viewed as a traumatic but essentially surface phenomenon, and the integrity of native society threatened but as yet maintained. (Brading 1991: 162-163; Clendinnen 1987a; Farriss 1984: 305)

The Maya recognized that certain Christian teachings were true and therefore must be accepted and incorporated into the native scheme of things. Thus, churches, church patios, and cemeteries were used as venues for offerings to pagan deities, and Christian objects, for example crosses and candles, were incorporated into native ritual. The crosses raised outside churches were adopted on purely Maya terms, with no hint of appreciation of the crucifixion story or the deep symbolic meaning of the sacrifice of God's only son. Accounts of the death of Christ in the Books of Chilam Balam reveal that the crucifixion has been transformed into a Maya event and partly assimilated to arrow sacrifice. The acts of human sacrifice by crucifixion carried out by Nachi Cocom, in which children had been fixed to a cross as a preliminary to having their hearts torn out, indicate how little Christian understanding informed them. Few of the patio crosses of the sixteenth century bore any representation of a crucified Jesus; in most a stylized face appeared at the junction of the arms. At some late stage, the great architectural crosses came to be identified with "Lord Dios," the supreme deity of the new order. But a much commoner, earlier, and more important association was with the worship of rain gods, with which the symbol of the cross had been linked in pre-Hispanic times, and so offerings were made to patio crosses for rain. The sign of the cross was also identified as a new version of the native symbol for Yax-cheel-cab or the Tree of the World, which in Maya mythology pierced the heart of the sun, the heavens, and the underworlds. The cross was also used on Maya maps as a boundary marker, just as native images had once been. The appropriation of the cross was a gradual, long-term process. Not until the nineteenth century did crosses emerge as independent deities, gifted with speech and addressed as Lord Saint Cross.

Another Christian figure assimilated on native terms was the Virgin Mary, who became identified by the Maya with the moon goddess Ixchel because of the Mother of God's common depiction on a crescent moon. In the Chilam Balam of Chumayel she is also associated with the Maya "Cord from Heaven" - the divine umbilical cord that signifies the link between the natural and sacred worlds, between Man and the gods. (Farriss 1984 306) The high Maya deity Hunab-Ku was reinterpreted as the Christian God the Father. These associations indicate that Christian elements had been accepted on native terms. The Christian saints were identified as Maya, always named with the pronominal ca meaning "our," for example, *ca yum san diego*, "Our Lord San Diego," or *ca yum santo*, "Our Lord Saint" when referring to the patron of the community. Thus, the purpose and meaning of the cult was entirely localized to the levels of home and community. There was a higher incidence of Virgin Mary household images than of male saints; and whereas the latter were usually given their Christian name, the Virgins were always referred to with the entirely Maya phrase *ca cilich colel*, "Our Holy Lady," or *ca cilich colebil*, "Our Holy Virgin," with almost never a mention of Mary or the use of a loanword. (Restall 1997: 153)

There is also the possibility that the figure of Christ could have been identified in the indigenous mind with the Maya deity Kukulcan, who was worshipped in the form of Venus, or the Morning Star of the East, at various centers on the East coast of Yucatán. His legend recounted how he died as a mortal but would return as the Morning Star, rising out of the eastern sea after a period in the underworld. The Kukulcan cult itself had originally been introduced from Highland Mexico (where Kukulcan was known as Quetzalcoatl), and the Maya had already achieved a syncretic merger with this alien cult well before the Spanish arrived. That the Aztecs may have viewed Hernán Cortés as Quetzalcoatl, or his emissary who had come to announce the deity's return, is a long established - if not universally accepted - proposition. The very fact that the East Coast of Yucatán was a strong cult center for Venus could have made the inhabitants there more receptive to Christian doctrine and ritual rather than less so. The concept of resurrection was not alien to the Maya, and the message that Christ died, rose again and will come again made sense. The traditional east-west orientation of Christian churches could have been interpreted as further evidence of the Kukulcan-Christ identification. It cannot be stated categorically that the East Coast Maya or any other Mesoamerican group, accepted Christianity as the fulfillment of the Quetzalcoatl-Kukulcan prophecies. But two historians conclude that there is enough resemblance between the symbolism and dogma of the two cults to help account for the receptivity to Christianity on the East Coast and elsewhere. (Miller and Farriss 1979: 239-40)

At the same time, rejection of or hostility to other Christian elements revealed Maya ambivalence. Small crosses and crucifixes closely associated with the friars were burned, perhaps expressing hostility toward any cross that was not an Indian symbol. Native priests who urged commoners to hide their children to protect them from the dangerous rite of baptism, themselves contrived to be baptized again and again, as if to test and augment their own spiritual force. Native lords set up illicit schools and churches where they pretended to teach Christian doctrine to their followers and to baptize and marry them, flattering the friars by mimicking them, but also showing disrespect by ignoring their monopoly in that area. An early attempt to capture the apparatus of Christian worship was made in 1610 by two Indians who, proclaiming themselves "pope" and "bishop," proceeded to offer their own masses in the local church (with the addition of a few native gods), to administer other Christian sacraments, and to ordain their own Maya clergy to assist them. These acts find echoes in the Tzeltal

Maya revolt of 1712 in Chiapas, in which native church assistants constituted themselves as a Catholic priesthood in the service of their own miraculous image of the Virgin. Arguably, though, the dominant aspect of these acts is the desire to seek to assert control over the new cult rather than reject it. (Farriss 1984: 318)

In other important ways, the Maya reaction to Christianity was not so different from in Central Mexico. The cult of saints signified to the colonial Maya, as to the colonial Nahuas, the same corporate bond with the supernatural that their ancestors had sustained. The saints on whom survival depended were not universal deities but community guardians whom an individual might approach on his own. Saints were not unfailingly benevolent; like pre-Columbian gods they were capricious, morally neutral beings whose well-being and good will required careful attention to their physical comfort and deference to their high status. The communal feasts sponsored by the community confraternities served as offerings to the saints, who would, by partaking of the food's essence, sanctify it for the other participants and, in return for this nourishment, ensure the continuing supply of maize and other food for all concerned. The food was served in the presence of the saint being honored, offered first to the saint and consisting of food expressly belonging to the saint - meat from one or more bulls raised on the saint's own estate and slaughtered during a fiesta bullfight (surely a form of sacrifice to the saint). Thus feeding the gods remained the main element in the Maya liturgy and the central element in the rites of the fiestas and even in the liturgy of the mass, both of which culminated in the ritual sharing of food and drink between deity and worshippers. Continuing to see survival as a collective enterprise, the Maya transformed the confraternity from a particular group of devotees pursuing personal salvation through individual contributions into public institutions supported by the entire community and dedicated to promoting the general welfare of the community through general obsequies to its sacred guardians. As in Central Mexico, the confraternity became an expression of the continuing existence of the village or municipal community. The Christian concept of personal salvation did not take strong root among the Maya. They did not anticipate in the eternal reward or punishment for a person's earthly life. The souls of the dead were subject to good and bad fates but an individual's fate was determined by the collective obsequies performed by others after his death rather than his own actions while alive. It was the survivors' obligation and in their interests to see that the disembodied spirits of the dead went to their place of repose without delay, for restless spirits could bring misfortune on the living. The observances of the Day of the Dead (All Souls' Day) when prayers were offered for the souls still waiting in purgatory reveals the merger between the Catholic concept of restless souls in purgatory and Maya notions of the afterlife. (Farriss 1984: 320-21, 323, 328-29, 334, 340)

A similar blending may be observed in requests in native wills for church burial and for said or sung mass, practices which both satisfied the requirements of the ecclesiastical authorities and also served to maintain a tradition of public religious ritual within the indigenous community. Maya testators were willing to pay double for a sung rather than a said mass to speed their souls through purgatory, both because they believed in the power of the mass and because it was culturally desirable and socially prestigious to be posthumously remembered in song. The Maya supported the mass because it was an acceptable ritual outlet and because they believed in its spiritual efficacy. The Maya reaction to Christianity was a long-term struggle not to reject its beliefs but to control the expression of those beliefs; religious hostility took the form not of paganism but of anticlericalism, often with Maya parishioners judging local priests for failing to live up to official standards of public behavior and professional practice. (Restall 1997: 158)

All these elements reveal a Mayanization of Christianity comparable to the Nahuatlization of Central Mexico. But the Nahuas and Mayas, who shared many similar religious traditions before the conquest, developed contrasting patterns of reaction to the same form of Spanish Catholicism: the former thoroughly integrated their own religious beliefs with Catholicism, whereas the Maya retained native religion as the meaningful core of their religion, which became incremented with varying degrees of Catholicism. In part this difference may be due to the circumstances surrounding conquest and evangelization, in particular the slower colonization of Yucatán and the difficulties the Spanish encountered in penetrating a society whose political and religious organization was highly decentralized. By the time the Spaniards began the conquest of Yucatán, Maya ceremonial centers were in decline and many of the temples had been abandoned. Hence the Mayas had no centralized theocracy comparable to that of the Nahuas, which the Spaniards wiped out with one bold stroke. The grass-roots religion of the Mayas was centerd in widely scattered hamlets that were generally more isolated and more resistant to change than the towns of the Mexican plateau. As a result, the religion and values of Maya culture survived the conquest more intact. (Madsen 1966; Lorenzen 1981: 13)

Comparison of the Nahuas and the Mayas indicates that Indianized Christianity attained a greater or lesser degree of completion among different groups or individuals at different times, and combined the two religions in different degrees of dominance and subordination. Some natives adopted a Christian worldview, identifying elements of Christianity as equivalent or complementary to analogous elements of the aboriginal religions. In some instances, this resulted in a complete conversion to Christianity, in which Christian doctrines were believed and understood, and in which participation in Christian rituals and associations replaced those of the pagan traditions. Equally, though, for others (maybe most), the process of conversion remained incomplete; these individuals understood the Christian worldview imperfectly and participated in Christian rituals without giving up fully their aboriginal practices. Yet others joined together, consciously and unconsciously, the elements of the aboriginal and Christian traditions into a blended pattern of religious life. (Vecsey 1996: 29)

Whichever pattern prevailed, native peoples interpreted Christianity according to their own understandings and their own circumstances, and were creative with the new religion on their own terms. They took what appealed to them, what made sense, what they could use. (Burkhart 1996: 80) By the end of the sixteenth century, Christianity had been thoroughly Indianized by natives who considered themselves genuine Christians, even as they worshipped many spiritual beings, disregarded the significance of the teachings on salvation, and continued to make this-worldly ends the legitimate object of their religious devotion. (Klor de Alva 1993: 174) This probably troubled them little. By acting as Christians, natives became Christians; they declared themselves to be Christians and Christianity to be what they did. (Burkhart 1996: 81)

10 Seventeenth-Century Blending of Two Religious Traditions

The extent to which elements of the old and new religions had blended by the seventeenth century may be demonstrated by reference to the activities of a native shaman, Juan Coatl, who was tried in the diocese of Puebla in 1665. Like his early-sixteenth century counterparts, Ocelotl and Mixcoatl, Coatl embodied the skills of the traditional man-god. He protected crops, regulated the flow of waters, organized the worship of native deities, celebrated rites of birth and marriage, kept track of the calendar and was even reported to sacrifice children. He communicated the messages conveyed by his god and interpreted the occult meaning of storms in the way expected of a man-god. He encouraged Indians to worship supernatural beings that he kept in a cave, including a painted canvas with an image of an Indian woman being adored by young Indians, kneeling at her feet, venerated under the name Soapile, and other paintings representing snakes (his name Coatl meant Serpent). He told Indians that these were their real gods and provided water and crops for them, and they should believe in them and not in the God of the Spaniards or the Blessed Virgin. He told Indians not to go to the parish priest since he, Juan, was more than the priest; he spoke with gods and provided what they needed. (Gruzinski 1989: 93) He even went by the name Cloud Serpent, recalling Andrés Mixcoatl, the man-god of 1537.

At the same time, Coatl incorporated Christian elements into his repertoire. He confessed, married, and baptized as if he was a Christian priest, even wearing white clothes. Although at one level Soapile can be seen as the anti-Virgin of the Christians, in that Indians were exhorted to venerate Soapile, not the Blessed Virgin, at the same time the name Soapile also designates a Christian Virgin, since her name was a corruption of Cihuapilli (Nahuatl for Señora or Lady), a term by which the Virgin Mary was addressed in Nahuatl (in, for example, the translation of the Hail Holy Queen into Nahuatl, where Cihuapilli stood for Queen of Heaven). Furthermore, Juan used a church ornament stolen from the Franciscan friary as an altar at Soapile's feet, and made offerings of garments to her at Christmas. He even invoked the Sierra of Tlaxcala, where Soapile was located, under the name of the Blessed Virgin. Soapile, the anti-Virgin, embodied, then, defiance of the cult of the Virgin Mary so characteristic of the seventeenth-century Mexican church, as represented by, for example, the Virgin of Ocotlán at Tlaxcala, of Guadalupe and of Los Remedios in Mexico. By preserving a sacred geography organized around a mountain and a mother goddess, Coatl maintained a territorial rivalry with the Christian church; as a response to the Christianization of the hill of Ocotlán that overlooks Tlaxcala, with its resplendent Virgin Mary, he nurtured a rival hill in the Sierra de Tlaxcala, La Malinche, which in former times had been the territory of the goddess Xochiquetzalli, and which now contained the cave where Soapile resided. Such is the symmetry and the mutual mimicry between native and Christian religions that one historian has even wondered whether the indigenous intermediaries (Juan Diego, Juan Bernardino) who played the key role in colonizing the native sierras with the cult of the Virgin may have been man-gods misled by Catholicism and converted into Marian oracles. Coatl was a native response to the miracle-working friars, made Venerable after their death, who roamed the hills and rural areas, successfully diverting some of the clients of mestizo sorcerers and Indian shamans. These Venerable friars themselves seem to have filled the gap left by the *nahualli*, shamans who before the conquest had led a life of sacrifice, fasting and sexual abstinence. Just as Christian miracle workers sought to replace native shamans by mimicking them, so the latter fought back by adopting their own mimicry. Thus, a century and a half of Christianity had led man-gods like Coatl to borrow far more from Christianity than was true of sixteenth-century predecessors; Indians of the area could only now be addressed using a language that drew on both religious traditions. For Indians, there was no discontinuity or contradiction in appealing equally to Soapile of the Sierra, the Virgins of their oratories, and those of their brotherhoods; all three were now extensions of each other. The dividing line did not run, as one might think, between Christianity and indigenous paganism, but much more between what Indians considered to be in their sphere - confraternities, holy images, churches, chapels, feasts, patron saints, springs, mountains, pre-Hispanic objects - and all the

rest, Catholic or Indian, all that remained foreign to their experience.
(Gruzinski 1989: 94-100; Cervantes 1998: 30)

Perceptive Spaniards in the seventeenth century were aware that native
religious rites had been revived and renewed, sometimes in defiance of
Christian influence, with indigenous principles reaffirmed,
uncontaminated by Christianity, but more commonly blended with
Christian elements to produce a mixture, which adapted Catholic rites
to fit the native religious world view. In 1629, Herando Ruiz de
Alarcón, the priest of Atenango in Guerrero, produced a treatise,
*Treatise on the Superstitions and Pagan Customs found today among
the Indians*, in which he collected evidence that, in settlements in the
hills and in thinly populated areas, ancient ritual was still practiced in a
great many areas of everyday life. Pre-conquest calendrical names and
the native pantheon of gods were still employed, sacrifices by self-
bleeding and offerings to the sun and spirits were still made, and
incantations - which Ruiz translated for his readers - were used for
productive activity - hunting, fishing, farming - and for divination and
curing diseases. Nearly all the incantations were accompanied by some
use of or reference to hallucinogenic or narcotic substances, such as
peyote (*Peyote tlapatl*) or *ololiuhqui* (morning glory seeds), whose
effects were attributed to possession by deities contained in the plant,
which sent the *tonalli* (vital force) of the person who partook on an
out-of-the body trip to the dwelling of the gods, most often in order to
diagnose illness and find an appropriate remedy. Those who were
called to this vocation suffered a transitory death by lightning, in an
epileptic attack, or during a serious illness, and obtained in the other
world the secrets of healing. (Ortiz de Montellano 1989)

Although Ruiz was more concerned about the survival of what he
understood to be idolatrous and superstitious practices from pre-
conquest times, the evidence he gathered actually reveals considerable
blending and inter-penetration of the native and Christian traditions.
He reported that hallucinogenic substances were often put on an altar
in the saint-house or oratory, as a sort of spiritual energy that could be
used for many different purposes. *Ololiuhqui* and peyote, which
became associated with Christ, Mary, Jesus and the Trinity, were to be

found alongside *copal* and native flowers at Christian altars, and wax candles brought by Christians might now be lit before a stone idol on a hilltop. Bees were to be revered because the wax they produce was to be burned before God. Some healers now had dreams involving Christian entities, and phrases such as "In the name of the Father, the Son, and the Holy Ghost" were added as a coda to the incantations (which remained in traditional vein). On occasions, Christian saints were held responsible for disease and had to be placated in a Christian manner with a new image, clothing, or celebration on the proper day. It is evident from Ruiz's treatise that a blending of Indian and Spanish medical practices had already taken place which he either missed or did not want to acknowledge. (Nutini 1988: 103; Ruiz de Alarcón 1984)

Unlike Ruiz, other Spanish priests in Indian communities occasionally remarked on an interplay between native and Christian beliefs. Pedro Ponce, the curate of Tzumpahuacan, who issued a treatise on idolatry which devoted special attention to the use of hallucinogens, commented on sacrifices that showed the honoring of the two traditions. He observed that, after midnight or at dawn on the eve of saints' feasts, Indians made sacrifices of birds over fire, which represented the god Xiuhtecutli; part of the bird was offered to the fire while the other part was taken to the church, and placed before the altar. (Duverger 1993: 205) The priest Jacinto de la Serna, who had thirty years of experience in Indian parishes in the valleys of Mexico and Toluca, noted in his textbook on idolatry that on the eve of festivities for a community's patron saint, the Indians offered to the fire the same food that next day was offered to the image of the saint in the church, and they would spill a little wine or pulque before the fire or the image, just as they did before the altars in their homes. He referred to an Indian healer who claimed to have been taught the art of healing by an angel that appeared to her in the form of a young boy, telling her that God had given her the gift so that she could survive. Every night the young boy crucified her on a cross and drove nails into her hands, and then taught her the means to cure. (Serna 1892: 165; quoted in Cervantes 1998: 26) Whereas Ponce was more troubled by what he regarded as the ignorant superstitions of his Indian parishioners than by the intertwining of beliefs, perhaps because the Son of God had acquired a privileged place in Indian religious practice, Serna was preoccupied with the comfortable coexistence of both systems in Indian minds. (Maurer Avalos 1983: 229) "[Indians] want to appear to be Christians even as they continue to be idolaters, believing as they do that these two things can coexist; they display great affection and esteem for the principles of Our Holy Faith, showing toward them veneration and respect; but they do not seem to forget about their old perverse beliefs and practices." (Serna 1892: 400) While the covert practices that these authors describe may indicate that the old religions survived behind a screen of Christian practice, or that they and Christian religions were thoroughly blended, another possibility is that old habits of conception survived in ways that could accommodate Christian devotions without great tension.

Even in the late-seventeenth century, pagan ceremonies routinely conducted by entire communities were uncovered, for example in the Sierra Zapoteca of Oaxaca, where an Indian "Pope" and his followers were jailed in 1679. Ten years later, the Bishop of Oaxaca observed that idolatry was so common in his bishopric and prisoners so many that a special ecclesiastical jail was needed in Antequera. In 1702, fifteen prisoners in San Francisco Cajonos were executed and their heads displayed in public after villagers had attacked the Dominican friary in order to put to death two fiscales who had denounced a pagan ceremony. An Episcopal visitation to the area revealed that native rituals mixed with Christian principles were still widespread in all the pueblos of the district. (Pita Moreda 1991: 234) Idolatry trials of Indians and mestizos conducted by the Inquisition in Oaxaca in 1739 and 1785 show the fusion of Mixtec-Zapotec religion with Catholicism, and throughout the eighteenth century both regular and secular clergy in remote regions of the Antequera bishopric documented renascent paganism. In Yucatán, investigations into Indian and mestizo idolatry continued far into the century, and there were trials in the 1720s and 1780s. Prosecutions continued also in Central Mexico.

The findings of Ruiz and others reveal that where Christianity left a niche unfilled - for example, in ceremonies for the prosperity of crops, or incantations for attaining health - pre-conquest beliefs and practices could survive in their original form, unchanged and untouched, with no Spanish loanwords. More commonly, though, some blending had already occurred, though not to the extent of producing a coherent and unified new set of practices. Thus, some Indians separated or maintained "in separate compartments" their native and Christian religious forms, and participated in one, then the other, according to need and situation, and used alternately the two systems of explanation. This form of religious interaction is called "juxtaposition," in which elements of the two religions coexist side-by-side and may be practiced by the same individual in different contexts. In this type of interaction, often the Christian challenge to native religion weakened the authority of the traditional system without fully substituting the new religion; in such cases, Indians were left stranded between a disfigured past and an unsatisfying present. Even so, juxtaposition has survived into the modern-day, and may be observed in present-day communities in Mexico, for example among the Maya.

The urgency of the extirpators' writings and of their warnings to fellow priests derived from their conviction that they were facing a diabolical reality, not a delusion or delirium provoked by poverty, ignorance or a primitive mentality. But, despite these priests' knowledge and attention to detail, their contemporaries did not take them very seriously. The extirpators lived at a time when the civil and ecclesiastical authorities in Mexico attached less and less importance to indigenous idolatry, and they were never able to persuade their superiors to share their fears and obsessions. Most of their writings were not published until the end of the nineteenth century. Neither the work of Ruiz, nor Ponce nor Serna was published in the seventeenth century. Despite the cry of alarm that they raised, there were no concerted campaigns of extirpation like those insistently demanded by Jacinto de la Serna, apart from some temporary commissions circumscribed to certain regions. Extirpation remained an individual, isolated enterprise, in the

face of the lukewarm attitude of the church and the indifference or
hostility of the crown. Here there was a stark contrast with the Andes.

11 Inti's Realm

Like Mesoamerican religion, Andean religion was an agrarian cult centered on the forces of nature. The most important deities were the gods of the heavens: Inti, the sun; Quilla, the moon, believed to be Inti's wife; Illapa, the god of thunder and of rain; and deities representing heavenly bodies, such as the Pleiades. (Katz 1972: 298) Then there were gods of the earth such as Pachamama, Mother Earth, who was considered the source of fertility and especially worshiped by farmers; and Mamacocha, Mother of Lakes and Water, especially worshiped by coastal fishermen. The major innovation of the Incas of Cusco was to spread an imperial cult of Inti, in which subject peoples were obliged to acknowledge that the solar deity was the ancestral divinity of the royal Inca dynasty, and that the person of the Inca ruler was a manifestation of Inti. Thus, whereas the Mexica commanded their subjects to recognize a local tribal god as identical to the sun god Tonatiuh, the Incas gave a self-serving twist to the mythology surrounding the solar deity Inti. Since the Andean sun god was already worshiped across the continent, the Incas probably had an easier task.

Andeans attributed sacred status to aspects of the natural environment, especially mountains, rivers, crags, rocks, and strange-shaped stones, or to unusual products of nature, such as human twins or triplets, or a double-headed corncob. Such shrines or sacred objects (*huacas*) were believed to be living manifestations of supernatural forces, which had to be propitiated by regular offerings. Some natural features, such as caves, were revered as the place of origin of the kin group (*ayllu*), and some stones were honored as petrified forms of mythical ancestors. Kin groups also preserved mummified remains of the dead with whom they frequently communicated, and whose propitiation was believed to be essential to ward off illness. These remains (sometimes bodies, sometimes little more than a few bones) were carefully preserved, wrapped in cotton with the face covered, kept in ancient resting grounds, such as caves or niches in rocks, and not brought out except for major festivals. As in Mesoamerica, households and individuals had their own domestic and personal gods. Domestic gods included rocks placed upright in the fields to protect them, and images, rocks or bound maize stalks that were believed to increase the fertility of the fields. Andeans offered sacrifices to their gods, but only to win their favor, rather than to provide essential nourishment or to protect the world from extinction, as among the Nahuas. Offerings were normally made of prized items (gold, silver, fine clothing, sea shells), animals (llamas, guinea pigs) or vegetable foods (maize, fermented maize beer, cakes, coca) rather than humans, who were only killed exceptionally on special occasions, such as the accession of a new ruler, or the incorporation of a new territory into the empire. As in Mesoamerica, those who did not make the required sacrifices to the gods and the ancestors, or who did not observe the obligatory fasts were understood to risk rupturing proper social relations and bringing adversity, especially sickness, upon the community. Offenders were required to recount their sins of commission and omission to native priests, who imposed penances, such as abstention from salt, pepper, and sexual relations. (Marzal 1993; Katz 1972: 300-01) As in Mesoamerica, the benefits sought from rituals were for the present life, not the afterlife.

Missionary strategies

The evangelization of the Andes was characterized by broadly similar goals and methods as that of Mesoamerica, but its timescale and geographical extent differed. The immensity of the Andean area and the challenges of its terrain, even greater than those of Central Mexico (which itself covered an area much bigger than Spain), set limits which were insurmountable for even the most enthusiastic and ambitious missionary. Consequently, during the sixteenth century evangelizing efforts were confined almost exclusively to the provinces between the Pacific Ocean and the mountain slopes. Toward the end of the century, missionaries penetrated some of the Amazonian territories where conquest by both Incas and Spaniards had been minimal, but these incursions were of a very limited nature. Repeated outbursts of violent conflict among the Spaniards in the wake of conquest disrupted the progress of early missionary activities and effectively delayed systematic efforts for two decades. As a result, the stages of the evangelization process differed considerably from those in Mesoamerica. There, the Golden Age of evangelization - the destruction of imperial and regional religions, the establishment of the church, the intensive study of native cultures, the in-depth evangelization of core areas - began almost from the beginning (in earnest from about 1530) and came to a close in the late 1560s/early 1570s, with the passing of the first generation of missionaries. There then followed a period of disillusionment and reevaluation. In Peru, by contrast, evangelization got off to a much more unsteady start. In the first stage (1532-51), the destruction of the official Inca cult, the establishment of the ecclesiastical hierarchy and the mass Christianization of the population of the former Inca Empire, were undertaken intermittently and sporadically on account of the civil wars between the supporters of the Pizarros and the supporters of the Almagros, and especially the great rebellion against the Crown by Gonzalo Pizarro in 1544-48. It was not until the second stage (1551-1606), particularly under the impetus of Archbishop Jerónimo de Loaysa (1537-75) who summoned the two first Lima Councils of 1551-52 and 1567, and Archbishop St Toribio Alfonso Mogrovejo who called the third Lima Council of 1582-83, that official imperial religion was dealt the death blow, native religious resistance movements were suppressed, the church's definitive organization emerged and missionary action became more uniform and stable. (Borges 1992, 2:507)

As in Mexico responsibility for missionary work fell to the mendicant orders. (Borges 1992, 2:508) The first conquistadors of 1532-33 brought in their wake both Franciscans, under Marcos de Niza, and Dominicans, under Vicente de Valverde (later archbishop of Cusco). (Malaga Medina 1992: 25) The missionary policy of rooting the church in the native religion found concrete expression in the erection of the first Dominican friary on the ruins of Cusco's Coricancha.[1] Despite the civil wars, Dominican friaries and missionary parishes proliferated in the first twenty years, and by the end of the sixteenth century, a chain of their foundations extended from one end of the Viceroyalty to the other, from Quito in the north down to Tucuman and Santiago in the south. (Armas Medina 1953: 141-44; Malaga

Medina 1992: 27) Similarly, from the moment in 1534 that they founded their first friary outside Cusco, the Franciscans extended their influence rapidly, thanks to solid internal organization and royal protection, acquiring a tremendous diffusion in the Andean area, from Quito to Rio de la Plata. After 1550, Franciscan missionary activity in the region was second to none and their numbers soon surpassed those of the other orders. Although the Mercedarians also opened their first friary in Cusco in 1534, their growth was held up by disputes with the Crown over their accumulation of wealth, and only after 1560 did the order expand. (Borges 1992, 2:506) Conversely, the later arrival of the first twelve Augustinians in 1551 worked in their favor since the civil wars had ended, and they were able to expand rapidly and, like the other orders, enter all regions of Peru. One of their most important centers was the Marian shrine of Copacabana on the southern shore of Lake Titicaca.[2] (Armas Medina 1953: 21-43)

The Jesuits, who arrived in Peru in 1569, when evangelization was already well advanced, adopted a different approach from the mendicants. Rather than acquiring permanent doctrinas (other than a few, for example at Santiago del Cercado outside Lima and Julí on the southwestern shore of Lake Titicaca, and (briefly) the area of Huarochirí), they preferred three other methods: transitory missions among Indians (of which they established hundreds); residences, founded in appropriate places, from which missions could emanate; and colleges for the sons of native lords. Despite their late start, the firm support of the Crown aided rapid Jesuit expansion and by the end of the century, their numbers began to approach those of the other orders. In 1595 there were three hundred and thirty-eight Dominicans, three hundred and ninety-one Franciscans, and two hundred and forty-one Jesuits in Peru; but by 1610 there were three hundred and forty-two Jesuits. (Armas Medina 1953: 171)

Proposals to share out the different regions of Peru among the mendicants were never put into practice, and as a result, there was no rigorous territorial division between the orders. Members of different orders existed alongside one another and disputed jurisdiction in the same regions and even villages. It was established, however, that where there were already foundations of friaries or secular priests, there should not be new foundations of other orders (1556, 1559, 1563). Once the civil wars were over, with greater numbers of missionary personnel and with the ecclesiastical hierarchy established, more organized and systematic evangelization could be conducted. At the First Lima Council (1551-52), clear rules for organized missionary activity were drawn up, later supplemented by the regulations of two more Councils (1567 and 1582-83). (Heras 1991: 57) In the third quarter of the century, large numbers of baptisms on the model of New Spain, although in lesser proportions, followed. In 1565 the viceroy calculated that three hundred thousand adults had been baptized, which amounted to almost all the adults of the region of Lima; as in New Spain, reference was made to individual religious who in one day had baptized prodigious numbers, for example more than ten thousand Indians. (Borges 1992, 2:595) A visit ordered by Viceroy Francisco de Toledo (1569-81) in 1580 concluded that in the majority of provinces there remained very few Indians unbaptized. Even so, despite the complacent self-congratulation of the colonial authorities, many religious chroniclers lamented the recalcitrant indifference of the natives to their preaching in Peru, and drew a stark and unfavorable contrast with the rose-tinted vision of Indian fidelity to the faith evoked by their counterparts in New Spain.

Since the systematic evangelization of the Andes began a quarter of a century after that of Mesoamerica, it was possible to take advantage of techniques used there. The methods of catechism, virtually the same in all the orders working in Peru, drew on the example of New Spain. (Borges 1992, 2:510) Indians were quickly admitted to the church after a very brief pre-baptismal instruction (baptism was administered in Latin but instruction was given in Castilian with a Quechua interpreter), and many missionaries administered the sacrament without first examining the nature of the Indians' faith. (Fernández García 2000: 117; Armas Medina 1953: 244) The Dominicans were the most vocal in their insistence on the need for a quality education in the faith. In 1545, Dominican Archbishop Jerónimo de Loaysa ordered that baptism should not be administered without previous instruction for at least one month in the Creed, Our Father, Hail Mary, sign of the cross, and explanation of the Articles of Faith and the Ten Commandments. Despite the First Lima Council's confirmation of this decision, many missionaries, including Dominicans, continued to flout these conditions when administering baptism. (Armas Medina 1953: 249-50) Much of the early missionary activity, though intensive, was extremely superficial. The Dominicans, for example, preferred to work briefly in many places, and in this way establish a certain right over them as missionary territories, instead of working in depth in just a few. (Meiklejohn 1988: 44) As in Mesoamerica, post-baptismal instruction was more thorough, at least in theory. Children were gathered daily, and adults three times a week, on Wednesdays, Fridays, and Saturdays to recite and learn doctrine; adults were also expected to meet for doctrine before or after mass on every important feast. As in New Spain, native lay assistants (*fiscales* and *alguaciles*) were appointed to assist missionaries in their duties, and the children of native lords were used as a vanguard for teaching catechism to their own families and for spreading the word to non-nobles. The Franciscan Mateo de Jumilla, for example, employed the services of fifty boys who prayed aloud and recited doctrine when he toured the villages of the large provinces of Cajamarca and Chachapoyas. Although Viceroy Francisco de Toledo ordered the foundation of schools for the sons of nobles, it was not until the seventeenth century that this ambition was realized, with two Jesuit schools established on the Mexican model, one in Lima (1620) and another in Cusco (1621). (Borges 1992, 2:513; Albó 1966: 275) These schools were never intended as potential seminaries; Indians might be trained to be future teachers and catechists, but in Peru there was never any support, not even among the Jesuits, for admitting Indians to the priesthood. (Albó 1966: 300-301)

12 Insertion of Catholicism in a Native Context

One field of activity where missionaries in the Andes were much slower and less ambitious than their counterparts in Mesoamerica was in their attempts to learn native languages and use them for evangelization. In the early years, missionaries were handicapped by lack of knowledge of Quechua and Aymara, the two principal Andean tongues. It was only in 1560 that Dominican friar Domingo de Santo Tomás published the first grammar and vocabulary in Quechua, written explicitly for missionaries. Before that, the friars were obliged to rely on other methods for catechism. Priests used drawings in order to explain the fundamentals of the religion, and composed their own simplified catechisms in Spanish, since there was no officially approved Catholic catechism before the Council of Trent (1545-63). Missionaries faced the familiar dilemma that catechisms in European languages would not be understood, whereas catechisms in the native tongue might misrepresent the faith, since so few priests had mastered indigenous languages. The publication of the Quechua grammar and lexicon meant that the early attempts to teach Indians Christianity in Spanish were supplanted by the practice of teaching in native languages. (MacCormack 1985: 447-50)

It was not until the Second Lima Council (1567) that priests in doctrinas were required to learn Indian languages so that they could teach doctrine to Indians and hear their confessions in the native tongue. Penalties were introduced to ensure more than lip service to the notion of a native-speaking missionary body. If priests failed to make progress in learning languages, they would be fined a third of their salary during the first year of negligence, with penalties increasing as the years went on. Priests were, however, allowed to hire multilingual assistants at their own expense. The severity of these regulations suggests the magnitude of the problem; there were undoubtedly many priests who could not carry out their duties in native languages. The Dominicans, for example, rarely heard confession by natives since few of them had acquired the necessary language skills, and of all the sacraments this was the one that required the most thorough knowledge of the native tongue. The regulations requiring knowledge of indigenous languages were more honored in the breach, apparently even among the Jesuits. (Meiklejohn 1988: 46, 260) This situation persisted despite official linkage of ordination to proven linguistic ability. In 1578 Philip II ordered the bishop of Charcas that nobody should become a priest without knowledge of an Indian language. (Albó 1966: 404) Chairs in Quechua were founded in Lima, Charcas, Quito, and Cusco in order to create centers of expertise. (Malaga Medina 1992: 52-54) By 1583, among one hundred and five priests in Peru, eighty knew Quechua. Even so, despite the prohibition imposed by the Second Council on the use of interpreters in confession, as late as 1611, in Yauyos, priests heard confessions by this method, casting doubt on the level of Quechua that in reality they had acquired. (Barnes 1992 69)

The greatest advance was made when the Third Lima Council (1582-83) ordered the preparation of an official manual of Christian Doctrine, a trilingual catechism (Spanish, Quechua and Aymara), and a confession manual, all written especially for Peru, and introduced as standard texts for the archbishopric of Lima. (Armas Medina 1953: 298-99) The catechism, modeled on the native language catechisms produced by the Provincial Council of Mexico in 1556, was published in two versions: a longer one for reference by teachers of doctrine, and an abridged version, which was to be taught every day to children younger than ten-twelve years old so that they could commit it to memory. (Barnes 1992: 70-71, 78) The texts were simple and direct, to attract the greatest number of converts. (Harrison 1994: 137) Although, henceforth, all catechisms had to be faithful translations of the original approved by the Council of Trent, provincial councils were free to insert culturally specific examples of sins, in order to make them relevant to their region. Similarly, the confession manual approved by the Third Council offered questions for parish priests to use as prompts when administering penance to Indians, but clerics were also free to respond to beliefs and practices current in their areas. The same principle was to apply to books of sermons; compilers in Peru drew on idolatry inspector Cristóbal de Albornoz's perceptions of native practices in devising questions and writing sermons. (Barnes

1992: 72) In the later years of the sixteenth century and early years of the seventeenth century, several important grammars, vocabularies, and books of sermons were published by Franciscans, Augustinians, and Jesuits, in both Quechua and Aymara.

But the Jesuits, in particular, remained ambivalent about using Quechua or Aymara terms to designate elements of Christianity, especially if they ran the risk of recalling indigenous beliefs or practices. (Albó 1966: 426) The great Jesuit theologian and missionary José de Acosta favored the use of Castilian neologisms for certain religious concepts, and this approach triumphed at the Third Lima Council but not everybody held this position. Inca Garcilaso, for example, referred to the Christian God as Pachacamac.[1] (Marzal 1992, 2:631) The use of native languages did lead to many mistranslations and errors in rendering Christian concepts. The concept of "communion of saints" became *hucllachacuininta* in Quechua, a word that young villagers in charge of teaching dogma transformed into *pucllachacuininta* or "game of saints" (*burla o trisca de los santos*, according to Arriaga), for which they were condemned by idolatry inspectors. Felipe Guaman Poma, a fervent Catholic of native origin, spontaneously transformed many of the Christian prayers in his Quechua versions, because a literal translation would have made no sense, so wide was the conceptual gulf between the two cultures. (Saignes 1999)

Missionaries in the Andes encountered the same dilemma as those in Mesoamerica: if certain ritual elements of native religions were admitted, they risked importing paganism into Christianity; but if they insisted on a clean break with the religious past, there was an equal risk that symbols of the culture which might allow transmission of the message would be destroyed, and profound evangelization frustrated. Missionaries adopted neither of these methods in an intransigent way, but with regard to the circumstances. Most, especially in the early years, were prepared to make practical accommodations with the Andean worldview. (Dussel 1974: 119) Some accepted aspects of pre-Hispanic iconography, particularly representations of animals, which for Indians were invested with the full force of the sacred. Rays of

105

light to represent divinity, which in the pre-Christian Andean system were identified with the Father Sun, began to be associated with the Christian God. (Salles Reese 1997: 40) The identification of God with celestial divinities, especially the sun, and of Mary with spirits of nature - mountains, lakes, rivers and springs - was explicit in early colonial iconography, and was actively fostered by the clergy, especially the Augustinians, whose founder had laid the foundations for such a strategy of evangelization. (Gisbert 1980: 12; Sallnow 1987: 70) As in New Spain, Christian supernatural beings took the place of native ones. Ticsi Viracocha, who according to native myth, had created the entire universe, was easily incorporated into the Christian God the Father (Salles Reese 1997: 38)[2]; the Virgin of Copacabana took on the rain-producing functions of the god Copacati at Lake Titicaca; and the Virgin of Pucarani was enthroned by the Augustinians to replace the god Cacaaca. Throughout the Andes, the Virgin Mary became identified with Pachamama, the Mother Earth; the Virgin of Copacabana, for example, shared some of her attributes, though by no means all (Pachamama was not virginal, chaste or pure). Several iconographic representations of the Virgin Mary, especially from the seventeenth century, show the Mother of God and Pachamama sharing the same artistic space, for example the Virgin appearing as the mountain of Potosí. This is more an assimilation than a substitution, since the latter entails the replacement of one thing by another, resulting in the absence of that which was replaced; but the cult of the Virgin of Copacabana did not put an end to the cult of Pachamama. (Gisbert 1980: 17, 21; Salles Reese 1997: 30, 32, 171)

The concept of Heaven/Earth/Hell was assimilated to the native triple concept of hanaopacha, caypacha and ucupacha. Caypacha was the earthly world. Hanaopacha was the afterworld or world above, where the dead plowed fields and tended flocks as in life, but never suffered hunger or want or pain; in the colonial period this place was believed to be the location of God, Christ, the Virgin, the saints and the spirits of the dead of exemplary life. Ucupacha was the underworld or world within, inhabited by small people and animals, and in the colonial period sometimes identified with the Christian Hell and the abode of Supay (a native spirit that Spaniards associated with the devil).

106

(Sallnow 1987: 128) Christian artists' representation of the Trinity by painting three equal Christ figures unintentionally recalled threefold pre-Hispanic divinities, for example, the deity Tancatanca, a statue with three heads (Calancha 1974-81, 2:1165) (the portrayal of the Trinity by a three-headed Christ, on the other hand, had a European origin). It is possible that the more traditional representation of the Trinity by three different figures - old man, young man, and dove - was avoided because the dove recalled the worship of zoomorphic gods. An interesting variant in the Cusco representation of the Trinity had three persons, each the same physically but with different attributes - Christ with a bare chest and a cross, the Holy Spirit dressed in white but with a dove on his shoulder, and God the Father in the center with a large sun on his chest. The use of the sun as a symbol of God derived from Augustinian texts but at the same time recalled pre-Columbian concepts. (Gisbert 1980 89-90) Another idiosyncratic interpretation of the Trinity, which drew on native religion, and which priests seem not to have opposed, was a trio of Sun-God, Virgin-Moon, and their Christ-Son. Sometimes Christ was even perceived as the older or younger brother of the devil. (Saignes 1999)

In the early years, Andean myths were admitted by some as a basis for the introduction of the new religion, since they were believed to contain intimations of a primitive Christianity, whose memory could be revived in native peoples and serve as means to make the Christian message familiar within the context of native culture. Tunupa, an Aymara celestial and purifying god, related to fire and lightning, usually understood to be either a manifestation of the (creator) god Viracocha, or alternatively his emissary, was rapidly identified as a Christian apostle, who was supposed to have evangelized the Americas in ancient times. Spanish chroniclers disagreed as to his precise identity. The Augustinian Antonio de Calancha identified him with St Thomas, whereas Guaman Poma and Inca Garcilaso believed him to be St Bartholomew. Another Augustinian, Ramos Gavilán, presented Tunupa as a saint, and a presumed disciple of Christ, who preached against idolatry and bad customs, but did not try to identify him (*History of the famous sanctuary of Our Lady of Copacabana*, 1621). Others expressed scepticism. In 1550, Pedro de Cieza de León was incredulous when he was shown the statue of a person at Tiahuanaco, alleged to have been the apostle who preached to the Indians before the arrival of the Spaniards, since he rejected the theory of a pre-Hispanic evangelization. (Cieza 1967, 5:11; MacCormack 1985: 460) But the story of the American apostle caught on and became widespread in the colonial Andes. According to his legend, Tunupa, usually portrayed as a tall, white, blond, bearded man, traversed the length and breadth of the Andes, from Paraguay and Tucumán to Chachapoyas and the valleys of Trujillo. Ramos Gavilán and Calancha related how he preached the worship of a single, universal, and true god, and how oracles were made mute by his presence and huacas ceased communicating with Indians. In many places the people wanted to kill this preacher but he was always saved by divine intervention. In Cacha he performed miracles and was stoned when he destroyed the idol there, but the heavens sent a rain of fire over the town. In Carabuco he preached and set up a miraculous cross that the Indians tried to destroy, first by fire, which failed but left scorch marks (which Calancha claimed to have seen), and then by burying it or by throwing it into the lake. Nevertheless, the cross remained intact. Tunupa escaped to the Island of Titicaca (now known as the Island of the Sun) where he was martyred. His body was tied to a raft, which was led by a beautiful woman to the shores of Chacamarca, where the land opened up to form a river. Here his body disappeared into Lake Poopó, near a volcano that was named after him (in another version, the saint was untied by beautiful birds which descended from Heaven, and then he spread his cape over the waters, entered the lake and traveled to Copacabana).

Tunupa's association with long pilgrimages, rejection of local idols, and miracles with water and fire made him ideal for assimilation to Christianity. His identification with St Bartholomew probably derived from shared attributes. Like Tunupa, the saint dressed in white and was associated with fire and Hell/underworld, since he was ordered by Christ to interrogate the devil about his fall. Bartholomew's appropriateness as a candidate for Tunupa was strengthened by that fact that he preached in the East, he silenced idols, and his corpse was thrown into the sea. The association with St. Thomas was probably a later development, possibly introduced by the Jesuits (though there are some indications that the tradition predated their arrival in 1569). A painting by Jesuit Diego de la Puente, finished before 1663 and originally housed in Cusco, shows St. Thomas with all the characteristics of Tunupa in his martyrdom on the Island of Titicaca, when he refused to worship the image of the sun. It is a fine illustration of the Jesuit policy of assimilating Indian myths to Christianity. A cult of relics even grew up around the myth. The cross at Carabuco was rediscovered after the conquest and was divided in two, with one part conserved in the church at Carabuco and the other in the cathedral at Chuquisaca; both were treated as if they were Christian relics. Furthermore, according to the Augustinian chroniclers, Tunupa's presence was marked in nine places by stones that preserved his footprints and by a mark left by his staff. Ramos Gavilán identified the beautiful lady of the myth as the Virgin Mary, prefiguring the Virgin of Copacabana, enthroned at the lake's shore in 1585 and in whose honor he wrote. The reutilization of myths referring to the region around Lake Titicaca may be understood as a recontextualization, an attempt to give historical continuity across a rupture caused by the conquest of the Andean world. By substituting Christian content for the old Andean content of the myth, these narratives were intended to become part of the Christian tradition and provide a basis for new evangelizing efforts. (Gisbert 1980: 40-42; Salles-Reese 1992: 185-86, 189, 190)

The idea of an apostolic pre-evangelization in the Indies obviated the need to explain why its inhabitants had not been included in the Christian cosmovision and offered the satisfying certainty that the Americas formed part of the history of salvation. Furthermore, if the Christian faith had existed in the New World in remote times, it allowed an acceptance of everything positive in the life of these peoples as the heritage of that ancient Christianity, rather than the work of the devil. (San Pedro 1992: 26-27) As far as we know, the earliest formulation of the theory of a pre-Hispanic evangelization occurred among the first twelve Augustinians who evangelized the people of Huamachuco in northwestern Peru. At times, these missionaries were so surprised by the complexity of native religion that they doubted the orthodox Christian interpretation of its diabolical origin; their barely concealed admiration for its richness led their chronicler to accept a previous evangelization as the only explanation for native beliefs. (San Pedro 1992: 14) Later advocates of the theory included Diego Durán (1581) and Jerónimo de Mendieta (1596), but in Peru it was the Augustinians, and especially Antonio de Calancha, who were most closely identified with it. Calancha suggested a double hypothesis: such beliefs and rites had Catholic beginnings through evangelization, though after the passing of years and the sowing of the seeds of demonic misinterpretation, there was corruption and degeneration; or the demon, like an ape introduced them from the beginning in order to mimic God. (Marzal 1996: 5) In his conclusion, Calancha defended the former hypothesis, explaining the later distortion of indigenous Christianity by comparing it to that which occurred in India and Persia, places that reportedly had also been evangelized by the apostles. Augustinian theology had always stressed the role of divine providence in human events. Its spokesmen in Peru did not remove the devil from the stage but they did take away his protagonism, allowing a positive evaluation of native life by the Europeans and a reconciliation of the Andean with his own past. (San Pedro 1992: 28; Marzal 1989: 334)

Some missionaries in the Andes sought native religious concepts that could be paralleled with Christian ones, with results as misleading as in Mesoamerica. They believed that they had found the equivalent of confession in the Andean practice of twice-yearly verbal acknowledgment of infractions of ethical rules in the presence of a native priest, but the motive behind this ceremony was quite different from Christian confession, since the well-being of the community was understood to depend on it, and if it was neglected, the springs would dry up and there would be no food. Their equation of sin with the Quechua concept of *hucha* was equally flawed. *Hucha* was committed if the duties of the ritual calendar were not completed or if one did not provide food and sacrifices to the sacred shrines, and was removed from the individual and the community by means of a ritual where the bad energy was carried off by the powerful rivers that flowed to the tropical forest. It signified damage to harmonious social relations, a concept that differed greatly from the Christian concept of sin, which affected the fate of the soul in the afterlife if it was not effaced by penance. (Harrison 1994: 143; Griffiths 1996: 200)

As in Mesoamerica, the missionaries and the church authorities actively encouraged the use of native dances, songs, and regalia in the celebration of Christian holy feasts. This was admissible because Spaniards believed that by distinguishing between the means of celebration and the object being celebrated, certain native religious behavior could be used to transfer worship from native supernatural beings to Christian ones. The Provincial Councils of Lima emphasized not the eradication but the utilization of native religious sentiment, and the careful application of a philosophy of substitution (see the third constitution of the First Council of Lima). Not only were crosses to be raised and churches built over the sites of native temples and shrines, but pagan seasonal festivals associated with sowing, rain, and snow were to be redirected into equivalent Christian celebrations which took place at the same time of year (Second Council of Lima). This willingness to build on and transform pagan practices is evident in contemporary descriptions of the Corpus Christi fiesta (a movable feast, celebrated in late May or early June, lasting more than two weeks if its novena – nine-day period immediately preceding the feast – and octave - eight-day period immediately following it - are included); the manner in which the feast was celebrated in Cusco in 1555 recalled pre-Hispanic religious ceremonies: (Dean 1999: 15-16)

"The chiefs from the whole district came into the great city to celebrate the festivity, accompanied by their kinsmen and all the nobility of their provinces. They used to bring all the decorations, ornaments, and devices that they used in the time of the Inca kings for their great festivals ... Each tribe brought the coat of arms of the family from which it vaunted descent. Some came dressed in lion skins, as Hercules is depicted, with their heads in the lion's head, since they claim descent from this animal. Others had the wings of a very large bird called cuntur [condor] fixed on their shoulders, as angel's wings are in pictures, for it was from this bird that they boasted of descending. Similarly, others came with painted devices, such as springs, rivers, lakes, mountains, heaths and caves, from which they believed that their earliest forefathers had emerged... and in the same way in my time, with such additions as they were capable of, they used to mark the feast of the Blessed Sacrament, the true God, our Lord and Redeemer. This they did with great joy, like people now truly disillusioned about their former heathendom...The Indians from each allocation marched past with their floats and accompanied by their kinsmen and friends, all singing in the special language of their province, not in the general language of the capital: thus each tribe could be told apart. They bore drums, flutes, horns, and other rustic instruments. In many cases the women of the province accompanied the men and joined in the singing and playing. The songs they sang were in praise of Our Lord God, thanking Him for the great grace He had granted to them of permitting them a true knowledge of Himself. They also gave thanks to the Spanish clergy, both regular and secular, for having taught them Christian doctrine. From some provinces no women came, but only men; in a word everything was done according to the custom in the days of the Incas. On reaching the cemetery which stands seven or eight steps higher than the square, they mounted the steps to adore the Blessed Sacrament, in their tribal groups, each ten or twelve steps in front of the next so that they should not get mixed. They came down into the square again by the other steps to the right of the platform. Each tribe mounted according to its seniority, the date of its conquest by the Incas, the most recent first, then the second and the third most recent until finally there came the Incas themselves. These went in front of the priests, a smaller and poorer band, since they had lost their whole empire and their private houses and estates." (Inca Garcilaso 1966, 2:1415-1417)

Thus, Indians accompanied Christian images organized according not to an Iberian model but on the basis of native affiliation, to one or other ethnic group of the region. Ethnic separatism was encouraged within limits, to provide a framework in which Indians could transfer allegiances from native to Christian deities. (Sallnow 1987: 57-58)

It has often been said that the Andean Corpus Christi was simply a continuation under Christian guise of Inti Raymi, the Inca festival of the Sun (Polo de Ondegardo 1916: 21-22). It is true that there were some similarities in dances, performances and songs, but the identification is highly debatable. Other chroniclers (including José de Arriaga and Hernando de Avendaño) associated Corpus not with Inti Raymi, but with an altogether different festival, Onqoymita, celebrated in early June to mark the appearance of the constellation of the Pleiades (whose heliacal rise was on 8 June), called Onqoy ("illness") in Quechua, and to pay homage to this celestial deity in order to prevent the corn from drying up just before the harvest. If an identification of Corpus with a pre-Hispanic festival is to be made, then Onqoymita is more plausible than Inti Raymi, given that the period prior to the summer solstice (21 June) was an agriculturally significant time, and that illness was expected in the Andes when the Pleiades were not visible, between late April and early June. (MacCormack 1988: 983; Dean 1999: 36) But to insist on either Inti Raymi or Onqoymita as the "true" pagan festival behind the Christian feast is to miss the point. Since the songs and dances performed at Corpus were generic festive behaviors (probably *qhapaq ucha* dances, performed not only for Inti Raymi, but also for other ceremonies to ward off illness, such as Ytu), no particular festival was duplicitously hidden under the guise of Christian celebration. Rather, Corpus became a festival of genuine importance to Andeans (and not merely a cover for something else) because it coincided with great celestial events (the reappearance of the Pleiades and the June solstice) and with essential terrestrial activities (the harvest). (Dean 1999: 37, 49)

Even more significantly, Spaniards no less than Andeans approvingly perceived the evident generic continuity between pre-Hispanic festivals and Christian ones. Inca Garcilaso (1966, 1:245) described how, in honor of Corpus in Cusco, a special version of an Inca victory song (*haylli*) was sung by eight mestizo schoolboys who appeared dressed in Incaic costume, each carrying an indigenous foot plow (*chakitaklla*). In pre-Hispanic times, this type of victory song had accompanied military or agricultural success; now, for the Catholic feast, it was refocused away from the Sun god and onto the Christian God, celebrating the conversion of those mestizo youths who performed in the costume of agricultural labourers. By replacing the principal Andean festival of the sun, the Christian feast re-channeled hitherto misdirected Andean religious sentiment. The remembrance of Inti Raymi was purposefully glimpsed and paraded at Corpus precisely to demonstrate how the Incas had prepared the way for Christianity and to highlight the triumph of the Christian God over his adversary, the Inca solar deity, and of Spanish Christians over Incas and their Andean subjects (remembrance of a lesser harvest festival such as Onqoymita would not do the trick). Native songs performed in indigenous costume but in praise of God testified to the Christianization of Incaic festive practices and constituted proof of a successful evangelization. No wonder, then, that Viceroy Toledo, in his ordinances of 1573, specified that each parish in Cusco would present two or three dances during the Corpus festival, for these exotic displays, as exhibitions of difference, affirmed the success of the conquest and conversion of the Andean region, and demonstrated the universality of the Christian triumph. (Dean 1999: 32, 38, 39, 46, 200-01

13 Andean Appropriation of Christianity

At the beginning of the evangelization, old ethnic constituencies remained largely intact, and Christian saints were installed in native communities alongside pagan gods. But Viceroy Toledo's resettlement program of the 1570s, whereby the inhabitants of scattered hamlets were gathered into small towns, produced vast native population movements, both as part of the relocation, and also as an act of resistance by those who fled to evade the labor requirements imposed on the new settlements. (Brading 1991: 102, 133) As ancient loyalties were weakened, there emerged new sets of attachments to community and locality, which were expressed in Christian religious observances. Andean villages were now populated by a panoply of Christian patron saints, who became the principal recipients of native religious devotion and the prime indicators of local prestige and rank. (Sallnow 1987: 60) In many cases, these new divine guardians were allocated to villages arbitrarily, according to the whim of the local priest. However, there is some evidence that on occasions Indians could exercise a decisive influence, at least in choosing which among several saints offered to them by Spaniards would become the object of their devotion. Calancha relates how in 1614 the Augustinian Fray Pedro Anbite placed an image of San Juan de Saagún on an altar at the hospital in the village of Anta (Cusco). A crippled Indian woman who gave alms for a mass to be said to the saint was miraculously cured of the affliction from which she had suffered for twelve years. The villagers asked the local priest, who had been absent from the village, to allow them to take the saint in procession to the church. When he refused, the Indians retaliated by hiding the image. Finally the priest agreed to accept alms from the Indians and, in return, allowed them to place the image on the main altar, where it remained. Calancha noted that thereafter the image continued to perform miracles, including the healing of all manner of illnesses. (Calancha 1974-81, 2:1127) The Augustinian reported many other examples of official recognition of the miraculous powers of an image as a result of the devotion and enthusiasm of ordinary Indians. Thus, native peoples were more than mere passive recipients of the process whereby local pre-Hispanic deities were replaced by communal patron saints.

Native protagonism was more substantial in the proliferating confraternities, which, in the Andes as in Mesoamerica, were encouraged by the colonial church in order to bind Indians more closely to Christian worship. (Kubler 1946: 405; Sallnow 1987: 61; Celestino 1981: 106) But, as in New Spain, an institution imposed by the ecclesiastical authorities for a colonial purpose was rapidly transformed by native Andean communities into one that primarily served indigenous needs. The religious brotherhoods largely replaced and took on the role of the ancient kinship groups. They did not represent simply the survival of archaic pre-colonial forms of reciprocity and competition, but rather were forms that responded to new social relations and revealed considerable social creativity. Natives used the colonial institution of the religious brotherhood for the preservation of social integration and indigenous forms of identity despite the traumatic cultural shock of conquest, cultural destruction, depopulation, and resettlement. (Dean 1999: 110).

An equally significant manifestation of the indigenous appropriation of Catholicism was the manner in which, during the second half of the sixteenth century, native sacred sites of the Andean landscape re-emerged in Christian form. (Sallnow 1987: 73, 175, 268) Regional gods that had been the object of long-distance pilgrimages before the conquest were replaced by important Christian shrines to Mary (Copacabana, Pucarani) or Christ (Señor de Wank'a: Lord of the Crag, situated not far from Cusco on the slopes of the Vilcanota valley; Señor de Qoyllur Rit'i), which became the recipients of miracle cults and the destinations for Catholic pilgrim journeys whose routes retraced those of former times. South Titicaca, because of its important pagan associations and its location on the transport route between Huancavelica, the source of mercury, and Potosí, where inferior ores were refined with that element, became the node of an interregional network of miraculous shrines. The appearance of this system of interrelated Christian shrines demonstrates that new divine personages do not emerge onto a religious tabula rasa but onto a historically configured ritual topography, a pre-existing pattern of sacred sites from which they draw significance. (Sallnow 1987: 72, 89) The relationship of the Christian shrines to pre-Hispanic sacred space is most evident in the symmetry of their arrangement in relation to Cusco city. Almost all lie on or near either the east-west or southeast-northwest axis of the city. Four of the five Marian shrines lie on the southeast-northwest axis on a line (*ceque*) linking Cusco with Tiwanaku-Titicaca. Nearly all the Christian sanctuaries are situated close to sites of native temples and shrines (themselves pre-Incaic shrines) used on the day of the June solstice as ritual stations by a group of Inca priests on long-distance pilgrimage from Cusco to Willkanuta. Like pre-Hispanic sacred sites, the shrines tend to be seen not individually but as members of sets, generally of three, four or most often five shrines, perceived as siblings, and ranked in order of fraternal seniority. Typically it is said that five brothers were wandering through the area, and that each stopped to rest at the spot where his shrine now stands, the oldest first and the youngest last. These shrines had their pre-Columbian counterparts in kindred huacas (as described in the Quechua narrative from Huarochirí, a region much studied by historians, lying between the coast and the Andes near Lima), and the wandering brothers are directly reminiscent of the itinerant sons of Viracocha. (Sallnow 1991: 145) The Christian shrines are also intimately related to Incaic and pre-Incaic mountain deities: the shrine of Señor de Wank'a is linked with Mt Pachatusan, and the shrine of Señor de Qoyllur Rit'i is associated with Mt Ausankati, which lies a few degrees south. (Sallnow 1987: 90) Thus, in progressive re-consecration of the regional landscape, there emerged miraculous Christian shrines, pagan sites transformed, with Catholic form but native religious meaning.

Miraculous Christian images also appeared in the cities and became recipients of civic cults. A famous example is the crucifix supposedly donated to the city of Cusco by King Charles I of Spain, which, following the earthquake of 1650, was enshrined as Señor de los Temblores (Lord of the Earthquakes). (Sallnow 1987: 73) This shrine, in Cusco cathedral, and that of El Señor de Qoyllur Rit'i (Lord of the Snow Star), far from the settlement on the mountain heights, shared the same crucification advocation. Whereas Temblores is honored by a civic cult, presided over by representatives of the political, military and church elites, Qoyllur Rit'i (which dates from the 1780s) has the reputation of being the most authentically Indian of all the important pilgrimages in the region. These two miraculous Christs have their titular feasts before Easter and Corpus respectively, both movable feasts, separated by an invariant span of sixty days. One historian has convincingly argued that the two feasts are Christianized fixtures of two key paired dates in the pre-Hispanic Andean calendar, the heliacal set of Pleiades (24 April) and their heliacal rise (8 June) - the former marking the death of the earth, and the latter marking the revival and the rebirth of the Sun at the June solstice. The two great pilgrimages of Pariacaca and Chaupiñamca in pre-Hispanic Huarochirí were affixed to these two astronomical observations. So through the apparent haphazard emergence of prodigious Christs and Virgins, an imperial matrix of suppressed pagan landscape gradually reasserted itself. The miracles were a vehicle for the acceptable re-sacralization of ancient pre-Hispanic sacred sites raised by the Incas to the status of imperial shrines. (Sallnow 1987: 91)

Therefore, these miraculous shrines are both Christian and Andean: Christian in iconography, religious meaning (to some extent), and clerical involvement; Andean in location in the sacred landscape and in belonging to a wider cult of earth divinities. When peasant pilgrims make their way as a group across the mountain trails to the miraculous shrine, they are recovering a sacred space in which they can redefine themselves in relation to one another and other groups. Andean pilgrimage, for the peasant, is an attempt to domesticate a sector of the Christian cult, to appropriate it and insert it into the socio-geographical matrix of their environment, recreating with Christian icons the non-imperial, trans-local domain of social relations. (Sallnow 1987: 269)

These miraculous Christian figures have been Indianized, not only by dint of their location in the landscape, but also by the protagonism enjoyed by natives in their emergence. The significance of the Virgin of Copacabana, and those regional virgins derived from her, is that they illustrate the partial appropriation of the Marian cult by Indians.

118

All the images were alleged to have been fashioned by the same sculptor, Francisco Tito Yupanki. They were, therefore, produced by an Indian, not a Spanish artist and were not merely franchise shrines of Spanish virgins (like those of Guadalupe at Pachacamac and Pacasmayo). (Sallnow 1987: 71) These images "belong" to Indians. Devotion to the image of the Virgin at Pucarani arose on account of a miracle performed for an Indian. Alonso Churaba prayed to the image for the cure of his crippled hands and feet and was rewarded by an apparition of the Mother of God, who took him by the hand, stood him on his feet and told him to ring the church bell eighteen times and to serve her for eighteen months. Another native, Lorenzo Llusco, who taught doctrine to the local Indians, was visited by the Virgin of Pucarani in a dream and exhorted to go to her church and expel a demon that was an interloper there. When he followed her command, he found himself cured of his lameness. Calancha noted that the Virgin chose for her work not a priest but a lame, poor, half-naked native so that Indians should learn of the love she had for them. He observed that it was precisely these images, made by a humble Indian, which God chose as the vehicle for miracles, since in this way incredulous Indians would learn of the omnipotence of his grace; at the same time God honored Indian devotions by making miraculous the very images that Indian hands had produced. (Calancha 1974-81, 4:1964-65, 1988) Ramos Gavilán's collection of miracles performed by the Virgin of Copacabana presented Indians as protagonists of the narratives in a majority of instances, and thus allowed them to participate actively in the conquering religion, and gave them an example to emulate rather than a diabolical image of themselves. In the miracle narratives, the Virgin always interceded on their behalf, healing them, bringing them back to life, freeing them, or making their lives bearable. As early as the beginning of the seventeenth century, Indians referred lovingly to the Virgin of Copacabana as "mamanchic," that is to say, "mother of all." (Salles Reese 1997: 161-162)

Even as native religion appropriated Christianity, it simultaneously adapted under the influence of the new religion. In an interesting parallel with Mesoamerica, as early as the middle of the sixteenth century, changes in shamanic practices had emerged as a response to

Catholicism. Sacred objects were manipulated in combinations that included both amulets and small statues of saints. Native healers, claiming to have received their power from God or the apostles, carried out ceremonies after Catholic confession. Wandering Indian medical men claimed to have received the church's approval. In the 1580s, one native "messiah," dubbed the Christ of Tacobamba (near Potosí), went about with apostles and female saints, telling his followers to drink maize beer as Christ's blood and eat achuma (*Trichocereus pachanoi*, also known as the San Pedro cactus, one of the most ancient hallucinogenic magical plants of South America). Countless shamans proclaimed themselves Santiago (understood to be a new manifestation of Illapa, the god of thunder and lightning) or the Virgin, or the "brother" of Christ. The mingling of native and Catholic elements in practices that were closer to Christian heterodoxy than to idolatry, and especially the underlying current of deep frustration at exclusion from the priesthood, reveal the internalization of the imported religious message. (Saignes 1999: 121-28)

The fact that Christianity made an impact which was often far from that intended by missionaries is revealed in an Indian story noted by the Jesuits that told how the volcano of Omate had tried to involve the volcano of Arequipa in a plot to destroy the Spaniards, only to be told by the latter that he could not take part since he was a Christian, with the name San Francisco, and that Omate would have to carry out the plan by himself.

Even where overt resistance was offered by native peoples to the new religion, the forms that this resistance took often betrayed the influences of the imported religion, and revealed accommodation with the object of resistance. The most important resistance in the sixteenth-century Andes was offered by the Taki Onqoy (dancing sickness) religious revivalist movement that arose in the Central Peruvian Highlands, around Huamanga (Ayacucho) in 1565. The *taquiongos*, or disseminators of the movement's message, preached that a pan-Andean alliance of deities would soon defeat the Christian god and restore to the Andean world its own principles of harmony and order, which had been so brutally shattered by the advent of the Spaniards.

The movement's message was given credence by the unprecedented outbreaks of disease that had afflicted native Andeans since the conquest. Only the wrath of the huacas, provoked by the neglect of their worship since the triumph of the Christian god, could explain the calamities that had befallen the native world. Now the huacas would wreak their revenge upon the Europeans by attacking them with the same diseases to which the Indians had succumbed. In order to escape the vengeance of the revitalized deities, native peoples were exhorted to return to traditional cults, to revile Christian worship and to reject all forms of cooperation with Spaniards.

Despite its self-proclaimed rejection of all things Christian, in many important respects the Taki Onqoy movement reflected Christian influences. For a start, the *taquiongos* presented themselves as counter-missionaries. They described themselves as messengers of the huacas, just as Spanish missionaries described themselves as messengers of the Christian God. The message that Indians were being castigated with disease for abandoning the huacas was a riposte to the Christian priests who attributed epidemics to God's punishment for idolatry (MacCormack 1988: 985-87) Their denial of the power of the Christian God to secure the material existence of Indians, which was the domain exclusively of the huacas, derived from the Christian emphasis on the powerlessness of native deities. The movement's ideas about incarnation and sainthood seem to reveal Christian influences. The native gods were no longer confined to rocks, water, or hills; now they became incarnated in natives' bodies and caused them to shake, tremble, and dance insanely (hence the name of the movement). Some female *taquiongos* were feted not as Andean huacas but as Christian saints, whose names (for example, Saint Mary and Saint Mary Magdalene) they adopted. One historian has observed that this phenomenon probably expressed a crisis of confidence in the capacity of Andean gods by themselves to control the course of events, and a desire to ally with some elements of the Hispanic supernatural world while simultaneously battling the Christian God. (Stern 1982) The consciousness of pan-Andean unity that the movement called for - indigenous affiliations to ayllu or ethnic groups should lose priority to a new Andean identity shared by all natives subordinated to Spanish rule - was also a startling innovation in response to Christianity. (Saignes 1999: 121-28)

"You have made the law which you preach to us odious"

The Taki Onqoy resistance movement should not disguise the reality that most Indians accepted Christianity, on their own terms, if not exactly on those of missionaries and idolatry inspectors. Does this mean then that the Andeans had been converted by the end of the sixteenth century? In contrast to the triumphalist optimism of Mexico, Spaniards in Peru were defeatist and pessimistic when it came to assessing the results of evangelization. All observers agreed that despite baptism the natives of Peru remained essentially pagan. Friar Antonio de Zúñiga wrote to Philip II in 1579 that the Indians confined themselves to a pretence of observance of Catholic ceremonies. Inspector Garci Diez de San Miguel found in 1567 that the majority of the Indians in Chucuito were not Christians, and that there even remained large numbers of unbaptized. (Wachtel 1977: 154) The superficiality of what the missionaries had achieved became evident in the early-seventeenth century when renewed attempts at the eradication of persisting native religious practices were considered necessary.

There were many reasons for the apparent failure of Christianity in the Andes to make inroads as great as in Mesoamerica. In the Andes, the initial missionary drive was only superficially effective. The Andean area was vast, with most of the population dispersed in high inaccessible valleys between soaring mountain peaks, or in impenetrable jungles. There was no equivalent of the plateau of Central Mexico with its highly densely populated settlements. Andean populations were dispersed in a larger number of smaller, more distant settlements. In general, there were too few priests (although this does not seem to have been true for some areas such as Chucuito). By 1569 the total number of priests and friars resident in the viceroyalty was only about three hundred and fifty, when the estimated need was for one thousand five hundred. New Spain, with a smaller population, already had more ministers. (Kubler 1946: 403; quoted in Sallnow 1987: 56) Many, probably most, of the secular priests received insufficient intellectual, theological, and linguistic training, and tended to be absent for long periods from their parishes, which were left to temporary replacements. The relative shortage of priests made more important the numerous local officers attached to the church (sacristans, administrators of church property, cantors, sponsors of saint festivals). Left to their own devices, these mediators promoted religious blending. Even among the missionaries, despite some notable exceptions, mostly among the Jesuits, proficiency in native languages was insufficient. Levels of commitment and enthusiasm were lower than in Mesoamerica, which may be attributed to the late start to evangelization in Peru, the protracted civil wars, and the fading of the initial currents of missionary optimism and ardor so characteristic of the early years in New Spain. As a result, the Andes had a briefer experience of the initial phase of zealous missionary activity that was so important in Mesoamerica. It is possible that the quality of the missionaries in the Andes was inferior too; Viceroy Toledo lamented that New Spain had taken the cream from the start. Missionary methods also contributed to slow progress. Once the initial impetus to gain conversions had waned, the trend among the Dominicans, for example, was to shift from baptism administered as soon as possible followed by indoctrination to the direct opposite, in other words beginning with instruction and postponing baptism. (Meiklejohn 1988: 45) This probably explains why Garci Diez found so many unbaptized Indians in Chucuito (though the upside of such a policy was that those who were baptized may have had a greater knowledge of what they had committed to). It has been suggested that other missionaries may have been less scrupulous than the Jesuits in ensuring that neophytes attained the fullness of Christian life as quickly as possible. It is also possible that, in contrast to the Jesuits, who believed in the need for explicit faith in Jesus Christ for salvation, the Dominicans were satisfied with some type of implicit faith. (Meiklejohn 1988: 261)

However, it is probably misleading to attribute too much significance to differences in methods between missionary orders. Other factors were more significant. The spiritual message of Christianity was reduced to memorization of basic prayers; instruction had to be simple, it was believed, otherwise Indians would not grasp it. This reduced Christianity left little chance that Andeans could acquire a deep understanding of the faith. The upheaval involved in the resettlement of population brought confusion and resentment that was not fertile ground for inculcation of lasting conviction of Christian truth. The most serious obstacle to an effective Christianization was the perception that evangelization and the church were deeply involved in the system of colonial exploitation. Too many secular priests undermined the relationship of trust with natives by engaging in trade transactions with them and treating their benefices as the first rung on the career ladder and a means to attain other economic rewards. Some clergymen refused to provide flocks with primary and religious education because education might reveal the unfairness in the Indians' condition and cause them to turn against their clergy. Although missionaries did not abuse their position in the same way, they were as willing as their secular counterparts to impose harsh punishments on the Indians, and were powerless to prevent lay Spaniards exploiting their charges, and largely supported their exclusion from certain sacraments such as communion and ordination. Native demands for a true evangelization were simply not met. (MacCormack 1985: 453-55; Saignes 1999; Meiklejohn 1988: 261)

The commitment of the church and missionaries to violent methods should not be underestimated as an important factor in limiting the enthusiasm of Andeans for the new religion. As in Mesoamerica, the use of force was an intimate part of the evangelization process from the very beginning. Jesuit José de Acosta reminded his contemporaries of St Augustine's dictum that "it is necessary to take the idols from the hearts of the pagans before they are taken from their altars"; and he warned them: "To make an effort to get rid of idolatry by force first, before the Indians have spontaneously received the gospel, has always seemed to me...to close, lock and bar the door of the gospel to those outside, rather than to open it." (Acosta 1954: 561; Marzal 1992, 2:595) Reality failed to conform to this ideal. The spontaneous destruction of native temples and shrines during the conquest, part and parcel of the process of seizing their treasures, was only the start of an ever-accelerating momentum of violence impossible to arrest. The sacred precincts of the Inca state religion were razed to the ground, their objects of reverence torn from protesting hands before being burnt, smashed and crushed, their ministers tortured and murdered. Resistance was violently suppressed; the Taki Onqoy movement provoked between 1568 and 1571 a swift and violent response by the idolatry inspector Cristóbal de Albornoz, who employed methods modeled on those of the Spanish Inquisition. Worse still, even those missionary campaigns designed to serve a didactic rather than destructive purpose and actively to win adherents to Christianity, began with acts of violence. Even if, theoretically, coercion was employed only to bring about the abandonment of old beliefs and not the adoption of Christianity, in practice the distinction was academic.

To some extent, resort to religious coercion was a by-product of the church's involvement with the state, which favored rapid evangelization and, if necessary, forced conversion; but it was also the outcome of a shift in position by the missionaries themselves. During the early decades of evangelization in the Andes, the model of conversion by persuasion was implemented by some missionaries, in particular by a follower of Las Casas, Domingo de Santo Tomás (who also believed that conversion to a European or Spanish way of life was not necessary). Subsequently this model was supplanted by an ever-increasing insistence on the authority of Christianity and European concepts of culture, as missionaries concluded that nothing could be salvaged from existing beliefs and practices. By the late-sixteenth century, missionary Christianity had crystallized into a rigid and self-contained body of doctrine impermeable to any influence from Andean religion. Quechua terminology used to describe Christian concepts had been eliminated from dictionaries, catechisms, and manuals of preaching to Indians. Whereas in 1560 Augustinian missionaries in Huamachuco could use Andean textiles from a destroyed huaca to adorn Christian buildings and images, so validating one part at least of native culture, and thereby acculturating Spanish Christian notions of beauty to the Andes, by the end of the century any such adaptation of Christianity had been rejected. The result was that missionaries failed to understand Andean life in such a way as to achieve conversion of the Indians from within their own system of values. As in Mesoamerica, despite an intellectual commitment to persuasion, missionaries opted for coercion, convinced that this was the only means to break the hold of demons over native peoples. Ultimately, this determination to anchor Christianity in the exercise of authority and force precluded real inner assent and probably presented the greatest obstacle to a genuine Andean commitment to the new religion. (MacCormack 1985: 446-62)

There is a telling quote, in this regard, attributed to an Andean named Tito by the priest Pedro de Quiroga in his *Dialogues of the Truth: causes and obstacles that prevent the conversion of the Indians* (1563). When the priest spoke to him, in a dialogue following classical Greco-Roman literary style, of the shortcomings of indigenous Christianity, Tito replied: "You have made the law which you preach to us odious by the things that you do to us, so contrary to that which you teach, that you rob the truth of its credibility...We are so resentful toward you and we hold you in such hate and enmity, that we cannot persuade ourselves to believe anything that you preach or say to us because in everything you have always lied and deceived us." (Marzal 1996: 6)

Historians have disagreed vehemently over the years whether the Andeans were truly converted. Much depends on the definition of conversion and of Christian. There is no doubt that by the end of the sixteenth century, almost all the Lupaqas, for example, had been Christianized in the sense that they had been baptized and instructed. It is more difficult to assess whether a true process of evangelization - of immersion in the meaning and values of the religion, of true understanding what it means to be Christian - had taken place. (Meiklejohn 1988: 250) In the past many observers believed that Indians adopted Christianity in appearance only, remaining almost entirely pagan under a veneer of Christianity, but today most historians agree that the new religion was adopted in substance and authentically, although they still differ as to whether this can be called a complete conversion, and if so, at what point the process was completed. Some emphasize the survival of purely Andean beliefs and rites to this very day and see two religions in coexistence, conceptually separate, both believed in sincerely; others see an eclectic accumulation of beliefs and practices from both religions but without any clear separation; yet others see the emergence of a mixed religion, in which either Christian or native forms have dominated, but with important elements from the other. One has suggested that each community or person is on a continuum between one pole of simple initiation in Christianity and another pole of authentic and conscious faith. (Dussel 1974: 128)

A common view today is that the majority of the Peruvian natives were not converted by the first missionaries but that they gradually assimilated and absorbed elements of the faith within the residue of their own religions. While Andeans did accommodate themselves to the invaders, they also persisted in constructing their own logically coherent and complete interpretation of their world and experience, and hence Andean ways of thought, like their forms of social and political organization, remained continuous with the past. (MacCormack 1988: 961) Natives admitted the Christian God, but they denied him any influence over human affairs, just as in modern Andean beliefs Jesus is separate from the Indians, and does not intervene in earthly matters, rather it is the ancient mountain gods that watch over and protect them.

14 Nightmare Conversions: Once and for All, Again and Again

Whereas in Mesoamerica, violent means dominated early in the evangelization and slowly receded, in Peru, aside from Taki Onkoy, there was little systematic, concerted use of violent repression until the early-seventeenth century, which witnessed a new missionary strategy - systematically organized ecclesiastical campaigns to extirpate idolatry. The change in approach was largely the result of a new suspicious attitude toward native religious practices. The glimpses of pagan remnants behind Christian celebrations that resulted from the evangelical strategy of substitution could evoke delight in the early years at how easily Christianity had been grafted onto pre-Hispanic practices, but those same glimpses in later years would provoke dark suspicion and deep unease that the strategy had only been half-fulfilled. The same native festivals which amounted for the optimist to proof of Christianity's triumph might also constitute for the pessimist evidence that Andeans were parading their duplicitous religious resistance beneath the Spaniards' very noses, and transforming, say, Christian Corpus into something entirely alien, pregnant with "pagan" possibilities. Could it be, Spaniards began to ask themselves, with increasing horror, that the conquered peoples had turned the tables on their victors, and Christianity had ended up being assimilated to native religion, and not vice versa? Christ in a royal Inca headdress could prompt the question: had these converts to Christ actually converted Christ to Inca? In this way, early evangelical practices created the context for the activity of extirpation that characterized the first half of the seventeenth century in the Viceroyalty of Peru and "set the table at which colonialist insecurities would later dine." (Dean 1999: 47, 50, 52, 55)

The idolatry investigations were sparked off by a denunciation made in 1609 by the mestizo priest of San Damián de Checa de Huarochirí, Francisco de Avila, to the archbishop of Lima that the inhabitants of his parish were secretly worshipping their former gods, Pariacaca and Chaupiñamca, chief mountains of the district, under the guise of

Christian celebrations for the feast of the Assumption of the Virgin Mary. In December 1609, in the presence of the populace, of the city's dignitaries and of the Viceroy, all gathered in the main square in Lima, Avila preached in Quechua against idolatry and put to the flame a large collection of confiscated huacas and ancestral mummies. As an example to others, the Andean religious teacher Hernando Paucar was tied to a stake in the square, whipped, and sent into exile. (MacCormack 1991: 389) The church authorities responded to the discovery of continuing native religious practices by launching visitations in regions of the Central Highlands within striking distance of Lima, conducted by priests who presided over judicial trials for the offense of idolatry, modeled on the procedures of the Inquisition (though without the death penalty). As a result, Avila, together with several other priests of Indian parishes, exchanged a life of parochial anonymity for an active role in the church hierarchy as idolatry inspectors, charged with testing Indian religious orthodoxy and rooting out pagan practices, not only in their own parishes but also across entire provinces. One of the most striking aspects is how this flurry of activity followed many years in which priests like Avila turned a blind eye to pagan ceremonies among their flock. In Avila's case this is indisputable, since, in or just before 1608, he had overseen the compilation of a Quechua text (untitled and anonymous, published in the twentieth century as *Gods and men of Huarochirí*, or *The Huarochirí Manuscript*), which comprised statements by informants who freely admitted that many of the villagers practiced native rites. (Brading 1991: 162) Like most local priests, Avila had reached an accommodation with his flock whereby he did not enquire too closely into their ceremonies and, in return, they acquiesced in his profitable use of local Indian labor in order to supplement his meagre stipend. When this cozy arrangement was upset by a lawsuit that the Indians brought against him, Avila used the accusation of idolatry as an act of revenge. Significantly, almost all his fellow idolatry inspectors had also been subjected to judicial proceedings by the communities for which they were responsible.

Avila's attack on native religion was only possible because he had privileged access to knowledge about it (it is possible that the Quechua manuscript was prepared with such an eventuality in mind). One of his principal sources of information was Don Cristóbal Choque Casa, a native lord of Huarochirí, who acted as Avila's ally. Don Cristóbal assisted him with the manuscript, preached Catholicism, denounced villagers who followed ancient religious traditions, and served as a friendly witness when natives litigated against their priest. Such behavior, which at first sight would seem to place him at odds with his own community, was by no means unusual for native lords in the colonial era, who were obliged to occupy an uncomfortable position as intermediaries between their people and the representatives of Spanish power. On the one hand, they had to prove to the priest that they were good Catholics if they wished to stay in political power and be seen as fit models for the Indians. On the other, they had to prove to their people that they were not abandoning the traditional ways of their communities. Some responded by sponsoring native religious celebrations in clandestinity, even as they maintained a public facade as good Christians. Don Cristóbal, as far as we know, was not one of these. His (conscious) religious affiliation was consistently Christian. But the need to reconcile his roles as good Christian and preserver of native traditions created considerable inner turmoil. The above-mentioned Huarochirí manuscript, the only known source through which early-colonial Peruvian Indians have left us an image of their culture in their own language, eloquently describes the severe mental conflict provoked in Don Cristóbal by the rival claims of Christianity and paganism. (Salomon 1992: 3) Don Cristóbal's father, Jerónimo Cancho Guaman, had been a backsliding convert. Having followed Catholic teaching since his youth, he prohibited the worship of the tutelary deity Llocllay Huancupa (according to local tradition, the child of the great coastal deity Pachacamac, who had come to protect the people of Checa) until a great epidemic swept the land (probably the first great epidemic of measles in 1558-59). Possibly because he believed that Llocllay Huancupa was responsible for the outbreak, he ceased scolding his subjects for their pagan ways, and allowed the Indians to revert to native gods. On his deathbed, he abandoned his ancestral beliefs and reverted to Christian rites. After the death of his father and his own elevation to the lordship, Don Cristóbal felt himself called by the indigenous deities. Although he was a model convert

131

who prided himself on scoffing at the old religion, he became plagued by visions and dreams in which angry native entities, the gods of his ancestors, tried to regain his allegiance.

Don Cristóbal recounted the conflict in two parts. In the first part, as in a vision, he encountered Llocllay Huancupa and engaged in ritualized combat with him, which apparently ended in conclusive victory for the native lord. He recounted how one night he went to Llocllay's "house" (his shrine) to see his lover, who was the daughter of the priest there. At that time, Don Cristóbal had abandoned worship of this god and did not think of him any more. While he was outside urinating, Llocllay appeared to him "like a silver plate which mirroring the light of the midday sun, dazzles a man's eyesight," flashing at him three times. Almost falling to the ground, he recited the Our Father and the Hail Mary and fled toward the house. When he was halfway there, the god flashed three times again, and then when he arrived at the house, three more times, making nine times in all. He rushed into the house and woke the priest's wife and her two children. Llocllay tried to overpower Don Cristóbal, resounding in his ears, with a noise so loud he feared it might demolish the house. Don Cristóbal invoked God, recited all prayers he knew at the top of his voice and said his doctrine over and over again, while Llocllay alternately lightened and darkened the inside of the house. As midnight came, he felt that the god was overpowering him and that nothing would save him, so, weeping and sweating, he invoked Mary, asking for the intercession of Jesus. Halfway through the Salve Regina, Llocllay flew away in the form of a barn owl. At that moment, it was as if it had dawned over the house, and all these terrors ended. The next morning, Don Cristóbal preached to the villagers, condemning Llocllay. "That Llocllay Huancupa whom we feared has turned out to be a demonic barn owl. Last night, with the help of the Virgin Saint Mary, our mother, I conquered him for good. From now on, none of you are to enter that house. If I ever see anybody enter or approach the house, I'll tell the Padre."

Don Cristóbal's weeping and sweating while invoking Mary and Jesus recall the teachings of the Jesuits in Huarochirí in 1571, encouraging people to pour out tears and sobs while conversing with the Lord. Don

Cristóbal probably intended his performance in the ritualized combat, and his homily the next morning, to conform to the Tridentine church's model of a good conversion, emphasizing, as it does, the favorite Jesuit motifs of proof of an idol's ineffectiveness, appeals to divine mercy, and above all, absolute abjuration of an old deity. But his story is also typically Andean in that it makes use of two ancient native myths. The first is the tale of victory (*atiy*) in which a new god and his human proteges supplant an older religion and its adherents; so, in Cristóbal's account, native gods are replaced with Christian deities through processes normal to local myth. The second myth relates to Llocllay's apparition as a silver disk that shines dazzling light onto Don Cristóbal; this follows the well-established myth of dazzling disks that foretell the fortunes of leaders. According to an ancient myth, the Inca ruler Pachacuti witnessed the fall of a crystal plaque from the sky which revealed a figure from whose head three brilliant rays like the sun's shot forth; the figure claimed to be his father the sun, and promised he would subjugate many nations (but in traditional disks the brilliance is solar, and presumably golden like the sun-disk of Coricancha). The meaning of the three flashes in Don Cristóbal's vision seems to be that Llocllay offers Don Cristóbal a future of power in return for his allegiance, but Don Cristóbal, unlike the Incas of myth, refuses. (Salomon 1992: 7-9; Molina and Albornoz 60)

The apparent conclusiveness of Don Cristóbal's victory over Llocllay and his allegiance to the Christian god is thrown into doubt by the second part of the account of the conflict. The night after the visionary encounter, the combat was replayed in a nightmare in which Llocllay tried again to conquer Don Cristóbal. In this nightmare, Llocllay sent a man who brought Don Cristóbal unwittingly to the door of his shrine, where an old lady told him that the deity wanted to know why he had repudiated him. Defiantly, Don Cristóbal asked why he should be obliged to honour an evil demon. At that moment Don Cristóbal dropped a four-real coin that was in his hand. While he was searching for it, he heard a man's voice calling him from outside the shrine asking him what he was doing there and telling him that his father was angry and was calling him to come at once. Don Cristóbal replied that he was coming right away, found the coin in haste, and was on the point of leaving when Llocllay flashed at him again from inside the shrine. Suddenly realizing that he could not save himself now, Don Cristóbal became very frightened. A voice inside the shrine said "it is our father who is calling you," the language used implying that the father was Don Cristóbal's too. Don Cristóbal felt very angry in his heart but he agreed to go inside and sat down close by the door. As he watched offerings being made to Llocllay, he found himself surrounded by a vision of endlessly repeating checkerboard patterns, pictures of llama heads alternating with tiny devils with silver eyes, in a dizzying repetition. When the offerings were finished, Don Cristóbal made invocations to Jesus and defied Llocllay to speak and to confirm that the Christian God was not the true god, and that he could defeat Jesus, but the deity remained mute. Then somebody threw an unidentified object at him, and not knowing if god or a demon had sent it, Don Cristóbal fled, protecting himself with it. Then he woke up. According to the manuscript, "from that exact time on, right up to the present, he defeated various gods in his dreams the same way. Any number of times he defeated both Pariacaca and Chaupiñamca, telling the people all about it over and over again."

The two versions - vision and nightmare - are mirror images. The first version replaces Llocllay with the Christian God, through a typically Andean victory. The new religion overcomes the old, but it does so through processes that belong to the native world. Christ and his family are absorbed just as Pariacaca had been in former times. But the second nightmare version suggests that the apparent victory may be an illusion. While it follows the plot of the first version, it also introduces three deviations. One is the reference to father figures. Traditionally the people of Huarochirí determined their religious and cultural identity by reference to obligations to ancestors on the paternal side. But Don Cristóbal's paternal inheritance was ambiguous. His father's divided allegiance seems to pull the dreaming Don Cristóbal in opposed directions and obliges him to choose between two fathers who both demand obedience - Llocllay, inside the shrine, and another father outside the shrine, who is God or Jesus or maybe his natural father Cancho Guaman. In the end, like his natural father, Don Cristóbal escapes from Llocllay and reaches the outside - Christianity - again. But since his nightmare did not reveal which "father" threw him the object that saved him, it reduces his seeming victory over Llocllay (in the vision) to a stalemate. The second deviation relates to the flashes. In native mythology, sovereignty was announced by a flashing plaque. In the nightmare version, the flashes related to a coin that becomes important at the moment Don Cristóbal must choose between two fathers, hence joining the coin, the flashes, and the paternal inheritance. The third deviation is the pattern of llamas and devils, which seems to suggest a repetition of the experience ad nauseam. Don Cristóbal does not find his own way out of the shrine, but is saved by an arbitrary event, an object thrown in by an unknown agent, and Don Cristóbal does not know who saved him, Llocllay or Jesus. In contrast with the first version, which brings the action to its logical culmination, but leaves Don Cristóbal in enough unease to cause nightmares, the end of the second version brings Don Cristóbal safety at the expense of a logical culmination. In the nightmare version, only an arbitrary end mitigates the sense of dilemma, circularity, and stalemate. (Salomon 1992: 11, 13, 14, 16)

The manuscript tells us that Don Cristóbal considers his nightmare experience as essential to his story as the visionary encounter, a fact that throws into doubt the completeness of his conversion to Christianity. The Third Council of Lima had recently laid down the doctrine that dreams are delusions and that converts should not look for religious meaning in them. (Salomon 1992: 10) Yet the title of the chapter in which the nightmare version is related starts with the phrase "Next, although a dream is not matter of value..." Don Cristóbal almost apologizes for the illicit but indispensable significance that he felt his nightmare to possess. His escape from Llocllay is inconclusive and he returns to a waking state only to resume the combat all over again, which, like the checkerboard pattern of llamas and devils, repeats itself any number of times, not only with Llocllay, but also, we are told, with other gods like Pariacaca and Chaupiñamca. This sounds like a circular process, repeated indefinitely. Rather than signifying victory and definitive conversion, it conveys an impression that the nightmare quality of endless repetition is transported back to daylight.

Here is Don Cristóbal's irresolvable dilemma: to atack Llocllay is to attack the ancestral connection conferring identity in family terms; but to yield to him means forgoing his ancestral inheritance, his father's authority as leader. The absolute demand of conversion is what makes it nightmarish; if the transition were complete, Don Cristóbal would cease to share in the identity of his forefathers. Don Cristóbal's predicament lies in his attempt, at one and the same time, to insert Christianity into his own culture on native terms, and, as a good Christian convert, to undermine the premises of native religion that made possible such an insertion. Thus, Don Cristóbal's Christian and Andean religious images are both antagonistic and inseparable, superimposed yet irreconcilable. Don Cristóbal says he repeated this struggle over and over. The historian who has drawn attention to this "nightmare conversion" concludes: "Perhaps the deadlock of the nighttime and the need for a daytime victory over the unacceptable, and politically inopportune, parts of his inheritance stirred him to attack without what he could not unseat within." (Salomon 1992: 17) In other words, the repetition could only be laid to rest by assisting Avila in his attack on native religion, and putting an end once and for all to Llocllay. This contradictory way of thinking is vital to understanding Andean peoples' ambiguous native Christian identity, and the mental conflict consequent upon trying to be both Andeans and Christians.

Revitalized Andean Religion

There were two principal periods of activity for the idolatry inspectors in the seventeenth century, the first between 1609 and 1622, and the second, more ambitious, between 1649 and 1670. The timing of this activity owes most to the personal commitment of the Archbishop of Lima to the objective of extirpation of idolatry, Bartolomé Lobo Guerrero (1608-22) and Pedro de Villagómez (1641-71), respectively. The rules for idolatry inspections were set down by a manual written by the Jesuit Provincial Pablo José de Arriaga entitled *The extirpation of idolatry in Peru* (1621), which resurrected and refined the methods employed by the priest Cristóbal de Albornoz in the elimination of

Taki Onqoy. Arriaga alerted extirpators to the fact that different kin groups revered different holy objects and followed independent ritual cycles, and also that these differences articulated community tensions and conflicts that could be exploited, since hostile ayllus might betray each other to the inspector. (MacCormack 1991: 391) Because of official unwillingness to fund the costs of extirpation, inspectors resorted to the enforcement of financial contributions from the communities subject to investigation in order to pay for the visitations. The frequent denunciation of the excesses of the inspectors testifies to their willingness to recover their costs and make their efforts financially rewarding at the expense of the Indians. This exploitative element cannot have led to anything but native cynicism and disillusionment regarding the Christian message that was supposed to be conveyed. To this problem was added another, the equation of indoctrination and punishment. During the first period, the judicial process was accompanied by a policy of preaching in native tongues and persuasive pastoral activity. The inspectors were accompanied by Jesuit priests, and ecclesiastical trials were preceded by sermons and teaching. However, the second period was characterized by a decline in missionary activity and an increased emphasis on the judicial function. The Jesuits withdrew their cooperation in the second period because of fears that the Indians' respect for them would be lost and their pastoral work would be undermined if they continued to assist the inspectors in their work. It would be too easy for Indians to conclude that the Fathers were passing on to the ecclesiastical judges the knowledge of native practices that had been revealed to them in the sanctity of the confessional. Participation in idolatry trials, which were fundamentally punitive rather than instructive, threatened to jeopardize the evangelizing missions. The fact that sentences decreed by inspectors at the close of their investigations often included supervised terms of doctrina classes for religious transgressors, an expression of the philosophy that saw instruction by love and by punishment as a complementary pair, can only have made rejection of the message much more likely. The inspections were counterproductive because they made Andeans more distrustful and dismissive of Christian religion. (Taylor 1996)

What did these idolatry investigations reveal about the state of Andean religion between a century and a century and a half after the beginnings of evangelization? Although no trace remained of Inca elite religion, local religious life, expressed in terms of place and descent, focused on sacred beings like rocks, stones, mountains, canals, springs, peculiar to particular communities, kin groups, families or individuals, had not only survived but had been reinvigorated. In many places, despite the material destructiveness of the inspections, the old religion had become a vehicle to resist Christianity. Idolatry inspectors hunted down images of gods and the corpses or relics of the ancestors, and ferreted out the ringleaders of native religious practices, smashing and burning thousands of images, and subjecting scores of native priests to ritual humiliation, public self-denunciation, flogging, and possibly banishment or imprisonment. But native religion proved more adaptable than the inspectors anticipated. Persecution of native religious leaders removed many but simply drove others into greater clandestinity. One native chief secretly engaged his niece, who had not received baptism, had never attended mass and had preserved her virginity, in the service of the communal god for more than thirty-five years. Her existence had been kept secret by not registering her in the parish book of baptisms, recording instead a child who had been born dead. Images which had been burned or smashed to pieces could nevertheless continue to be worshiped; they might be replaced by substitutes, often rationalized as "children" of the destroyed gods, or reverence would be offered at the spot where their ashes had been buried. This phenomenon was so widespread that idolatry inspectors were forced to resort to extreme measures, such as the grinding down of the stone remains and their disposal in fast-flowing rivers. Even this strategy could be overcome by native communities, which insisted that the spirit (*camaquen*) of the god or ancestors lived on. One native priest, Hernando Hacaspoma, testified in 1656 that he had told the Indians of his village (San Pedro de Hacas) that they should continue to make sacrifices to the gods and ancestors burned by the idolatry inspectors because their "souls" (*camaquen*) were immortal and were watching over them and would be present to receive offerings. Two communal deities that had been removed by the Spaniards continued to receive the sacrifice of a llama kid in the identical place because their *camaquen* was said to inhabit the spot. The physical destruction of images or the mummified remains of ancestors did not prevent their "posthumous" survival in purely spiritual form, or through association with those indestructible repositories of divine power that lay in natural phenomena. Jesuit Francisco de Patiño highlighted the insuperable obstacles facing missionaries when he recounted how an Indian inquired of him, "Father, are you tired of taking our idols from us? Take away that mountain if you can, since that is the God that I worship." Mountains have remained until this day receptacles of irresistible forces, whether benevolent or hostile, whether of Andean or Spanish origin. The sacred Andean landscape could not be obliterated. (Griffiths 1996: 190, 198, 263)

The relationship between the Indians and the Christian God represented the most serious challenge for native priests. Since the competence of Christian supernatural forces could not be denied, native priests attempted instead to discredit the Christian God, minimize his importance for Indians, or maintain a clear separation between the Spanish and the Indian supernatural worlds. Augustinian Antonio de Calancha reported that native priests told the Indians that God was not always good, nor did he look after the poor, nor did he forgive great sins. Indeed, he had created Indians to live in sin, and they were not capable of being good. Events occurred by the will of the sun, moon, and the huacas, not God. Just as the Christians had their images, so the Indians should worship their huacas; the images in the church were the idols of the Christians (a view which demonstrates once again how native religious priests adapted their message in order to respond to Christianity). Much of what the Catholic priests said was not true but was designed to frighten the Indians, and there was as much reason to believe the native ancestors as there was to believe the ancestors and writings of the Christians. Some preached that it was acceptable to worship Jesus and the devil at the same time, since they were brothers and had made an agreement between themselves. (Calancha 1974-81, 2:858) Hernando Hacaspoma taught the Indians that they should not worship the Christian God because he had not created them or their agricultural plots. Although the saints might be effective as guardians for the Spaniards, they could not serve the

139

Indians' needs. They were, after all, only dumb wooden objects, incapable of communicating with the Indians in the way that their own images did. Most native priests preached that their gods had forbidden the Indians to worship the god of the Christians and that they should not go to church because it was a dirty place. However, since Indian attendance at church was enforced, they had to make concessions. Hacaspoma told his followers that while performing their fasts and sacrifices they should not enter a church to pray lest the sacrifices be nullified; but if the priest should come at that time and oblige them to go, then they should attend "in body only and not in spirit." They were forbidden to receive the sacraments of communion and penance "with all their hearts" but were instructed to do so "in mockery." No compromise was admitted during the first five days of native fasting, when they were not to go to church to pray or worship even in outward appearance. Nor were Indians allowed to go to church immediately after worshiping the native gods. (Griffiths 1996: 204)

If Indian attendance at Christian worship could not be entirely avoided, it could at least be contextualized within the native tradition by requiring that Indians actively seek the permission of native deities for participation in Catholic religion. Before the celebration of the feasts of Corpus Christi and Saint John the Baptist in the village of San Juan de Machaca, the religious leaders took offerings to the mallquis (mummified remains of the dead) and requested their permission for the coming feasts. On the day of the fiesta, the Indians poured the first cups of chicha (fermented maize beer) in their name and reminded them that the celebrations were in their honor and not that of the Spanish god. In San Pedro de Hacas, the stewards of the religious brotherhoods were instructed that, before celebrating the feasts of the patron Saint Peter or Corpus Christi, they should supply offerings of llamas and guinea pigs for the mallquis and beg their permission, since 'they had to show greater respect to their huacas than to the saints.' The first act of the celebrations was to dedicate some chicha to the mallquis, the huacas, and the ancestors buried in the church. Then they performed traditional ceremonies to commemorate their ancestors, in which all the ayllus passed through the village singing, dancing and beating drums and relating the past deeds of their mallquis. In this

140

way, the fiesta fulfilled a dual role, honoring both the Christian saint and the native huacas. It seems legitimate to conclude that Christian elements had been incorporated into native religious behavior. Though the acceptance of the Christian saint was genuine, not a duplicitous cover for a purely native ceremony, as the idolatry inspectors feared, it does seem that the native deities held the dominant role in maintaining the natives' allegiance. Significantly, the image of Saint Peter was taken to the house where the mallquis were kept (not vice versa) so that it might witness the offerings made to the native deities and be present at the dedication of the fiesta to them. Two other religious festivals celebrated in San Pedro de Hacas - Pocoimita (held in January when it began to rain before the Indians began to prepare the agricultural plots) and Caruamita (held at Corpus when the maize began to mature), which respectively opened and closed the Andean religious and agricultural cycle - were initiated each year upon or near the huacas and the sites of the mallquis, demonstrating that the most important native observances were isolated from the main village, and not incorporated into the Catholic realm. Thus, although aspects of Catholicism were becoming sources of sacred power in the Andes - saints were adopted as additional protectors and intermediaries, and village celebrations merged the observance of the official church calendar and the Andean religious and agricultural cycle - this occurred by means of a process whereby the native religious system absorbed the alien supernatural deities into its own structure, and an accommodation was made between the two religious systems on native terms. (Griffiths 1996: 204-206; Mills 1994: 74, 84-85)

Thus, even as Christian elements seeped into native religious consciousness, the indigenous religious worldview continued to be upheld by Andeans. In many of the villages investigated by the idolatry inspectors, as late as the final quarter of the seventeenth century, human material survival continued to be secured by the participation of the whole community in native religious rites, dedicated to the sun, the huacas and the mountain deities. Traditional rites of name-giving were reasserted to combat the conquests of Christian baptism; Indians were encouraged to abandon their Christian names and take the names of their gods. They were obliged to keep the native practice of verbal acknowledgment of infractions of norms, which were still defined by native criteria such as failing to make sacrifices to the gods, and, at the same time, they were instructed to obstruct Christian confession by only revealing trivia to the Catholic priest. Ancient views on the appropriate treatment of the dead still held sway. Andean tradition required careful conservation of the dead, dressed, and adorned with indigenous textiles, in caves, niches carved out of rock, or funerary towers, where they were regularly visited, feted and offered llamas, guinea pigs and maize. Christian burial was rejected on the grounds that the dead suffered greatly under the weight of the earth on top of them, and that it precluded feeding and clothing of departed kin and hence condemned them to starvation as well as suffering while they decayed. If their welfare was neglected, they would curse their descendants and deprive them of food and crops. One of the constant preoccupations of Catholic priests was to prevent bodies of the dead being removed from Christian cemeteries and returned to the native resting grounds, which were invariably located near the former villages and sacred sites. One idolatry inspector, Bernardo de Noboa, discovered the existence of separate native resting grounds for baptized and unbaptized Indians near their former villages, an adaptation in response to Christianity that ensured that the ancestors were not "contaminated." The struggle over the resting place of the dead continued until at least the end of the seventeenth century. (Griffiths 1996: 199; MacCormack 1985: 459; Saignes 1999: 112-17)

Although the practices of native healers and sorcerers adapted under the impact of Christianity, they continued to conform broadly to Andean tradition throughout the seventeenth century. Magical activities included the use of coca, corn, and talismans, combined with the use of tobacco and wine; and divinations, where the ancestral figures of the Inca and others were summoned together with God, Saint Martha, Jesus Christ, the devil, Saint Anthony and Saint Nicholas. Most idolatry inspectors treated native healers and sorcerers as frauds and tricksters who hoodwinked their clients and, although they were prepared to accuse them of pacts with the devil in order to scare them, in general they did not believe in a genuine demonic presence in their acts. As a result, they tended to underestimate the

142

importance of these practices within the indigenous world. (Griffiths
1996: 125) However, the depositions that they preserved in trial
documentation have allowed historians, to some extent, to tease out the
native content of the acts of the accused. The relationship between
healer and tutelary lord (often a mountain spirit or a spirit that emerged
at a spring, described as Indians in native dress, or native American
animals such as the jaguar, condor or llama) was often described as
one of feeding the latter, with coca leaves or animal blood, in return
for the granting of special powers. Although the practical aspects of
healing were taught by a human master, the neophyte still required an
ecstatic experience in which the guardian spirits demonstrated his or
her chosen condition as a healer. This experience, whether in dreams
or in a waking state of altered consciousness, typically took the form
of conversations with the spirits and the souls of dead shamans. Healer
Catalina Suyo confided to her pupil Juana Icha that her initiation had
occurred when, as a young girl tending her llamas, she had been
swallowed by a spring on the mountain Julcan, wherein she remained
for several days in the company of a golden-haired man who invited
her to feed him thereafter at that spot. Felipe Cupeda described how
one day, when he went fishing, his body began to tremble and he fell
into a doze beside some stones near the river. During his sleep, his
soul abandoned his body and entered a huaca, where a black man and a
mestizo took him to a huge table where many people were eating.
When they tried to persuade him to remain with them, a Franciscan
friar entered and told him to go home. The diners protested, but the
friar silenced them, telling them to leave the Indian alone since he
knew nothing. Cupeda's soul remained three days inside the huaca
before returning to his body. Several defendants recounted initiation
experiences in which the tutelary lord revealed to them hidden or
future events and imparted privileged knowledge about the healing
qualities of plants and other substances. As a young girl, Leonor
Rimay had fallen gravely ill after the apparition to her of a black
llama, which had followed her from the river to her home.
Subsequently an old man with a bushy beard came to her in dreams
and taught her how to cure with plants and guinea pigs and how to
divine using saliva in her palm. On other occasions he appeared as a
"lion" (puma) and told her to bring offerings to a white stone near her

house, in return for which he would furnish her with the necessary replies for the demands of her clients. She believed that this huaca could communicate to her the whereabouts of lost objects, sensing 'in her heart' if the item was to be found or not. Fernando Carvachin had been initiated into the secrets of healing by an old Indian who had appeared to him and given him a string of blue and black beads, telling him always to take them with him when he went to worship his huacas and to offer some of them to ensure the effectiveness of his cures. Two months later, an Indian shepherd, passing near a spring, was startled to witness the emergence of a rainbow and fell ill from fright. Carvachin, remembering the Indian's exhortations, ground up some of the beads and sprinkled the powders at the spring, begging for the health of the shepherd, who, after some weeks, underwent a complete recovery. Both Rimay and Carvachin acquired such a reputation that they were consulted by Indians from all over the valley. (Griffiths 1996: 127-32)

However, the trial documentation also reveals that the invasion of the indigenous consciousness by Christian images had caused disharmony and a crisis of confidence in the relationship between healer and spirit. Fernando Carvachin protested that by day his tutelary spirit appeared to him in the fields, with his fierce burning eyes, and beat him, scolding him in his native tongue for neglecting the magic which he had taught him; and by night his guardian came to him in dreams in the form of a donkey and transported him to Lima, taking him to every church, and bidding him to enter alone whilst it remained outside. Like Don Cristóbal's encounter with Llocllay, and Felipe Cupeda's descent into the huaca where the inhabiting spirits disputed over his soul with a Franciscan friar, Carvachin's journey pitted two competing religious allegiances against one another. Another defendant, Maria Ticllaguacho, grumbled that her guardian would appear to her in the form of a ferocious lion with bulging, fiery eyes, and scold, whip and beat her, leaving her half dead, for believing in the Spanish god.

Andean deities had always been capricious and ambivalent, but, whereas in the pre-Columbian era, native religion provided the only spiritual remedy, in the colonial period Christianity competed as an alternative source of supernatural power and offered the opportunity

144

for native healers to switch between religious traditions, or even combine the two. Some had difficulty in deciding where they stood in relation to the two traditions. One native religious leader, Juan Gutiérrez, had been convinced that the Christian faith was untrue and that the saints were only for Spaniards until the death of five of his sons led to a change of heart and he learned to pray. He told his interrogators that now he remained in doubt both about the powers of his huacas and the mysteries of the Faith. In the village of San Pedro de Pilas, when those who made sacrifices to a mountain in response to the outbreak of an epidemic nevertheless rapidly succumbed, one defendant admitted that, as a result, he no longer knew if he should believe that the huacas had the power to end epidemics. Others experienced little difficulty in switching allegiances. One Indian became disillusioned with traditional methods when a native healer told him that despite the offerings he had made to a rock, formerly worshipped by his ancestors, his sick daughter would die as a punishment. Deciding that both the healer and the rock were a fraud, the man denounced the healer to the priest, helped the latter to set fire to the rock and cover it with crosses, and requested a mass for the health of his child. Even so, the withdrawal of confidence reveals native disillusionment with the huacas rather than indifference or complete disbelief, and less rejection of the huacas than a bewildered incomprehension at their inability to counter the enormity of the epidemics. Insofar as Indians still expected the huacas to help them and were enraged at their failure to do so, Christian repression had not altered native expectations in relation to their gods. Native Andeans may have lost their trust in the ability of native deities to protect them, but they had not abandoned their faith in their very existence. (Griffiths 1996: 206-17)

Yet others managed to reconcile the two traditions in such a way that Christianity validated rather than undermined recourse to native supernatural entities. In 1710, healer Juan Vasques told his interrogators that his knowledge of the healing properties of herbs had been conferred on him by a guardian spirit in the form of an old white man who had come to him in his dreams, and that since that time he had been able to perform cures, whereby he discerned from a client's

145

spittle and from his pulse the origin of his ailment and the most appropriate herb for its treatment, as clearly as if it had been reflected in a mirror, or as if human bodies were open to the eye. His most startling claim was that he had been instructed to practice this skill by a Catholic priest, who had reprimanded him and refused to absolve him in confession until he used his talent as a gift of charity for others. He insisted that he always prayed the Creed before performing these cures, the success of which he attributed to the will of God. It is not implausible that a Catholic priest might have given his approval to Vasques' cures since there was nothing unorthodox in official tolerance of the scientific aspects of native healing rites. The great Dominican scholar, Francisco de Vitoria, considered many cures made with special herbs to be efficacious on the basis of their natural virtues, a tolerance reflected in the resolutions of the Council of Lima of 1567 which condemned sorcerers, who acted in league with the devil, but stipulated that healers whose cures derived from 'empirical' experience were to be provided with written permission to practice, as long as they did not employ 'superstitious' words or ceremonies. Thus, Vasques's appeal to Christian authority for his cures may be more than a convenient defense; it may represent an original attempt to reconcile the two religious traditions. For Vasques, the two traditions were not antagonistic and contradictory, but complementary and mutually sustaining. By seeking the blessing of the Catholic priest for practice of the native healing tradition, Vasques obtained Christian authorization for his engagement in the indigenous supernatural world. Once again the indigenous religious tradition had both adapted and reaffirmed itself. (Griffiths 1996: 135-46)

Christianity's role as an alternative source of supernatural power allowed missionaries to present themselves to native peoples as powerful intermediaries with magical forces. Outbreaks of disease and the fear of imminent death provided an unequalled opportunity for demonstrating both the superior magic and the superior medical and therapeutic techniques possessed by the emissaries of the Christian God. When a terrible epidemic broke out in the village of Los Reyes (Province of Chinchacocha), the Jesuit missionaries responded with two mutually supporting strategies, one medical/therapeutic and the other magical. They supplied material aid in the form of food and medicines which were distributed from house to house, and they persuaded the inhabitants to seek to placate God by making a vow to celebrate the day of Saint Ignatius, and to make an image of him to adorn the altar (JL 1613). By these means they sought to discredit the native religious leader who had sacrificed to native deities so that the epidemic would cease. On many occasions the Fathers explicitly highlighted the failures of native healers and their own successes in order to bring about a transfer of native allegiances to Christian magic.[1] Indians who tried to conquer illness by making offerings to huacas recommended by curanderos without any success, or whose sufferings were made worse by native healers, were targeted by the missionaries, and encouraged to abandon the huacas and attended confession instead. In this way, the Jesuits challenged Indians to judge native deities according to the competence of their earthly representatives. However, by attempting to outperform the native healers, by suggesting that natives should accept Christianity on the basis of the missionaries' abilities as physicians and magicians, the Jesuits effectively conceded that they would fight native sorcerers and healers on their own territory, and, even more significantly, allowed Indians to continue to believe that they should seek, in native fashion, reciprocal bonds with supernatural entities, merely substituting Christian deities for native ones. This should be considered one of the more significant adaptations that the missionaries made to the native worldview.

The willingness of the Fathers, their satisfaction even, that they were seen as powerful shamans may also be demonstrated by their attempts to outshine their native rivals in other spheres of activity. The Fathers took great pride in their apparent success as more efficient rainmakers. Indians were encouraged to address their pleas for rain to figures of the Christian pantheon rather than the indigenous one. Missionaries from the Lima College convinced the Indians to pray to God for assistance in times of drought. In one village, there was a great shortage of water at sowing time. On the day that the Holy Sacrament was brought in procession into the village, the entire population joined in prayer, seeking a resolution to their predicament. "Rain fell in such great quantities that all recognized the benefits conferred by the new arrival." (JL 1625) The rainmaking talents of Father Ignacio Martínez from the college of Cusco were legendary. In one village it had not rained for more than six months. Although Martínez assured the Indians that it would rain on the following Thursday, they began to perform "superstitious ceremonies" in order to encourage rain. In the morning the women danced and sang half-naked at the river while some young boys sprinkled them with water; in the afternoon they did the same in the main square. Exasperated at their defiance, the Father told them that, despite the encouraging appearance of the skies, it would in fact not rain. He added that he was determined to pray to God for such a result. It did not rain all afternoon. The following day, which was the one on which he had told them it would rain, he sent word that they should not dance. But when the sky had turned ashen black and a downpour appeared imminent, some of the Indians began to dance so that the forthcoming rain would be attributed to them. Immediately the Father implored the Lord to prevent rain; miraculously, the clouds dispersed and the sky cleared. When the Indians came shamefaced to his house and asked him to beg the Lord for rain, he scolded them, telling them that in punishment God had postponed the rain for a week. Indeed, one week later it rained as the Father had said, which, he claimed, earned him great respect among the Indians. (JL 1635)

The conclusions that Indians drew from such events were not necessarily those that the Fathers attributed to them. For example, some Indians came to believe that medication would not be effective unless personally administered by the Fathers themselves. Clearly they believed that the effect lay not merely in the plant or herb but in the personal quality of the priest. Since priests insisted that only they could administer the magic of the ceremony of the mass, it is not surprising that Indians drew such conclusions about other aspects of their activities. The conclusion that the Fathers wished the Indians to draw from their success in healing illness or bringing rain was that the incompetence of native curanderos and shamans suggested the impotence of their deities, and the superiority of the Christian God. But it is likely that the Indians simply came to see the Fathers as

148

powerful witches. They might have proved not the invincible power of Christianity, but rather a more personal feature, their own spiritual force. The irony is that not even the figure of the priest himself was immune from assimilation to the native religious worldview.

15 First Spanish Shaman in America

In the spring of 1536, some Spaniards hunting slaves in what is today the northwestern Mexican state of Sinaloa encountered a black man and a white man, both dressed as Indians, traveling with an Indian retinue. Barely able to contain himself, the white man told an extraordinary tale. He was Alvar Núñez Cabeza de Vaca, one of the sole survivors of an ill-fated expedition to Florida, which had foundered eight long years before. Since that time, he had completed an odyssey that had taken him across the North American continent, and through a series of adventures remarkable even by the standards of conquistadors. He would later recount the details in his *Relation*, first published in 1542, but even now, the historical significance of his trek was clear: this was the earliest report of contacts between Europeans and Amerindians beyond the northernmost frontiers of New Spain. (Cabeza de Vaca 1999, 2:xvii)

A man of about forty, and a native of Jerez de la Frontera in Andalucia, Cabeza de Vaca landed on the Florida coast, near the entrance to Tampa Bay, in the spring of 1528, as second-in-command on the expedition of conquistador Pánfilo de Narváez, who, with some four hundred men and eighty horses, was executing instructions from the Crown to explore, conquer and settle lands on the northern Gulf Coast. Distracted from his primary purpose by the prospect, tantalizingly offered to him by the local Timucuan Indians, of finding gold to the northwest, Narváez failed to establish a permanent base and instead marched along the Florida coast, while his ships sailed on ahead, intending to make a rendezvous. When the land and sea parties subsequently failed to reunite, the vessels searched in vain for a year before giving up and sailing for New Spain. Narváez and three hundred men continued northwest to "Apalachen," the chiefdom of Apalachee (near present-day Tallahassee) where they turned the native inhabitants against them by seizing their chief. Finding their numbers inexorably reduced by disease and Indian attacks, the party made the unlikely decision to try to reach Mexico by following the coast. At Apalachee Bay, they launched five makeshift barges onto the sea, and

two hundred and forty two survivors of the three hundred who had
started north from Tampa sailed along the coasts of present-day
Florida, Alabama, Mississippi, Louisiana, and Texas. A month and a
half later, in November 1528, the occupants of just two of these craft,
having survived storms, Indian attacks, thirst and hunger that had
taken the lives of the rest, including Narváez, were washed up on or
near Galveston island off the Texas coast. Here, in a curious reversal
of roles, the coastal Karankawas expressed shock at the evidence that
the starving Spaniards had eaten the flesh of their dead fellows
(although the Spaniards would later describe these Indians as
cannibals, there is no evidence to support this charge) and enslaved the
survivors, who by now lacked horses, firepower, or swords. Over the
next few years, most of Cabeza de Vaca's companions died or
scattered so he lost touch with them. In his travels among the coastal
peoples, he located three other survivors, Andrés Dorantes, Bernardino
del Castillo and the black Estebanico or Estebanillo, who joined him,
and together they began their long trek across the south of the present-
day US and the north of present-day Mexico. (Weber 1992 42-44)

One of the most remarkable aspects of this odyssey is the relative
detachment with which Cabeza de Vaca described and evaluated the
native peoples among whom he passed. As one analyst has observed,
Cabeza de Vaca's cultural bias is much lighter than that of other
famous chroniclers, such as Gonzalo Fernández de Oviedo or
Francisco López de Gomara; and, in contrast to most contemporaries
who looked for similarities between native peoples as a way of making
sense of this bizarre new world, Cabeza de Vaca focused on
differences, not only between American and European, but among
American cultures which he knew with unusual immediacy (most
evident in his description of linguistic variety). (Pupo-Walker 765,
773) He is also unusual in that he claimed to have found a complete
absence of human sacrifice and idolatry among all the Indians he
encountered. In fact, his account is largely devoid of the many
negative assessments of native cultures found in most others. More
than any other conquistador, he suspends his own cultural assumptions
and exhibits a considerable degree of assimilation into native culture.
These characteristics are clearly to be attributed to the several years he

spent alone among the Indians of the Texas coast. No other Spanish explorer or conquistador that later wrote an account of his experiences had undergone such a long and intense experience of isolation from his own culture or immersion in native culture. When he re-encountered his fellow Spaniards in July 1536, he identified with Indians, not with Spaniards. He spoke on behalf of the Indians, numbering some six hundred, in his retinue, and defended their interests against those whom he disparagingly referred to as "Christian slavers." His native companions held him in such esteem that they were unable to believe that he belonged to the same people as the Spanish slavers and were extremely reluctant to entrust him to these white strangers. In the course of the trek, Cabeza de Vaca crossed the divide into native culture to such an extent that he became not only an inspiration, and even a leader, for the natives from a variety of different ethnic groups who accompanied him on his journey, but also even acquired a sacred status among the native inhabitants of the region.

The most extraordinary manifestation of this sacred status was the manner in which Cabeza de Vaca and his companions acted as healers for the ethnic groups that inhabited the regions between the coasts of Texas and the area near Culiacan in the north of New Spain. According to Cabeza de Vaca, the survivors of the Narváez expedition learned indigenous curing techniques at the Isle of Malhado off the Texas coast, during the winter of 1528. After the Spaniards' arrival, a stomach ailment befell the Karankawas and carried off half of their population. Speculating at first that the Spaniards were responsible and should be killed, the Indians changed their minds, concluding that if the Spaniards had such power, they would not have allowed so many of their own to die (only fifteen survived from among the eighty who had arrived on the island), and since so few of them remained, it would be best to leave them alone. (Cabeza de Vaca 1999, 1:107) Having decided not to kill them, the logical alternative was to enlist their help in curing:

"On that island about which I have spoken [Malhado], they tried to make us physicians without examining us or asking us for our titles, because they cure illnesses by blowing on the sick person, and with that breath of air and their hands they expel the disease from him. And they demanded that we do the same and make ourselves useful. We laughed about this, saying that it was a mockery and that we did not know how to cure. And because of this, they took away our food until we did as they told us...In short, we found ourselves in such need that we had to do it, without fearing that anyone would bring us to grief for it." (Cabeza de Vaca 1999, 1:113)

Cabeza de Vaca's account leaves the reader in no doubt that he and his companions joined in the healing process only under duress. When he protested his ignorance of cures, one Indian shaman told him that he did not know what he was saying, and that if he (the shaman) could restore health and remove pain, it was certain that the Spaniards had greater virtue and capacity. Since starvation was a threat in the area at this time of year, becoming shamans was an effective way to secure food and assure the friendly attitude of the natives despite the population losses they suffered. (Adorno 1991: 168)

Accounts of healings and even resurrections of the dead were frequent in missionary writings of the period for northern New Spain, but Cabeza de Vaca's account is different because he provides detailed descriptions of how they were carried out. (Adorno 1991: 172) His method, which was to mimic the native curing techniques he had observed, inserting Christian prayers and gestures, placed the cures simultaneously within both Indian and Christian ritual, and almost certainly constituted the first instance in North America of a healing tradition which blended elements from both old and new religions.

"The manner in which we performed cures was by making the sign of the cross over them and blowing on them, and praying a Pater Noster and an Ave Maria, and as best we could, beseeching our Lord God that he grant them health and move them to treat us well. Our Lord God in his mercy willed that all those on whose behalf we made supplication, after we had made the sign of the cross over them, said to the others that they were restored and healthy, and on account of this they treated us well, and refrained from eating in order to give their food to us, and they gave us skins and other things." (Cabeza de Vaca 1999, 1:115)

Thereafter there was a break in healing activities.[1] Cabeza de Vaca spent about four and a half years alone among the Indians of Malhado, from the winter of 1528 to the spring of 1533, after a thirteen-man party departed along the coast, leaving him behind because he was too ill. (Cabeza de Vaca 1999, 1:123) Only three men survived from the thirteen-man party - Castillo, Dorantes and Estebanico - with whom Cabeza de Vaca was reunited. Sometime later in 1533, Cabeza de Vaca and these three survivors made their way farther down the Texas coast, where the Mariames and the Yguazes held them captive. They lived among the Mariames for at least eighteen months during 1533-34 and learned to speak their language, before the neighbouring Avavares rescued them from starvation and danger.

It was among the Avavares that Cabeza de Vaca and his companions began to heal again (alternatively, if we accept recent revisionist interpretations, this is the moment when they first began to heal). (Ahern 1993: 217) Accommodated on the day of their arrival in the dwellings of two shamans, Castillo was called upon that night to cure severe headaches from which some of the natives were suffering. When he made the sign of the cross over them and commended them to God, they declared that they were cured. As a reward, they brought prickly pears and venison in such quantity that Cabeza de Vaca did not know where to store them. The news spread fast and many other sick people came to be cured that night. Castillo repeated his curing procedure and they too went away as if they had never suffered any malady. (Cabeza de Vaca 1999, 1:155-61) Cabeza de Vaca himself was asked to cure a man who to all appearances was dead; shortly afterwards, it was said that the lucky man had revived and was able to walk about, eat, and speak. (Cabeza de Vaca 1999, 1:163-65) It should be noted that Cabeza de Vaca did not say that he actually "cured" the dead man, but that the natives said that the man recovered.

"In all this time people came from many areas looking for us. And they said that truly we were children of the sun. Until then Dorantes and the black man had not performed any cures, but on account of the great demands made on us, [the Indians] coming from many places to look for us, we all became physicians, although in boldness and daring

155

to perform any cure I was the most notable among them. And we never cured anyone who did not say that he was better, and they had so much confidence that they would be cured if we performed the cures, that they believed that as long as we were there, none of them would die." (Cabeza de Vaca 1999, 1:165)

Most of those that came to be cured complained of maladies of the head and the alimentary tract. The party remained with the Avavares for eight months during the years 1534 and 1535, advancing from one prickly-pear grove to another, and meeting tribes of many different languages. (Ahern 1993: 218)

What are we to make of these cures? It seems likely that the shamanic ritual improvised by the four survivors was followed by the alleviation of psychosomatic maladies, such as the headaches of which the natives complained. One initial coincidental "cure" could be sufficient to set off a series of successive corroborations that, though imaginative and not verifiable by Western standards, were nevertheless credible for the community. The criteria for "success" depended on the expectations of the group. The phenomenon of the innocent bystander becoming a shaman is not unknown in the modern era, as illustrated by an example, cited by anthropologist Claude Levi Strauss, among the Zuni of New Mexico, in which an innocent young boy, accused of shamanism, deflected the potential fatal consequences by confessing his magical powers and satisfying his accusers of their reality. In this way, an individual who at first appeared to threaten the security of the group, served to corroborate its system of belief. (Levi Strauss 1967: 167-75; Pupo-Walker, 764, 769) The principle was the same in Cabeza de Vaca's case. As physician, interpreter, even "psychoanalyst," Cabeza de Vaca reconstituted and reaffirmed for the native groups that asked him to heal the principles by which they made sense of illness and its connection to the material and supernatural worlds. (Pupo-Walker 1987: 774-75) It is not that he and his fellows became great shamans because they performed cures, but rather that they performed cures because they were perceived to be great shamans. Group expectations imposed the role of shaman on them, and the cures inevitably followed. Like the young boy among the Zuni, those that threatened the community were neutralized, by being forced to confess their magic and use it for the benefit of the community. It is ironic that Cabeza de Vaca played a role that reaffirmed native religious beliefs even as he undertook a journey later characterized as an evangelical enterprise involving successive conversion of indigenous communities. (Pupo-Walker 1987: 772) The number of cures cited by other sixteenth and seventeenth-century travelers through the area supports the notion that the healing served to compensate for the unclear threat, implicit or explicit, in the white man's presence. (Adorno 1991: 173) The natives feared the Europeans because they feared the death that these strangers often brought by their presence. It is significant that epidemics and death preceded or accompanied the Spaniards both when they were initiated into native healing on Malhado and when they were later prevailed upon to resume curing in northwest Mexico. From the natives' perspective, since the Spaniards did not die, they had power over death and the power to extend it over others. (Adorno 1991: 191)

After the Spaniards departed from the friendly Avavares, they probably struck toward the southwest, where they met the Arbadaos, north of the Rio Grande. From this point on, whenever they departed from a settlement, they did not do so alone but in the company of other Indians who had come from farther ahead on the route and who guided them on their journey. The survivors were at the beginning of a process by which they were escorted almost as sacred objects in the Indians' ritual passage of them from one village to the next, a process that carried them from the Gulf of Mexico to northwest Mexico. (Cabeza de Vaca 1999, 2:260) Part of the explanation for this phenomenon may lie in the exceptionality of Cabeza de Vaca's situation. Apart from the curing powers conferred upon him, he possessed much more direct knowledge about surrounding tribes than did the Indians among whom he passed. Thus, on account of his awareness of Indians, Spain and Europe, and his know-how in healing, he represented a remarkable source of information. (Pupo-Walker 1987: 770) Here is a perfectly natural explanation for the wisdom that the natives found in him.

Traveling north again, as they crossed the plains near the river Nueces, the survivors were presented with two pierced gourds with stones inside, which were said to come from the sky and to possess great virtue. (Cabeza de Vaca 1999, 1:195) This was the insignia of the Indian shaman, which invested Cabeza de Vaca and his companions with the authority of the physician. The travellers used the gourd rattle as a symbol of healing prowess and knowledge, in order to effect the safe passage of their party from tribe to tribe through the Greater Sonoran Desert. They also accepted the privileged status of leadership that the gourd conferred, and from this time exercised their medical functions with greater authority: (Pupo-Walker 1987 768) Assuming the mantle of the native shaman to the full, Cabeza de Vaca also promised to command the heavens to rain. (Cabeza de Vaca 1999, 1:225)

It is clear that when the native peoples said that Cabeza de Vaca and his companions "came from the sky" (Cabeza de Vaca 1:231-33) they meant not that the Europeans came from Heaven or that they were gods, but that their origin was unknown. The strangers were seen as agents of death and destruction rather than as heavenly visitors, as some later commentators tried to suggest. (Adorno 1991: 184)

In the spring of 1536, Cabeza de Vaca finally came upon Spaniards from a slave-raiding party: "I reached four Christians on horseback who experienced great shock upon seeing me so strangely dressed and in the company of Indians. They remained looking at me a long time, so astonished that they neither spoke to me nor managed to ask me anything" (Cabeza de Vaca 1999, 1:245) Recovering their composure, the slave-raiders took Cabeza de Vaca to their captain. This long-awaited moment is presented in such a matter-of-fact fashion that it amounts to a considerable anti-climax. The reason for Cabeza de Vaca's brevity becomes clear from the details that Pérez de Ribas provides:

"In the province of Sinaloa, they encountered Captain Alcaraz (the name of the soldier who had been raiding for slaves). One of his soldiers who had gone ahead saw Alvar Núñez and his companions in

the distance, and thinking that he had run across the Indians they were
looking to capture, he sounded the call to arms and summoned Captain
Alcaraz. Here were four unknown travelers who in dress and
appearance were indistinguishable from the Indians. They had not
worn clothes for years and were just as sunburned and longhaired as
the barbarians with whom they were traveling. Alvar Núñez Cabeza de
Vaca recognized the Spanish soldiers by their weapons and uniforms,
so he went up to the front of his company of Indians. Wishing to
defend them, he got down on his knees, and using whatever language
he could remember in order to be recognized, he spoke in halting
Castilian, which he and his companions had nearly forgotten. They
stated who they were and whence they had come. This speech kept
them from the slave chains and collars." (Pérez de Ribas 1999: 103)

A few days later, Dorantes, Castillo, and the others arrived with six
hundred Indians, who were natives of settlements that the Spanish
raiders had caused to ascend into the highlands. From this point,
Cabeza de Vaca's behavior made sense more within the context of the
cultures through which he had passed on his journey than his native
Spanish culture. His familiarity with native ritual signs made him an
intermediary between the slave-raiders and the Indians. Under
instructions from the captain, Cabeza de Vaca called the people of the
villages on the bank of the river Petatlan and commanded them to
bring food. (Cabeza de Vaca 1999, 1:247) The Indians brought many
other items too, but Cabeza de Vaca took only the food and gave
everything else to the captain's forces. In his account, he wrote: "We
gave everything else to the Christians," a turn of phrase which
identified with native ways of looking at Europeans; as a matter of
course he referred to his fellow Spaniards in this way in the rest of his
account. Taking the part of the Indians who had accompanied him, he
entered into considerable dispute with the raiders in order to dissuade
them from enslaving his native companions. (Cabeza de Vaca 1999,
1:249) When the main body of Spanish troops arrived, Cabeza de Vaca
initiated the meeting with the same cultural code of ritual giving by
which they had survived, cured, and traveled since he left the Gulf
Coast - he gave the Spanish party cow skin (i.e. buffalo) robes and
other objects. His Indians were reluctant to return to their homes but

insisted on accompanying Cabeza de Vaca's party until they could leave the survivors in the care of other Indians, as they had been accustomed to do throughout the journey. They feared that if they returned home without doing this, they would die, whereas if they accompanied Cabeza de Vaca, they feared neither Christians nor their lances. In a revealing passage, Cabeza de Vaca observed:

"The Christians were disturbed by this, and they made their interpreter tell them that we were of the same people as they, and that we had been lost for a long time, and that we were people of ill fortune and no worth, and that they were the lords of the land whom the Indians were to serve and obey. But of all this, the Indians were only superficially or not at all convinced of what they told them. Rather, some talked with others among themselves, saying that the Christians were lying, because we came from where the sun rose, and they from where it set; and that we cured the sick, and that they killed those who were well; and that we came naked and barefoot, and they went about dressed and on horses and with lances; and that we did not covet anything but rather, everything they gave us we later returned and remained with nothing, and that the others had no other objective but to steal everything they found and did not give anything to anyone...finally it was not possible to convince the Indians that we were the same as the other Christians." (Cabeza de Vaca 1999, 1:249-51)

So great was the integration of Cabeza de Vaca's party into native cultural references that the Indians could not believe that the survivors were of the same people as the slave-raiders. Nevertheless, Cabeza de Vaca managed to persuade them to return to their villages and sow and work the land. He and his party were sent off under guard and taken through depopulated areas so that they could not converse with Indians and find out that the slave-raiders had decided to attack the Indians whom he had sent away with assurances of peace.

The climax of Cabeza de Vaca's account was his mediation of peace and resolution of a regional conflict by means of the signs of the gourd rattle and the cross. Melchior Díaz, the alcalde mayor (chief justice and civil official of the province) of Culiacan, regretted the bad treatment that Cabeza de Vaca had received from the Spanish slave-raiding party, and begged him to persuade the Indians who had accompanied his party to return from their refuge in the sierra. (Ahern 1993: 223) Since none of the Indians who had traveled with him on the great trek remained, he gave the task to some Indians who had learned from the others of:

"the great authority and influence that through all those lands we had possessed and exercised, and the wonders that we had worked and the sick people we had cured...And so that they could go in safety and the others come forth, we gave them a very large gourd of those that we carried in our hands, which was our principal insignia and emblem of our great estate. And taking this gourd they set out and went through the area for seven days, and at the end of them, returned and brought with them three lords, of those who were taking refuge in the sierras, who brought along fifteen men.   And they brought us beads and turquoises and plumes. And the messengers told us that they had not found the natives of the river (Petatlan or Sinaloa) where we had come out because the Christians had again made them flee to the highlands. And Melchior Díaz told the interpreter to speak on our behalf to those Indians and tell them how we came on behalf of God who is in Heaven, and how we had walked through the world for nine years, telling all the people we had found to believe in God and serve him because he was Lord of all things in the world..." (Cabeza de Vaca 1999, 1:255-57)

When the Indians were told that if they became Christians they would be treated well and would not be taken out of their lands, but if not they would be carried off as slaves, they responded that they would be good Christians. When asked to what they gave reverence and made sacrifices, "they responded that it was to a man who was in the sky," whose name was Aguar, who had created the whole world and all things in it, who sent water and all good things. Their ancestors had imparted this knowledge to them long ago. In an act of assimilation of the native deity Aguar, the Spanish interpreter told them that the one to whom they referred was called God by Christians, that they should call him by this name, and serve and adore him as they were commanded, and that they should come down from the sierras and populate the land and, in the midst of the houses, make one for God and put a cross at the entrance "and that when Christians came there, to come out and receive them with the crosses in their hands, without their bows and without weapons, and take them to their houses and give them whatever they had to eat." In this way, the Christians would not do them harm but be their friends. They accepted all they were told and agreed to comply. The children of the most important lords were brought for baptism, and the Spaniards swore not to take slaves in that land. (Cabeza de Vaca 1999, 1:259-61)

It was Cabeza de Vaca's use of the natives' sign of their own spirituality, the gourd rattle that compelled the Indians to send their leaders to listen to his transmission of the Spanish official's request that they return to their lands and accept Christianity. By sending ahead of him one of the ritual gourds that he had been given months before as a sign of healing prowess - gourds whose great power he had witnessed in the hands of many shamans during the previous three years - he elicited a response which no other Spaniard could have achieved - three chiefs of those Indians who had been in the mountains came to dialogue with him. It was Cabeza de Vaca who probed for the name of their supreme deity, Aguar, whom he equated with the Spanish God, and entreated them to mark their villages with a Christian emblem and to meet the Spaniards with crosses, not bows. Thus, ironically, a native sacred symbol, the gourd rattle, was appropriated in order to convert Indians to Christianity; Indian signs were employed to relay Spanish conversion messages. Cabeza de Vaca's inversion of the function of the ceremonial rattle must be one of the earliest documented examples of the Spanish strategy of turning native expression back on itself. His knowledge of the signs and symbols (cross and gourd) of two separate and apparently contradictory religious systems gave him power over both, and enabled him to pacify and (apparently) convert Indians in an area that still lay beyond the military control of New Spain. It was his success as a healer and the power that it signified which enabled him to act as a cultural mediator in this way. (Ahern 1993: 224-25, 232)

According to the historiographers of the Jesuits, Cabeza de Vaca became a very saintly man; for the Avavares, he was Son of the Sun, a being of great sacred significance. By becoming an iconic figure for both cultures, he succeeded in bridging the gap between them. The Avavares obliged Cabeza de Vaca to make "miracles" (whose authors were really Indians) and then persuaded him (whatever his reservations in writing) that he had done them, from which suggestion arose the later European literary tradition. Cabeza de Vaca was probably the first living example of religious mixture. (Lafaye 1997: 83-84)

16 Temples of Disease

Cabeza de Vaca's precocious incursion into the unexplored north of New Spain failed to serve as a preface to further exploration, still less organized settlement or evangelization during the sixteenth century. Missionary efforts in this region encountered several obstacles. The terrain was far from propitious; the Sierra Madre Occidental mountain range runs like a great backbone through the northwest of New Spain, hindering ready access from one side to the other. The native peoples were divided into a large number of ethnic groups, and even the sedentary populations were highly dispersed. Furthermore, the available missionaries were few in number. Whereas in Central Mexico all the inhabitants had been evangelized by the second half of the sixteenth century, in the north there were still groups that had not been visited by a single missionary even at the beginning of the eighteenth century.

The formation of the mission system was characterized not by steady, continual growth but by cycles of rapid expansion; violent native resistance was swiftly quelled and then followed by renewed efforts at expansion. (Merrill 1993: 139) Whereas in Central Mexico missionaries arrived at the same time as (or after) conquest, in the north, by contrast, they were a vanguard. Indeed, their purpose, as far as the state was concerned, was to pacify, settle, and domesticate Indians amongst whom other more violent methods had failed. (Powell 1991: 300-302) Although the Franciscans were the first to breach the northwest frontier, ultimately it was the Jesuits who conquered it. (Hu-Duhart 1981: 22) The Fathers expanded through an arc taking in all the regions of the northwest, including the northern parts of Nayarit, the western parts of Durango and Chihuahua, all of Sinaloa and Sonora (which were converted into almost exclusively Jesuit mission territory) and (eventually) Baja California. (Borges 1992, 2:168) The first missions were established in the decade following 1591 around Durango, among the Sinaloas, Tepehuanes, Xiximes and Acaxees, but only after 1614 did there begin a coordinated process of expansion, which continued for the rest of the century. Between 1614 and 1620,

the Jesuits founded twenty-seven missions in the present state of
Sinaloa, among the Cahitas of the rivers Sinaloa, Mocorito, Fuerte,
Mayo and Yaqui. The rapid occupation of this area is explained by the
high density of the native population, by the natural conditions which
allowed agriculture with simple techniques, by the increase in the
number of missionaries (eleven in 1613 grew to twenty-six in 1623)
and by the efficient cooperation of the Captain-General of Sinaloa,
Diego Martínez de Hurdaide, who wished to conquer all the Cahitan-
speaking people of these valleys. Some, for example the Mayos,
entered into an alliance with the Spaniards, but most groups resisted, if
briefly. The Yaquis, proved the most formidable, defeating Hurdaide
three times in campaigns between 1608 and 1610, prompting the
captain to abandon their subjugation. In the final encounter,
Hurdaide's fifty mounted Spaniards and four thousand Indian troops
were routed by the Yaquis, who were reported to have put seven
thousand fighting men in the field. Nevertheless, the victorious Yaquis
agreed to maintain an alliance with the Spaniards (and hence with their
former enemies, the Mayos) and asked that Jesuit missionaries be sent
to them. The first two Jesuits, Andrés Pérez de Ribas and Tomas
Basilio, sent after some delay seven years later, were accompanied by
no military escort but only by four baptized Zuaque Indians from the
Fuerte River. Within two years, almost the entire Yaqui population of
thirty thousand had been baptized. Within six years - by 1623 - eighty
small settlements (agricultural villages) had been reduced to eight
larger villages. (Spicer 1961: 20-21)

After 1619, the Jesuits penetrated Sonora and by 1653 they had
founded forty-six mission villages in Pimería Baja and Opatería, along
the rivers and valleys between the mountains and the coast. The
advance was less spectacular here than in the Cahita area on account of
the greater extension of territories inhabited by the Pimas and Opatas;
the lower density of population; the mountain terrain, which made
communications difficult and demanded more complicated agricultural
technology than in the coastal valleys; and the modest increase in the
number of missionaries (from twenty-six in 1623, the number had
increased only to thirty in 1638 and thirty-five in 1657). After a lapse
of almost twenty years (1654-72) during which there were no new

166

foundations, expansion continued from 1673, and by 1680 eight new villages were founded. There was also notable expansion in the states of Durango and Chihuahua, though not as great as in Sonora, including the consolidation of the missions of Lower Tarahumara (on the east of the Sierra Madre) and the establishment of those of Upper Tarahumara (on the north of the Sierra Madre). The former had begun as early as 1608, when two missions were established in the easternmost and lowest part of the Sierra Madre; further missions had been set up in 1630 and 1639, and by 1678 there were thirteen. The missions of Upper Tarahumara began in 1673, and by 1682 there were thirty churches and eight missionaries. (Borges 1992, 2:172) The mission frontier expanded northward to the Pimería Alta region only in the 1680s, although the northern Pima had already been in intimate contact with the Spanish frontier society of Sonora for at least fifty years. Between 1687 and 1699, under Eusebio Francisco Kino, twenty-five mission villages were founded in Pimería Alta. From the mission of Dolores on the river San Miguel, Kino advanced to the northeast to the valleys of the rivers Alisos, Magdalena, Altar, Sonoyta, and Santa Cruz. (Ortega Noriega 1996: 48-50)[1]

This extraordinary expansion led to the baptism of hundreds of thousands. By 1631, forty years after their first arrival in Sinaloa, Jesuit missionaries had baptized one hundred and fifty-one thousand, two hundred and forty Indians. Pérez de Ribas recorded in 1643 that, amongst the Acaxee and Xiximes, fifty thousand had been baptized by that time. By 1654, more than four hundred thousand had been baptized in the whole Jesuit mission system. (Dunne 1944: 12, 73)

The establishment of missions accelerated the process of demographic collapse that had already begun in the decades following the Spanish conquest of central Mexico in 1521. There is little doubt that Old World diseases had already claimed a large part of the Indian population of northwest New Spain, even before missionaries set foot there. The establishment of Jesuit missions led, within a few decades of the arrival of the Fathers, to even greater collapse in the native population. In the period 1600-50, which was the most active for the missionaries, the indigenous population of northwest New Spain

167

declined by seventy to seventy-five percent (on top of the losses before 1600). (Reff 1998: 21; Reff 1992: 268) Lest there be any doubt about the role of the Jesuit mission system in the chain of disease transmission, the correlation between the spread of illnesses and the foundation of Jesuit missions can be precisely demonstrated. Epidemics of smallpox, measles, typhus, pneumonia and other maladies swept through the mission system and beyond at regular five- to eight-year intervals (1593-94, 1601-2, 1607-8, 1611-13, 1617, 1623-25) and on many occasions during the decades that followed. Smallpox had probably become endemic in the southwest borderlands by the early seventeenth century, and measles also occurred frequently. (Cook 1998: 167, 192) As the mission system grew, epidemics became more destructive and far-reaching. Particularly hard hit were the Zacatec, Tepehuan, Acaxee, and Irritila. The Irritila, in the Jesuit missions of Santa Maria de las Parras (Durango), to the north and west of Zacatecas, are thought to have lost one third of their population prior to missionization in 1598. At that time, the Irritila numbered between sixteen and twenty thousand. Following missionization, and as a consequence of disease, particularly the epidemics of 1607 and 1623-25, the Irritila declined to one thousand five hundred and sixty nine in 1625.

The rapid diminution of the Irritila was not unusual. Neighboring groups in the mountains and along the eastern slopes of the Sierra Madre all suffered dramatic population reductions during the opening decades of the seventeenth century. In 1638, the Jesuits reported that while they had baptized three hundred thousand Indians, only one third survived. After that same year, when a new wave of epidemics began in northern New Spain, many thousands more perished. By 1678, Jesuit missionaries had baptized some five hundred thousand Indians in Sinaloa and Sonora, yet there remained only about sixty-three thousand Indians still living in the missions, indicating a rate of depopulation of seventy to eighty percent. (Jackson 1994: 163) By that year, the Zacatec, Irritila, Tepehuan, Acaxee and Xixime were too few in number to survive as distinct cultural entities, and most populations in northern Sinaloa and Sonora were largely destroyed by that time. (Reff 1992: 269) The decline in the native population of northwestern

New Spain for the sixteenth and seventeenth centuries as a whole was ninety-four percent. (Ortega Noriega 1996: 60) It is hard to avoid the conclusion that missionization, by nucleating Indians and thereby increasing the likelihood of greater mortality when disease broke out, in fact killed the Indians. (Lovell 1992: 432)[2]

Since disease swept so extensively in advance of the mission frontier, the Jesuits found only the vestiges of once populous and developed cultures. It is important to remember, then, that missionaries did not erupt into a static, unchanging, disease-free environment; on the contrary, they encountered a native world torn apart and disordered by unprecedented disease. It was a deeply traumatized Indian population that received the Jesuits and their Christian message. Demographic contraction had provoked profound alterations in the economy and social organization of communities, and in relations with each other. (Ortega Noriega 1996: 62)

The warm welcome that some native peoples bestowed on missionaries was a direct consequence of the disease environment; it was motivated less by interest in Christian religious teachings than by a wish to gain access to the priests' supernatural power to cure or prevent Old World diseases. Indigenous peoples understood baptism as a ceremony that healed, or that conferred additional protection against disease. The desire to gain its benefits in times of epidemics made native communities more open to Christian overtures. In late 1607, the Tepehuanes from the Sierra de Ocotlán sought baptism, just at the time that the smallpox epidemic claimed many victims. Similarly, smallpox and measles epidemics in 1616-17 prompted the Yaquis, some of whose shamans considered baptism to be a curing ceremony, to invite the Jesuits to reside among them. Another Jesuit missionary, Father Juan Agustín, reported that it was the presence of an epidemic at Laguna Grande de San Pedro, near the mission in Santa Maria de Las Parras, that led the inhabitants to invite him to go and baptize the sick, and provided the opportunity for him to teach doctrine in the local tongue. (Pérez de Ribas 1999: 660) Such factors motivated natives throughout the seventeenth century. Like the Indians of the Lower Tarahumara area in the early 1600s, so too those in the Upper

Tarahumara areas in the 1670s requested the presence of missionaries in the belief that they could cure the diseases that afflicted their societies. (Merrill 1993: 141)

The central objective of the Fathers was to prove that they possessed techniques and medicines that were both scientifically and spiritually stronger and more effective than those of the Indians' own shamans. Pérez de Ribas suggested that the secret of his fellows' success lay precisely in the combination of material and supernatural assistance. The Fathers seized the opportunity provided by the epidemics to demonstrate their selfless and untiring devotion to the Indians' welfare, intending that a sharp contrast would be drawn with the behavior of the native shamans. Religious ministers provided the sick with food, using the stipend they were given for their own maintenance. (Pérez de Ribas 1999: 673) Because the Jesuits coupled prayer with clinical care of the sick, they had an advantage over Indian shamans, who had little or no experience with acute infectious disease. From the point of view of the average Indian, it made sense to hedge one's bets, to maintain a balancing act that could garner as much protection as possible without inviting retribution from any of several supernatural beings. (Deeds 1998b: 6-7)

Epidemics not only had profound demographic consequences, but also undermined the structure and functioning of native societies, including the authority of Indian shamans and other elites, who could neither explain nor prevent the unprecedented suffering coincident with Old World diseases. Whereas native cultures had elaborated few behaviors and beliefs to confront the unprecedented destruction wrought by maladies such as smallpox, the Jesuits, by contrast, brought rituals and beliefs (for example vows, relics, saints, shrines, prayers, and scourging processions) that had evolved in the Old World over the course of a millennium precisely in order to enable the faithful to come to terms with the trauma of recurrent fatal disease. (Reff 1995: 71) The Fathers were able to assume many of the rights and responsibilities of native elites because they were better able to account for and deal with disease, whereas indigenous chiefs and shamans had little experience in this regard. Furthermore, whereas Indian elites were swept away by disease, priests lived long lives. (Reff 1998: 27) Thus, the collapse of native society provoked by epidemic disease greatly assisted the Jesuits' assumption of authority. The Fathers followed in the wake of epidemics, reconstituting native subsistence practices and socio-political organization, supervising productive activities and the redistribution of surpluses and trade goods, much as native chiefs had done prior to contact. In addition, at times the Jesuits genuinely sought to promote natives' welfare, protecting them against Spanish encroachment on their land and restraining indiscriminate uses of their labor, for example among the Yaqui. (Reff 1992: 272) If the survivors of high mortality viewed the Jesuits as useful in providing a model for social, economic and cultural reorganization, it was largely on account of the impact of decades of dramatic change in most Indian societies induced by the epidemics. (Jackson 1994: 163)

However, the remorselessness of the epidemics could work against the missionaries as well as in their favor. Just as the impotence of native priests in the face of Old World diseases encouraged natives to turn to the Jesuits, so in turn the missionaries' failures in this field led to disillusionment and rejection. It cannot have helped that the measures taken by the Jesuits, especially bloodletting, were counter-productive. Although some decided they had little to lose by getting the Christian God on their side, many other natives became disillusioned with the many deaths, especially of young children, that followed baptism. (Deeds 1998a: 40) It was commonly believed that the priests were the sorcerers of the Spanish, that baptism caused illness and death, that church bells attracted diseases and that conversion would render the land sterile. Among the Tarahumaras, these ideas were diffused widely among Indians outside the mission system, and so missionary visits to unevangelized areas produced intense debates between community members who favored accepting the missionaries and those who were ambivalent or opposed them. (Merrill 1993: 135-38; Cook 1998: 139) The missionaries countered that death would be visited upon those who were not baptized. The persuasiveness of these arguments must have depended in part on local configurations of Christian and non-Christian deaths. (Deeds 1998b: 14)

In Sinaloa, an outbreak of smallpox in 1594 was blamed on the Jesuits, and the natives rose in revolt, burned the church, killed Friar Gonzalo de Tapia, stuck his head on a pole, and paraded it on a circuit of neighboring settlements. This event was not exceptional: as many as fifty Jesuits were martyred in various New Spain missions during the colonial period. (Cook 1998: 162) In the mission of Santa Maria de las Parras, the sorcerers proclaimed that the new doctrine that the priests had brought to the land was the reason why the people were dying of smallpox. (Pérez de Ribas 1999: 673) Father Diego de Acevedo reported that during a typhus epidemic among the Acaxee in 1612-13, a very sick man died immediately after confession, whereupon his sons concluded that the priest had been the cause of the man's death. They spread it about that he was a sorcerer, and that whenever he spoke to sick people they died. (Pérez de Ribas 1999: 521) Sorcerers among the Indians of Sinaloa and among the Yaqui persuaded the Indians that baptism killed children and that when the blessed salt was placed in the infant's mouth it was a kind of spell that the priests used to kill the young. (Pérez de Ribas 1999: 96, 348) One former Yaqui sorcerer, who had been baptized and had encouraged others to submit to the sacrament, reverted to native religion around 1622 and engaged in counter-evangelization, devoting himself to undoing the spells that the priests cast during baptism. He preached that the faith was pure fiction, that heavenly bliss was a lie, that Christian souls did not go to Heaven but rather descended below the earth, and that if the Yaqui gave themselves over to vice they would still be very happy in the next life. He exhorted Indians to kill priests, burn churches, and throw in the river the bells that were used to call people to catechism. (Pérez de Ribas 1999: 369-70) Thus, the Jesuits could fill the void created by the failure of native priests and shamans only in part. (Reff 1995: 71) Communities now sought to get rid of individuals who seemed unable to prevent or halt epidemics and were now taken not as saviors from epidemics but as the cause of them.

In the seventeenth-century northwest, missionaries, as well as the broader Spanish colonial system, became the object of attack in succeeding waves of revolts by indigenous people, including the Acaxees in 1601-04, the Xiximes in 1610, the Tepehuans in 1616-20, and the Tarahumaras in 1690-1700. Three of the revolts - Xixime, Tepehuan and Tarahumara - had in common that they occurred within a generation or two of the first serious demographic invasions by Spaniards and were responses to the cataclysm of resettlement, population decline and labor demands. In each rebellion there were leaders and participants who had experienced firsthand the transition from pre-conquest to colonial conditions, and therefore could call with some authority for a revival of traditional beliefs and structures. Most fomenters and leaders of revolt seem to have been former religious and war leaders who resented the Jesuits for having displaced them as spiritual leaders, and for having prohibited proven, familiar rituals. They now exhorted their followers to reinstate pre-contact ritual activities that aimed to restore spiritual and material balance. In each case, too, continuing high rates of decline from disease allowed the disaffected to turn the tables by pointing to the association between conversion, baptism, and death. (Deeds 1998b: 1, 11-12, 23;)

The link between rebellion and traumatic disease-induced depopulation is clear. Jesuit sources reveal that epidemics claimed tens of thousands of lives among the Acaxee, Xixime and Tepehuans in the 1590s to early 1600s. The Acaxee rebellion occurred in the period of greatest demographic decline due to disease. (Deeds 1998a: 45) The Xixime revolt broke out in the context of the spread of smallpox and shamans' allegations that association with Spaniards would bring death. Rebels were promised immortality only if Jesuit churches, construed as temples of disease, were destroyed. (Deeds 1998b: 5) The Tehueco revolt of 1611 coincided with an outbreak of smallpox among their neighbors, the Sinaloa, and was fed by Tehueco doubts about the efficacy of Christianity, particularly in dealing with unprecedented epidemics. (Pérez de Ribas 1999: 236) The Tepehuan revolt coincided with a major epidemic which decimated a population already severely affected by disease-induced mortality; it has been estimated that on the eve of the uprising, the Tepehuans and their neighbors had been reduced in population by eighty percent or more, from over one hundred thousand at contact to fewer than twenty thousand. Attracting support from other Indian groups, including the Acaxee and Xixime apostates and some Tarahumara non-Christians, the revolt posed the most serious challenge of the seventeenth century to Spanish settlements in Nueva Vizcaya, leading to the violent deaths of three hundred Spaniards (including eight Jesuits) and the destruction of missions, mines, and settlements throughout the Sierra Madre Occidental, and the temporary Spanish loss of control of a large part of present-day northwestern Mexico. (Deeds 1998b: 6; Reff 1995: 63-64) Seeking to turn the tables, the Tepehuanes convinced many Acaxees in 1617 that their Sun God had brought the recent epidemic of pestilence and measles to those converts who refused to join their rebellion. (Deeds 1998b: 11-12) The shaman leader Quautlatas, baptized but relapsed, told his followers that if they killed priests and Spaniards, who had stolen their lands and enslaved them, they would be safe and would be victorious over the foreigners. Any Indian warrior killed in battle would be resurrected after seven days and once the victory was achieved, all the old would become young again, but those who failed to obey would succumb to disease. (Reff 1995: 70; Pérez de Ribas 1999: 594; Deeds 2003: 30) The leader, who also sought to stir up the Acaxee and Xixime nations, promised to create storms at sea and prevent any more Spaniards from reaching these lands.

In the mid-seventeenth century (1648-52) and again between 1690 and 1700, Tarahumara opposition to the expansion of the Jesuit mission system exploded into a series of organized revolts, which accompanied mortality rates as high as thirty percent since the first Spanish entry a half-century earlier. (Vecsey 1996: 47; Deeds 1998b: 16) The rebels in these revolts were, for the most part, baptized Indians living within the mission system rather than non-Christians from outside the missions, as had been the case in the Tarahumara revolts of mid-century. In the earlier rebellions, the rebels were almost exclusively Tarahumaras, whereas in the later period a number of different Indian groups were allied. The later revolts did not succeed, as the earlier ones had, in expelling the Spanish from the upper Tarahumara region. In his history of the Tarahumara rebellions, Father Joseph Neumann attributed the outbreak in 1690 to the machinations of a messianic leader who promised that any Tarahumaras who were killed by Spaniards would be resurrected in three days. Although Neumann's assertion is not corroborated by the interrogations of Indian participants in the rebellion that began in 1690, it certainly fits with the aspects of religious blending in previous Nueva Vizcayan first-generation revolts. (Deeds 1998b: 16)

These revolts were, then, not only a violent reaction to Spanish exploitation and the missionary suppression of native religion, but also revitalization and millenarian movements that stemmed from the profound dislocations caused by disease-induced population collapse.[3] Among the Acaxees, Xiximes and Tepehuanes, messianic leadership and millenarianism provided the ideological underpinning for the rebellion. (Reff 1995: 65, 72) But even as the revolts sought to revitalize native culture and religion, they exhibited at the same time accommodation of the object of their resistance. The rebels believed that they were called to action by supernatural beings that promised social and individual revitalization if certain injunctions and rituals were practiced but personal and social catastrophe if they were not. (Reff 1995: 69-70) However, unsure of the relative power of Christian and indigenous supernatural forces, many Acaxees hedged their bets by continuing old practices while at the same time incorporating new ones. (Deeds 1998a: 37) According to Pérez de Ribas, the Acaxee revolt of 1601 was sparked off by an Indian sorcerer who both rejected and appropriated Christian elements: "The false and diabolical liar began making speeches to the rest of the Indians against the doctrine preached by the missionary priests. At other times he persuaded them that he himself preached the same doctrine as the priests. Throughout the land they addressed him as 'Bishop.' He rebaptized the Indians that had already been baptized by the priests." (Pérez de Ribas 1999: 505) The shaman appointed disciples to spread the word and carried an icon he called the Son of God and that resembled Jesus on the cross. He also carried two letters said to be from God the Father, which exhorted the Indians to rise up against the Spaniards, an interesting demonstration of the idea that the Indians perceived European literacy as magical power. If the Indians failed to respond, God the Father (also called the Sun God) would exact retribution through plagues or famine. Even as the rebels appropriated Christian symbols, they also denigrated and destroyed them. They laid waste missions, killed priests and mutilated their bodies, flogged statues of Virgin, used crucifixes and crosses as targets, urinated on the Host, and held mock processions in which Indian women dressed as the Virgin.

The use and abuse of Christian elements demonstrates not only a rejection of these elements but also certain ambivalence about their power and how it could be undermined. Religious icons themselves became focal points of rebellion, both to defy the Spaniards' claim to imperial dominion and to acquire the spiritual power that flowed through these sacred objects. The degree to which Christian symbols were incorporated varied widely; the Tarahumaras, for example, borrowed little. Interestingly, the figure most often quoted by the missionaries as responsible for the revolts - the devil (when talking idols began to appear, calling for the worship of ancient gods, the Jesuits attributed this to demons) - does not seem to have been appropriated by the rebels. (Deeds 1998b: 8, 9, 25; Radding 1999)

17 Native Christianity on the Northwest Frontier

Whereas a minority accommodated only certain elements of Christianity in order more effectively to resist and reject the new religion, its missionaries and its secular lords, the majority accepted the central aspects of Catholicism - especially icons such as the cross, the rosary and the saints - but imposed traditional indigenous meanings on them. Christian symbols and rituals were appropriated in ways that reveal simultaneous accommodation and resistance, adaptation and defiance. Crosses came to adorn informal places of worship maintained by Indians distant from churches and where they had no need to dissemble. Oratories and stones piled along roadways that invoked the protection of spiritual powers for travelers and pilgrims were often crowned with simple crosses; among the Cahitans sudden deaths at the hands of the Apaches or due to other misfortunes were marked with wooden crosses. Indian attachment to the rosary marked for the missionaries a sign of their success, yet for natives the rosary may have carried the power of the new Christian god to their homes and to their own bodies when they wore it as a protective talisman. (Radding 1999: 121-22)

Natives more often than not successfully resisted efforts to eradicate or significantly transform their religious beliefs or cultural values. Although they made superficial adjustments to please the missionaries or to win the favor of the Christian God, such as participating in Catholic rituals or changing burial customs, neophytes on the seventeenth-century Spanish frontier apparently retained the integrity of their religions. The Yaquis accepted readily the form of what was offered by the missionary but attached to it quite different meanings. The cross was not conceived as the missionaries understood it, but was associated with a female deity whom they called "Our Mother." At least one form of the cross, carved from a mesquite trunk, and used at the spring festival the Finding of the Holy Cross (on May 3rd), was treated overtly as a female requiring dress and ornamentation. (Spicer 1980: 34) Baptism became of deep importance in Yaqui culture but largely because it was integrated with existing ceremonial sponsorship rites. Belief in Hell was difficult for the Yaquis to reconcile with ancestor worship, but was accepted in greatly modified form. Very probably, Jesuit religious ideas constituted alternatives for most Yaquis during most of the period. (Spicer 1961: 31-34) Insofar as neophytes interpreted the message of exclusive conversion as an alternative resource for religious strength and insight, they to some extent retained control of the conversion process. (Merrill 1993: 131) It was natives who determined which aspects of Christianity and European culture they would embrace and which they would reject. As a rule, those native societies which had not been vitiated by war or disease adopted from the friars what they perceived was both useful and compatible with their essential values and institutions. Ideally they sought to add the new without discarding the old, or to replace elements in their culture with parallel elements from the new. Some natives underwent sincere conversions; others found a way to synthesize the old and new religions. Most commonly mission Indians practiced both the old and new religions simultaneously. (Weber 1989: 436)

This was only possible because the Jesuit policy was to convert each people within the context of their ethnic diversity, and so the Fathers retained, albeit modifying when necessary, many aspects of native life, even in the field of religion. True, the Jesuit mission program entailed radical change in native settlement patterns (formerly dispersed, mobile groups were gathered together in a single fixed location), in social, political, and economic relations and in the scheduling of daily life. It also involved the eradication of certain practices such as polygamy and drunkenness that were contrary to Christian teachings and European values. But at the same time the missionaries did not intend the complete replacement of the indigenous way of life. "Although the Jesuits did not explicitly acknowledge their indebtedness to native people, and indeed, many were loath to consider such a possibility, subconsciously at least, they recognized the logic and utility of many native behaviors and beliefs, particularly those that were consistent with Church teachings." (Reff 1998: 31) The Jesuits employed the same strategies as the apostles and medieval saints,

178

accommodating as much as destroying pagan beliefs and ritual. For example, missionaries found it expedient to place biblical stories in natural settings that resonated with native cosmologies. Since caves were holy places and played a central role in Sonoran creation myths and religious practices associated with curative rites and sorcery, Fray Francisco Barbastro placed the birthplace of Jesus in a cave in his Christmas sermon to the Opatas of Baviacora. (Radding 1999: 122)

The Fathers also encouraged the performance of native rituals that they felt complemented or reinforced Catholic practices. (Merrill 1993: 135) Among the Yaqui, the Jesuits tried to retain and incorporate some indigenous music and dances into the new Christian festivals they introduced. (Hu-Duhart 1981: 13) Among the Zuaque, the Fathers encouraged the natives to light bonfires in the central square of the pueblo of Mochicahue, and with the dances and drums that once called them to war against the Christians, now celebrate festivals for Christ and His Most Holy Mother. (Pérez de Ribas 1999: 225) Pérez de Ribas noted approvingly how the Indians of Santa Maria de las Parras and surrounding areas were invited to dance together at Christian feasts such as the Nativity, and how at a celebration, in Mexico City, of the beatification of Saint Ignatius in 1610, two or three thousand Mexica Indians danced a *mitote*.[1] (Pérez de Ribas 1999: 669) In Santa Maria de las Parras, during Christmas 1598, Jesuit Juan Agustín was delighted that Indian converts, together with pagan Indians, celebrated the *mitote*, adorned in traditional costumes with plumes and feathers and holding arrows in their hands, calling out in their own language what the missionary called "divine praises." Agustín stated with satisfaction that they now honored God with ceremonies that before they performed to honor Satan. (Dunne 1944: 28)

Pérez de Ribas often referred to instances where missionaries "successfully" substituted Christian for native rituals and beliefs. He recorded how Indian residents at the Jesuit seminary of San Gregorio in Mexico City celebrated Carnival by performing the *mitote* of the emperor Moctezuma, which although formerly dedicated to gentile purposes, was now a Christian celebration dedicated to the honor of Christ. Fourteen dancers, attired in the garb of ancient Mexica princes, performed before the emperor, shaking rattles and waving and raising the crests of feathers, while richly dressed boys swept the way for the emperor and threw flowers at his feet. Regaled by the music and the words "Come out, Mexica, and dance; We have the King of Glory here," the emperor took his seat on the stage on a golden stool while the dancers bowed before him, a genufluction which, Pérez de Ribas noted, was now performed to the Most Holy Sacrament of the Altar, since "Moctezuma was converted." Pérez de Ribas observed approvingly: "This festive dance is now being employed in the service and recognition of the King of Kings, Jesus Christ. This was what prompted me to record it here, and the Catholic faithful cannot help but be pleased to see the ancient Mexica heathenism cast down at the feet of their redeemer, whom before the gentiles did not know but now worship and recognize with all possible demonstrations of happiness." (Pérez de Ribas 1999: 715)

A comparable process of substitution can be observed in the case of a celebration for adopted children held among the Indians of Sinaloa, in which they danced and sang, and sat on the sand and painted different figures with loose sand of varying colors, apparently depicting the Cahita origin myth (a similar phenomenon has been observed among the Navajo). They painted mainly two figures that appeared to be human, Vairubi (a mother) and Variseva (her son). When they spoke about these figures, "it even seemed that they spoke of them with a glimpse of God and His Mother, for they referred to them as the first beings from whom the rest of mankind was born." One of their leaders showed the priest the figures that his ancestors revered, those whom they asked to safeguard their planted fields from the snakes, toads, and animals that were painted there. (Pérez de Ribas 1999: 117)

The role of epidemics in awakening Indian interest in Jesuit missionaries is a good illustration of the fact that natives responded most positively to mission formation and baptism during times of crisis, when the advantages of the mission program appeared to outweigh the disadvantages. (Merrill 1993: 139) Aside from Christian medical and supernatural assistance in the struggle against disease, another important motive for inviting missionaries was to seek the protection that a series of laws and royal decrees afforded Christian Indians and their communities against military conquest, enslavement, and encroachment by non-Indian settlers. For this reason Indians tolerated missionaries as a lesser evil, and, interestingly, some invited them even in a position of strength. After their rout of the Spanish army in 1610, the Yaquis requested a Jesuit presence among them. Their objective was to secure Jesuit missionaries without military and political submission to the Spaniards. For the next hundred peaceful years, the Jesuits served native interests by working hard to limit Spanish settlement in the area. (Deeds 1998a: 47) Similarly, encroaching Spanish settlement in the Lower Tarahumara region in the 1640s, and fear of the Spanish military in the Upper Tarahumara region after the revolts of the 1690s, seem to have encouraged Indians in these areas to seek the protection of the mission system. (Reff 1992: 272)

But in the absence of threatening Spanish soldiers or encroaching Spanish settlement or other adverse conditions, the Indians were more reluctant to enter the mission system. (Merrill 1993: 141) Missionaries were often resented for their ineffectiveness in protecting their charges from labor service and from other acquisitive demands of the Spanish community and in some instances were perceived as a means of collecting royal subsidies and taking Indian lands. (Merrill 1993: 135-38) The Tarahumaras, who may have felt more hostility toward the Jesuits because they represented the first significant Spanish presence in their territories, stated on more than one occasion that the Jesuits were no more than advance agents of other Spaniards who came to take their labor and their lands. They should be contrasted with other native groups - like the Acaxees and the Tepehuanes - who initially saw the Jesuits as buffers between themselves and a civilian population that had already begun to exploit them. (Deeds 1998b: 27)

Where native communities perceived that the Jesuits could serve their purposes, profound changes in all aspects of life and society could result. The best example is perhaps the missions among the Yaqui, where between 1610 and 1740, possibly on account of the lack of Spanish settlement either within or in close proximity to Yaqui territory before the end of this period, natives and Jesuits coexisted in a state of adaptive or accommodative resistance. The impact of the missionaries was to provide political stability and stimulate wider integration among the Yaquis at a community level, creating a more precise definition of their territorial boundaries and a stronger sense of cultural unity. By 1623, and without a coercive military presence, the Jesuits had reorganized the Yaquis from about eighty dispersed settlements into eight mission villages. Yaqui culture was transformed from a loose federation to a tighter-knit unit speaking the same language and sharing the same social development. A fundamental change in Yaqui identity took place, as the Yaquis made the mission towns the focal points of the ethnic territory they thenceforth so staunchly defended. (Spicer 1980: 292) It has even been suggested that Yaqui culture and identity, as modified by the mission system, actually supplanted most traces and erased most memories of their aboriginal or pre-Jesuit past (the Yaquis' own historical memory in the modern period dates back to the era of Jesuit reorganization, but not earlier). The profound impact of the long, intense Jesuit missionary experience must be judged decisive in explaining the survival of the Yaqui people as a culturally intact and politically autonomous people at the end of the colonial period. (Spicer 1961: 24, 27; Hu-Duhart 1981: 23, 24) The imposed experience compressed in time social developments that would have taken much longer in a more natural evolution. (Hu-Duhart 1981: 3) However, the case of the Yaquis seems to be exceptional among natives evangelized by the Jesuits.

An influential expert concluded that differences in missionary methodology were ultimately responsible for the differences in the degree of cultural interaction that resulted among Indian groups exposed to Jesuit and Franciscan evangelization. For example, in Jesuit missions among the Yaquis, political linkage was weak, and coercive sanctions were relatively mild. Franciscan mission communities were structurally stable, but Jesuit communities shifted from scattered settlements to compact towns. The differences appeared to be of great importance in influencing cultural change. (Spicer 1961: 527) There is some historical evidence to substantiate a difference in method (though Spicer was unaware of it): a report in 1715 by a contemporary investigator, Don Pedro Tapís, Bishop of Durango. The document is nearly unique in mission literature for comparing methodology between the orders. The findings are significant because they are made by an interested, critical observer who had reason to desire complete success on the part of both religious orders. In the Jesuit missions, he found that the Indians had been well educated, that there was nothing in which to correct the Fathers, and he expressed the wish that all missions and doctrinas could be under their care. By contrast, in the Franciscan missions, the churches were run down and poorly adorned and the Indians had little instruction. The major difficulty was that the superiors changed the missionaries at every chapter, or before, and so no Franciscan missionary remained in one place more than two or three years. The Franciscans also made little effort to learn native languages, or even to teach the Indians Spanish. Tapís took a position on methodology similar to those of Pérez de Ribas and Kino. He stressed the importance of personal communication and warm, mutual acceptance. The Franciscans did not fail, in his estimation, because they had employed the wrong method. Their error was in not communicating effectively and in showing minimal concern about acceptance because their assignments were too temporary. (Polzer 1976: 54-56)

More recent writings have emphasized that differences in the pre-existing native culture and society, and differences in the circumstances of contact between missionaries and Indians, are more likely to be important in explaining the form and characteristics of the mission system in different areas. Spanish missionary will was not sufficient for the process of change; a response by natives to the action of the religious was necessary, and this response depended - among other things - on cultural conditions at the moment of contact. The cultural level of the native groups of Sonora, with their knowledge of agriculture and their previous forms of social integration, provided a base for missionary action which was lacking among, for example, nomad groups, such as the Seris and the Apaches, where the mission system never could have established itself. The natural resources of the provinces of the northwest were a decisive factor in the establishment of the mission system. The existence of precious metals in Sonora and

Ostimuri led to the creation of mines that became the market for the products of the missions; the aptitude of these regions for agriculture and ranching allowed the development of the economic base of the missions in the first place. Where these conditions did not exist, such as in Baja California, the Jesuits did not succeed in establishing dynamic and self-sufficient communities, nor did the natives integrate into the Spanish colonial system. Conflictive relations among native groups also influenced the acceptance of the Spanish, since some sought military alliance. Factors such as these played a more significant role in determining the form of the mission system than differences in methodology between the orders. (Ortega Noriega 1996: 73-74)

18 Christian Shamans Among the Guarani and the Strategy of Seduction

In the frontier region of the South American continent, the Jesuits established missions among several ethnic groups including the Guarani, the Guaira and the Itatin, in the region of Asunción; the Chiquitos and the Mojos, in the region of Santa Cruz de la Sierra (the present-day Bolivian department of Beni); the Maynas, in the Upper Amazon basin, in the region of Quito; and the Casanare, in the region of the Orinoco. Of these, the reductions among the Guarani of Paraguay have acquired universal renown.[1] After 1610, the Fathers began sustained mission efforts among Guarani communities that lay in an area between and on both sides of the Parana and Uruguay rivers, south-east of Asunción, and extending into the present Misiones province of northern Argentina, and over into southern Brazil. Advocates have eulogized the reductions as a temporal and spiritual utopia, the achievement of the ideal, sought by many other American evangelizers, of educating the Indians totally apart from the Spanish and Creole population, subject only to the religious, social and civil authority of the Fathers, who devoted themselves disinterestedly to the welfare of their charges. Critics have denounced the creation of a private empire, an expression of the Jesuits' determination to control and dominate the Guarani in the interests of their own order. Whichever view one holds, it is clear that the reductions in Paraguay were the closest approximation to what the Fathers considered to be the ideal situation for a successful evangelization. This is not to say that conditions were favorable. The constant depredations of slave raiders from the region of Sao Paulo (called paulistas, mamelucos or bandeirantes) not only disrupted but also obliterated the early mission communities. By 1631, of eleven reductions in Guaira, nine were totally destroyed by paulistas, assisted in their raids by Tupi Indians, leaving only San Ignacio and Loreto. The missionaries calculated that in the previous three years, two hundred thousand Indians had been lost, some captured, or killed, but the majority dispersed through the woods. The subsequent relocation and re-foundation of the missions in

The Misiones area, nearer to the Spaniards and further from the paulistas, reduced but did not eliminate the attacks, which continued in 1636, 1638 and 1641. By 1652, of forty-eight villages organized by the missionaries, twenty-six had been destroyed and another twenty-two remained (twenty of which were in Paraguay-Parana), with a total population of about forty thousand Indians. By the beginning of the eighteenth century, there were seventeen villages beside the Uruguay and thirteen beside the Paraguay, with over one hundred thousand Indians; the most populous villages had about five thousand Indians. (Borges 1992, 2:679-682) The constant threat to the physical integrity of the missions placed limitations on what the Jesuits could attain among the Guarani. But nowhere else in the Americas did the Fathers establish such total control over the mission populations.

The missions among the Guarani and those of northwest Mexico are the two most significant Jesuit enterprises in the history of the Americas. In both of these regions, the Jesuits were able to establish a largely self-supporting mission system that encompassed several hundred square miles and dozens of missions. Despite the small numbers of missionaries - there were never more than eighty to one hundred missionaries working at any one time in either region - the Guarani missions and those in northwest Mexico, at their height, each had between one hundred thousand and one hundred and fifty thousand Indians under Jesuit tutelage. (Reff 1998: 19) Over the course of a century and a half, the Jesuits persuaded more than a half-million Indians in each region to accept baptism and missionization. It has been assumed that it was military organization and protection that enticed the Guarani to settle in missions. But it is important that the most significant parallel between the mission frontiers in northwest Mexico and Paraguay is that they were disease environments. (Reff 1998: 20)

As in northwest Mexico, the population of the area of Paraguay, and the broader Rio de la Plata region, had been decimated by Old World diseases before systematic and sustained penetration by missionaries occurred. The region was afflicted by repeated epidemics that apparently originated in adjoining areas, specifically highland Peru, where population densities were much greater, and where Spanish mining activity at Potosí encouraged frequent movement of goods, people, and disease agents to Paraguay. Within a year or two of an epidemic in highland Peru, the same disease was often reported by the Jesuits of the Rio de la Plata region. (Reff 1998: 21-22) Around 1560, an epidemic killed more than one hundred thousand Indians in the region of Asunción, and by the end of the sixteenth century, there were no more than three thousand Indians in a radius of thirty kilometers around the town. (Haubert 1986: 23) In the mission era, severe smallpox epidemics continued to strike the native inhabitants (notably in 1618, 1619, 1635, 1636 and 1692). In 1630, the Jesuit missions in Paraguay were inundated by a disease (which could have been measles, smallpox or typhus) that killed more than twenty percent of the population. The mission of Candelaria, with seven thousand Indian converts, was struck by an epidemic infection that took off one thousand Indian victims. (Cook 1998: 177) A number of scholars have suggested that the Guarani population was reduced by upwards of ninety percent by 1732 - from roughly one million to one hundred and forty one thousand. It is estimated that, in the Asunción region alone, the Guarani population declined between 1556 and 1688, from more than one hundred thousand to fewer than twelve thousand. (Reff 1998: 24) However, it is difficult to be sure since the size of the original Guarani population is unknown. (Reff 1998: 23) There are more reliable statistics for the eighteenth century. In 1733, the Jesuits counted twelve thousand nine hundred and thirty three smallpox victims among children alone, and in 1737 there were more than thirty thousand deaths, a figure equivalent to the total population of several reductions. (Caraman 1976: 143) There is no doubt that introduced diseases had a profound impact on the Guarani. Related tribes near the coast fared even worse. Already by the end of the sixteenth century, the Tupinamba were nearly extinct on the littoral of Rio de Janeiro, and the Tupiniquim faced a similar destiny on the Sao Paulo littoral. (Cook 1998: 154)

The relentless effects of European diseases created an opportunity for individuals who were able to offer expertise in medical and spiritual healing. In reality, there was little effective medical assistance that the

Jesuits could provide against the inroads of smallpox. But the Fathers' knowledge of pharmaceutical and herbal remedies - both European and indigenous - was sufficient to provide some relief against most other illnesses. In the absence of imported drugs, the priests devised cures from material at hand - shrubs, trees, the intestines, or other parts of wild animals - and rapidly built up considerable expertise in their application. They found that the intestines of the cayman, or South American crocodile, dried and reduced to powder, gave instant relief from stones; that the soft hair of the water-hog could assuage sciatica, gout and bowel pains; and that small stones from the head of the iguana, ground to powder and swallowed with water, could dislodge blockages in the kidney. What made this growing expertise more than a collection of ad hoc remedies was the semi-professional medical status of many of the Fathers, and the intellectual framework within which they operated. Although there were only two doctors for all the Parana and Uruguay reductions, it became standard for each mission to have its own infirmarian, whose medical skills were often considerable. Juan de Montes, for example, studied medicine and practiced surgery in Europe before becoming a Jesuit; another, Domingo Torres, was an enthusiastic herbalist. Pedro Montenegro, probably the greatest pharmaceutical botanist of Jesuit Paraguay, wrote several books in both Spanish and Guarani, of which only two have survived: one book on surgery and another on the properties and virtues of the trees in mission provinces, the most quoted work on herbalist medicine of the period. He belonged to the school of naturalists founded by the great missionary leader Antonio Ruiz de Montoya, who himself devoted three chapters of his *Spiritual Conquest* to animals and one to herbs. (Caraman 1976: 143-149) There is no doubt that on occasions the remedies that the Fathers prescribed were effective and saved many lives. When, in 1616, virtually the whole township of San Ignacio Guazu went sick with influenza, Father Juan de Salas concocted a syrup that healed them. But, crucially, their remedies for smallpox - which included sulfur, alum, salt, tobacco, sugar, pepper, the fat of hens, and even gunpowder - were ineffective except in mild cases. The limits on what they could achieve medicinally in the face of this greatest scourge obliged the Fathers to have recourse largely to spiritual and therapeutic assistance. As in northwest Mexico, it was the combination of the skills of the physician and of the magician that cemented their identification as powerful shamans.

It is possible that nowhere in the Americas did shamans play such a large part in the lives of Indians as among the Guarani. For one thing, a large percentage of the population acted as one sort of shaman or another. In the seventeenth century, as among the contemporary Guarani, shamans did not belong to a closed caste nor was their gift hereditary. Although nobody could become a shaman except by inspiration (and not through learning), this path was (and is) potentially open to all. Every Guarani was to a greater or lesser extent a prophet. Traditionally, the Guarani were divided into four classes: those, mainly adolescents but also a small number of adults, who had not yet made any contact with spirits and had not received any inspiration at all; those who had access to spirits, had received one or more songs and could direct some minor dances - this category included most adults of both sexes; the ritual leaders called *paje* (or *page*), who officiated at typical religious functions in order to find the name of a newborn, to cure diseases, to lead a ritual ceremony, to speak prophetically concerning the way things are and the way they ought to be, and to remember traditional mythical stories; and the *karai*, or great shamans, who could only be men, who lived in solitude, spoke little and undertook immense fasts, and were the only ones who could direct the most important dance, Nimongarai, designed to protect living things from harm. These exceptional individuals were not only the most accomplished healers but were also considered as saints, prophets, even messiahs, with great miraculous powers. They were reputed to dry up rivers, provoke floods, change themselves and others into birds or animals, rejuvenate the old, and resuscitate the dead. These powers marked them out as man-gods, manifestations of the mythical ancestors or civilizing figures of Guarani myths, who returned to the earth in order to bestow benefits on humans, such as the cultivation of manioc. The same term, *karai*, was used to describe both the mythical culture heroes and the great shamans, and the Jesuits reported that the latter's bones were often revered as holy objects. The quality of perfection of speech, a remarkable ability with the word

"that fulfills, magically or persuasively, what they say" was attributed
to them, together with the authority of a father who knows how to give
counsel, organize a feast, provide resources and take decisive
measures for the life of the community. They were often the only
chiefs, whose authority extended over several villages. Thus, more
than healers and miracle-workers, they were also religious and
political leaders. (Melia 1996: 189-190; Clastres 1975: 40-52)

Perceiving the missionaries - both the Jesuits and their forerunners, the
Franciscans - as more powerful than their own shamans, the Guarani
conferred upon them the title of *pa'i* (father, sorcerer) or *karai* (great
shaman). Friar Luis Bolaños, who evangelized from 1575 in the
province of Guaira (now part of Brazil), was called "Pai Luis," and
"God's sorcerer," and was attributed with supernatural powers over the
elements, nature, and men. According to native legend, when the
waters of Lake Ypacarai flooded the region, the friar was able to
contain them; and a spring emerged miraculously when Bolaños
ordered Indians to lift a stone on the spot. The Franciscan chronicler
Cordoba Salinas attributed to Bolaños the power to exert influence
from a distance and the power of ubiquity, and stated that the Indians
had seen him levitate, surrounded by light and his face shining, while
he was praying. The reference to his shining face indicates that the
friar was identified with Maire-Pochi, the personification of the sun
among the Tupinamba, or Nyanderuvusu, the civilizing god of the
Apapocuva, whose breast illuminates the darkness. Significantly, the
Jesuit Antonio Ruiz de Montoya was also considered a shining sun.
Thus, the evangelized peoples "Guaranized" the friars and the Fathers,
recreating them by means of their myths and legends, and adopting
them in a way that reveals that they did not see them as alien (it is
telling that the Guarani referred to the Franciscan prelate as *pa'i
rubicha*, where *pa'i* means father or sorcerer, and *rubicha* means
headman or lord). A further indication of the assimilation of the
Fathers to the *pa'i/karai* is the fact that the title "killers of jaguars" -
normally conferred on the shamans - was applied to them, as a result
of their apparent success in securing the intercession of Christian
saints so that jaguars would fall into traps or cease to bother villagers.
In revenge, the jaguars punished the pagan villages that had refused to

accept Christ, and would frequently devour Indians who failed to go to
mass. Both the friars and the Fathers assumed the leadership mantle of
the great shamans. There was an important similarity between the
friars' way of acting, and especially their commitment to poverty, and
what was expected of native lords, who had to be generous and
magnanimous, and contrary to elsewhere in America, were the ones
who possessed the least. The Jesuits' authority resembled that of a
lord, since their pre-eminence was marked by acts of generosity, by
powers of eloquence and by force of character. All these
characteristics confirmed that they fell into the category of great
shaman. Furthermore, like the native civilizing heroes, who were also
called *pa'i*, the Jesuits led an ascetic life, and taught the Guarani new
techniques and introduced new plants and tools. (Necker 1979: 71-73,
87, 189; Cayota 1998: 132; Caraman 1976: 179)

However, the claim that the missionaries made to powerful
supernatural magic, and the coincidence of their arrival with the
outbreak of disease meant that, in many areas, they were seen as
agents of destruction. In Brazil, Francisco Pires wrote in 1552 to his
Jesuit superiors that the ravages of disease among the first converts
near Bahia had left very few survivors, and as a result the shamans
were able to convince the Tupi peoples that the Jesuits were the cause
of death and destruction. "The sorcerers delude them with a thousand
follies and lies...preaching that we kill them with baptism, and
proving this because many of them do die." (Cook 1998: 150) Father
Manuel da Nóbrega, Superior of the Jesuit mission in Brazil, reported
in 1549 that the shamans were telling the Indians that baptismal water
was the cause of the diseases that were beginning to afflict villages at
the time. In another village near Salvador, sick children were hidden
from the Jesuits because the sorcerers said that they would be killed
through baptism.

As a response to missionary incursions, and also as a reaction against
colonial domination and slavery, during the second half of the
sixteenth century new religious cults emerged led by indigenous
prophets, and characterized by messianic and millenarian aspects. The
Jesuits gave the name *santidade* (holiness or saintliness) to these

movements, which evoked Tupi-Guarani myths and traditions, exalted warfare and promised abundant crops and game. In 1559, Father Nóbrega reported the outbreak of such a movement on a plantation near Salvador, where an Indian from one of the early Jesuit missions spread an insurgent message among slaves. He preached that a saint would appear who would transform the master and other whites into birds and free the subsistence plots of caterpillars and other pests. The Jesuits were to be spared, though Indians were to destroy the church, dissolve their Christian marriages, and take on many wives. In the wake of the serious epidemics of 1562-63, another movement arose in the backlands of Bahia, led by the shaman Santo. In a manner reminiscent of the Taki Onqoy cult of the central Andean highlands during the same decade, the movement rejected outsiders and called for a return to the old order. It promised that food would grow without labor and that Indians would be freed from slavery and would become masters of the whites, who would be turned into game to eat. The movement gathered momentum and continued as a regional force into the next century. (Cook 1998: 152)

Another santidade cult emerged around 1580 near Jaguaripe, a sugar-producing zone south of the Bay of All Saints, led by the charismatic Antonio, a Tupinamba who had run away from a Jesuit reduction south of Bahia. Since the cult acquired a considerable non-Indian following on the plantations, an inquisitorial visitation was conducted in 1590-91, which has allowed details of this movement, unlike others, to pass into the historical record. One witness, a white woman called Luisa Barbosa, confessed that, at the age of twelve (ca. 1566), she was drawn into a santidade cult which taught that Indians should not work because food would grow by itself, that white people would be transformed into game, and that anyone who did not believe in the movement would be converted into sticks and stones. Firmly based on traditional Tupinamba political and religious components, the santidade of Jaguaripe borrowed heavily from the hierarchical order introduced by Jesuits and slave owners. Raised by Jesuits in the Tinhare mission, Antonio incorporated significant new elements in the prophetic experience; declaring himself "pope" and one of his wives "mother of God," the prophet established a parallel church, complete

192

with bishops and vicars. New members were accepted to the cult
through a sort of reverse baptism, in which Christian names were
replaced by names given by the leader. Beyond the usual appeal to a
world of abundance, where crops would produce themselves, where
arrows would shoot spontaneously through the air slaying game, and
where the enemy would fall easily captive to heroic warriors,
Antonio's message also concerned colonial oppression. Using an
incomprehensible language invented by members of the santidade,
possibly in emulation of the Latin ritual of the Jesuit missions, and
inspired by a stone idol, the cult leaders claimed that their god was to
come immediately and free them from slavery and make them masters
of white people. Although some have depicted the santidade as a
single, unified movement that spread along the coast and throughout
the backlands over the course of several decades in the sixteenth
century, it seems more likely that many different phenomena were
called santidades, ranging from traditional Tupi-Guarani shamanistic
rituals to manifestly anti-colonial resistance. These movements are
important because they consciously combined tradition and revivalism
with historically new elements in order to forge novel strategies that
aimed to restore indigenous collective identity in a dynamic fashion.
(Monteiro 1999: 1009-15)

It is clear, then, that in the Rio de la Plata region, as elsewhere in the
Americas, even those Indians who advocated rejection of the Christian
message showed accommodation to the object of resistance.
Conversely, those Indians - such as the majority of the Guarani in the
Jesuits missions of Paraguay - who avowedly internalized the Fathers'
teachings and respected their benevolent supernatural power,
nonetheless remained discriminating in their adoption of Christianity,
accepted or rejected elements of what they were told, according to
native criteria, and showed thoughtfulness, skepticism and even
incredulity. Recognition of the Jesuits as powerful shamans did not
necessarily mean that the Guarani adopted the beliefs and practices
that these respected men wished to impose, in precisely the form in
which they were presented. A Mocobi Indian who agreed to be
baptized openly admitted that his purpose was to see his ancestors
again. When the Jesuit priest told him that they were burning in Hell,

he replied that if his ancestors could put up with that, then he could as well, especially since none of them had come back to complain to him that they could not stand that great fire. Many Indians were astonished to learn that they were destined for Hell, even though it was the whites that killed Jesus. Father Francisco García was asked by a Guanoa sorcerer, how God, if he was so merciful, could have left the Indians for so long in darkness, allowing them all to be condemned? He seems to have been unmoved by the reply that the judgments of God must not be scrutinized but respected. Moreyra, a famous Charrua sorcerer, when told that he had one foot in Hell, exclaimed that the Jesuit's god was his best friend, for if it were not so, how was it that he had conferred on him so many favors, protecting him against death, thunder and wild beasts? A Mocobi lord, Cithaalin, when told that to go to Heaven he must not have more than one wife, lie, deceive, steal or kill, replied that he found all these faults and worse amongst the Spaniards, even though they had been baptized. Many Indians were put off by the Christian doctrine of love for all men, even those of other tribes. The Guanoas agreed to convert in order to please Father García but they wanted to wait a few weeks since first they had to make war on the Yaros. Indians were often concerned to know if all Spaniards went to Heaven, perhaps because they feared being in their company for all eternity. Sometimes they confessed that they were not interested in being good. One Indian said he wanted to live and die as a good Pampa, and not as a bad Christian. Other times their reaction was more violent - the Guarani of Tayaoba threatened to kill Antonio Ruiz de Montoya when he spoke to them of paganism and their sin, and in the ensuing flight, seven of his companions were killed by arrows. (Haubert 1986: 59-60)

As elsewhere in the Americas, both the Franciscans and the Jesuits who followed them chose to root evangelization in native culture by translating the Christian message into Guarani. Franciscan Luis Bolaños produced between 1582 and 1585 the first Guarani grammar, the first vocabulary and the first prayer book, as well as translating sections of the catechism (all of which corresponded with the books issued by the Council of Lima in 1583). (Caraman 1976: 26) The first Jesuits in Paraguay made use of Bolaños's catechisms and produced

194

their own grammars and vocabularies. (Haubert 1986: 105) From the earliest days, native terms were used to express Christian concepts. Manuel da Nóbrega reported in 1549 that the Tupi who lived on the Brazilian coast gave to thunder the name Tupana, which meant divine thing, and that the missionaries could find no term more appropriate to speak to them about God than "Father Tupana." In both Brazil and Paraguay, the missionaries adopted the word Tupan to designate the Christian God in their preaching and catechisms, and ultimately the term was used by the Indians themselves in this sense. (Clastres 1975: 18) Antonio Ruiz de Montoya defended the use of the term Tupan since he believed it had designated the true God whom the Indians had perceived in their heathen state:

"They knew of God's existence, and even in a certain way of his unity. This is gathered from the name they give him, Tupa. The first syllable, tu, expresses wonder, while the second, pa, is an interrogative; thus it corresponds to the Hebrew word Man-hu, "What is this?" ... they never had idols, though the devil was already imposing upon them to venerate the bones of certain Indians who had been famous magicians during their lifetimes...They never offered sacrifice to the true God, nor did they have any more than a simple knowledge of him. In my own view, this was all that remained among them from the preaching of the apostle St. Thomas..." (Ruiz de Montoya 1993: 49)

In a later work, *Apology in Defense of Christian Doctrine*, Ruiz de Montoya wrote that conceiving of the incomprehensibility and inexplicability of God as a result of the preaching of St Thomas, the Indians' use of only these two sounds to refer to Him actually said more about God than if they had used many words and concepts to define Him, since in this way they worshiped what could not be understood or explained. Indeed, the word Tupan was better than Dios, since the latter referred both to the true God and to false idols, whereas Tupan referred only to the former, since the Guarani had no idols. Leaving no ambiguity in his position, he reminded his readers that a name that comes from one language might not be as appropriate in a foreign language. If the Jesuits were to try to introduce the word Dios, the Indians might not accept it, thinking that it was a vile name, or the name of some man or idol, "making the same mistake as those who believe Tupan to be the name of an idol." Defending the appropriateness of the term on the grounds of its universal use, he insisted that the word Tupan was found everywhere among these peoples, not invented by discoverers or passed by them from one group to another. (Marzal 1992, 2:632-33)

Ruiz de Montoya's view was shared by some, but not all Jesuits. Father A. Thevet reported that, although the Tupi believed that there was a God in Heaven, they did not honor him since he was the god of the Christians and did good for them and not for the Indians. They called this God Tupan, but did not confuse him with their own god of thunder, or believe that he had the power to make it rain or thunder. (Clastres 1975: 19) Even if this were the case, the use of a native term which already had its own meaning served to present the Christian God in terms of the indigenous religious worldview. The Indians may or may not have disassociated Tupan from thunder, but this was largely irrelevant, since his true significance lay elsewhere. Tupan was the most sacred entity of all to the Guarani, since he was the agent of the inevitable and imminent destruction of the world, and hence the true master of their destiny. The missionaries were not wrong about the transcendental importance of Tupan to the Guarani - he did rule over their religion - they were mistaken only about his meaning - he was a cosmic destroyer, and nothing could be further removed from the Christian idea of the benevolent creator. The god associated with creation, Monan, played a secondary role. Thus the missionaries probably erred when they assumed, in Paraguay as elsewhere, that religion must be defined in relation to a creator god. (Clastres 1975: 36)

Jesuit assimilation of the devil to the native Anyan, one of a class of malign spirit which troubled the living, haunted graves, preyed on the souls of the dead, and was no less mortal than man, must have been equally misleading. Reference to Anyan entirely failed to convey the essence of the Christian notion of sin, which was alien to the Indians. There were good and bad men, but the latter were considered a nuisance, to be chased away or killed, since they put in danger the

well-being of the group. Individual actions were seen as the result of
fate, and not of moral responsibility. The Guarani hoped to go to a
mythical paradise, but they attached no idea of remuneration for their
conduct on earth, and if they did not get there, it was the result of cruel
fate or of the soul falling victim to numerous perils that await it on the
way. (Haubert 1986: 57-58)

As elsewhere in the Americas, the missionaries adopted a strategy that
while it might allow error to slip through, at least held out a chance
that an evangelization, however imperfect, might occur. Some
contemporaries strongly disapproved. Bishop Bernardino de Cárdenas
cited the Jesuits' willingness to introduce Indian words into their
catechisms as proof that the Society was prepared to lead the Indians
into heresy in order to assuage their thirst for domination. An assembly
of linguists and theologians convoked in Asunción in 1656 cleared the
Society of such offences, thus implicitly supporting the Jesuit
evangelization strategy. (Haubert 1986: 106)

The strategy of admitting elements of native culture, such as language,
also extended to assimilating native cultural heroes to Christianity. As
in Peru, so among the Guarani there was a belief among many
missionaries, with Ruiz de Montoya a notable example, that the
Indians had conserved a tradition, handed down from their ancestors,
of an evangelizing apostle, probably St Thomas. According to this
tradition, they had been visited long ago by a wise man, called Pay
Zume by the Guarani (and Sume by the Tupis) who carried a cross,
performed miracles, and wanted to teach them a new religion. They
refused to listen, and tried to kill him. Before leaving, he warned them
that: "In time you will lose the doctrine that I am now preaching to
you. But after a long period, when some priests who will succeed me
come carrying a cross as I do, this teaching will be heard by your
descendants." (Ruiz de Montoya 1993: 74) The Indians would be
assembled in villages and forced to follow new norms, such as taking
only one wife, and would learn to love each other, but until then they
were destined to misunderstand one another as a punishment for their
lack of faith. Ruiz de Montoya adduced as grounds for giving credence
to the tradition the name that the Guarani gave to their priests - *Abare* -

which meant a man removed from sex, or a chaste person, which in no way reflected the practices of their own ministers but rather those of Christian priests; the firm tradition of the apostle among the Portuguese and indigenous settlers of Brazil; and the tradition in Peru of a wise man known as Pay Tume, as recorded by Alonso Ramos Gavilán. (Ruiz de Montoya 1993: 74-80) It is generally accepted that the missionaries themselves imposed the interpretation of a visit by an apostle onto a native tradition of a cultural hero; the belief that this wise man had taught them how to plant manioc, which would only mature after a whole year instead of some months, confirms that Pay Zume was a personification of the civilizing hero of the mythology of the Tupis-Guaranis. (Haubert 1986: 56-57)

The Jesuit approach was predicated on the assumption that adoption of some elements of native culture was admissible in order to attract the Indians to the faith. The Fathers employed "a strategy of seduction," based on the idea that "similarity is to be embraced," a principle enunciated as early as 1549 by Manuel da Nóbrega in Brazil, and defended against its critics on the grounds that there was no harm in taking advantage of some native customs which were not against the faith, for example singing in native languages, or preaching in the indigenous fashion. Nóbrega never assumed the irremediably corrupt nature of the Indians or their insuperable demonic allegiance. His writings show that he believed that the Indians could be genuine Christians, and that the difficulties were more of a cultural than natural root. However, as time passed, he came to rely increasingly on subjection and fear to achieve his ends. (Chambouleyron 1999: 37-47)

The Jesuits were not the only order to attempt to present Christianity to the Tupi-Guarani in terms of their pre-existing religion, as is revealed by a dialogue between the French Capuchin Ivres D'Evreux and various Tupi-Guarani wise men (Pacamao, Tapuytapera, Tacupen and others of the Tupinambas) in Brazil in 1613. In one conversation, Pacamao asked the Capuchin who the dead person on the crucifix was; when told that he was the Son of God, he asked "Like Tupan? Is it possible for God to die?" The missionary said that God lives eternally, and it was only the body that died, so that God could conquer Jeropay,

a malignant god or being in Tupinamba beliefs. He added that Jeropay
had dominated humans for a long time and continued to do so among
the Tupinambas. Pacamao wanted to know why this was so, if God
was so powerful, why death and the god's blood were needed to
cleanse and liberate men, and how enough blood could flow from one
man to cleanse all humans. The Capuchin told him that he was still
very obtuse to understand these mysteries. The Indian answered,
perhaps without D'Evreux noticing the possible irony, "You and other
Fathers know great things, you are wiser than us." This exchange
shows not only that missionaries were prepared to use native concepts
like Jeropay, but also that attempts to convince the Indians by means
of dialogue and reason could raise as many problems as they solved.
(D'Evreux 1929: 337-40)

Like other ethnic groups conquered by the Spaniards, the Guarani
incorporated elements from the new religion into their own without
difficulty, whether they were sacred objects such as the cross, religious
personages like the great Noah (Noendusu), or Jesus Christ (Pa'i Tani)
or Christian concepts such as paradise. In all of these cases, though,
the "re-Guaranizing" of these elements is so strong that the Christian
significance is hardly noticed, while meaning is imputed to them by
the Guarani system; it is always the Guarani meaning that prevails.
(Melia 1996: 203-04) The only missionary theme that found an
immediate echo among Indians was the promise of eternal life after
death, which rapidly became assimilated to the (very different)
Guarani concept of the Land without Evil. The Land without Evil was
(and is) understood to be a land of abundance, prosperity, harmony,
and eternal youth, where maize grows by itself, where arrows hunt
animals without human agency, where nobody has to work, and where
there is no death. Crucially, this land was believed to be located on this
earth, usually somewhere to the west or to the east. The identification
with the Christian paradise after death came about without difficulty,
since the Spanish chroniclers understood the Land without Evil to be
an afterlife where souls went, while the Indians believed that they
recognized their own myth of the Land without Evil in the story of the
Christian Heaven. The fact that, unlike the native Land without Evil,
the Christian version was not to be sought on this earth may have been

the key to the extraordinary success of the Jesuits among the Guarani. The Jesuits replaced the native prophets in the same enterprise, and possessed the means to surpass them. They intended to liberate the Guarani from the encomienda, and they announced that the Land without Evil was accessible but after death. (Clastres 1975: 37, 63, 99)

Christian supernatural entities, such as the saints and the Virgin, were incorporated into Guarani religion, and at the same time, Christianity was Guaranized. A very good example is the image of the Immaculate Virgin of Caacupe, which had a role in evangelization from the very beginning, as patroness of both the Franciscan and Jesuit reductions, and which retains great significance today, as a shrine to which many Paraguayans make a pilgrimage on foot every year on the eighth of December, in order to honor "the mother of the people." The legend of the image contains elements that demonstrate continuities with native religious thought, and is therefore worth retelling. In the legend, a Guarani from Tobati-Tava, who is being pursued by the Mbayaes, a feared ethnic group of Chaco, takes refuge behind a tree and promises the Virgin to make an image of her if she saves him from danger. He survives and, in fulfillment of his promise, makes two images, one for the church of Tobati and another, smaller one for his own house. Some time later, the waters of an immense flood from the lake Ipacari (quelled only by the conjuring of Franciscan Luis Bolaños) carry a cedar wood box to the feet of a Guarani carpenter named José, from the Franciscan doctrina of Atyra, who finds inside, and intact, the household image of the Immaculate Virgin, which, with the permission of the missionaries, he takes to his own home. In search of good wood for construction, José discovers a place called Ka'aguy Kupe (behind the woods) and decides to move there with his family. He takes the image with him and builds a hermitage for it in the new place. After José's death, a relative takes his widow and child back to Tobati and places the small, household image next to the larger one in the church. After a century of silence, a descendant of José returns the small image to Ka'aguy Kupe, where an oratory is erected. From then on, the movements of the image, before finally arriving at Caacupe, are documented.

The legend is significant in several respects. First, it is the story of an image that migrates from one place to another, thus recalling the history of forced migrations of the inhabitants of Tobati, and serving as a paradigmatic history of the Guarani people in that period. In the present, this story resonates in the context of the forced migration of thousands of Paraguayan peasants to Argentina and Brazil. (Bremer 1998: 141-142) Therefore this is a Virgin who is very much of the Guarani.

Second, it is a story that manifests important continuities with ancient concepts of the sacred that derive from pre-Hispanic times. In the legend, the Virgin performs two miracles of protection - the first by means of a tree, and the second by means of a cedar box - that involve sacred materials. The tree, and in particular, wood from the cedar tree, have uncommon religious significance among the Guarani. Trees are attributed with the power to interfere in human life. In the creation myth of the Apapokuva Guarani, trees and wood played an important role in the process of creation. The creation of the world began, in the myth of the Twins, when Nyanderuvusu placed two crossed poles, made of cedar wood, which gave sustenance to the world. At the end of the myth, Tupa, god of storms, summoned by "Our Mother" Nyandesy, "embarks" on his *apyka*, or wooden seat (also made of cedar), and circumnavigates Nyandesy's house, and "disembarks" in front of it. The seat is in the form of a canoe in which Tupa navigates in the sky and attracts thunder from the west. Today, the apyka serves as the sacred seat of Guarani shamans, to whom it transmits the co-creative power to seat a new soul on the earth; it is here that they sit when they seek the name of a new born child, and ascertain his future role in the community (a moment which witnesses the very beginnings of the process of reciprocity, so central to Guarani social life). (Bremer 1998: 147)

In another important Guarani myth, that of the destruction of the world, cedar wood also played a crucial role. When the waters rose, forcing Guarypoty and his family to flee, Nyanderuvusu trod on a tree and made Iaboticaba appear, a fruit tree from which the family could eat. Not forgetting their obligation to others, they left one branch for those that would come after them; despite their hunger, they were faithful to the rules of reciprocity. But they failed to find this reciprocity in others, who refused to assist them in constructing a floating house; completing the task by themselves, they rose above the waters and reached the sky, saving themselves while those who had failed to help were drowned. In this myth, the fruit tree and the houseboat (recalling the tree and the cedar box of the legend of the Virgin) provide two opportunities to practice reciprocity. In another Guarani myth, the creator engendered the earth from his staff of indestructible wood. Today, the staff of the Mby'a Guarani shaman is the sign of power that Nyanderuvusu has given him to maintain and promote life and harmony in the community. Thus, traditionally, the tree and wood play a mediating role between Creator and created, and are an instrument for man to communicate with God. (Bremer 1998: 148)

Of all woods, cedar has the greatest sacred significance. It is the material from which were made the crossed poles, the wooden seat, the houseboat, and the shaman's staff. In the Chiripa version of the myth of the destruction of the world, a cedar tree emerges miraculously after the great flood, and from it all other plants and even animals are engendered. Thanks to the cedar, the earth becomes habitable again. Cedar was used to make canoes to bury the dead among the Guaranis of the east. Among the Mby'a, young children who die prematurely are buried in coffins of cedar. Thus, cedar has the power to produce new life from death, and to communicate with God. (Bremer 1998: 149) It is of great significance, then, that the ancient sacred power of the tree and of cedar wood is contained in the legend of the Virgin of Caacupe. Just as the tree is an intermediary in the realization of the law of reciprocity, the Immaculate Virgin is an intermediary between God and the people, and protector of those lacking protection. The fact that she was crafted from cedar wood signifies that she bears in herself the promise to be faithful to the practice of reciprocity.

Third, her legend blends the spiritual messages of Christianity and Guarani religion. Luis Bolaños translated the Virgin's name into

Guarani as Tupasy Maraney, or "Mother of God without Evil."
(Bremer 1998: 143) "Mother of God" was a concept unknown in
Guarani religious experience, but the ancient myth of the Twins
contains an important mother figure, Nyandesy, in search of whom the
two young men undertake a long, wandering journey, and at whose
house they finally arrive at the end of the story, thanks to the mutual
aid that they have given to each other on the trip. The arrival at her
house is identified with arrival at paradise, whose characteristics also
coincide with those of the Land Without Evil. Thus, there arose a close
relation between the Land without Evil, the Christian paradise, and the
Mother of God. Significantly, today, the Chiripa refer to paradise as a
Big House (Oga Vusu) where Nyandesy lives. The contemporary
journey on foot to the shrine at Caacupe is conceived as a journey
toward Tupasy, or Nyandesy, who are the same, and also a journey
toward the realization of the goal of total harmony. In the myth of the
Twins, the lessons that the two young men learn on their journey
enable them to discover how to live together in a community. In this
sense, arriving at Nyandesy's house is to arrive at understanding a
particular way of living in reciprocity. Similarly, to walk toward the
Land without Evil is to learn to practice reciprocity in all aspects of
human life and hence to reach the fullness of life in the community
intended by the creator. The Virgin of Caacupe becomes a model of
immaculateness that manifests itself as human fullness without any
room for imperfections. So, to walk toward Caacupe means to walk
toward the Mother of God without evil (Tupasy Marane'y), and to
seek, as the people of Nyandesy, a Paraguayan Land without Evil. As
a result of contact between Christianity and Guarani religion, the
Virgin has become accepted within the category of Land without Evil,
and the gospel has been understood as the new form of seeking and
recuperating the path toward that sublime destination. (Bremer 1998:
145-46)

According to Mby'a-Guarani myths, the cedar grows in paradise, and
hence is not only a sacred tree but is the true Tree of the Creator God.
The cedar is the agent of the permanent renovation of life, since its
roots are in the waters of life in the interior of the earth. Those who
inhabit paradise bathe in the water that falls from this tree in order to

renew themselves permanently. (Bremer 1998: 150) By analogy, the Immaculate Virgin is the cedar that sprinkles over the earth the drops of eternal water (the spirit of God) that emanate from her; and as from a mother to her children, from her flows the reciprocity which gives sustenance to communal fraternity.

19 The Taming of Jaguars

The acceptance of Christian elements reinterpreted according to the native religious worldview is found among South American frontier peoples other than the Guarani. The Mojos, also evangelized by the Jesuits, provide examples of phenomena comparable to those among the Guarani and the mission populations of northwest Mexico. Among the Mojos, initial contact between the Indians and Spaniards, in general, and missionaries in particular, was sought on native terms; and sustained evangelization depended upon native peoples allowing the continued presence of missionaries for motives that had little to do with acceptance of Christianity per se. The first sustained Jesuit contact with the Mojos in the 1640s (as opposed to the brief and rapidly abandoned contact of the 1590s and early seventeenth century) originated in the Indians' own desire for trade with the Spaniards in order to buy directly from them the tools for use in the fields, which they had hitherto secured indirectly through their neighbors, the Chirihuanas. (Borges 1992, 2:576; JL 1688) The principal motive for seeking commerce with the Spaniards was in order to gain an advantage in their war with the neighboring Caracuraes peoples. The arrival of some Mojos in Santa Cruz de la Sierra in search of tools in 1647 induced Jesuit Juan de Soto to accompany them on their return to their lands. A request for help against the Caracuraes led to a new expedition of eighty soldiers entering the region in 1668, accompanied by two Jesuits, José Bermudo and Juan de Soto again, who, once the Mojos' enemies were defeated, founded there the village of Santísima Trinidad. The mission became definitively established with the baptism in 1682 of some six hundred natives, and the foundation of the mission village of Nuestra Señora de Loreto, which became the chief settlement of the mission, and whose economic subsistence was guaranteed by the introduction of cattle raising. By the end of the century, the Jesuits had founded eight Mojos villages, with more than twenty thousand inhabitants. (Borges 1992, 2:576-77)

Just as the Jesuits were welcomed when it served native purposes, so too when circumstances changed, and the Fathers became perceived as more of a threat than an opportunity, they were rejected on native terms. Gradually the Indians became convinced that the purpose of gathering them together to receive instruction, and of forcing them to live in a smaller number of larger villages, was so that they could more easily be handed over to the Spaniards, and with the encouragement of their shamans, they began to withdraw from the doctrina. Gaining in confidence, the shamans told them that their deities had given instructions to kill the Fathers, in the same way that their ancestors had murdered a Franciscan many years before. If the Indians were finally dissuaded from this course of action by their lord, it was less out of respect for the Jesuits than fear of the consequences of such an act, namely retaliation by Spanish military forces (though the Jesuit account firmly insisted that the decisive factors were the apparition of a very beautiful woman who persuaded them not to harm the Fathers, and the vivid memory of the death of the ringleaders of the earlier murder, many of whom had perished in the clutches of a single jaguar when they were out hunting, which had been recognized by all as the manifestation of divine retribution). Prudence inclined the Mojos against violence. Expulsion of the Fathers was also rejected for fear of punishment for deception in making the missionaries come in vain at such great expense. Since they did not wish to be Christians, as the Jesuit account itself acknowledges, they decided to flee to the depopulated regions where they were sure that if the Fathers followed them, they would perish. Faced with such resistance, the Jesuits gave up and abandoned the mission. These events demonstrate that the Indians had little interest in Christian doctrines per se but wished to manipulate the missionaries for their own purposes. Acceptance of the mission was a strategy to placate the Spaniards and thereby gain access to their tools and support, but once the Mojos understood that the price was to be abandonment of their gods, and when it became convenient and possible to do so, they obliged the Jesuits to withdraw. (JL 1688 and 1696)

The return of Jesuit missionaries in 1674 and 1685 signified no newfound enthusiasm for Christianity on the part of the Mojos. The Fathers made little progress, despite using an interpreter, and were forced to spend two years learning the native language in order to communicate effectively, during which time they were unable to begin their task of spreading the gospel. The discovery that the house in which they were accommodated had been (or still was) the native temple led them to believe that they had supplanted the old gods and their ministers. But it seems more probable that the Indians purposefully placed the Fathers in the native place of worship either because the temple seemed the appropriate place to locate representatives of an alternative supernatural power, or in order to pit them in battle against their own deities (the effectiveness of this strategy seems to be confirmed by the fact that shortly after learning of the purpose of their house, one of the priests fell so ill from fever that he saw the "face of the Devil" appear to him within the walls of the dwelling). In either case, the natives assimilated the Jesuits into their own religious worldview. When shortly thereafter the river broke its banks and the house was swept away, forcing the Fathers to relocate, one wonders how surprised the Mojos were.

It is true that, by 1687, the Mojos had apparently abandoned their desire to kill or to drive away the Jesuits. One lord spoke with great regret about the murder of the Franciscan missionary, lamenting that, if only such a terrible deed had not been committed, their fathers would have been Christians and they themselves would have had their eyes opened and there would no longer be shamans to pervert them (it is worth noting that the shamans provided a convenient scapegoat for Indians to explain their departure from the true faith). However, the change of attitude toward the Fathers may more probably be attributed to the protection that their presence provided rather than to the inherent benefits of Christianity, which in any case had had insufficient time to become evident or to take root. As long as the Mojos had missionaries among them, they were freed from assaults by Spanish slavers from Santa Cruz and were defended against depredations by more powerful native adversaries. The missionary presence also provided dependable access to a wide variety of European manufactures, and regular deliveries of metal implements. In many ways the missionaries behaved like European traders, introducing numerous utilitarian and ceremonial goods to the savanna: musical instruments, medals, axes, knives, machetes etc. The activities of the Fathers were as much a material as a spiritual conquest, and European material culture was an integral part of the conversion process. (Block 1994: 124; Bitterli 1989)

As among the Guarani, the Jesuits provided defense against disease, even if most of the benefits were therapeutic and spiritual rather than strictly medical. The Fathers were not inhibited about mixing European and native cures; quinine was widely prescribed in the Mojos missions for the treatment of tropical fevers. (Block 1994: 120) As in northwest New Spain, the most appreciated characteristic of the Fathers was probably the close attention they paid to the sick rather than the effectiveness of their cures. Here too there was a strong link between the incidence of disease and the willingness to receive baptism. The mortality occasioned by the smallpox epidemic of 1702 allowed the Jesuits to baptize five hundred people. As elsewhere in the Americas, it was the supernatural and magical qualities of the missionaries, rather than strictly medical ones, which drew the disease-afflicted Indians to them. Once again, the Fathers allowed themselves to be interpreted as analogous to native shamans, and hence moved squarely onto native territory.

The importance of Christian magic in attracting the Mojos to the Fathers may also be observed in the use that they made of it, with the express approval of the missionaries, in order to fend off natural calamities. When the village of San Ignacio was afflicted by terrible plagues of maggots and locusts, the Indians made a procession for Christ, sprinkling holy water on their crops and placing crosses as guardians. Shortly afterwards, the plagues ended. (JL 1702) Invocations were made to figures of the Christian pantheon, especially the Virgin Mary, in order to provide good fortune. If an imminent downpour threatened the hunt, the Mojos would call on the assistance of the Virgin and often they were overjoyed to see the clouds departing to discharge themselves elsewhere. Some went to the church before going hunting in order to plead for the help of the holy image in finding something to take home to eat. (JL 1688) Once again the Christian God and his ministers risked being turned into a native deity and his shamans.

The phenomenon of promoting Catholicism on native terms was most noticeable with regard to the success that the Fathers claimed in Christianizing the sacred relationship between the Mojos and the jaguar. Traditionally, entry to the ranks of the most revered shamans was achieved by those who fell into the clutches of one of these felines and succeeded in escaping; these special individuals were considered to be chosen and protected by the gods, as if, the Fathers noted dryly, the animal's teeth possessed "a sacramental character" by which a minister could be selected and endowed with special powers over illness and universal knowledge of the names of all jaguars. Initiation involved long fasts, lasting one or two years during which abstinence from ají, fish and women was required; failure to comply would be punished by falling to one of these beasts. All those who killed a feline consulted these experts to learn the name of the slain animal in order to take it for themselves, and be known by this name instead of by their baptismal name. The slain jaguar was feted with great ceremonies, in which the victorious killer would undertake a long fast, cut a part of his own hair and remain for some days without returning to his home in a special place devoted to the making of chicha for the jaguar god. This deity would sit in a corner at night emptying the pot of chicha, out of sight of all ("although such shyness on his part should be put down to the lies of the shamans"). The Jesuits marveled, and encouraged their charges to marvel, that, whereas in pagan times the Indians had been constantly troubled by these ferocious beasts, since baptism, and under the protection of the holy cross which they now placed at the doors of their houses, the Mojos were no longer molested by these wild felines.

Not only was the presence of the jaguar marginalized, but, more significantly, its sacred significance was redefined. Following the Fathers' teaching that the danger of jaguars could be overcome by invocation of Christian supernatural entities, one Indian who saw a feline in the mountains invoked Jesus and the Virgin, and the animal disappeared in a flash of fire and smoke, "thus revealing who he was." (JL 1702) Only those who sinned by, for example, going hunting instead of attending mass, continued to fall into the clutches of these fearsome beasts, an event whose edifying lesson - that it was divine retribution - was drawn by the Indians "without the need of any interpreter." (JL 1688 and 1696) Perhaps. But the danger of allowing the Mojos to see the Jesuits as jaguar shamans was that they were likely to draw inferences consistent with the native belief system. A man who fell into the clutches of a jaguar might be a sign of divine displeasure, as the Fathers taught; but equally, according to traditional native beliefs, and validated by Jesuit recognition of the sacred bond with the jaguar, his fate was punishment for neglecting age-old reciprocal duties to the gods (native or Christian). Similarly, the willingness of Indians to come to confess before any absence from the village in order to ensure security on the journey from the frequent dangers of wild animals may illustrate Jesuit success in establishing the regular habit of confession, as they believed, or alternatively it may be a new form of the native custom of purifying oneself in order to secure protection from the gods' vengeance on a journey. (JL 1713) An important aspect of the process whereby Christian elements were accepted and interpreted according to native criteria was that both sides - natives and priests - could continue to believe that the other accepted its own religious worldview. By such means Christianity became indigenized almost without anybody noticing.

20 Comparison of Core and Frontier Regions

The frontier regions of Spanish America (northwest Mexico, eastern Paraguay, region of Santa Cruz de la Sierra in present-day Bolivia) have been differentiated here from the core regions (Central Mexico, Maya highlands and lowlands, Central Andes), not because one was more important than the other but because there was a distinction in the type of interaction between Christianity and native religion in the two areas. The core regions, especially Central Mexico, shared an earlier and more intense "Christianization" (baptism and instruction) and a higher degree of interpenetration of the two religions, in comparison with the frontier regions. Did this result in a more genuine "evangelization" (immersion in the meaning and values of the religion, and true understanding of what it means to be Christian)? On the one hand, the natives were well exposed to the new religion and came to regard themselves as Christians. On the other, their understanding of the post-conquest spiritual world owed much to a recognizably pre-Hispanic worldview. But, even in the core regions evangelization occurred within an essentially native framework. It was in these regions that Christianity made the greatest inroads, but also where the new hybrid religion emerged most clearly. This leads one to believe that Christianity succeeded where it could most effectively mould itself to native spiritual needs. Precisely those missionaries who allowed the most adaptation were those who achieved the greater integration of Christianity. Should this be judged a success - greater acceptance of Christianity - or a failure - greater adaptation?

The question is made harder to answer by the fact that whereas Christianization can be said to have a beginning and an end, evangelization is a process that has continued imperfectly up to the present day. Are the native peoples truly evangelized even today? Historians differ considerably in their evaluations. For example, in the Andes some see an intensive Christianization in the sixteenth century, and the formation of an integrated Andean Christian system (an effective evangelization) after 1660. (Marzal 1988; Wachtel 1977) One analyst concludes that the popular religion in present-day Bolivia is more or less a finished product, rather than representing an early stage in the conversion process and it is no less Christian for all the "pagan" elements that it so unequivocally contains; native Andean elements of Corpus Christi in highland Bolivia are indispensable to the feast's Christian character, rather than subversive of it. (Platt 1987) But others emphasize the survival of purely Andean beliefs and rites to this very day, and believe that one can at best speak of religions in coexistence. (Borges 1992; Saignes 1999)

There were significant differences within the core regions, notably between the Central Mexican and Andean experiences. Central Mexico was the region where the greatest interpenetration of religions occurred. This is related to two factors: first, it was here that the greatest contact occurred anywhere in colonial America between a sizeable Old World immigrant population and a much reduced but still relatively large indigenous population, with high rates of ethnic mixture and cultural blending, both within and outside the sphere of religion. Second, the Nahuas had more cultural common ground with the Europeans than any other indigenous group did, enabling them to "build their adjustments on their own traditions in almost every sphere and leading to a tightly interlocking system that tended to evolve as a unit." (Lockhart 1999b: 227) This is one of the best illustrations of the fact that the character of the interaction between Christianity and native religions owed most to the pre-existing indigenous culture and religion. Interpenetration of religions occurred in the Andes to a lesser degree than in Central Mexico, despite the former region having undergone an early and intense Christianization (though not as early or intense as in the Nahua region). Parts of the Andes maintained Christianity and native religion in "separate spheres," far less integrated than anywhere in Central Mexico after ca. 1550.

The Spanish American frontier regions, by contrast with the core regions, reveal more sporadic, less intense, and less thorough Christianization and, consequently, a more defective evangelization. However, there were disparities within the region: the Yaqui of North Mexico seem to have undergone a more complete evangelization than other inhabitants of the frontier regions, and even than many natives in the Yucatán or the Andes. The case of the Yaquis seems to be exceptional among natives evangelized by the Jesuits. Since the seventeenth century, the Yaquis have accepted and integrated into their own culture the central figures of Christian doctrine and ritual. As a result, present-day Yaqui religion is a combination of Catholic doctrine and liturgy with strong elements of pre-Hispanic beliefs and behavior. Whereas other Indians of the southwest, like the Pueblos, have kept Catholicism relatively separate from native practice, the Yaquis have fused native and Catholic traditions into a coherent whole that constitutes a distinctive religion. Yaqui religion is Catholic in that they believe that Jesus suffered on behalf of mankind and that grace from Heaven is vital. No supernatural entity deriving from the pantheon of the pre-Christian religion is worshipped in any church. But the Yaqui also believe that much of Jesus' suffering took place in the Yaqui country when he went about curing natives there, and that grace is symbolized by flowers which grew from blood that fell from the wound of Jesus on the Cross. Many Yaquis believe that their people have always been Catholic, since long before the coming of the Jesuits, or even Christ himself. Most see no inconsistencies in their expression of religion. (Spicer 1980: 59; Vecsey 1996: 76, 79-80)

Like the Yaqui, the Guarani also experienced profound evangelization. It is debatable whether these successes owed more, on the one hand, to the identity of their missionaries, the Jesuits, and their policy toward learning native language and accommodating native culture, or, on the other hand, to the characteristics of the pre-existing native culture and religion. The Jesuits lived in close intimacy with both the Guarani and the Yaqui, and the periods of greatest harmony between missionary and native occurred when there was lack of Spanish (and/or Portuguese, in the case of the Guarani) settlement either within or in close proximity to Indian territory (the Yaqui, between 1617 and 1740; the Guarani, from the 1650s through 1750). The indigenous concept of the Land Without Evil allowed Christian ideas to gain a unique purchase among the Guarani. This people also redefined themselves as a result of contact with the Jesuits, but not to the extent of eliminating their aboriginal past (as among the Yaqui); on the contrary, the missionaries seem to have been successful because they reinvigorated it. The case of the Guarani is also different because of the constant threat to the integrity of the Jesuit missions, especially in the first half of the seventeenth century, their violent end, and the forcible relocation of the Guarani after 1750.

Taking a broader view, frontier Spanish America shared with core Spanish America the creation of many native Catholicisms rather than just one. There may have been as many outcomes of the interaction of Christianity and native religions as there were different ethnic groups. Even today, each community, even each person, is on a continuum between the pole of simple initiation and the pole of authentic and conscious faith; the nearer one is to the former pole, the greater the pagan elements will be. But, for one historian, this represents neither a juxtaposition nor a mixture, but an "eclectic accumulation," a spectrum on which nobody can judge where one hew shades into another. Christianity was adopted by the mass of the Indian population, not superficially nor in appearance only, but rather substantially and authentically. Catholic doctrine and liturgy prevail, but within the cult of saints, for example, elements of the former religion - local shrines on the sites of former pre-Hispanic cults - are much in evidence. Rather than signs of corruption or degradation, these are creations at the popular level designed to create a fuller system of meaning. (Dussel 1974: 127-132) The adoption took place on native terms, since indigenous peoples judged that Christianity provided new answers to old spiritual questions.

PART TWO

French and British America

21 Peoples of the Northeast

The peoples of the northeast were the first natives of North America to come into contact with Europeans, from the 1520s, and in a sustained fashion from 1610. The major distinction among the native peoples of the northeast is that between the Indians of the Algonquian (or Algonkian) family of languages and the Indians of the Iroquoian family of languages. The Algonquians occupied a vast territory between the Atlantic and the Mississippi, north to the latitude of James Bay and south to that of Cape Hatteras. The northern part of the area, now the eastern half of Canada, was inhabited by the Algonquin (or Algonkin), Chippewa (or Ojibwa), Cree, Montagnais-Naskapi, and Ottawa peoples. Whereas the term Algonquian designates Indians belonging to the same family of languages, the term Algonquin refers to one particular tribe within that family (rather like the difference between the Germanic languages and the Germans).[1] The east coast region, extending from the St. Lawrence River to North Carolina, now US territory, was occupied by the Abenaki, Delaware, Maliseet (Malecite), Massachusett, Micmac, Mohegan, Nanticoke, Narragansett, Passamaquoddy, Pennacook, and Penobscot peoples. One of the first to come into contact with Europeans was the Micmacs who lived on the Gaspé Peninsula, in present New Brunswick east of the drainage basin of the St John River, and throughout Nova Scotia, including Cape Breton Island, as well as on Prince Edward Island.[2] Closely related to the Micmacs were the Maliseet-Passamaquoddy (or Etchemins) who lived in the area straddling what is now the border between Maine and New Brunswick, and who, like the Micmacs, belonged to the Abenaki family of Algonquians. The Abenaki were culturally divided into Western and Eastern groups. The Eastern Abenaki lived in Western Maine along the Kennebec, Androscoggin, and Saco Rivers. Members of the only enclave of Eastern Abenaki to survive within their traditional homeland are known as the Penobscot Indians. The Western Abenaki lived mostly in present-day New Hampshire, but also in Vermont and Quebec, between St Francis (Odanak) and the present border with the US. The Montagnais-Naskapi were Cree-speaking nomadic hunting peoples who inhabited a region ranging from the north shore of the St. Lawrence, from the Atlantic seaboard to the St Maurice River and extending north to James Bay and the Arctic Ocean. The Naskapi inhabited Labrador, whereas the Montagnais (given this name, which means mountaineers, by the French because of the nature of their homeland) occupied heavily forested inland regions around Quebec. The Algonquins were a tribe, made up of six major bands that in the early-seventeenth century lived north of the St. Lawrence, on the northern tributaries of the Ottawa River, west of present-day Montreal. They were situated between the Montagnais in the east and the Ojibwa in the west. Up-state New York was home to the Mohegans (confusingly renamed Mohican in popular writings), while further southeast, in the area of the Massachusetts Bay and Narragansett Bay, were to be found, amongst others, the natives after whom these two geographical features were named.[3] (Trigger 1978, 15: 109-17, 137-40, 156-60, 166, 168; Dickason 1984: 100-104, 109; Tooker 1979: 8)

The term Iroquoian embraces the broad linguistic grouping to which the peoples of the Hurons and Iroquois belonged, as well as the Cherokees, Eries, Neutrals, Petuns, Susquehannock and some other groups. The Iroquoian tribes lived in the area of Lakes Huron, Ontario and Erie, and in the north of present-day New York state. The Iroquoian linguistic grouping of tribes must be distinguished from the Iroquois, who were one (albeit the most important) of its constituent groups (themselves made up of five separate tribes). The tribes of the Iroquoian family can be distinguished from the Algonquians not only by a shared kinship of language, but also by their common sedentary trait, in which the chase supplied only a small part of their subsistence, and by their comparatively well-developed social and political structure, in which there were varying degrees of development from tribe to tribe. (Trigger 1968: 109) The Algonquians, by contrast, generally lived in societies that were less sedentary, in which the chase played a greater role, and in which socio-political development tended to be less complex. (Trigger 1985: xii; Moore 1982: 20; Kennedy 1950: 23-25; Rooy 1965: 157; Conkling 1974: 2; Smith 1988: 52; Bitterli 1989: 93)

The Iroquois, the best-known of all the native northeastern peoples, inhabited the Mohawk and Hudson Valleys, south and east of lakes Erie and Ontario, in present-day upper New York State, and held the waterways connecting the Hudson and Ohio rivers and the Great Lakes. They consisted of a confederacy of five separate tribes, hence the name 'Five Nations', as they were commonly called by the French, though their self-designation was 'The Long House' (a longhouse was a long bark lodge, which served as a place of residence for families, and the focus of social, political and religious life). Moving from east to west, the five tribes were the Mohawks, Oneidas, Onondagas, Cayugas, and Senecas.[4] The 'Long House' was unique since, unlike Algonquin or Ojibwa leagues that functioned solely in time of war, the Iroquois association remained continually in effect, and represented the achievement of permanent peace among its participants. Their settled association lent Iroquois attacks a force far out of proportion to their numbers.

The Iroquois had neighbors who were also members of the Iroquoian linguistic group. One of the most important was the Hurons (as the French called them) or the Quendat or Wendat (as they called themselves, meaning 'the one language', 'the one land apart' or 'the one island').[5] By the early-seventeenth century, the Huron heartland covered a relatively small but highly resource-rich and productive area, extending south and east from Georgian Bay on Lake Huron toward Lake Simcoe, in what is now Ontario (about three hundred and forty square miles).[6] Other Iroquoian peoples included the Petuns (Tionnontate or Khionontaternon), who lived to the southwest of the Hurons, and shared the same culture as their neighbors, even though they were not members of their confederacy; and the Neutrals, whose territory lay southeast of the Petuns, in the eastern Niagara Peninsula of Ontario and in the northern Niagara frontier of western New York.[7]

Man and the Manitous

Some early European observers, and some later historians, denied that the Indians of the northeast had any form of religion at all, or claimed that they had only superstition: "Our barbarians were indeed without religion - that is without regulated and ordinary worship of the divinity...therefore they had neither temples, nor Priests, nor feasts, nor prayers and public ceremonies...but relying only on superstitious means..." So wrote Jesuit missionary Joseph Bressani in 1653 about the Algonquins near Quebec. (JR 39:15) But as Thomas Hobbes said: "The fear of things invisible is the natural seed of that, which every one in himself calleth religion; and in them that worship, or fear that power otherwise than they do, superstition." (Hobbes 1946: 69) In short, one man's superstition is another man's religion. One prominent historian has concluded that, since superstition has no objective reality but is an aspersion used by one group to denigrate the religion of another, it is best dropped from the historian's descriptive vocabulary. (Axtell 1985: 13) Indian spiritual life was no less a religion for the fact that it did not seem familiar to Europeans. The Hurons, like other northeastern peoples, lacked specialists who performed regular religious ceremonies on behalf of the whole community, and did not construct special buildings, shrines or altars for religious purposes. This does not mean that religion was unimportant; it merely indicates that instead of having its own institutionally delimited sphere, as it had in European culture, religion was indissolubly a part of all the things the Hurons believed and did. Their religion and way of life were one and the same. (Trigger 1976: 75) The native groups of the northeast each possessed a religion in that they performed "a set of rituals, rationalized by myth, which mobilize[d] supernatural powers for the purpose of achieving or preventing transformations of state in man or nature." (Wallace 1966: 107; Axtell 1985: 13) Indian religions were capable of explaining, predicting, and controlling the world in emotionally and intellectually satisfying ways. Despite their linguistic and cultural differences, they shared enough beliefs and practices to allow generalization. At the same time, there were many variations on common themes, so it is often best to describe the beliefs and practices of a particular group in order to appreciate common types.

In the religious beliefs of the northeast, humans were not the only persons in the world, but rather they shared the universe with non-human, or other-than-human, persons, which included all plants, herbs and animals (bears and other animals were often spoken of as relatives) as well as some stones, clouds, natural phenomena and other entities which Westerners would call 'things', but which in the native view possessed both body and soul, and enjoyed life and power. In short, Indians of the northeast had a concept of animate beings that was far broader than that of Europeans. Other-than-human persons such as game animals, trees, or the wind possessed spiritual power that could be turned to human advantage or human destruction. These beings could willingly aid people - animals might give themselves as food, trees might allow themselves to be carved into masks that helped cure disease, winds might keep lakes calm to allow one to cross in a canoe - but in return they demanded respect. Furthermore, human persons participated in the world on an equal level with non-human persons, and were obliged to maintain a proper relationship with them. Humans fitted into the universal order; they did not rule over it. In order to survive and prosper, they had to ally themselves with the sources of spiritual power that pervaded their universe. (Richter 1992: 25)

One of the most important other-than-human persons was called *manitou* in Algonquian, and *orenda* in Iroquoian languages (henceforth designated manitou), which is to say entities that inhabited the local surroundings, personifications of the mysterious powers or forces operating in man's environment. "Spirit" is the normal translation, though it should be remembered that the manitou was not immaterial (material and immaterial were not native thought categories). The manitous were persons, living beings with souls, acting under the same motivations as humans, only with incomparably more power. They were essential prerequisites for the continuance of life, the fount of human existence, the ultimate sources of daily food, of hunting success, of medicinal powers and of human health. They took manifold physical forms. Among the Ojibwa, for example, the most powerful and important included the Four Winds (which controlled weather conditions), the Underwater Manitou (which controlled the waters), the Thunderbirds (which provided thunder), and the Owners of animals. (Mooney 1965: 217) Humans' existence depended on their ability to establish and maintain relations with the manitous, since these beings were responsible for most inexplicable

221

events; indeed, there were as many manitous as phenomena to explain. (Vecsey 1983: 4) Man's role was to conciliate them humbly, both by making offerings and by not giving unnecessary offence. It was very important to avoid offending the Owners of the animals lest living animals no longer permitted themselves to be caught. Thus, animal and fish bones were not burnt nor were they fed to the dogs. If humans neglected their reciprocal obligations and offended these beings, the result could be hunger, sickness, injury, or death. In human dealings with all beings that had access to spiritual power, the same principles of reciprocity characteristic of life in the village prevailed. The most common offering was tobacco, which was usually thrown on the fire or into rapids as a sacrifice to the manitou of the waters. Tobacco smoke was a gift that pleased spirit beings as reciprocation for their blessings. The substance induced a state of mind that opened one to supernatural forces, hence smoking, in appropriate ceremonial contexts, was a religious act. (Richter 1992: 24-25, 28) Before going to war, it was essential to appeal to the manitous to secure a promise of success, without which victory would surely elude the warrior. Individuals, chiefs, divines, bands, and tribes had their manitous, usually but not exclusively animals. Relationships with these entities were highly personal, and each person was expected to establish his own contacts. An individual entered into a relationship with a personal manitou through a rite of initiation. Among the Ojibwa, every child, male and female, fasted between the ages of nine and eleven in order to achieve visions of at least one personal manitou (and preferably several), which would reveal itself and promise lifelong support and protection. Acquisition of the personal manitou at puberty was the most important spiritual relationship for many native groups. Without it, a person was completely unanchored and at the mercy of events, natural and societal, in their most cruel forms. Success in the chase depended on the relationship with the manitou acquired by the hunter in his puberty dream-vision, and for that reason all young men underwent a vision quest (the ritual seeking of communication with the spirit world by a solitary individual) alone in the woods. Manitous were friendly benefactors, intercessors between the one undertaking the fast and the universe. (Radin 1972: 115; Vecsey 1983: 72-73, 136; White 1991: 9, 25; Bailey 1969: 134; Campeau 1967: 161-64)

Traditional initiation by means of a manitou occurred without consultation or guidance from human teachers. But it was native shamans (usually men) who communicated more frequently with the manitous by means of visions that required prolonged fasting and the avoidance of sexual intercourse for a period of time. (Vecsey 1983: 160) Not even the most powerful shamans ever practiced sexual continence for life, or even for long periods, and there was no equivalent of the European concept of religious celibacy. (Trigger 1976: 79) The primary roles of shamans were curing, divining, interpreting dreams, controlling the weather, and finding game. (Dickason 1984: 98) Burial of the dead and communication of myths were also important.[8] These services for the kin community were not rewarded financially, though outsiders might be charged for cures. The shaman worked for prestige, not pay. (Vecsey 1983: 162) The role was not a full-time occupation and there were no families of specialists; nor was it hereditary, as it called for special personal qualities, and could be attained only after a long apprenticeship. Above all, shamans owed their powers to the blessings and protection of the manitous. Unlike Christian priests, the native shaman had personal supernatural power that allowed him to manipulate the spiritual cosmology on his tribesmen's behalf. (Axtell 1985: 17) Since almost every Ojibwa was a visionary, the shaman had to demonstrate special gifts and charisma; he was a highly successful visionary in a community of visionaries.

Indian religions of the northeast did (and do) bear a family resemblance to one another, but there were (and still are) many unique Native American societies, each with a distinctive culture. The principal distinction, in religion as in economy, was (and is) between the hunters and the horticulturalists: the former are oriented toward animal ceremonialism, personal quests for power, shamanism and annual ceremonies of cosmic rejuvenation; the latter toward rain and fertility ceremonies, priestly ritual, medicine societies and calendrical rites. Whereas horticultural societies, in keeping with sedentary living patterns and the collective nature of agriculture, emphasize traditional bodies of religious knowledge and practice, collectivism and cooperation, hunting societies are strongly oriented toward individualism. The guardian-spirit complex, whereby individuals seek a personal link with the sacred to aid them in their personal lives, can at times attain the level of an almost individual religion. At the time of contact, there were several hundred separate worldviews with associated ritual systems and applications to everyday life. For example, the guardian-spirit complex that was important among northern Algonquian groups appears to have been absent on the coast. (Dennis 1993: 91) Within major geographic regions, cultures were broadly similar, yet each society offered a variation on a theme. Therefore the brief survey of the religious cultures of the Algonquians and Iroquoians outlined above is not intended to be a comprehensive description of the spiritual life of the northeast (still less of North America as a whole), but rather to furnish representative examples.

22 Black Robes of New France

Unlike in Central and South America, the Jesuits dominated missionary activity in French America from the beginning. Although for the first third of the seventeenth century, the Fathers struggled to gain a foothold, after 1632 (the return of Quebec to the French by the English), they obtained a virtual monopoly over evangelization in New France for a quarter of a century, and led a vigorous expansion in missionary activity, radiating in all directions from the axis of the St. Lawrence. After 1690, the impulse to expand subsided, and the missionaries concentrated on strengthening posts already established.

The Jesuits rapidly moved from a policy of living among Indian bands in the winter to encouraging them to join permanent mission settlements, on the model of the reductions in Paraguay. The establishment (in 1638, re-established in 1640) of the Jesuit residence of St. Joseph at Sillery, near Quebec, the first Indian reserve in Canada, was the most ambitious project to bring a sedentary life to the Montagnais and Algonquins. By 1642, there were about thirty-five to forty Indian families living at Sillery, though hunting and trading expeditions took them away for several months a year. A far greater number of Indians merely passed through each year to reaffirm their faith or to receive their first catechism. Another important mission center for the Montagnais was, from 1640, at Tadoussac, a favorite harbor and trading station for the French. (Grant 1984: 27; Moore 1982: 19; Ronda 1972: 391; Axtell 1985: 61; Campeau 1967: 465-67; Ronda 1988: 13; JR 17-18)

The Fathers' most important effort was the mission among the Hurons. By 1640, there were fourteen Jesuit priests, a figure that rose to nineteen by 1648. Unlike most other efforts, the Huron mission benefited from great continuity of personnel - nineteen of the twenty-four priests who came to Huronia (Huron country), beginning in 1634, either died there or remained until the end of the mission in 1650. Of these, ten were there for a decade or more. (Codignola 1994: 40; Trigger 1976: 666)

The Hurons admitted Jesuit priests, having rejected them earlier, because trade with the French had become central to their exchanges with neighboring Indians. In northeastern native culture, stable relations were promoted between tribes that wished to be trading partners by the exchange of a few people, both as a token of friendship and to assure each group that the other intended to behave properly. Very often, these hostages were children. Hurons whose sons or nephews were sent to the Jesuit seminary in Quebec boasted that they were relatives of the French and for this reason hoped for preferential treatment when they went to trade on the St. Lawrence. They were not disappointed. Huron converts were sold European goods at lower prices and were allowed to buy guns. Thus, there was a close correlation between conversion and direct involvement in the fur trade. (Salisbury 1992: 504-05; Ronda 1988: 15; Bowden 1981: 88; Conkling 1974: 11-12; Salisbury 1982: 73; Trigger 1968: 114-15, 120; Trigger 1985: 201, 227;Grant 1984: 55) Hurons consented to be baptized more as a trading strategy than out of interest in Christian teachings. Jesuit Pierre Biard had already noted that the converts among the Acadian Micmac "accepted baptism as a sort of sacred pledge of friendship and alliance with the French" but had no notion of its deeper theological meaning. One group understood the term "baptized" but not "Christian." For the Hurons, as for the Micmacs, it was the political meaning that was important. Many converted because they had friends or relatives who had done so. Even those who appreciated that there was more to Christianity than trading perks or family solidarity seem to have understood the cult to be only one more ritual society, akin to their own curing societies, in which membership could simply be added to that of others. In short, most Hurons became Christians in order to obtain guns and better trading relations, or to join dead relatives in Heaven. As yet, the Hurons saw no reason to change their way of life; the missionaries (as opposed to the traders) provided nothing that the Hurons wanted and yet criticized their behaviour and challenged their most cherished beliefs. The Jesuits were aware that their acceptance by the Indians was principally a demonstration of native interest in trade, and they expressed no disapproval of this motive. (Trigger 1976: 496, 707; Trigger 1968: 125)

226

The fact that the Jesuits were tolerated rather than enthusiastically embraced is demonstrated by the paucity of converts before 1640. Prior to that year, only those on the point of death allowed themselves to be baptized, but thereafter increasing numbers of people who were in good health began to convert. Between 1640 and 1643, the Jesuits baptized approximately one hundred Hurons each year, and subsequently the number increased to about one hundred and fifty annually. Taking account of those who died, by 1646 some five hundred Hurons were professing Christians. These conversions were also more permanent. Whereas few of the more than one thousand Hurons baptized in 1639 still professed to be Christians by the spring of 1640, of the one hundred Hurons baptized between 1640 and 1641, about sixty survived illnesses and misfortunes to become professing Christians. (Trigger 1976: 702; Trigger 1968: 133; Trigger 1985: 255)

The improved conversion rates after 1640 can be attributed to two factors: the growth in the Iroquois threat and the decimation of the Huron population as a result of the epidemics of the 1630s. The relationship between Indians and French was to be transformed in the period after the restoration of Quebec by the spread of disease. It is almost certain that population collapse did not begin in the northeast until the second decade of the seventeenth century (and not in the sixteenth century, as one historian suggests), but even if epidemics were delayed for several decades in the northeast, compared with Central Mexico, their effects were similar. Overall mortality from the 1616-19 and 1633-39 epidemics was no less than eighty-six percent of the Indian population of the areas affected, and in some localities much higher, reaching ninety-five percent or more for this twenty-three year period alone. The pre-epidemic population of the Hurons has been variously estimated (ranging from twenty to thirty-five thousand in the early 1600s), but whatever the original number, by 1640 their numbers had been reduced to between seven and nine thousand, a loss of thirty-five to sixty-seven percent, depending upon the original figures chosen. Disease affected virtually all Jesuits and Hurons, yet while the Europeans recovered quickly, it was lethal to many of the natives. (Cook 1998: 165; Snow 1988: 23, 24, 28; Trigger 1976: 499, 500, 526)

The series of epidemics of unusually severe proportions that the Hurons suffered between 1634 and 1640 contributed to the success of the Jesuit conversion effort but also seriously undermined native social cohesion. (Trigger 1965: 40; Cook 1998: 194) Sudden, profound population losses resulted in the vacating of traditional tribal leadership roles held by older men and women. In the face of this leadership vacuum, there was no legitimate means whereby younger Hurons might acceptably gain power within the tribes. Political factions developed and there were splits between Christians and non-Christians, and between those who wished to sever all links with the French and those who wished to retain them. (Trigger 1985: 255) Converts were required to destroy their charms and forbidden to use dreams as guides to their actions. They resisted participating in curing ceremonies, and making gifts or performing actions necessary for the efficacy of shamanistic healing rites. Because they could no longer consult with shamans, Christians were deprived of an important means for resolving personal frustrations within the context of a highly conformist society. Converts were not allowed to participate in public feasts and celebrations which meant that they ceased to be an integral part of their community's network of economic reciprocity and redistribution. They were also forbidden to contract ritual friendships with non-Christians. (Trigger 1985: 257; Trigger 1965: 44) Chiefs who converted initially had to give up their public offices, since they would have been obliged to preside over traditional rituals. Later, much to the Jesuits' satisfaction, an agreement was reached whereby Christian chiefs continued to manage public affairs, but transferred their pagan religious functions to a subordinate deputy. Occasionally pagan chiefs would tell Christians not to attend a feast that involved pagan rites. (Trigger 1965: 45) By the early 1640s, many Hurons refused to be buried alongside pagan members of the tribe, which was seen as a rejection of community solidarity. The converts insisted that if others wished to retain the corporate identity, they could accept baptism and be united with regenerated Indians in Christian burial. (Bowden 1981: 90) Most serious of all, Christian warriors refused to take part in pagan divinations associated with war or to fight alongside traditionalists in war parties against the Iroquois. As a result, the effectiveness of Huron resistance to the Iroquois was weakened, and division grew in the face of the impending Iroquois threat. (Trigger 1985: 256) All in all, Christians became an increasingly isolated minority within their communities, and an unprecedented segregation came to pervade Huron society.

The impact of the epidemics, the availability of guns, and the need to find new sources of furs for the trade all contributed to increasing aggression on the part of the Iroquois, who now aimed to unite all other related groups into one nation, within the territory of the Iroquois Confederacy, to replace the people they had lost through epidemic diseases, to acquire the fur-bearing regions of the Canadian Shield, and to curtail French encroachment on their territory along the St. Lawrence River west of Trois-Rivières. (Parkman 1997: xiii) This involved destruction of the Hurons, the Neutrals, and the Eries as sovereign political entities. In 1649, the Jesuit mission among the Hurons ended when a party of Senecas and Mohawks attacked and destroyed the Huron villages of Saint Ignace and Saint Louis and forced the inhabitants to abandon Huronia. (Grant 1984: 28)[1] Even with the great population losses that they suffered (in the 1640s the Mohawk population fell by at least sixty percent), by the early 1650s the Iroquois had practically destroyed the Montagnais between Quebec and the Saguenay, the Algonquins of the Ottawa, and the Hurons, Petuns and Neutrals. By 1665, the Iroquois reigned supreme over their neighbours. They had subjugated adjacent regions from the Connecticut River to Lake Michigan, and from Ottawa to the Carolinas. They now represented the next missionary challenge.

Only when the Iroquois felt threatened by attacks on either side from the Eries and the Susquehannocks, and feared that while thus engaged their northern victims might revive for combined vengeance, did they send overtures for peace to Quebec in 1653 and invite missionaries. The fact that both now and later in the century Iroquois requests for French missionaries came during peace negotiations demonstrates that, like the Hurons, these Indians regarded the Jesuits among them as hostages, to cement the peace. Furthermore, their motivation in inviting missionaries in 1655 was to encourage adopted Huron Christians to remain among them, and to lure to Iroquoia the Catholic

Huron refugees living near Quebec at Lorette. (Richter 1985: 3) Once many surviving Hurons left French protection at Lorette for new homes in Onondaga and Mohawk country, many Iroquois decided that the services of priests were no longer required. (Richter 1992: 108) The political context was entirely different from that which prevailed among the Hurons. The French acquired neither the economic control nor the military ascendancy that was necessary to achieve the Jesuits' goals. The Iroquois traded with the Dutch and later the English, so it was impossible for the Jesuits to use a system of rewards and punishments to encourage conversion, as they had done with the Hurons. (Trigger 1985: 291) The Jesuit presence among the Iroquois depended upon peace with the French, and when hostilities broke out again in 1658 the priests were forced to leave. (Moore 1982: 33)

More sustained efforts took off after the peace agreements of 1665-1667 allowed the dispatch of French missionaries to each of the Five Nations. (Richter 1985: 2) The Iroquois were now sufficiently weakened by the French, and decimated by the smallpox epidemic of the 1660s that the Jesuits could once more enter their regions to do missionary work. (Cook 1998: 195) By 1668, all five Iroquois tribes had received missions, and these lasted for nearly twenty years. But most Iroquois felt under no pressure to convert, and for a long time Jesuit teachings made little headway. Even those who proved to be the most successful converts, such as the headman Garakontié, only asked for baptism in the late 1660s, after more than a decade of close relationships with French priests. (Richter 1992: 115) Most Iroquois came to view the Jesuits as a pro-Five Nation faction among the French, and so the pro-French factions that existed within the five tribes valued the Fathers' presence. The Iroquois treated the Fathers respectfully when they wished to be on good terms with the French, but when relations deteriorated they developed an aversion to the priests and their teachings, which frequently led to overt hostility. (Trigger 1985: 291) Once the enemy Susquehannocks were defeated in 1675, relations between the Iroquois and the French became strained, and war broke out after 1680. The missions were recalled, and the last was abandoned in 1686.

During the Jesuit presence, many Iroquois villages became deeply divided into two factions that often cut across kinship lines (lineages and clans) and severely disrupted village politics. Members of a minority faction were traditionally expected to yield rather than disrupt village peace and consensus, but Christian converts did not do so. Instead, tenacious in clinging to their position, they boycotted or disrupted the village and confederacy rituals that bound together the Iroquois of different clans and nations. (Richter 1992: 117-118) During the 1670s, some converts were stripped of their chiefly titles; others were abused or assaulted. While traditionalist ranks solidified, the Christian forces shrank through departures for mission villages in the St. Lawrence Valley. Migration grew to a flood after 1673 when the Jesuits altered their missionary tactics and encouraged Christian factionalists to depart; eager to go were disaffected adoptees. Hundreds of Francophiles among the Iroquois, many of who were the most dedicated Iroquois Catholics, departed for the mission villages in Canada. (Richter 1988: 54) By 1684, only a handful of Iroquois Catholics remained and most of the priests, feeling their lives to be in danger, abandoned their posts in Iroquois villages. Migrations to the mission communities did not end political struggles in Iroquoia, since many of the Jesuits' supporters, both adoptees and natives, remained. For them, kinship ties with factional opponents, economic considerations, and commitment to traditional ways of life outweighed devotion to Christianity. The effect of migrations was neither neatly to divorce one community from another nor ultimately to heal factional wounds, and deep divisions remained within Iroquois villages. (Richter 1992: 128)

From the early 1660s, the Jesuits pushed past the Iroquois to Lake Huron and the Lake Michigan region. Here the Ottawas and Ojibwas were to be the focus of Jesuit attention, mainly because after 1649 these peoples replaced the Hurons as the pivot of the French fur industry at Sault Sainte Marie, a settlement where Lake Superior joins Lake Huron, and where there was a Jesuit presence from 1641. Those who after 1670 were to become the Ojibwas possibly numbered thirty-five thousand at this time. Their settlement pattern was of numerous, widely scattered, small autonomous bands; the term tribe is applicable in terms of a common language and culture, but not in the political sense that an overall authority or unity was present. (Trigger 1978, 15:743) As a result of contact with the French, the various communities reduced their isolation from one another, amalgamated with other groups, established villages near Sault Sainte Marie, intermarried with greater frequency, and even absorbed French traders into their families. Although the early fur trade modified the aboriginal community framework, it did not radically alter it, and even the missionaries did not significantly upset the indigenous organization. (Vecsey 1990: 12, 19, 20) Father René Ménard, who died on mission work in the region in 1661, was followed by the so-called "apostle" of the western tribes, Father Claude Allouez, who spent the years 1665-89 working among the Indians of the west. (Moore 1982: 33) It was through his efforts that the Petuns, Ottawas, Potawatomies, Ojibwas, Miamis, Sioux, Cree, Illinois, and other ethnic groups, including some Hurons who had fled west, were reached.

As a result of these efforts, many hundreds of peoples in the Lakes region were baptized. The Jesuit Relation for 1669-70 recorded that, in the previous two years, three hundred Indians had been baptized at the Sault Sainte Marie. But, as elsewhere, it is debatable to what extent these baptisms signified a genuine religious change, since they were motivated by the desire to cement an alliance with the French king and with the fur traders who brought wealth. Any religious change brought about was superficial, if not accidental. It is significant that Father Allouez effected the baptism of the Ottawas, and probably Ojibwas, at Chequamegon by threatening to leave them; the Indians knew that the fur traders would leave with him. (JR 52:205-07) Such baptisms probably had no lasting effect on the religion of the whole of the Indian communities. Observers around Lake Superior in the early nineteenth century could find no solid trace of Christian beliefs or practices among the Ojibwas. If the seventeenth-century Indians had converted, they had not passed down their faith to their descendants. (Vecsey 1990: 49, 52, 53)

The Jesuits also returned to work among the Indians of the north. The Micmacs had been among the earliest of the peoples of the northeast to

232

come into contact with Europeans, yet they managed the best of all the coastal peoples in accommodating to Europeans. They maintained themselves in their ancestral lands as middlemen in trade and later as guerrillas in colonial rivalries. It is true that they suffered severe population losses in the early-seventeenth century. From a pre-contact population of possibly six thousand, they declined to less than two thousand according to Biard's estimate in 1612, though he revised this figure four years later to between three thousand and three thousand five hundred. But a century and a half later, the number was almost the same, with no further decline. The Micmacs embraced Christianity with an enthusiasm that pleased the missionaries. In 1673, the Jesuits established their Acadian mission headquarters at Port Royal, and by 1700 claimed that all the Acadian Indians were Christians.

Headway was also made among the Abenaki. Europeans came into contact with the eastern Abenaki in 1602, and with the western Abenaki in 1642 (the latter's interior location prevented encounters with the earliest explorers). After the 1617 epidemic, speakers of eastern Abenaki coalesced around the Kennebec and Penobscot drainages. (Dickason 1984: 105) In 1646, Father Gabriel Druillettes was sent to the Kennebec, at the invitation of converted Abenakis who had been at Sillery, and over a period of eleven years he was very successful in gaining converts. (Morrison 1984: 80) Thereafter the Jesuits concentrated upon trying to draw Abenaki converts to Sillery. Despite the grant of the seigneury of Sillery to the Indian inhabitants themselves in 1651, the settlement proved a failure at establishing a permanent population of agriculturalists. By 1663, few Indians remained and most of the site had been granted to French families; in or around 1670, the inhabitants were wiped out by smallpox. (Cook 1973b: 500) The Fathers abandoned the site in 1685, and relocated the mission to St. Francis de Sales, at the falls of the Chaudière, further away from Quebec, which soon became almost exclusively an Abenaki mission. During the second half of the seventeenth century, all the inhabitants of the country from the Merrimack river (in southeast New Hampshire) to Lake Champlain (in northwest Vermont), that is, the western Abenaki, began to drift up to Canada, settling in Montreal, Trois Rivières and at St. Francis. Some eastern

Abenakis from the Chaudière mission also settled at St. Francis. (Dickason 1984: 107)

Jesuit missionaries followed Druillettes to the Abenaki territories in the 1660s. Father Jacques Bigot went to Penobscot in 1667, and his brother Vincent replaced him shortly after and evangelized the Penobscots and Kennebecs. In the 1680s, Sebastian Rasle undertook missions to the Kennebecs. (Moore 1982: 35) In 1694, Bigot established a permanent mission at Penobscot, and Rasle founded the Nantansouock (Norridgewock) mission on the Kennebec River. As hostilities developed with the English colonists and increased with the Iroquois, the Abenaki joined French expeditions, in alliance with their former enemies, the Micmac, to fight against the Five Nations and to lay waste New England's northern frontier. Jesuit activity was severely affected by the Treaty of Utrecht (1713), which stripped New France of Newfoundland, Acadia and Hudson Bay. (Kennedy 1950: 51) At Nantansouock, now deep in English territory, Rasle struggled against English Protestant divines for the souls of the Abenakis. So vast was his influence among the Abenakis in their relationship with the English that Massachusetts sent an expedition to wipe out the French presence, killing Rasle and destroying the mission and its chapels in 1724. Chief Bombazine, an Abenaki warrior, was killed defending the priest. (Lapomarda 1990: 98-99) Thus ended the last permanent French mission in New England and the majority of the Kennebecs migrated to the mission at St. Francis de Sales. (Kennedy 1950: 52; JR 15) In the end, the Abenaki were reduced to a fraction of their pre-contact population and lost their ancestral lands.

Unlike Francis Xavier in India and the Far East, or the missionaries in Spanish America, the French Jesuits deliberately adopted no policy of mass baptisms. As one historian has noted, "contrary to Protestant mythology, the Jesuits were as hard-nosed about admission to baptism as the staunchest Puritan." (Axtell 1988: 113) Father Paul Le Jeune was explicit regarding the reasons: "We dare not yet trust baptism to any except those whom we see in danger of death, or to children who are assured to us; for, not yet being able to fully instruct these barbarians, they would soon show a contempt for our holy mysteries, if they had only a slight knowledge of them." (Axtell 1985: 277; Bailey 1969: 126; JR 7:275) In 1616, Pierre Biard recorded his refusal to baptize too soon, and his conviction that the sacrament was to be given cautiously, only after candidates had passed through the requisite preparatory stages; above all, Indians should not be baptized while still ignorant of what the sacrament entailed. (O'Neill 1989: 131) He pointed to the example of Mexico and Peru, where the natives were baptized very readily, the result being that "these who were too soon baptized willingly came to Church but it was to mutter there their ancient idolatries"; and he lamented "O how those who have come since, have been obliged to toil there where these tares might quickly and easily have been eradicated at first, if the field had been well ploughed before sowing it. I mean by observing the ancient practice of the Church in giving Baptism cautiously, first having Postulants and Seekers, then Catechumens, and at last Baptism." He made an approving reference to the Spaniard José de Acosta who had "very properly observed this fault." (JR 3:143-45)

Nor was this noble sentiment merely theoretical. In Canada, the first adult Huron was admitted to the rite after only three years of careful catechism and testing. There were only two instances in which baptism was administered more liberally: in epidemics, when those at death's door were sprinkled without extensive instruction, in order to ensure their salvation; and in battle or under attack when priests and/or Indians were about to be killed. Otherwise, as the Jesuit Relations make clear, the Fathers resisted French pressure for conversions en masse, and were highly selective in baptizing able-bodied adults and healthy children whose parents were not proven Christians. (Richter 1985: 8) Candidates for the sacrament were obliged to undergo a probationary period of instruction that normally lasted for one or two years before being carefully tested prior to baptism at a major Christian festival. (Trigger 1985: 254) Only those candidates who demonstrated their ability to lead a Christian life and who proved that they were unlikely to revert to their former ways were to be baptized. (O'Neill 1989: 132; Trigger 1965: 42) The Fathers could have baptized the whole country if they had wanted to, yet they claimed to have administered the sacrament to around sixteen thousand natives between 1632 and 1672, some twelve thousand in Huronia alone (at least a third of these baptisms were of infants, children and adults who soon expired). (Axtell 1985: 122)

This approach derived from the Jesuit view that the Hurons had a complex religion that had to be counteracted, discredited, or destroyed in order to effect a genuine conversion. It was also necessary to make the Indians wish to be baptized, even if initially their motives were not spiritually acceptable. Indeed, the potential converts' strong desire to receive the sacrament could be used in order to compel them to submit to a long period of instruction and demonstrate their ability to live as Christians. (Trigger 1985: 254) Jean de Brébeuf recounted how it was customary to restrict baptisms to cause the sacrament to be more highly respected, and how individuals could be constantly denied baptism in order the more to stimulate their desire. The Jesuits' knowledge of the true faith and their virtual monopoly over conversions meant great power. In controlling the sacrament, they assumed a powerful influence over Indian lives and used this power to force changes in native cultures. (O'Neill 1989 135-36)

23 "All Things to All Men"

The Jesuits did not share the view of most other Frenchmen that conversion entailed "civilization," that is to say, the native adoption of French culture. (Moore 1982: 138; Healy 1958: 151-52) During the early part of the seventeenth century, it is true, the Jesuits experimented in fostering cultural contact between the Indians and the French, but they rapidly became convinced that almost any interaction with the immoral and corrupting European settlers could only be harmful to the Indians, and by mid-century they expressed virtually total opposition to the spread of French civilization among converts. (Moore 1982: 187, 190) From the 1640s, the establishment of new mission sites at arm's length from French urban centers was accelerated. The disappointing results of the mission at Sillery were attributed to the attempt to settle Indians next to Europeans, providing further indication that segregation was the best policy. Guided by the successful precedent of the mission among the Guarani of Paraguay, which respected the integrity of local cultural traits such as kinship relations and social values, the Jesuits of New France aimed to eliminate, or replace, only those customs that did not accord with Christian teachings and morality. (Trigger 1976: 468) In this respect, the Fathers followed a long and respectable tradition within the church, beginning with St. Paul, who sought to incorporate into Christianity whatever in a given culture did not directly contradict it. This approach assumed that Christianity was compatible with many, perhaps most, aspects of traditional native culture, which should be left largely intact and become the context for a new expression of Christianity. (Moore 1982: xi) In this way, Indian identity would be preserved, converts would absorb the faith at their own pace, and an indigenized Christianity belonging exclusively to the native inhabitants would emerge. (Bowden 1981: 85; Pomedli 1987: 281)

Rather than condemning native cultures outright, the Jesuits preferred to observe them closely to determine how they could use indigenous ideas and customs in fostering new Christian expressions, and how they could build on common denominators in order gradually to reshape native ways toward closer approximations of a Christian norm. Thus, they did not insist that conversion to Christianity should represent a clean break with the past, and were not unduly troubled by carry-overs from the pagan religion. Although (ostensibly) they would not compromise on Christian principles, they accepted that some element of accommodation would apply not only to the Indians but also to themselves. When Father Jerome Lalemant exclaimed in 1642 that it was required of the Jesuit to become a "barbarian" with the Indians if he were to win their souls, he reflected Christ's admonition to "be all things to all men in order to win all," and expressed the willingness of the Fathers to adapt themselves and their message to the native cultural environment, and to seek out ideas familiar to the new converts that could be used as starting points for the explanation of Christianity. (Axtell 1985: 77; Axtell 1975: 278; Moore 1982: xi, 39, 42, 72, 75; Grant 1984: 44; Bowden 1981: 83, 84)

Methods of instruction were adapted to native culture. Chants in the native tongue were tolerated as part of Christian ceremony. Since native pictographs, unlike the spoken word, showed great uniformity across ethnic boundaries, the missionaries chose to communicate the new religion (sometimes themselves adding new symbols) through this medium, which seemed especially appropriate, as it had formerly been used to record shamanistic songs and rites. (Moore 1982: 132, 135)

As elsewhere in the Americas, the acceptance of native culture included the use of native languages as a vehicle for evangelization. (Hanzeli 1969: 45) Brébeuf produced a Huron translation of the Christian Doctrine. (Axtell 1985: 106) Rather than teach the meaning of French words, the Fathers opted to coin words approximating to the native language, a strategy preferred by the Hurons and Iroquois. With the exception of a few proper names, such as Jesus and Mary, all of the Christian concepts used by the missionaries were translated into a native word or phrase. According to a Jesuit dictionary written in the last quarter of the seventeenth century (Shea 1860), the word for Christian meant "He has caused me to be good," the word for Virgin signified "she does not know a spouse," and the closest approximation for "sin" was "mistaking one matter for another." In works produced by other missionaries, the Hurons referred to the soul as "our medicine" and a rosary as "Mary's necklace" (with connotations of a collar of wampum). (Axtell 1985: 108) Father Le Jeune coined words (although we are not told what they were) in order to translate into the Montagnais tongue the story of the Creation, the Pater Noster, the Ave Maria, the Creed, the mysteries of the Holy Trinity, and the Incarnation. (JR 5:117, 187; 11:149-67) The preference for native self-expression threw up problems of translation. The obligatory use of person markers ("my," "your," "her" etc.) in Huron made impossible a literal translation of the expression "Father, Son and Holy Ghost." The Jesuits suggested that the phrase might be translated "our Father, his Son, and their Holy Ghost" (JR 10:119) but the implementation of this proposal required approval from ecclesiastical officials in Europe. Huron linguistic etiquette also had to be learned and respected. This included not referring to God as "Father" in the presence of a Huron whose own father was dead, since this would be a serious affront. (JR 10:121; Trigger 1976: 511-12)

Dreams were tacitly acknowledged as valid grounds for accepting Christianity when, for example, Hurons saw Heaven or Hell in their sleep. Sometimes the Jesuits even took the lead in adapting traditional practices to Christian ends, for example when they claimed that in dreams they had seen all the Indians converted, in order to counteract shamans who had dreamed the opposite. (Axtell 1985: 111; JR 11:203) During a hunting expedition, Le Jeune was told by his host that he had dreamed that they would find no food and that the Father would be abandoned in the midst of the woods. Fearing that they would leave him just to prove that the man was a prophet, he decided to counter this dream with one of his own. He said that he had dreamed the opposite, seeing in his sleep two moose, one already killed and the other still living, and so which dream would be found to be true? Despite his admonition that dreams were lies and that no dependence should be placed on them, the Father revealed his willingness to adapt to native views on their importance. (JR 7:169) On another occasion, one of the Fathers expressed pleasure that in one village the inhabitants had erected a large cross in the middle of an open space, since a local prophet had dreamed that this should be done in order to protect the villagers and defend them against their enemies, who would never be able to conquer them as long as it stood there. (JR 53:161) Another Father expressed no qualms when an Indian who had refused his attentions changed his mind after in dreams he saw the Father offering him medicine beneficial to his health; the Jesuit gave him baptism instead, but failed to condemn the dream. (JR 55:81-83)

The Jesuits also adapted new Christian forms to old functions. Crucifixes, medals, rings, rosaries and relics, especially those of saints and Jesuit martyrs, replaced traditional stone amulets. (Axtell 1985: 112) The use of the rosary became particularly popular among Indians, probably because it resembled wampum (cylindrical beads fashioned from the central column of whelk shells, for the white variety, and from the violet area of quahog shells for the black variety), whose characteristics it acquired (for example, as a symbolic gift) and could be used as a kind of mnemonic device. It was often worn by a neophyte not only as a symbol of his own devotion to God and love for the Virgin, but also as a symbol of the pledge of God's love and protection to him. (Moore 1982: 136-37) The cross was another symbol that was assimilated to ancient forms with missionary approval. When a native sorcerer, Sondacouane, broadcast that demons were responsible for the disease that afflicted the Indians and that the remedy was to hang masks and figures of men, like scarecrows, in the doorways of houses, the Jesuits responded by instructing the Indians to use the cross in order to ward off the demons and the contagion, effectively presenting the Christian symbol as the equivalent of native supernatural protectors against disease. (JR 13:227-33)

The policy of adaptation meant that the Jesuits allowed traditional native rites to continue, but ostensibly with a Christian content. The Fathers were present on many occasions when tobacco was ceremoniously offered to God by being thrown into the fire, a rite that was tolerated as part of Indian social life. (Moore 1982: 96) Yet they were aware that this was a Christian form of an old native practice. They knew that the Ondatauauat (an Algonquian people), for example, threw tobacco in the fire as an offering to "He who created the sky,"

240

whom they believed to be different from the one who created the earth. (JR 33:227) Most likely the Christian God had been assimilated to this native supernatural being, but in such a way that his act of creation was perceived in native terms. In 1673, Father Louis André persuaded Indians among the Menomini, in the region to the west of Lake Michigan, to replace an image of the sun - to which they made offerings to improve the catch of fish in their nets - with an image of Jesus crucified. Despite the substitution of the image, the context remained the same; the native offering was made for the same purpose, according to the same rite. (Moore 1982: 146)

Burial customs that maintained the placing of symbolic possessions - such as a comb, a tomahawk, or a wampum collar - in the grave for use in the afterlife were also tolerated. In 1635, the Huron Feast of the Dead (a ceremony performed every eight to twelve years, whereby the bones of the dead were transferred from village burial sites to a central burial ground) was effectively sanctioned by Jean de Brébeuf when he allowed the bodies of about twenty Christians to be brought to the new burial site, and oversaw the recitation of the *De profundis*, a Christian hymn for the dead. His justification was his hope that the feast would cease or would be replaced by a proper Christian ceremony. Although he insisted that the bodies were interred in a separate pit on consecrated ground, his mere presence at the rite and his acquiescence in the removal of Christians conferred authority on the ceremony, and certainly was far from condemnation. (Moore 1982: 154-55; JR 10:301-07)

Traditional native feasts might be Christianized by omitting sacrifices and by using the customary welcome speech to ask God for health. Jean de Brébeuf took advantage of a feast, given among the Hurons at the time of the baptism of the first healthy adult, in order to present his teachings to village leaders. It became customary for families to give feasts in order to announce officially their intention of embracing Christianity, and for dying Christians publicly to proclaim their steadfast belief in Christianity at an *athataion*, or death feast, a feast customarily given by a Hurons as death approached, where one sang and ate well in order to show that one was not afraid. (JR 34:113) The missionaries themselves opted to give such a feast when the outbreak of disease among the Hurons, blamed by the natives on the Jesuits, led to death threats against them, in order to convince the villagers that the Fathers would rather meet death than flee. (Moore 1982: 178 Thus, the Jesuits approved of efforts to reinterpret traditional practices in keeping with Christian concepts.

Another ceremony tolerated by the Fathers was the resuscitation rite, common to the Hurons, Iroquois, Montagnais and Algonquins, whereby, when a man died, his name, and with it his responsibilities and honors, were bestowed on someone deemed worthy of them, who was thenceforth referred to as if he were that person. The Jesuits interpreted the rite as a means of perpetuating the name and memory of the deceased, and for providing for the care of widows and orphans. (JR 22:289)

Not only did the Jesuits allow this ceremony to continue, but they even participated in it themselves, and encouraged their converts to do likewise, in order to advance the faith among the unconverted; as a result, a Christianized version emerged. When an unconverted chief was resuscitated in his convert brother in Huron country in 1642, the missionaries took an active part in the ceremony, presenting gifts intended to restore the voice of the deceased, which would now be that of a Christian. The Fathers sought to instill in converts a symbolic relationship between the resuscitation rite and the church's doctrine of the resurrection of Jesus Christ and of faithful Christians. This was especially appropriate if the deceased had been a convert, since the rite became an "image" of the resurrection. Convert ethnic leaders used rhetoric to this effect in the "Christianized" rite, for example, setting to chant melodies the words "He who is to bring me back to life is he who consoles me." Converts were also encouraged to draw parallels between the passing on of certain characteristics at the rite, and the taking of a saint's name at baptism; the convert was to imitate the saint as the native had been taught to imitate the deceased whose name he bore. After his death in 1646, Father Isaac Jogues was resuscitated among his former neophytes when his Indian-given name of Ondesonk (meaning "bird of prey") was transferred in the rite to Father Thierry

Beschefer in 1666 (having in the meantime passed through Father Simon Le Moyne). Beschefer wrote that he hoped God would let him inherit Jogues's virtues, and referred to the ceremony in which he had participated as his "baptism." A similar process occurred when Jean de Brébeuf died in 1649, and the Hurons conferred his name of Echon (after a tree with medicinal properties) on Father Chaumonot. The granting of the native name represented adoption into the tribe, membership in a recognized clan or family. The Jesuits were eager to be subject to the rite since nobody would listen to their teachings if they were not considered officially part of the native group. (Moore 1982: 183-185; Axtell 1985: 83-84)

The process whereby Catholic missionaries pointed out parallels between Christian precepts and concepts of Indian belief, so that native catechumens might more quickly and easily grasp the new religion often resulted in the unintended indigenization of Christianity. When the Montagnais were told that the great Captain, He-Who-Made-All, gives us light with the Sun, maintains fish and animals, forms bodies in the womb and creates souls by his word, Christian belief was presented in such a way as to fit the native worldview. (Morrison 1986: 17) Many converts came to understand God or Jesus as the Great Creator, the Garden of Eden as a native paradise, baptism as a ritual which offered a measure of protection, like a talismanic aid (hence the not uncommon belief that the more water used, the more healthful the consequences; Dickason 1984: 253), and the burning of incense as a ritual of purification akin to the burning of tobacco. This process was furthered by the Jesuits' eagerness to have converts express Christian dogma by means of Indian language and thought structure. One Algonquin compared the Christian concept of "grace" to a beautiful robe of beaver fur with which God clothes the souls of his good children. The selection of a beaver robe is significant, since much of Huron and Algonquin religion centered on this creature. The Indian had merged the Christian concept of grace with the Indian view of the life-giving beaver. (Ronda 1972: 388)

A prominent historian observes that, although the initiative for most religious mixture came from the natives, "the Jesuits allowed or

243

encouraged a certain amount of syncretic blending of old and new beliefs and practices, hoping thereby to ease the natives' transition to the new faith." (Axtell 1985: 110) Missionaries were confident that this would not undermine true Christianity, first, because they, not the Indians, dominated the conversion process (or so they thought), and, thus, if traditional or pagan elements were carried over, they were translated piecemeal as isolated elements rather than religious complexes or systems, since it was the missionaries who allowed them to pass; and second, these practices were regarded as temporary expedients, until they could show the natives a "purer" way. (Axtell 1988: 118)

It is worth noting that the circumstances of evangelization in French North America encouraged an approach that accommodated native cultural realities. Since the Jesuits were greatly outnumbered, they could not hope to use methods that might alienate neophytes, and still less compel natives to convert. The only approach available, other than emphasizing the benefits of cooperation with missionaries (medical care, growing trade, military assistance against enemies), was to make Christianity appealing by adapting methods and message. (Axtell 1985: 71) Though the missionaries claimed that they only adapted their approach in matters of cultural "indifference," and admitted no compromise with the word of God, pope, and church, it is likely that they compromised perhaps more than they intended or even realized.

24 "A Better Acquaintance with the Manitou"

It is in their adopted role as shamans that missionary adaptation to native realities is most marked. We have already seen how Cabeza de Vaca legitimized his presence among the Indians of the North American southwest by conforming to their expectations regarding the healing powers of the Europeans who seemed to possess a particularly potent magic. From the earliest days of contact between Europeans and natives in French America, a similar phenomenon occurred. About fifty Iroquoian Indians from Stadacona (Quebec) died during an epidemic in 1535. According to one account, the chief of Hochelaga believed that the foreigners, led by explorer Jacques Cartier, might be able to effect a cure. The chief, who was completely paralyzed and deprived of the use of his limbs,

"Showed his arms and legs to the Captain motioning to him to be good enough to touch them, as if he thereby expected to be cured and healed. On this the Captain set about rubbing his arms and legs with his hands. Thereupon this Agouhanna [chief] took the band of cloth he was wearing as a crown and presented it to the Captain. And at once many sick persons, some blind, others with but one eye, others lame or impotent and others again so extremely old that their eyelids hung down to their cheeks, were brought in and set down or laid out near the Captain, in order that he might lay his hands upon them, so that one would have thought Christ had come down to earth to heal them." (Ronda 1996: 39; Kellogg 1917: 129)

Cartier responded by making the sign of the cross over the Indians and reading aloud from a prayer book and the Gospel of St. John, praying to God to give the Indians knowledge of the faith. He then handed out hatchets, knives, beads and other trinkets, and had trumpets sounded, at which the Indians rushed to offer provisions. (Biggar 1924; Cook 1998: 163) If Cartier could be taken for a shaman, how much more was this true of the missionaries, who claimed to possess medical and therapeutic skills, to act as intermediaries with Christian supernatural beings, and to be blessed with specialist knowledge of the workings of demonic power. Thus, in 1665, when Father Claude Allouez advised a Fox man that his parents, who were dangerously ill, should be bled, the Indian poured powdered tobacco over the priest's gown and said: "Thou art a spirit; come now, restore these sick people to health; I offer thee this tobacco in sacrifice." (Axtell 1985: 10; Kellogg 1917: 155-56) Not only were the Jesuits seen by the Indians as comparable to, and more capable than, their own shamans, but the Fathers themselves encouraged this perception and deliberately assimilated themselves, letting the Indians believe that they had greater and more effective spiritual power at their disposal.

This was possible because the Jesuit religious worldview meshed in many important respects with that of Native Americans. Both believed in the immediate reality of an invisible world and the constant intervention of supernatural forces in earthly affairs; both accepted reports of flying shamans, talking stones or bleeding altar cloths. (Reff 1998: 16, 29) Both shaman and missionary called on the aid of forces from the spiritual world - the former appealed to the manitous, the latter to God, the angels, and the souls of the dead, for strength and protection. Like the shaman, the missionary used "charms" - the sacraments, the relics of the saints, and material objects infused with divine power, such as holy water, medals, statues of saints, and rosaries, objects that served as special channels through which spiritual power passed into the physical order. (Moore 1982: 106, 118) Thus, the association between Jesuits and shamans derived from real analogies in the functions of the two groups.

This analogy was not simply tolerated by the Jesuits but was actively exploited in order to win the allegiance of the Indians to their own God. Missionaries deliberately and purposefully employed their own "magic" to outdo and discredit their shaman rivals. (Conkling 1974: 13; Dennis 1993: 92) Indeed, the missionary was successful only to the degree that his power exceeded that of the shaman, a fact demonstrated by the fierce contests in which they often engaged with native sorcerers. (Martin 1974: 20) When Father Le Jeune scoffed at the power of the Montagnais shaman Etienne Pigarouich to consult with spirits called *Ka-Khichigou Khetikhi* ("those who make the light") who

246

were reputed to shake the shaman's tent, the Indian challenged the Jesuit to a wager that the tent would move, although neither he nor anyone else should touch it. The priest accepted the wager, insisting on betting three times as much as his adversary suggested. At this, the assembled Indians became enthused, some averring that he would lose, others insisting that he was a "greater sorcerer" than Pigarouich. Astutely, Le Jeune told them that he did not wish to gain from his wager, and so when he won he would give the sorcerer's losses to them; as a result, the Indians placed themselves squarely behind the priest. The Jesuit warned the sorcerer that he would force the demon in the tent to confess his impotence against those who believe in God, which might provoke him to harm or even kill somebody in his fury. The two men agreed to face each other the next day, but the sorcerer failed to appear at the appointed hour, perhaps because he already believed that the Jesuit was a shaman like himself, and feared that he might unleash his power on him. The priest indicated no distress that the Indians concluded from this confrontation that the French were greater sorcerers. Indeed, he repeated his tactics. Some days later he used his knowledge of how a lodestone could attract needles to demonstrate the superiority of his magic, and he warned Pigarouich not to carry out his plan to kill one of his enemies by charms since, when the devil discovered that he could not do him harm because he was under the protection of God, he might discharge his wrath upon the sorcerer. As a result, Pigarouich made up with his enemy. Subsequently he destroyed his ritual paraphernalia, and explicitly recognized that the Jesuits were greater sorcerers than himself, promising to observe exactly their techniques for curing the sick and for ensuring a good hunt. (JR 11:255-67; 12:11) Although the Jesuits presented him as an exemplary convert, his loyalty to the Christian God derived from an appreciation of His power over aspects of life traditionally important to Indians, such as protection in battle against the Iroquois and success in the chase. (JR 11:267) The story of Pigarouich is a good illustration both of how native shamans reacted to Christianity according to their own understanding of the functions of supernatural power, and of how the Fathers moved onto native ground in order to attract converts.

Even if the sorcerer-shaman was an impostor, he was no less dangerous for it. However hollow his claims to real power, he held the Indians in his thrall, and constituted the single greatest obstacle to successful evangelization. The missionaries were obliged to discredit him, by proving that they, not the shamans, provided effective supernatural protection. Since one of the major functions of the shaman was healing, the Jesuits recognized that their ability to demonstrate superior medical techniques was crucial in the struggle for the Indians' souls. François Joseph Le Mercier observed: "The most ordinary of our occupations was that of Physician, with the object of discrediting, more and more, their sorcerers, with their imaginary treatments." (JR 15:69) The role of physician was appreciated by the first two Jesuit missionaries in French America, Pierre Biard and Ennemond Masse, who used care for the sick as a means to spread their teachings. When they restored to health the son of Membertou, the local Micmac chief, merely a nominal Christian, the youth became a convert, his father committed himself more enthusiastically, and many others of the tribe were attracted to the faith. (Moore 1982: 4; JR 1:213-15) Many converts were made through healing, despite the fact that for medicine the Fathers made do with what was at hand - lemon peel, raisins, sugar, prunes, and perhaps theriac and senna. Some Jesuits attempted bleeding, such as Father Simon Baron who practiced the art among the Hurons in 1636-37. They also provided material assistance to many of those who fell ill during major epidemics, bringing them food, water and firewood. It is impossible to know whether the missionaries had, in fact, any more success in curing disease than native specialists, but the evidence suggests that whatever results they apparently achieved did impress at least some of the Indians, who soon believed that the Fathers had healing powers and withdrew their trust in their own shamans. (Cook 1998: 195; JR 15:69) The Hurons, for example, interpreted baptism as a healing rite, similar in nature to those performed by the Atirenda or Awataerohi curing societies, and becoming a Christian was viewed as analogous to a sick person joining one of these societies. (Trigger 1976: 505) The Hurons readily borrowed rituals of all kinds from each other and from neighboring peoples and incorporated these rituals into their society alongside existing ones. They initially viewed Christianity as a ritual society and the Jesuits as its adepts. (Trigger 1976: 848)

One of the best examples of the powerful influence exerted over the Indians by a successful Jesuit physician is Father Gabriel Druillettes among the Kennebec Abenaki. When a particularly virulent epidemic struck, Druillettes gave close personal attention to the sick, and confounded and discredited his rivals when some of those he baptized survived. Consciously aiming to outdo the native shamans, he reversed their traditional social role to his own advantage. Understanding that shamans required payment for their attentions and did not nurse the sick, he eschewed gifts and lavished care, thus undermining the shamans' prestige. Because the Kennebecs believed that beneficent power rested in manifest social concern, his behavior proved he was more humane than the medicine men. It was the Jesuit's psychotherapeutic skills, as much as his medical ones, which earned him respect. Druillettes's role as a curer, and his resistance to disease and the threats of shamans, made him a formidable charismatic figure, to whom even the shamans themselves succumbed. One sent for Druillettes when he fell ill and allowed himself to be baptized, and had his drum and charms destroyed, after which he recovered. This act conferred tremendous authority on the Jesuit since the drum was the heart of ritual power; the Abenaki word for shaman means "sound of drumming," and the word for "drum" refers to the act of beseeching supernatural powers for help. (JR 31:197; Speck 1919: 240-41) Druillettes was compared favorably with shamans because he acted as the man of power that the Kennebecs expected him to be, and because he addressed the tribe's sense of crisis and offered solutions that accorded with the Abenaki's opinions of good and evil. (Conkling 1974: 13-14; Morrison 1984: 80-85; Morrison 1981: 244-45; JR 38:37)

As well as seeking to outshine their adversaries in the sphere of illness, the Fathers also assumed the mantle of shaman by presenting themselves as more efficient rainmakers. During a drought among the Hurons in 1635, one sorcerer named Tehorenhaegnon told the Fathers to take down a cross in front of their door, because it was hindering him from making it rain, and warned them that if the crops did not mature, they might be beaten to death, as often happened to sorcerers in the region. The missionaries assembled in their cabin the men and women of their own village, since they alone had not resorted to native sorcerers, but instead had always asked the Fathers to make it rain, believing that nothing was impossible for them. Father Jean de Brébeuf told them that only God, not the priests, could bring rain or fine weather; that the cross had not hindered rain as it had often rained since it was erected; that perhaps God was angry because they spoke ill of him or had recourse to sorcerers, who either had no power, or, perhaps themselves had caused the drought by their intercourse and pacts with the devil; and that they should undertake a procession every day to implore God's help. The Indians marveled to find that their processions had to be cut short on account of the rain which lasted, on and off, for a month. Another procession during a drought later that year also produced enough rain to cause the corn to form perfect ears and ripen. The Indians enthusiastically told the Fathers that they were good and that God was good, and that they would serve God and not their soothsayers.

This event was not exceptional, as indicated by a similar incident in 1628. At that time, during a severe drought, Tehorenhaegnon attributed his failure to bring rain to the fact that the red painted cross in front of Brébeuf's cabin was frightening the thunderbird, "like a fire burning and flaming," and causing the rain clouds to divide in two as they passed over it. The elders of the village told Brébeuf to take down the cross, so that the thunder and the clouds could no longer see it and fear it. He refused, and warned them not to touch the cross in case they made God angry, but recommended that they paint it another color to see if the sorcerer spoke the truth. Even when it was painted white, there was no rain for several days. Brébeuf told the Indians to assemble to honor the cross, and each to bring a dish of corn to make an offering to God, which should afterwards be distributed to the poor of the village. As instructed, they honored and kissed the cross and "on the same day God gave them rain, and in the end a plentiful harvest." (Trigger 1976: 407; JR 10:35-49) Brébeuf's insistence that no man, but only the creator, could bring rain fell on deaf ears; the Hurons remained unconvinced and persisted in their belief that the missionaries had influenced the supernatural.

In any case, Brébeuf, like his fellow Jesuits, was only half-hearted in asserting the orthodox Christian view that it was not they who brought rain but God. More often than not, through their actions rather than their words, the Fathers made it clear that they did expect natives to look on them as more reliable conjurers of rain. Brébeuf himself, for example, was proud of his considerable reputation as a rainmaker. (Trigger 1976: 388-89) It is evident that the Indians were won over on their own terms; they deferred to the missionaries because of their superior access to rain magic. (Jaenen 1974: 279)

The Jesuits also did little to discourage the Indians from ascribing to them, as they did to their own shamans, the ability to prophesy the whereabouts and number of game. (Conkling 1974: 15) Recounting how he had asked Huron hunters to translate two Christian prayers into the native tongue in order to ask God for success in finding game, Le Jeune observed that "these people promise you faithfully that, if you will help them, they will believe entirely in you, and that they will obey you with all their hearts." These words seem to recognize the legitimacy of the natives' expectation that obedience to God was conditional upon aid in hunting. (JR 7:147-53) Conversely, natives who rejected God did not find game. One young Indian, while disputing with Father Brébeuf, defied God to oppose his taking beavers and elks, since he would not fail to take them. After this, the man killed neither beaver or elk, fell sick, which the Fathers pointed out to him was God's punishment, and later died. (JR 7:277-279)

The Jesuits were often exasperated that dreams played such an important role in preparation for the hunt. One Father commented: "They show such fixity of purpose that they will not desist until they have seen in a dream what they desire - either a herd of moose, or a band of Iroquois put to flight - no very difficult thing for an empty brain, utterly exhausted with hunger, and thinking all day of nothing else." (JR 50:291) The missionary response was to attempt to persuade the Indians that prayer was more effective than dreaming. Father

Jacques Marquette observed that God helped Hurons who went to hunt and led them to places where they killed a great number of bears and other animals. If they dreamed of bears they did not kill any on account of this, but after they had recourse to prayer, God gave them what they desired. (JR 57:261) It is hard to avoid the conclusion that Marquette allowed the Indians to see prayer as a form of hunt magic which brought better results than relying on dreams, as their own shamans recommended.

Similarly, Father Druillettes sought to win over the Kennebec Abenaki by assisting them in the hunt. When the native sorcerers put it about that the priest and all those who prayed with him would be taken by the Iroquois, they were confounded "not only did those who prayed to God incur no disaster, not only did the Father and his people not fall into the ambushes of the Iroquois, but God further favored them with a successful hunt; and some sick people, at a distance from the Father, having had recourse to God in their sufferings, had received the blessing of very unexpected health." (JR 31:193-97) This was no isolated example. On another occasion, when his native companions lost their way and found themselves without provisions, Father Druillettes begged God for help, offering a mass to save them. "The Father...had recourse to the God of men and animals, offering him the sacrifice of his Son in those great forests; and conjuring him by the Blood shed by him for those people to succor them in their necessity." Just as Druillettes finished mass, the Abenaki hunter returned with news that he had killed three moose. (JR 37:245; Morrison 1984: 86) As the imagery used in this statement powerfully declares, priest and shaman barely differed; whether curing sickness or conjuring game, Druillettes conformed to native expectations of the shaman.

The Jesuit priests' assumption of the charismatic status of the shaman allowed Christian beliefs to be not merely imposed but legitimized. (Murray 1999: 10) Druillettes achieved an authority over Abenaki society that he could not have secured in any other way, making it possible for Christianity to receive a sympathetic hearing. But the accompanying danger was that the new religion was accepted only insofar as it could be assimilated to the old. The Fathers' determination to present themselves as better providers of game than indigenous shamans encouraged natives to identify God and Jesus with the manitous. The Christian God was frequently referred to as the "Great Manitou," and Jesus began to appear in dreams to promise a successful hunt. One Father was told by two Indians that they had seen "his Manitou" and "his Jesus," who had promised a good year for beavers and elks, providing that the priest gave them tobacco to sacrifice. (JR 9:213) Others called on God during hunting and fishing expeditions, using titles such as "You who have made all" and "You the Master of animals." (JR 15:87) One Abenaki told his people that "He who is the master of all the animals gave us meat"; (JR 37:251) and one Montagnais of Tadoussac prayed to God that he might make a kill because God was "the sovereign Lord of animals." (JR 37:195) It is clear that God was understood as a new version of the native Owners of animals.

The Jesuits themselves contributed to this process by urging Indians to redirect their prayers from the Master of Game to He-Who-Made-All. One Indian, instructed by Druillettes, prayed to "the great spirit, the master of men and the lord of war" and offered him the heads of animals; (JR 57:223) thus, the same offerings which had once been made to the manitous at feasts were now dedicated to Christ. The Indian who told Le Jeune that his favourite prayer was "Mirinan oukachigakhi nimitchiminan: Give us today our food, give us something to eat," was surely expressing the assumption, tolerated by the Fathers, that food and feasting had strong spiritual connections, and that God could provide food like a Manitou. (JR 8:37; Murray 1999: 15) Another Indian told the Father that he had always been aware that Divine Providence watched over him, since when he went to visit the traps that he had made in order to catch beavers and bears, he would always find his prey, and never returned empty-handed, even though his comrades often took nothing. He asked himself: "Who is that one who gives me to eat so liberally? No doubt he loves me and wishes me well; I would much like to know him, in order to thank him for it." When he heard from the Fathers about the existence of a God who has made everything, and who governs all, he immediately thought that it was He who had looked out for him and was attracting him to His acquaintance by the care that He had for him. (JR 24:131) This Indian was interpreting God in terms of the traditional native guardian spirit.

Although the priests denied that God and Christ were manitous, they themselves often behaved as if they accepted native premises; for example, they neglected to challenge the indigenous logic of why fish or game appeared or did not appear, but instead, denied credit to the manitous and gave it to Christ. One Father remarked approvingly on the common Indian custom of thanking God for game, since if the natives had recourse to the Lord, his goodness would not abandon them. (JR 18:207) Le Jeune had no qualms about telling the Indians that if they believed in God, then it would snow and they would find moose; or that if they found no food, they should fall upon their knees and promise God that they would believe in him if he would assist them. (JR 8:33-35) In this way, he effectively encouraged the Indians to apply native criteria for accepting Christianity, and risked giving tacit approval to the native assumption that Christian supernatural beings should be accepted only insofar as they could provide game, that Christ was a potent manitou but his aid should be sought only as long as he delivered it reliably. On this basis, Christian priests and their God could fit easily into the existing religion. If Jesus was a powerful Master of Animals, then natives did not need to repudiate their basic supernatural assumptions in order to embrace Christianity. Indians were not so much being converted to Christianity as Christ was being converted into a manitou. (Morrison 1986: 16; White 1991: 26-27)

The same dangers attended the Jesuit approach to disease. Many, if not most, Indians, like the Ottawas and Ojibwas who received baptism as a result of an epidemic which Druillettes claimed to have cured in the early 1670s shortly after his arrival in Sault Sainte Marie were in awe of the Jesuits largely on account of their supposed healing powers. (Vecsey 1990: 53, 157; JR 55:117-31; 57:219-37) It is highly likely that many who sought baptism did so in the hope that by earning the Jesuits' goodwill, they would be spared in any future epidemic. (Trigger 1976: 567) The notion that baptism was a curing ritual refused to die. As late as the 1670s, when it might be supposed that the missionaries had communicated the purpose of baptism, Father Julien Garnier complained that without medicines, he could not be sure of baptizing any child. He lamented: "Why have I not a quantity of medicines, and of what is needed to sweeten their bitter lot! It would be a bait wherewith to secure nearly all the dying. There are some who, when they find that they are given no medicine, turn their backs to me, and say that I have no pity on them; and after that they cannot be approached." (JR 57:173-75) The underlying assumption was that the Fathers were direct providers of health rather than intermediaries with God. That the lesson drawn from Christian healing was often not that intended by missionaries is illustrated by the Kennebecs' observation to Druillettes: "How may times have we seen persons in the last extremity, whom we thought bewitched, restored to health upon praying to him who is the master of all the demons." (JR 38:37) The Fathers' attempt to prove themselves more powerful agents in countering epidemics entailed a risk that the Indians would attribute cures to the powers of Christian manitous, and, at the same time, accept the Christian God only insofar as he provided effective healing. "It must surely be," said the Kennebecs, "that the God whom this Father [Druillettes] announces to us, is powerful, since he so perfectly cures the greatest and the most contagious diseases - which the Manitou or Genii, whom our sorcerers invoke, cannot do." (JR 31:203)

The belief that the sacred waters gave health to the sick and restored the dying to life coexisted alongside the diametrically opposed belief that baptism caused death. This may not be the paradox that it seems. In native eyes, all spiritual power was double-edged; the power to cure could also be used to destroy. Like traditional shamans, the "white manitous" were both healers and sorcerers, to be revered and feared at the same time. (Axtell 1985: 100; Axtell 1988: 91; Conkling 1974: 13) Whether Indians determined that baptism was life-restoring or life-endangering depended on the presence and severity of epidemics. If the Kennebecs did not fear that baptism was actually the cause of death (Morrison 1984: 83), it may be because they did not suffer so severely from epidemics. Villages that were spared epidemics after accepting the sacrament looked favorably on the rite; those that were struck believed their acceptance of baptism to be responsible. Among the Hurons, hostility to the sacrament ebbed and flowed in tandem with the incidence of the epidemics. Once the epidemics subsided, baptism began to lose connotations of sorcery and came again to be viewed as a means by which initiates were able to join relatives in Heaven rather than in the traditional villages of the dead.

Sometimes an undeniable logic lay behind Indians' fear of baptism. One Huron reasoned, if baptism were the path to Heaven as the Jesuits claimed, then he would die as soon as the ceremony was performed. (Dickason 1984: 253) He told the Fathers that on one occasion when he fell sick, he saw the soul of a young Frenchman, who had conferred his name upon one of his children, calling him to go to Heaven: "When I recovered my senses, I concluded that I would not fail to go there as soon as the door should be opened to me. Now, as you told me that Baptism was the door to Heaven, I was in no haste to enter, seeing that I had to pass thither by death. The road is not very pleasant, though its end is most delightful. But that is all over; in resolving to receive Baptism, I am resolved to die." One day, while he was hunting beavers and wished to take a rest, he heard a voice that said to him: "Thou art a dead man if thou art baptized." Since he also believed that newly baptized Christians are soon attacked by death, or by some serious illness, if they fail, however slightly, in keeping the promise they have made to God to follow his will, and that he himself did not have sufficient strength to observe the Laws of Christianity, and to render so strict an obedience, he looked upon Baptism "in the same light as we look upon death or illness." (JR 22:103)

The Fathers themselves expressed the view that belief in the health-giving qualities of the sacrament - assisted by the diminution of the epidemics and the recovery of more of the baptized - was gradually replacing the belief that it was fatal. "They are beginning to lose the dread they had of baptism, and the belief that this sacrament must cause them to die." (JR 9:99; see also 51:23 and Axtell 1985: 123) However, the evidence of the Jesuit Relations suggests that it was peoples who had only a limited experience of the missionaries that believed that baptism granted health. Those peoples who had more sustained contact with the priests often changed their minds and attributed the spread of disease and death to the sacrament. Where the Jesuits had arrived recently, Hurons seem to have regarded baptism as a healing rite; but where their teachings were better known, increasing numbers of people rejected this explanation. (Trigger 1976: 531)

It is clear that the belief that baptism caused death remained throughout the seventeenth century. In the 1660s, there was still a widespread belief that those who had embraced the faith had been destroyed almost as soon as they had become Christians, and most of those who had received baptism had died a short time afterwards. (JR 54:55) In the 1670s, the Iroquois still believed that baptism either hastened death or prevented them from going to the native Heaven. (JR 57:177; see also 64:161-65, 191) The Fathers' standard response was that those who died were on the edge of death anyway, and that not one of those who had been baptized while in health had died suddenly, but on the contrary, some sick people had recovered. (JR 11:201) But their own behavior - for example the emphasis that they placed on the afterlife in the instructions that preceded baptism, which suggested that the sacrament might be a ritual designed to send the soul of the sick person to the realms of the dead - contributed to the view that no one could hope to recover from an illness after being baptized. The Jesuits' description of baptism as showing the way to Heaven linked the sacrament with death in the minds of the Hurons. This interpretation was reinforced by the Jesuit emphasis that baptism was a medicine not for the body but for the soul. The Hurons maintained that it was not right for the Jesuits to ask a sick man if he wished to go to Heaven or Hell; instead, they should wish for his recovery. (Trigger 1976: 506, 531)

The belief that baptism could cause death was a manifestation of the broader belief, encountered almost universally, that the Fathers were the cause of the epidemics. According to Father Brébeuf, tales were spread among the Hurons that the Jesuits were the origin of the pestilence which had struck severely that year, and that the priests' sole purpose in coming to their country was to wreak destruction. (JR 11:15) Father Lalemant reported that the sorcerer Tonneraouanone accused the Jesuits of being the cause of the epidemics, adding that this was the sentiment even of those of the Fathers' own village, who said that when they were getting better the priests gave them something that made them die. In 1646, Father Isaac Jogues was killed by a faction of the Iroquois that accused him of spreading disease and corn worms. (Trigger 1965: 46) During an earlier period of captivity among the Mohawk, he had acted the part of the shaman, caring for the sick and practicing Catholic ritual. He had thus acquired a reputation as a man of great supernatural power. Subsequently, he returned to the Mohawks on a diplomatic mission, and when he departed, he left behind a chest of personal belongings to signify his intention to come again. Shortly thereafter, worms infested Mohawk corn and people began to fall sick. Believing that the "French shaman's box" had caused these misfortunes, the natives seized him when he revisited the town later in 1646, and put him to death. (Richter 1992: 113; JR 30:227-29)

As late as the final decade of the seventeenth century, Father Jacques Gravier was accused by Indians in the Illinois mission of using toads to kill the sick. Whereas in the beginning, he was well received, told that prayer was a good thing, and invited to instruct the women and children to pray well so that no disease might break out, once the contagion spread, he was looked upon as a bird of death, and held responsible for the sickness and the mortality. (JR 64:173-77)

The Algonquins, with a logic that proved hard to refute, pointed out that they had not suffered from such terrible epidemics before they heard about the Fathers' God:

"'It is a strange thing', said they, 'that since prayer has come into our cabins, our former customs are no longer of any service; and yet we shall all die because we give them up.' 'I have seen the time', said one, 'when my dreams were true; when I had seen moose or beavers in sleep, I would take some. When our soothsayers felt the enemy coming, that came true; there was preparation to receive him. Now, our dreams and our prophecies are no longer true - prayer has spoiled everything for us.' Others...said, 'We see well that God is angry at us, and that he is right - for we do not do what he says; inasmuch as it seems hard to us, we disobey him, and so he becomes angry with us and kills us. But you, you are the cause of it; for if you had lived in your own country without speaking to us of God, he would not say a word to us, since we would not know him or his will. You would then do much better to return to your country and live at rest; for it is you who kill us. Before you came here, the French did not say so many prayers; they only made the sign of the Cross, and even then, all did not know how to make it. They did not have all those prayers which you are introducing; it is you who have brought in all these novelties, and who teach them to the Savages, and overturn their brains and make them die. Besides, if you called to prayers only once in ten days, we would have some respite: but you have no regard to either rain, or snow, or cold; every day you are heard shouting for the prayers. It is a strange thing that you cannot remain quiet..'..The majority...were furious with spite against the Father, and said that he was a greater sorcerer than their own people; that the country must be cleared of such; that they had clubbed three sorcerers at the island, who had not done so much harm as he." (JR 24:209-13)

The Jesuits were rumored to spread disease by the most ingenious methods, including the presentation of deadly gifts, the contamination of drinking water and the distribution of poisoned sugar (or "French snow" as native sorcerers called it) to the sick. (JR 13:209; JR 14:51-53) Word spread that the Fathers' own servants confirmed that they were the sole authors of the sickness, which emanated from a toad or a serpent that they kept hidden in their house, or from a demon which was concealed in the barrel of an harquebus, and could be fired off in any direction. (JR 19:95-97) Deadly spells were said to emanate from the baptismal water and the food and drugs that the Fathers distributed, and harmful influences were thought to emanate from the paintings and images in Jesuit chapels and penetrate the chests of those who looked at them, as well as from communion wafers, which were rumored to be pieces of human flesh that had been brought from France as instruments of sorcery. In 1637, a rumor spread that death among the Hurons was caused by a corpse that the Jesuits had brought from France and which they kept in the tabernacle in their chapel. (JR

12:237-39; 15:33; Trigger 1976: 537) Dreams were reported in which the Black Robes had been seen unfolding certain books from which issued forth sparks of fire that spread everywhere and caused disease. (JR 20:33) Missionaries were said to write down the names of children in order to cast spells on them, and to make marks of charcoal on people's bodies, which, as they gradually became defaced, would cause those bearing them to be afflicted with ailments until they died. Disasters always gave rise to charges of witchcraft among the Huron themselves, and the epidemics of the 1630s were no exception. (JR 42:135; 12:169, 237-39; 14:51-53; 15:33; Trigger 1985: 247)

Since the Jesuits were thought to be responsible for the epidemics, it was also assumed that they could prevent them. One Algonquin elder sent news to the Fathers that he was intending to travel to Quebec to see the French governor in order to obtain some letters that he had heard could prevent people from dying. When he arrived, he was keen to know why his people were becoming visibly depopulated when the French, on the contrary, lived so long. "It must be," he averred, "that thou knowest some secret for preserving thy people, and that thou hast an intimate acquaintance with the Manitou." The governor sent him to the Fathers, telling him that if his people did as the priests taught them, they would learn the secret of preserving their nation, and of diminishing the number of deaths. (JR 12:183-85)

Le Jeune observed that even distant nations considered the Jesuits to be the masters and arbiters of life and death. One Algonquin tribe (probably the Nipissing) sent a special embassy to the Fathers with presents, to beg them to spare their lives. The Jesuits refused the offerings and told the Indians to address themselves to God. When subsequently many of their people died of disease, they attributed their misfortune to the fact that they had once robbed French trader and interpreter Etienne Brûlé of a collar of two thousand four hundred wampum beads, and decided that they should return it to the Fathers and beg them to spare the few who had survived. The Jesuits commended their desire to make restitution but explained that they could not accept it since it had not been stolen from them, and there was no one who could receive it in the name of the deceased owner.

They also explained candidly that it was too dangerous for the Fathers to receive presents from strange nations at that time since the people of this country would soon get wind of it, and would not consider it a simple restitution, but rather some secret understanding to their disadvantage. Acceptance of the collar might be injurious to the Jesuits if from that time the Algonquin tribe began to recover; and if, on the contrary, the sickness continued, they would be regarded as impostors for not having fulfilled expectations. As if to confirm the wisdom of this decision, no sooner had this group departed satisfied than other representatives came who, observing an image of the Day of Judgment which depicted the damned, concluded that the multitude of men, desperate and heaped one upon the other, were all those that the Fathers had caused to die during the winter, that the flames represented the heat of the pestilential fever, and that the dragons and serpents were the venomous beasts that the Black Robes made use of in order to poison them. One asked if it was true that the Fathers were raising the malady in their house as if it were a domestic animal. (JR 14:99-105)

There were many factors that lent credence to the native view that the Jesuits were able to control the diseases. First, the priests presented themselves as men of extraordinary spiritual power, and, as a result, were taken by the Indians to be great sorcerers, even "the greatest sorcerers on earth." (JR 19:93) "The name of Echon resounded on all sides as that of one of the most famous sorcerers or demons that had ever been imagined." The Hurons related that "when Echon set his foot in their country for the first time, he had said: 'I shall be here so many years, during which I shall cause many to die, and then I shall go elsewhere to do the same, until I have ruined the whole land.'" (JR 21:207-11) Brébeuf was widely believed to have come from France with the express purpose of casting spells to bring illness. The wampum collar that he presented to the Attignawantan in 1636, in order to show them the way to Heaven, was interpreted as a clear sign that he intended to kill them. (JR 34:169-71; Trigger 1976: 535) The same maleficent sorcery was attributed to other Jesuits. Father Le Jeune was asked if he could provide a deadly powder so that the Hurons could eliminate a man who had caused disease among them, and was regarded as the author of the death of an Indian who would not obey him. (JR 6:195; 16:53)

The Black Robes' alien manners and behavior, particularly their dress, gait, and gestures, seemed to confirm that they were sorcerers. (JR 21:219-21; 18:41; 56:59-61; Moore 1982: 23) Their antisocial behavior was typical of that of witches. Their refusal to give presents to satisfy the desires of people's souls was proof that they wished to see individual Hurons suffer and die. The frequently closed door of their cabin, and their refusal to admit Huron visitors except at specified times of day strongly suggested that sorcery was being practiced within. Christian prayers were taken to be the spells and incantations of magicians; although Christians drew a clear distinction between prayer and spell, the belief of the Jesuits in God's intercessionary power was barely distinguishable from a magical act as a coercive ritual. (Murray 1999: 12) The Fathers themselves admitted that Indians were less scared by the fires of the other world than they were by the thought that the priests might communicate with God and cause their death, as native sorcerers tried to do with those who refused them. (JR 33:27) Their celibacy also suggested that they were nurturing great supernatural force.

Second, a degree of control over disease was suggested by the fact that the missionaries either remained mysteriously unaffected by the epidemics, or recovered far more rapidly than Indians. The relative speed, compared to the Indians, with which the Jesuits recovered from their own bouts of influenza in 1636, for example, seemed to demonstrate their power over the affliction. The Hurons believed that the Fathers had a secret understanding with the diseases, since they alone were full of life, although they constantly breathed infected air. (JR 19:91-93)

Third, the Jesuit insistence on baptizing only the dying (in the case of children, often surreptitiously, due to parental opposition) led the Hurons and others to assume a cause-and-effect relationship and to see baptism as a form of murder by witchcraft.

Fourth, the Fathers themselves sometimes claimed to exercise power over epidemics. They performed religious rituals which at times apparently succeeded in halting or diminishing the impact of diseases; hence, it was easy to conclude that failure on other occasions to combat disease could be attributed to malice rather than incompetence. Their special knowledge about the providential purpose behind the diseases, and particularly of the Christian God's intentions, contributed to the Indian assumption that they had some control over the epidemics. During the influenza epidemic of 1636, Brébeuf told the Hurons that they should make a public vow that if God ended the contagion, they would agree to serve him and in the following spring erect a cabin (chapel) in his honor. (Trigger 1976: 529-30) Such suggestions communicated to the Indians that the priest held special influence with the spirit causing the disease. Le Jeune wrote with satisfaction that almost at the same time as a Huron assembly of elders spoke against the Fathers and issued murderous threats, the scourge of deadly disease fell upon the family that had said the most against the priests, serving as chastisement "for a long time due them on account of the contempt they had always shown for our holy mysteries." (JR 13:215-17) This was a point of view that the Jesuits did not conceal from the Indians; on the contrary they broadcast it freely. The Fathers made much of the fact that when convert Etienne Pigarouich encouraged other Indians to pray to God, only those who obeyed him remained free from the pestilence stalking the land, whereas all those whom infidelity or fear of public opinion had prevented from having recourse to God were carried off. (JR 18:189-91) This created the impression that Christian magic secured protection; and the emphasis that the Jesuits placed on the role of ex-sorcerers in attracting Indians to the faith lent credence to the view that these individuals had simply become Christian sorcerers. Later in the century, Father Gravier responded to accusations that he was the author of the widespread sickness by asserting that the disease had only begun after the Indians started practicing native ceremonies, and, in mockery of his sprinkling of the holy water, performed an impious sprinkling in public. He reminded them that, in punishment, an old woman had died a few days after she had imitated Christian ceremonies, and that disease and death had entered the cabins of all the most superstitious. (JR 64:183-85) By suggesting that those who spoke against the faith were punished, it is clear that Le Jeune led the Indians to believe that the Fathers did in fact have some effect on the incidence of disease. And by affirming that the disease was selective, Gravier intimated that the Jesuits had some special understanding of how the sickness worked, and therefore encouraged the idea that they could control it. It is not surprising if the Indians also believed the Black Robes to be responsible.

Finally, the French insistence that the missionaries should reside among the Hurons could most plausibly be understood as an attempt to undermine the communities from within. Many Indians asked themselves what possible motive the Black Robes could have for coming to Indian lands. Why would they leave France and come so far and suffer hardship without apparent profit? Clearly their resolution must originate in some object of great importance, and what else could this be than the ruin of the country? When the Jesuits told them that it was for blessings after death, the fact that death entered into their speeches confirmed the notion that the priests made them die - even some of the Christians thought that the Fathers brought them death through love and their desire to reveal God to them the sooner, and to give them the enjoyment of the blessings that they valued so highly. (JR 17:125-27) Others claimed that the Jesuits wished to lead to Heaven as many Indians as they could in order to burn and roast them there at their pleasure; this was the sole recompense that they expected in return for the pain and hardship that they had undergone in converting them. (JR 42:151) Revenge for their murdered fellows was another motive that could plausibly be attributed to the Black Robes. One rumor held that a woman, believed to be the sister of the late Etienne Brûlé (murdered in 1633), had been seen infecting the whole country with her breath, in order to avenge her brother's death. (JR 14:51-53)

The Jesuits noted with some perplexity that the course of events lent considerable plausibility to the widespread accusations that they were the agents by which the epidemics were being spread. Their arrival coincided so clearly with the outbreak of epidemics that the Indians could not fail to connect the two. During their first year in Huron country, the Jesuits remained popular and their presence was sought after, but this welcome turned sour after the outbreak of the epidemics. Although the contagion was probably carried into the interior from Quebec by traders, the natives blamed the resident missionaries, who shared an intimate lifestyle with them. "They observed, with some sort of reason, that, since our arrival in these lands, those who had been nearest to us, had happened to be the most ruined by the diseases, and that the whole villages of those who had received us now appeared utterly exterminated." The sad truth is that the Fathers almost certainly contributed unwittingly to the spread of disease by scurrying from the bedside of one sick Indian to the next, and by carrying contamination from one village to the next on their shoes and robes. (Richter 1992: 107) The Jesuits showed some awareness of the possibility that disease was spread by means of clothing when they counseled that a suit that they had sent to France as a gift for the Dauphin should not be presented to him since smallpox was rife in the colony. (JR 15:237)

The Fathers admitted that there was some truth in Indian perceptions: "where we were most welcome, where we baptized most people, there it was in fact where they died the most; and on the contrary, in the cabins to which we were denied entrance, although they were sometimes sick to extremity, at the end of a few days one saw every person prosperously cured. We shall see in heaven the secret, but ever adorable, judgments of God therein." (JR 19:91-93) "Never have the Algonquins or the Hurons had such recourse to God as now, and never have they been afflicted with greater misfortunes. The more we advance in the Faith, the more do we walk amid crosses. It seems as if everything were about to perish - at the very moment, perhaps, when God intends to save everything." (JR 22:273)

The Fathers recognized that this paradox was not lost on the Hurons:

"Since we have published the law of Jesus Christ in these regions, plagues have rushed in as in a throng ... How many times have we been reproached that, wherever we set foot, death came in with us! How many times have they told us that they had never seen calamities like those which have appeared since we speak of Jesus Christ! 'You

265

tell us' (exclaim some) 'that God is full of goodness; and then, when we give ourselves up to him, he massacres us. The Iroquois, our mortal enemies, do not believe in God, they do not love the prayers, they are more wicked than the demons - and yet they prosper; and since we have forsaken the usages of our ancestors, they kill us, they massacre us, they burn us, they exterminate us, root and branch. What profit can there come to us from lending ear to the Gospel, since death and the faith nearly always march in company?'"

When told that death and war afflicted both Christians and infidel, they answered that the Iroquois did not die despite holding prayer in abomination. Before the new religion appeared in Huron country, they lived as long as the Iroquois, but since some had accepted prayer, there were no more white heads, and they died at half the age. Informed that the Iroquois were being used as a whip to correct them, and that when they were wise, the rods would be thrown into the fire, and the Iroquois too would be chastised if they did not reform, some asked why God did not begin with the Iroquois and try to give them some sense first, since the Hurons had so much already but their enemies none at all. They were told that God preferred them to the Iroquois; he gave a life of pleasure to those who died after baptism, but cast all the Iroquois into the fire. (JR 25:35-37)

The assumption of the mantle of shaman allowed the Jesuits to enter the native supernatural world, but it also made it more difficult for the Fathers to persuade the Indians that they were not simply new and more effective counterparts of native sorcerers, and that their practices were not merely so many new techniques for calling on supernatural power. Le Jeune expressed the dilemma most succinctly:

"Because we predict to them the Eclipses of the Moon and Sun, which they greatly fear, they imagine that we are the masters of these, that we know all future events, and that it is we who order them. And with this idea, they address themselves to us to know if their crops will succeed; where their enemies are, in what force they are coming, being unable to persuade themselves that we are not wiser in all things than their sorcerers, who profess to discover such secrets. And what confirms them still more in their notion is that - it being the custom of the country in public necessities to have recourse to the most famous Sorcerers, and these not hesitating to promise wonders, provided they are given presents - we cannot at such times keep silent, especially since we have Christians who are found to be engaged and involved in such matters; we speak therefore, and say what we ought. But forthwith, according to them, we are declared arraigned and convicted of that of which they accuse us - of intending nothing else than the destruction and the ruin of the world, since we will not deliver them from their troubles, nor permit them to provide themselves with the ordinary remedies employed in their country from all time against their misfortunes, especially when, in their belief, it is we who are the cause of these...This throws them into despair; for, on the one hand, they cannot resolve to abandon these remedies without giving up therein the hope of living, which is, however, their sovereign good; on the other, they see persons who threaten them with the anger and the Justice of God, if they continue to use them." (JR 17:117-23)

Missionaries like Father Pierre Millet, who used his knowledge of an eclipse of the moon in January 1674 to awe Oneida men and women in a contest with their shamans, proved that they were formidable purveyors of supernatural power. (JR 58:181-85; Axtell 1985: 101-02) Other Jesuits also predicted the lunar eclipses of 1637 and 1638. When Le Jeune was able to explain that an eclipse of the moon was caused by the interposition of the earth between it and the sun, and that the changing color of the sky was caused by light passing through clouds, his interlocutor exclaimed: "You are Manitous, you Frenchmen; you know the sky and the earth." (JR 12:143; Trigger 1985: 252) The possibility that the Jesuits' power might be domesticated and made benign, that missionaries could be transformed into men promoting health, reason, and security, encouraged the Indians to accept them for a while. But, because the line between the beneficent and the malignant, between medicine and witchcraft, was easily crossed, the Jesuits were as likely to be perceived as witches, more evil than good. (Dennis 1993: 91-92) Attributing French technology to the possession of magical powers that essentially were no different from their own, some Hurons seem to have believed that by identifying themselves with the Jesuits they could acquire their magical powers, even if they incurred the enmity of their own people. Thus, missionaries were valued less for the message they brought than for the magical powers that they were believed to possess. (Trigger 1976: 566-67)

In their efforts to discredit the Indian shamans, who possessed charismatic qualities, the missionaries, like Druillettes, took on the special extraordinary cast of a typical charismatic leader. (Conkling 1974: 2) If priests behaved like shamans, then Christian magic was likely to be understood as the expression of the personal shamanistic power of the priest. The result was not only that God's power became conflated with the missionary's own personal power, but also that attention was directed to the person of the missionary rather than to the message he preached. (Richter 1985: 6) Since European priests could apparently manipulate the spiritual cosmology, the Christian view that the priest was a mere intermediary whose only strength lay in supplication and explanation was not appreciated. (Axtell 1985: 17) For all that Jesuits like Father Le Jeune might insist that the missionaries had a much higher calling than native shamans - "they think only of the body, and we of the soul" (JR 5:239) - the seduction of the Indians by means of the Jesuits' skills as healers conveyed a very different message. As Le Jeune recognized, when the Indians saw how easily the Fathers challenged and defied their sorcerers, they attributed it to "a better acquaintance with the Manitou." (JR 12:9)

25 Native Religion Renewed

Evangelization can be best understood as a dialogue between Indian individuals and priests, whereby natives adopted those aspects of Catholicism that made sense in traditional terms. The two religions were not dogmatically incompatible and exclusive. Natives saw traditional belief and Catholicism as compatible systems of religious power. The Jesuits presented their teachings, but natives weighed their options and decided what did or did not make sense. (Morrison 1986: 17) The result was that Native Americans accepted some aspects of Catholic teachings while often rejecting or modifying the ideological message of Christianity. (Ronda 1979: 2)

Christian ritual objects were accepted for their magical properties and were appropriated in order to serve as equivalents or replacements for traditional counterparts. The symbol of the cross could easily supplant native sacred pole symbols, such as the manitou pole or the grave post. After evangelization, the Menomini replaced the sun symbol with the cross, and attributed a successful sturgeon catch to this symbol of Christ. (Kurath 1959: 214; Keesing 1939: 60-61) Saints' images were interpreted as new types of *oki* (spirit). Le Jeune reported that the Hurons called certain saints' statues at Quebec *ondaqui* (which is the plural of *oki*) and believed them to be living things. The Hurons asked if the tabernacle was their house and if they dressed themselves in the ornaments seen around the altar. (JR 5:257) Crucifixes and rosaries took the place of native amulets. (Bailey 1969: 143) Indians applied rosaries and crosses to the body of a Micmac chief during his illness (JR 45:63), just as the Jesuits themselves saved a Montagnais woman in child labour by placing a relic of St. Ignatius about her neck, after which she delivered without pain or difficulty. (JR 31:151; Bailey 1969: 144) However, these ritual objects were not always employed in ways approved by the missionaries. Once in circulation, they could be put to uses that were uncontrolled and unauthorized by Catholic priests. One Micmac woman enhanced her own shamanic status by giving out beads of jet that were the remains of an unthreaded rosary, claiming that they were from Heaven. Another who claimed that her rosary beads were a gift from Heaven was debunked by Christien Le Clercq who responded with an act of conjuring, making a bead appear and disappear, demystifying the beads but at the same time, ironically, playing the role of the 'juggler' or shaman he was trying to discredit. (Murray 1999: 57-58; Le Clercq 1910: 230-33)

Not only Christian ritual objects, but also Christian concepts were assimilated because they were interpreted in native terms. Both God and the devil were referred to as manitou ("good manitou" and "bad manitou"), indicating that these figures were subsumed into native categories. (JR 12:7) If the persons of Jesus and He-Who-Made-All were accepted so readily, it was largely because they reinvigorated the traditional hunting economy, based as it was on reciprocal relations between human and animal persons. Even the more abstract aspects of Christianity could be absorbed if analogies existed in native beliefs or mythology. The central Algonquians could understand that the holy wafer became the body of Christ since their cultural hero Nanabozho had turned bits of his own or his wife's flesh into raccoons for food. (Bailey 1969: 135; Leland 1884, 1:338) And there was little difficulty for the Hurons in accepting the Jesuits' claim that those who had been baptized went to Heaven rather than to the traditional villages of the dead, since they had always believed that the souls of people who died at different stages of their life or in different ways were separated. (Trigger 1985: 252) Similarly, the tortures of Hell, despite the best efforts of Catholic missionaries, were equated by the Hurons and Iroquois with their own ritual tortures, which conferred respect and honor on those who withstood them bravely and therefore carried positive connotations. (Murray 1999: 14) This is a good example of how some Christian concepts were incorporated on native terms in ways that radically altered their meaning.

Important Christian and native personages or mythical figures could be assimilated to one another in a process of mutual reinterpretation. The mother of Christ was not only assimilated to the native concept of *orenda*, or powerful spirit, but also, more specifically, to the daughter of the Sky Woman of the Huron and Iroquois creation myths, who was mysteriously impregnated by a sacred being, gave birth while still a virgin to twin sons, and was revered as the mother of Huron and Iroquois humankind. This native Virgin Mary bridged Christianity and the autochthonous religion. Many Huron and Iroquois Christian women appeared to define her in both Catholic and native ways; she was seen as the intercessor in the way that the Jesuits taught, at the same time as she was supplicated as an *orenda*. Christian Iroquois women clung to traditional medical practices but, if these failed, were also prepared to turn to the Virgin Mary as a more powerful *orenda* for relief and cure. Thus, she was interpreted as a repository of supernatural power accessible to meet indigenous needs. (Hart 1999)

It was the chronic moral and social crisis that beset Native Americans after contact that created an opportunity for the Jesuits to act as agents of reform and renewal. By the 1630s, the Montagnais, among the first northeastern Native Americans to come into regular contact with Europeans, were faced with disintegration as a result of French encroachment, commercial displacement, Iroquois attacks, depletion of food resources - especially beaver, due to over-trapping - and the inroads of European diseases. Although inclined to blame the French for their troubles, they also worried that they themselves might have been at fault and felt the need to examine themselves for personal responsibility for the deepening crisis. Taking Jesuit criticism seriously, they began to attribute their troubles to their own irresponsibility, particularly in refusing to accept baptism. (Morrison 1986: 12, 14, 15) It was clear that traditional native ritual no longer placated offended animal persons and hostile humans, whose anger had brought starvation, sickness, and death at the hands of enemies. Only French Christian ritual, and in particular the sacrament of baptism, seemed to offer the prospect of reviving social solidarity and cooperation and renewed positive relations with animals and other humans. Those who had acquired baptism demonstrably benefited from improved hunting, smoothed reciprocal relations with the French and assistance against threatening Indian enemies. (Morrison 1990: 416-17) Although fear of baptism was still common, the number of cures associated with the sacrament had begun to increase. Equally important, baptized children were educated among the French, and some received French godparents, demonstrating that the sacrament

271

extended the bonds of social solidarity. Thus, baptism operated like many traditional native rituals that aimed to create and maintain alliances among all classes of people. French godparents reserved the right to name the newly baptized, and here too French custom meshed with Montagnais tradition; changing one's name had always been a powerful way to declare personal transition. Since the Jesuits taught that the baptized went to Heaven rather than to the traditional land of the dead, some Montagnais - particularly parents who had lost a loved child - sought baptism as a way to ensure continued contact. (Morrison 1986: 14; Morrison 1990: 421)

The ritual may have been new, but what was reinvigorated was the traditional religious world. Christian power merely emerged as a new manifestation of the ancient category of person. The Jesuits brought awareness of powerful new other-than-human persons who offered real assistance in return for moral obedience. But the mutual obligations between human and other-than-human persons remained, and the native concept of power itself did not change. Rather the Christian concept of grace was understood as an expression of native concepts of power. For example, the dramatic increase in the number of baptisms from twenty-two in 1635 to over a hundred in 1636 was attributed by Paul Le Jeune to a vow that the priests had made to the Virgin; the Montagnais no longer resisted the baptism of their children because they were impressed by the workings of this Christian power, rather than by Christian beliefs. (JR 12:9) This was the foundation of the adaptive process whereby the Montagnais accepted the efficacy of Catholic ritual, but utilized it in a traditional context. (Morrison 1990: 419, 431; Morrison 1986: 17)

A comparable process of self-examination and revitalization went on in the 1640s and 1670s among the Abenaki people of the Kennebec River. As with the Montagnais, the early contact period brought social disruption. Alternating epidemics of smallpox, measles, and plague (beginning as early as 1616) revealed their vulnerability, the fur trade created domestic conflict, commerce pitted the bands against one another, and the liquor traffic disrupted family relations. Disagreements among religious leaders about how to react to the newcomers bred shamanistic rivalries, with some threatening to inflict sickness on any of their people who collaborated with the outsiders. Although the Abenaki did suspect that the colonists were responsible for the recurring sickness, their traditions related illness to social discord, and hence they believed that their own moral disunity had unleashed the epidemics and disorder. Since traditional means had proved ineffective in countering post-contact disease, drunkenness, and discord, the Abenaki felt an urgent need for ethical renewal. (Morrison 1984: 72-74) Early in the 1640s, they visited the Montagnais mission at Sillery and returned to their people with an appreciation of the Christian message. (Morrison 1981: 243) As a result of their request for a priest, Gabriel Druillettes was sent to their region. On his first visit, he remained only during the winter of 1646-47, yet when he returned in 1650, he found abundant evidence that his teachings had taken root. Many Abenaki had come to believe that prayer was powerful; even in his absence, they continued to recite prayers that he had taught them, and they had invented and taught each other methods to remember the ritual imagery of Catholicism. Druillettes believed that the Kennebec interest in Christianity was genuine, and he was all the more impressed because they could expect neither economic nor military aid from the French. Since the Abenaki were excluded from the fur trade, they had no hope of reaping temporal advantage from the coming of the Jesuits. The French did not admit the Kennebecs to the Canadian fur trade until 1665. (Morrison 1984: 82)

Druillettes was critically important to Kennebec religious regeneration. The extraordinary powers which the Indians attributed to him, such as his ability to acquire their language in a couple of months, with more ease than visiting Algonquians (JR 31:203), led them to believe that he was not a man but a *Nioueskou* (JR 37:253), which is to say, one who is blessed or holy, a spirit or extraordinary genie. (Morrison 1984: 85) As a result, like missionaries elsewhere, he was able to usurp the role of a shaman-sagamore (a sagamore was a chief or headman), and exercise not only religious but also political leadership. For example, he helped arrange a treaty between the Kennebecs and the Sokoki Indians to the south. His charismatic authority allowed him to spark a

Christian revitalization movement across the ethnic boundary, which, at least for a time, had as much revolutionary impact as any indigenous revitalization movement among other North American tribes. (Conkling 1974: 2, 15) His success lay in the convincing explanation for the crisis that his message provided, expressed in a form that the Kennebecs could readily understand. He struck a resonant chord when he attributed the sickness and the social disruptions of alcohol to sin. Rather than immersing them in Catholic dogma, he made specific proposals for their regeneration - prayer, abstinence from drinking, quiet submission to adversity, and maintenance of peace - which made sense because they were understood to have the power to conquer the demons of social enmity, drunkenness, perverse shamanism, and even sickness, and thus addressed the causes of their crisis in the 1640s. Druillettes met them on their own territory and spoke to them in their own terms, in particular in helping to identify their sense of responsibility for their own social problems. (Morrison 1981: 246; Morrison 1984: 85) The best missionaries were at once the best teachers of the Christian alternative and the best students of Indian culture. (Axtell 1985: 286)

The Abenaki did not simply accept the Catholicism which Druillettes presented; they took from his teachings only what would restore their own self-esteem and revitalize their religious identity. If the Jesuit had engendered a religious revival among the Kennebecs, it had been accomplished by reinforcing traditional beliefs. Catholicism ensured the success of the Abenaki's hunting economy; tribes would not have embraced any religion that failed to validate their reciprocal relations with animal persons. (Morrison 1984: 82, 91) The pattern of religious revelation remained the same. Dreams and visions were as commonplace in Abenaki experience after Druillettes's preaching as before, even if the symbols did sometimes become Christian; for example, children who died immediately after baptism appeared from Heaven to encourage parents to embrace the truths of Christianity. (Morrison 1981: 247) Although traditional shamanism was undermined, it did not wither but evolved; Druillettes learned that one man received old shamanistic powers over sickness in a new, Christian form. When one Abenaki avowed that Druillettes had driven away by his prayers a demon who wished to take his life, he merely admitted that prayer was more powerful than, rather than different, from traditional medicine. (JR 37:251) What the priest identified as demonic forces, the Kennebecs had long recognized as malevolent other-than-human persons who worked through viciously anti-social shamans. In any case, the priest's ridicule of traditional medicine merely confirmed the conclusions that the Kennebecs had already reached and which had prompted them to seek a priest in 1646.

Despite Druillettes' impressive results, the Kennebecs did not immediately embrace Catholicism en masse, but from the 1670s the intensification of their communal crisis led the Abenaki to react more profoundly to Catholicism than they had thirty years earlier. (Morrison 1984: 88) After war with the English in 1675-77, which thoroughly disrupted their hunting and agricultural economy, entire families arrived from Maine and chose to settle permanently at Sillery, where the Jesuits offered them a community base far removed from the hostilities, and where they were allowed to remain culturally distinct. By June 1681, nearly one hundred Abenaki had moved to Quebec, and in 1683 a new Abenaki mission was established on the water route to the Kennebecs. By 1689, six hundred Abenaki resided in Canadian missions, where they freely participated in religious activities even though the Jesuits provided little aid. (Morrison 1984: 90; Morrison 1981: 253) Conversion to Catholicism followed kinship lines. Abenaki villages near French centers of population became what their summer villages had been long before European contact: not only the physical locus of economic and political life, but also the seasonal center of communal religious expression. Many embraced Catholicism because they fervently believed that community health stemmed from the moral integrity of its individual members. The widespread practice of self-mortification, encouraged by the Fathers, suggests how deeply they had internalized their own responsibility for the post-contact crisis. The mission also encouraged the Abenaki to foster among themselves a reinvigorated tribal order because it provided them with both a religious and a social critique of the insidious alcoholism which traditional values alone had been unable to contain or eradicate. (Morrison 1981: 252)

Christian revitalization movements were more successful than native equivalents, of which traces appear in the Jesuit documents. Anti-Catholic cults spread rapidly throughout Huronia during the epidemics to provide ideological resistance to the new European religion. These native movements focused on visions of native prophets and renewed zeal for ceremonies, re-emphasizing traditional ways and attempting to marshal opposition to Christianity, while simultaneously adopting elements of it. Huron versions of the rite of baptism became part of a native healing cult. During a twelve-day fast on the shores of a lake at the time of the smallpox epidemics of 1637, the shaman Tehorenhaegnon learned a curing ritual which he and his associates subsequently practiced, which involved sprinkling the sick from a kettle filled with water and fanning them from a distance with a turkey's wing. The sprinkling of the sick may have been an imitation of baptism, or could have derived from a blending of Christian elements with a pre-existing equivalent Huron ritual. The revelation by a lake recalls rites performed by the Iroquois Otter Society, which is dedicated to propitiating water animals that are believed to influence health, and which practices a rite whereby the sick are sprinkled with spring water. Tehorenhaegnon's innovation may have been to combine elements that mimicked the powerful magic of the Jesuits with traditional healing practices. (JR 13:241; Trigger 1976: 533) Another rite involving dispensing ritually prepared water from a kettle to treat the sick was reported a few years later. The deity Iouskeha appeared in a vision to one Huron while he was fishing and informed him that he was the master of the earth, and none other than the spirit that the Jesuits wrongly called Jesus, but whom the French knew inadequately. The deity attributed the disease that was assailing the natives to the Jesuits who traveled two by two throughout the Huron country with the design of spreading the affliction until all the Indians were dead. First the Black Robes were to be driven away. Then the Indians were to perform a ritual in which a great kettle of ritually treated water was carried through the village, from which the sick should be encouraged to drink. The man reported the vision to the village council, which gave orders that the ritual be performed. These rites are the first recorded attempt by a Huron group to reassert traditional beliefs and denigrate those advocated by the Jesuits. They provide glimpses of ideological resistance to Christianity and reinforcement of the basic tenets of the Huron tradition. (JR 20:27-31; Trigger 1976: 594; Jaenen 1974: 278)

The spread of illness encouraged a revival of healing practices by specialized medicine or curing societies among the Hurons and the Iroquois. Each society specialized in curing certain types of illness, and membership was open to those who had been cured by a particular society, and thereafter remained hereditary in the individual's family. True to native tradition, the content of the victim's dreams revealed which medicine society was to be summoned. For example, among the Iroquois, dreams of dwarf spirits indicated a need for the "dark dance" of the Little Water Society; dreams of bloody birds were properly diagnosed as wishes for membership in the Eagle Society; and dreams of face masks called for the rituals of the Society of (False) Faces, so-called on account of the members' grotesque wooden face masks which symbolized supernatural beings (this society is popularly known as "False Faces," but its members speak simply of "Faces"). Wearing these masks and equipped with tortoise-shell rattles, the medicine men moved about the village accepting tobacco from the inhabitants and curing the sick. (Hultkrantz 1979: 100) Members of the society performed dramatic pantomime at New Year's and Green Corn ceremonies; in spring and fall they conducted a public exorcism of disease, high winds, malevolent witches, and ill luck; and they cured illness at any time of year. Membership included a large share of the community, for all those who had been saved from disease through its work or who had dreamed of membership became members. The society probably evolved in response to the threat of periodic epidemics of introduced diseases for which the Iroquois had no immunity, and hence was a post-contact phenomenon. (Fenton 1987: 505) The earliest wooden masks, which may have originated as representations of personal guardian spirits revealed in dreams, probably date from the sixteenth century. Champlain first saw them among the Hurons in 1616, and a Dutch trader came across them among the Mohawks and Oneidas in 1634. They are not mentioned among the Seneca before 1687, but there is no reason to suppose that they did not have a similar antiquity here. (Wallace 1970: 67, 71-72,

79, 81) Among the Hurons, the Atirenda society, which had about eighty members in the 1630s, including six women, was famous for treating ruptures. The performance of dances by individuals dressed as hunchbacks and who carried sticks and wore wooden masks suggests the existence of a curing society similar to the Iroquois Society of Faces. Another Huron society was the Awataerohi, whose members were held in awe for their ability to handle fire and use it to cure. (Trigger 1976: 80-81) Among the Ojibwas, curing societies, such as the Midewiwin, also seem to have been of post-contact origin.

Further evidence of revitalization appeared in 1645-46 in several Huron villages. (Ronda 1988: 16) One was based on the alleged revelation of a Christian woman whose ghost had returned from the dead to report that Huron Christians who went to Heaven were tortured there by the French: (Trigger 1965: 45)

"It was said that a Huron Christian woman, of those who are buried in our cemetery, had risen again; that she had said that the French were impostors; that her soul, having left the body, had actually been taken to Heaven; that the French had welcomed it there, but in the manner in which an Iroquois captive is received at the entrance to their villages - with firebrands and burning torches, with cruelties and torments inconceivable. She had related that all Heaven is nothing but fire, and that there the satisfaction of the French is to burn now some, now others; and that, in order to possess many of these captive souls, which are the object of their pleasures, they cross the seas, and come into these regions as into a land of conquest, just as a Huron exposes himself with joy to the fatigues and all the dangers of war, in the hope of bringing back some captive. It was further said that those who are thus burned in Heaven, as captives of war, are the Huron, Algonquin, and Montagnais Christians, and that those who have not been willing in this world to render themselves slaves of the French, or to receive their laws, go after this life into a place of delights, where everything good abounds, and whence all evil is banished. This risen woman added, they said, that, after having been thus tormented in Heaven a whole day - which seemed to her longer than our years - the night having come, she had felt herself roused, near the beginning of her sleep; that a certain person, moved with compassion for her, had broken her bonds and chains, and had shown her, at one side, a deep valley which descended into the earth, and which led into that place of delights whither the souls of the infidel Hurons go; that from afar she had seen their villages and their fields, and had heard their voices, as of people who dance and who are feasting. But she had chosen to return into her body, as long as was necessary to warn those who were there present of such terrible news, and of that great misfortune which awaited them at death, if they continued to believe in the impostures of the French. This news was soon spread everywhere; it was believed in the country without gainsaying...it was an article of faith for all the infidels, and even some of the Christians almost half believed it...and in order to confirm this truth more substantially, they said that in reality the place of the fire is not the center of the earth, but rather the Sky, to which we see fires and flames ascend. They added that the Sun was a fire, and that - if he makes himself felt from so far, if he warms or burns according as he approaches us - one cannot doubt that he makes a powerful conflagration in the Sky, and that he furnishes flames more than are required in order to burn all the Hurons whom the French try to send hither." (JR 30:29-33)

Another area of native religious life that showed resilience and revitalization was dream interpretation. Peoples of the northeast looked to their dreams for guidance in all the important affairs of life. Dreams were believed to be the language of the soul, a source of revelation of the 'secret desires of the soul.' Dreams foretold future events; prescribed feasts, dances, games; and provided supernatural guidance for the conduct of daily life. No Huron would act counter to the dictates of his dreams. The hidden desires revealed therein had to be fulfilled if people were to enjoy health, happiness, and success. (Wallace 1970: 59-75; Axtell 1985: 15) Failure to do so would lead to illness, madness, and if untreated, even death. Diseases attributed to this cause could be cured if a shaman could determine the nature of the desire and satisfy it, either by seeing that the object of desire was obtained for the sick person or by performing suitable rituals, in what amounted to a sophisticated form of psychotherapy. The role of the shaman was to help to interpret the dream and to assist in its fulfillment. Communal feasts, sports contests, and even sexual orgies might be called to satisfy a sick person's dream and thereby effect his cure. Among the Hurons, there was a formal ritual of gratification for sexual wishes expressed in dreams. In 1639, Le Jeune met an old man who was dying of an ulcer; he desired a feast, the climax of which was to be mating of men with girls, including one for himself.

A common desire of the soul was for curing rituals to be performed. Each winter, among the Hurons, a large part of the population of a community would take part in a three-day festival called *ononharoia*, 'the upsetting of the brain', which required the guessing and fulfillment of the dreams of the whole community. Bands of people would stream through the village, acting out their dreams in pantomime and demanding that the dream be guessed and satisfied, and claiming objects (a dog, a canoe) or requiring acts to be performed (act of murder, act of sexual gratification) that they had seen in their dreams. The ceremony was usually precipitated by the illness of a well-known person. At the end, the participants retired to the woods outside the village to cast out their madness, hoping that the sick person would recover. This ceremony probably served as a means to give vent to pent-up emotions. It also led to a redistribution of wealth, because objects taken during these days were not returned. (Trigger 1978, 15:373)

But some desires could not be fulfilled in the form in which they were asked, either because the object could not be obtained, or because the desire was destructive to the petitioner or to others. In these cases, a symbolic equivalent was suggested by the shaman. If a warrior dreamed that the enemy was burning him at the stake, he would seek to avoid this happening in reality by having his fellow villagers go through the preliminaries of torturing him but a dog would be killed in his place. (Trigger 1976: 82) In 1661-62, Father Lalemant reported an Indian who had himself tied to a scaffold and the fires lit (though no burns), another who had his house burnt down, and another who also had himself burnt, with fire applied to his legs so he took six months to recover from his burns, all to satisfy dream visions. (Wallace 1970: 64-66) A young man whom Brébeuf had told that he was on his way to

Hell dreamt that his life could only be saved if he killed the missionary. To appease his dream, the village council presented him with the recently taken head of an enemy, thus satisfying his soul wish and diverting his anger from the Jesuits. (Trigger 1976: 592) Whereas dreams in which hostility was directed at members of other nations could be satisfied by acting them out both in pantomime and in reality, dreams in which hostility was directed at the dreamer's own community could be acted out only in symbolic form, which had a prophylactic effect. (Wallace 1970: 66) The idea was that a wish was fateful, and the only way of forestalling the realization of an evil-fated wish was to fulfill it symbolically.

Intuitively, native peoples had achieved a great degree of psychological sophistication. They recognized conscious and unconscious desires, and were aware that the frustration of these desires could cause mental and physical (psychosomatic) illness. They understood that these desires were expressed in symbolic form, by dreams, but that the individual could not always properly interpret these dreams himself. They had noted the distinction between the manifest and latent content of dreams, and employed what sounds like the technique of free association to uncover the latent meaning. And they considered that the best method for the relief of psychic and psychosomatic distresses was to give the repressed desire satisfaction, either directly or symbolically. (Wallace 1970: 63; Wallace 1958: 238)

The effectiveness of the Iroquois dream therapy was admitted in some cases by the Jesuits themselves. One woman saw the moon transform itself into a tall, beautiful woman and demanded presents from the Hurons and their allies for the dreamer, including dressing her from head to toe in red. The chiefs decided this dream should be satisfied since it expressed the wishes of the moon-lady. The disease from which the dreamer was suffering was diagnosed, from her symptoms of giddiness, as requiring the Dream Feast or *Ononharoia*, and messengers collected the articles she required. She underwent the five-day ritual, received gifts, and had her last desire guessed and satisfied. Le Jeune noted that the woman's condition was much improved after the feast though she was not cured, a circumstance that the Indians attributed to some lack or failure in the ceremony. (Wallace 1970: 69-70; Wallace 1958: 244)

But the failure of shamans to protect natives against disease meant that Hurons looked to Christianity and the Jesuit priests who presented themselves as substitute shamans. Such was the hold that the priests were able to secure over native peoples that they were able to become extremely influential in native groups' attempts to adapt their religions. Revitalization movements were led by the priests, not native shamans. (Conkling 1974: 1) Indian society contained the means to regenerate itself and, indeed, did so; the major instigators of this transformation, however, were not aboriginal leaders but the missionaries. The revolutionary change in the Abenaki's social forms was not entirely imposed from outside the society, therefore; on the contrary, it was also wrought from within. The power of the French missionaries was conceded by the Abenaki because these men met their own idea of charismatic qualification for an authoritative role in their society. It is this that explains the profound conversions of many of these Indians, who remain steadfast Catholics today. (Conkling 1974: 20)

26 "They will Believe All You Please"

Did the Jesuits convert the native peoples of the northeast? Some historians remain stubbornly optimistic. They point to the Fathers' remarkable success both with large, powerful, sedentary groups around the Great Lakes and with mobile hunting bands all over New France. By the beginning of the eighteenth century, one hundred and fifteen Jesuit fathers and numerous lay brothers had established some thirty missions across New France (from Nova Scotia through Maine, Quebec, Ontario, and New York to Michigan, Wisconsin and Illinois); considerably more than ten thousand natives had been baptized, of whom a large proportion, we are assured, were bona fide converts. Indian Christians not only left their homelands to embrace Catholicism, but after the fall of New France in 1763 the vast majority remained in the faith at times with no priests to guide them. The majority of the Algonquian and Iroquoian peoples converted by the French missionaries have preserved their identity as Catholics to the present day, and the former Laurentian reserves are still Catholic, more than two centuries after the British Conquest. (Axtell 1985: 276-77)

This interpretation attributes the major credit for the success to the Jesuits themselves, and extols their superiority over all other missionaries in eastern North America. The Fathers are held clearly to have outshone their English Protestant rivals and their Catholic rivals in Canada and Louisiana, in terms of numbers, wealth, education, and skills. (Axtell 1988: 73) They have been credited with the best intellectual preparation among missionaries; the development of superior linguistic skills by comparison with their rivals, for example the Recollects; the most rigorous means of testing Indian candidates to ensure that converts were genuine; and the most efficacious techniques of conversion, including their mastery of the written word, their ability to predict and therefore apparently control eclipses, and the intelligent use of tools and weapons, images and paintings, clocks, magnets and magnifying glasses. (Grant 1984: 33; Axtell 1985: 72)

There is much in this portrayal of the Jesuits that is true, but some important qualifications should also be noted. The Fathers also overestimated the extent to which they overthrew the shamans' power; ultimately the shamans outlasted the Black Robes. Many Indians consistently preferred treatment by their own healers, even when it came to unfamiliar, introduced diseases. Indian techniques for treating wounds and injuries were at least as good as, and in some cases better than, those of Europeans, and there were many cases of Indians recovering faster than Europeans, when using their own curative techniques. Furthermore, the tribal memories of the descendants of those who were the objects of the missionaries' attentions creates an image quite at variance with that created by the Jesuits. (Trigger 1976: 708; Dickason 1989: 91-93)

The destruction by the Iroquois of the most important Jesuit endeavor, the missionary experiment in Huronia, made impossible the Jesuit goal of establishing a firm base in the heart of North America from which the gospel could be spread. But the fact that Huronia collapsed should not obscure evidence that the Jesuits succeeded in bringing about a Christian transformation of Huron culture before the confederacy ceased to exist as a cultural entity. In some areas, Christianity made significant inroads. Converts abandoned shamans, biblical cosmology largely replaced the world of Aataentsic, totems and *oki* gave way to saints and angels, and the priest was coming to replace the native sorcerer as an object of awe and respect. Many Huron converts appear to have been imbued with sincere zeal to change and reform their own culture. However, this did not involve passive submission to wholesale changes in their cultural orientation. Rather than capitulate to an entirely different set of ideas and actions, they borrowed Christian elements selectively to enhance a native life-style without suffering complete disintegration in the process. Their own economy, kinship, language, architecture, and dress remained substantially intact. Compared with many other native groups, the Hurons enjoyed strong cultural bonds that allowed for "conversions manifesting a New World expression of the Old World faith." (Bowden 1981: 89) No doubt the size of the Huron confederacy and its isolation from unsupervised contact with Europeans did much to prevent the deterioration in self-confidence that is obvious among many weaker tribes. Had other circumstances not been adverse, one expert believes it would have been possible for Jesuits to transform Huronia successfully into a nation that was both Christian and Indian. (Trigger 1968: 134)

At the same time, the Hurons demonstrated that their religion could resist the new faith and even become reinvigorated as a result of the contest. Although the many deaths from disease - especially after 1637 when the population fell by more than half - contributed to the number of conversions, most natives did not abandon their own religion but reacted in the traditional manner, killing suspected witches and performing ancient rituals in the curing societies. (Bowden 1981: 91, 94; Trigger 1985: 245-46; JR 13:155-7 and 227-43; 14:37-9; 15:53) The failure of particular native rituals to cure the sick did not discredit the Huron religion, a fact that the Jesuits commented on with some exasperation:

"They believe most diseases arise from their desires or from witchcraft. This is because if natural remedies fail to produce effect, they conclude that the disease must be due to some cause that is not natural. As the desires of the soul are infinite in number, and so too the spells that might prevent a cure, they can drive out ten or twenty spells from the sick person's body, but if they see that the disease continues, they attribute its cause to some other spell, which is still more concealed and cannot be removed by their art. In spite of that, their jugglers retain their reputation among the Hurons, as much as the most skilful physicians do in France, although in many instances they do not restore health." (JR 33:199-203)

Shamans were spurred to communicate more intensively with the spirit world in an effort to discover rituals that would be effective. While many of these were in turn discredited, each epidemic did eventually subside, thereby giving credit to the rituals that were performed at that time and reinforcing the traditional beliefs on which they were based. (Trigger 1985: 248) The interest displayed by shamans in monitoring the effectiveness of their cures indicates that more was involved in these rituals than the charlatanism ascribed to them by the Jesuits. The "decade of death" never led many Hurons to become seriously disillusioned with their own religion, but only to believe that they had not found the appropriate counter-magic to use against the Jesuits. The epidemics neither terrorized them into submission to the European newcomers, nor so overwhelmed them that native religious beliefs and the traditional social order that they sanctioned no longer appeared to be valid. The possibility must be considered that what held true for the Hurons must apply even more so to native peoples who did not have in their midst missionaries trying to undermine their traditional religious system. (Salisbury 1992: 504-06; Trigger 1985: 242-43, 258)

Likewise, at Sillery, the mission obtained a few dedicated converts, but the majority of Montagnais clung to the old beliefs, and traditionalists maintained an active religious underground and managed to resist Jesuit teachings for the better part of ten years. Christianity in Sillery was always a minority belief rejected by most as a strange, complicated, and potentially dangerous ideology, not least for the divisiveness it provoked. Those who recovered from illness after they accepted baptism began to draw apart from those who clung to tradition. The Jesuits' insistence on the dominance of Christian Indians in Sillery introduced new conflicts into Montagnais life. Although the Christians were in a minority, through outside help from the French they managed to achieve a majority among the newly elected village officers. These Christian leaders insisted that acceptance of the French and Christianity was the only means to halt the eventual destruction of the Montagnais people and that those who opposed would be driven from the village. The Christian Indians began to scrutinize their traditions, such as polygamy, for the workings of evil demons, and refused to participate either in war feasts or in any occasion that had a ritual character. They adopted courtship customs more acceptable to the Jesuits, and even refused to permit traditionalists to marry their daughters. Native traditions of consensus were being replaced by coercion. Christian Indians wished to use prison sentences and public floggings for transgressors of moral codes, especially those who abided by traditional courting practices which sometimes involved sexual intercourse. Even the threat of execution was used to force adherence to their orders. When Jesuits counseled moderation, they were accused of being cowards and backsliders. The Christian challenge produced a traditionalist reaction that portrayed converts as petty and power-hungry, bent on dividing the group. For the first time in their history, the Montagnais were split into two rival and hostile ideological factions. The ideal of a peaceful, united Christian Sillery was already a failure by 1641, since many Indians had come to believe that to be a Christian was to lose one's identity as a Montagnais. The Sillery experiment failed not simply because of war, disease, and lack of funds but because, contrary to the original intentions of the Fathers, it demanded cultural suicide. (Ronda 1979: 9-15; Morrison 1986: 1; Morrison 1990 429)

It is clear that on the basis of their order's experiences in India, China, and Japan, the Jesuits had underestimated the problems involved in making Christianity acceptable to the tribal societies of North America. The brand of Christianity propounded by seventeenth-century missionaries, Catholic and Protestant, did not easily cross the cultural divide that separated European from Native American. Christian doctrines were based on ideas of authority, hierarchy and punitive justice which Europeans took for granted; to express them in a way that was compatible with the beliefs of people whose whole way of life was founded on directly opposite principles - consensus, equality, persuasion - required more than linguistic skills which could translate the Christian message. It required "the remolding of Christian teaching to fit a different social code." (Trigger 1976: 393-94) Even though missionaries adopted an alien language and way of life, they found great difficulty in conveying the substance of Christian faith to a mentality that differed in crucial respects from the European one. Instead, the Jesuits concluded that the implantation of Christianity required that native societies be transformed, as they had begun to do at Sillery and Ossossané, from an egalitarian social order governed by consensus, into a hierarchical one. The far-reaching interpenetration of religion and everyday life meant that whether the Jesuits wished it or not, if the conversion of native peoples was to be effective, it required major alterations in aspects of their culture that the Jesuits, on the basis of previous experience, had no reason to suspect had anything to do with religion. (Trigger 1985: 294, 296; Trigger 1976: 847; Richter 1992: 109; Bitterli 1989: 103; Conkling 1974: 16)

The scale of the transformation ultimately involved in true conversion proved to be greater than the Jesuits had first anticipated, a fact that they only gradually came to perceive themselves. Le Jeune, basing his estimate on the experiences of Jesuits in Brazil, thought a generation would be a realistic estimate for conversion. By 1642, Jerome Lalemant confessed that the early impressions of easily converting the Amerindians were mistaken. The Jesuits required of their converts a massive reorientation of both belief and behavior. Changing native religion meant changing the whole native way of life. The exclusivity inherent in Christianity, the inability of seventeenth-century Europeans to distinguish Western culture from Christian religion, and the close relationship between native beliefs and their everyday life combined to require converts, in many instances, to do no less than renounce their Indianness. Missionaries who had set out intending to respect native cultures ended up finding themselves obliged to try to alter them. Thus, the Jesuits' initial willingness to adapt to the traditions of their converts was replaced by a doctrine more similar to what English ministers called "civility before sanctity." As Father Jacques Fremin told the headmen of a Mohawk town in 1667, the missionaries' purpose was "teaching them to live like men, and then to be Christians." The Jesuits professed to allow Indian converts to retain customs that were compatible with Christianity, but in practice few traditional ways measured up. (Dickason 1984: 251; Richter 1992: 109)

Despite the enormous obstacles in the way of effective communication between Indian and priest, there was genuine interest in the religious message on the part of at least some natives. It was difficult for Christianity to penetrate the religious life of inhabitants of tribal societies, but those who insist that it was impossible surely overstate the case. Furthermore, it is too simplistic to suggest that all natives were interested in French missionaries *only* because they provided access to French trade. Although the effects of Jesuit missions proved as destructive for the Indians of the northeast as did Puritan programs of directed culture change, paradoxically, the priests were admired as often as scorned, and the effects of positive dialogue between Indian and priest must be assessed along with those which accompanied hostile polarization. Considerations that induced Indians to become Catholics certainly included social and ideological disorientation resulting from disease and other aspects of European contact, as well as material benefits and the superior supernatural powers of the Christian God. But perhaps the explanation is both less complex and more profound. An initial attraction must have frequently become a heartfelt conversion simply because of the Jesuits' ceaseless efforts, evident dedication, and willingness to share in the lives of their charges. A message delivered often enough and sincerely enough by a respected figure was bound, sooner or later, to win adherents. Possibly twenty percent of the eight thousand six hundred Iroquois surviving in 1670 became sincere Catholics; perhaps, given the substantial obstacles, this is not such a dismal figure. Despite the yawning chasm between European and native cultures, the priests seem to have connected in surprising ways. For example, despite the inherent patriarchal bias of the Christianity taught by seventeenth-century missionaries, Catholicism, with its cult of the Virgin Mary, its veneration of female saints, and its sisterhoods of nuns appealed strongly to the matrilineal principles of Iroquois culture. This was so even though the messages were delivered almost entirely by males - nuns played no formal role at the Canadian mission villages. Christian communities (Caughnawaga, La Montagne, Cataraqui, Lorette) paradoxically provided a social environment in keeping with the cherished values that now seldom seemed to exist in the faction-ridden towns of Iroquoia. In these Canadian mission communities, traditional hospitality and reciprocity reigned, and there was little factional strife. In Iroquoia, as in Huronia, the St. Lawrence Valley, and elsewhere, the priests made many sincere converts, but they won support on the basis of diplomatic, political and religious considerations that were essentially Indian and traditional rather than European and Christian. (Morrison 1979: 52, 74; Richter 1992: 115, 116, 125, 128; Richter 1985: 4)

For every group of Indians who found, like those at Sillery, that to be Christian meant no longer being Indian, there was another who became Christian in order to remain Indians. The Abenaki warmly embraced Christianity on their own terms, and largely remain both Catholic and ethnically distinct to this day. The Kennebecs, in particular, responded so warmly to Catholicism that they seem to support the traditional view that the Jesuit missions led to the benevolent transformation of Indian peoples. Nor does it appear that the Abenaki missions triggered a vehement, nativist backlash, as occasionally occurred in other French missions. Yet the Abenaki's unequivocal acceptance of Catholicism does not mean that they either rejected or supplanted their traditional religiosity. Contact with the Jesuits enabled them to adapt creatively to post-contact threats against their identity. Although it was Father Druillettes who catalyzed the Kennebecs' experiment in cultural adaptation, they themselves controlled the direction of religious change. (Morrison 1981 235-36)

It is important to remember that, unlike in Spanish America, Indians in New France were under no direct compulsion to embrace Christianity; there could have been no native Christian communities unless they had voluntarily converted themselves. During the colonial period many Indians became Christians, both genuine and nominal, and adopted in some degree European ways, because they were persuaded that the Christian faith spoke more to their spiritual and cultural condition than did traditional religions. In every setting, particularly Canada, where material seductions were small or nonexistent, Indians converted because they were persuaded - by the missionaries and the logic of the situation as the natives saw it - that the Christian answers to the urgent, new questions of life were intellectually and emotionally satisfying, at least more so than the outmoded explanations offered by their traditional wise men. Conversion represented not so much a rejection of the old way as a conviction that Christianity offered more powerful magic for a changed situation. (Axtell 1985: 283-84; Grant 1984: 44)

Christianity offered some (not all) natives of the northeast something that traditional religion alone could no longer provide: a means of reintegrating societies in which old standards had broken down.

"Conversion to Christianity," as one historian has memorably argued, "was essentially a phenomenon of the moon of wintertime, when ancestral spirits had ceased to perform their expected functions satisfactorily and angel choirs promised to fill a spiritual vacuum." Christianity offered a new diagnosis and cure for native ills, but one that made sense in terms of traditional social and moral assumptions. It not only furnished the medicine of an apparently more powerful people, but also a dynamic view of history that helped to make change comprehensible, as well as documents whose permanence and uniformity made traditional myths seem evanescent and unreliable. "The Great Spirit has not given you any such book, but he has given it to us" was an argument that the Indians found difficult to answer. Furthermore, Europeans by their very presence compelled Indians to try to make sense of a cosmos broader than their mythology envisaged, and only Christianity seemed well equipped to meet this need. While the European associations of Christianity were the most formidable obstacle to its acceptance, they also constituted its chief attraction. (Grant 1984: 244-45)

Conversion meant different things to different people, but three typical meanings should be distinguished. First, for some, conversion signified a deliberate break with the past. Second, for others, it meant appropriation of Christianity on terms consonant with native modes of thought and relevant to perceived needs. An Indian who sincerely accepted everything the missionaries said might also interpret what he heard in terms of presuppositions at odds with those of the missionaries; apparent agreement might conceal fundamental differences of understanding. A priest might be regarded not merely as a dispenser of sacraments over which he had no proprietary right but as a shaman giving and withholding blessings at will. The word of missionaries might be accepted on the understanding that it had come to them directly in dreams. It was through dreams that many conversions of individuals took place, demonstrating the distinctively Indian way in which Christianity was adopted. What was embraced was so different from Christianity as the missionaries understood it as to be classified more properly as, at best, a blend neither quite Christian nor traditional. (Grant 1984: 241, 246, 263)

Third, for yet others, it represented an opportunity not to discard traditional ways but to supplement them. For many (perhaps most), the profession of Christianity was a subtle but effective way of rejecting it. Such a possibility lurks behind Father Le Caron's summary of the Huron response: "they will believe all you please, or, at least will not contradict you; and they will let you, too, believe what you will." One Huron confessed in 1670 that, though he had been taken for a good Christian for more than twenty-five years, he had been one in appearance only. He had given this impression in order to gratify the Jesuits and so they would stop trying to convert him: "I said to you 'Yes, I will be converted'; but I must reveal a secret to you. You must know that we have a 'yes' which means 'no', a sort of long-drawn and languid 'yes.' When we say aaao, although we seem to yield what is asked of us, yet that aaao, thus prolonged, means, 'I will do nothing of the sort.' On the other hand, when we accede to anything in earnest, we cut the word shorter and say Ao, 'yes.'" (JR 55:297) That this could be found out in 1670 is an indication of the gap in understanding that must have separated the Jesuits from those they baptized in the 1630s. (Trigger 1976: 531) The 'yes that means no' places a question mark after a fair number of Indian conversions. But even this possibility is not necessarily so incompatible with genuine adherence to Christianity as it appears. Was it always Christianity itself to which their yes meant no, or could it sometimes have been the frame in which it was mounted? Although it might be argued, on the one hand, that authentic Christianity is incompatible with some pagan beliefs and practices and must therefore always be in tension with the culture in which it is set, on the other hand, it can be argued that Christianity has not really taken root in a community until it has fused with its culture sufficiently to make possible its appropriation in distinctively indigenous ways. If this argument is valid, the success of Christian penetration can never be measured simply on a scale of displacement. (Grant 1984: 247-51)

27 Land of Hobbamock

At the time of contact, the region that came to be known as New England - broadly speaking, stretching southwest along the Atlantic coast from Saco Bay, Maine, to the vicinity of the Housatonic river, in Connecticut, and from Long Island inland to southern New Hampshire and Vermont - was occupied by groups of Indians who shared, with minor exceptions, a single cultural pattern. All spoke closely related Algonquian languages, obtained their food by combining maize-beans-squash horticulture with the collecting of land and sea fauna and wild plants, and engaged in similar social, political, and religious practices. Above the village level, multi-village alliances played an important role, but it is not clear if these were enduring or highly structured enough to be classed as true 'tribes.' Pre-contact socio-political units were probably small, each consisting of a number of extended families exploiting the lands around individual river systems; the larger more formal 'tribes' of the seventeenth century almost certainly developed in response to new needs that arose with the fur trade and European settlement. Thus the emergence of 'tribes' only occurred after, and as a result of, the arrival of the Europeans. It was also to the advantage of each European colonial administration to emphasize, and even to enhance if possible, the power and territorial limits of the particular Indian leaders from whom it obtained treaty rights and deeds to land, in relation to other Indian leaders. This suggests that Europeans, out of self-interest, may have exaggerated the cohesion of native peoples into recognizable 'tribes.'

Daniel Gookin, superintendant of the Indians of Massachusetts Bay colony from 1656 to 1687 listed five principal nations of New England: Pequots; Narragansetts; Pokanokets (or Wampanoag); Massachusetts; and Pawtucketts. He also made reference to the Nipmucks, to the west of the Massachusetts. Two other peoples worthy of note were the Mohegans (confusingly renamed Mohicans in popular writings) and the Montauk (of Long Island). (Trigger 1978, 15:160, 166, 168) The inhabitants of Cape Cod, and of the islands of Martha's Vineyard and Nantucket, were related to, if not a direct offshoot from, the Wampanoags. Those on Cape Cod were sufficiently distinct to be set apart as the Nausets. The islanders were different linguistically and politically from the Nausets and more closely resembled the Wampanoags. (Cook 1976: 40) The Narragansetts have always been considered the largest single tribe in New England. Their core territory embraced the modern state of Rhode Island, west of the main channel of Narragansett Bay and Lower Blackstone River.

One of the most important factors in determining relations between the English and native groups was the spread of disease. By the late-sixteenth or early-seventeenth century, the northeast constituted a single disease interaction sphere subject to a pattern of severe but localized outbreaks of epidemics, sometimes taking years to spread across the entire region. The total population for the northeast (defined as east of the Hudson River and within the present limits of the US) at the beginning of the seventeenth century has been variously estimated, with figures ranging between thirty-four thousand and one hundred and forty-four thousand.[1] Although the total population is a matter of great dispute, it is fairly certain that, in the seventeenth century, four fifths of the New England Indians died of various disease epidemics, and some Indian groups were reduced by up to ninety-five percent. (Cook 1973b: 493, 494, 501) Mortality was extreme among coastal groups from the eastern shore of Narragansett Bay northward into southern Maine, particularly among the Massachusetts and Wampanoags. By the mid-seventeenth century, the coastal Massachusetts and the Narragansetts taken together had been reduced by eighty-six percent in comparison with their population levels in 1610 (from forty-four thousand to six thousand four hundred). (Cook 1976: 37) The greatest killer in the northeast between 1610 and 1640 was smallpox, which at intervals flared into epidemic proportions as it reached new Indian tribes, or attacked non-immune younger generations in older territory. In addition to the devastation wrought by sudden, catastrophic epidemics, the natives suffered even more severely from endemic disease in the form of respiratory ailments (tuberculosis, pneumonia, influenza) and dysentries, to which they remained appallingly susceptible. While American Indian medical care was sophisticated enough to handle diseases present before the

Europeans, it was not able to deal effectively with "crowd-type" diseases, that is, diseases developed in large, dense human populations such as those brought from Europe. Medical care was grossly inadequate. Also, certain American Indian disease treatments, such as sweathouses and plunging into cold water for smallpox, often only increased mortality rates. (Thornton 1987: 47)

As elsewhere in the Americas, native peoples were stunned by the huge population losses consequent upon the spread of European diseases. The traditional source of assistance against sickness was the shaman or *powwow*. With one recorded exception, all shamans were male; they were called to their role in a dream or vision experience, which may have been induced by herbal infusions. The shaman had the power to cure both physical and mental illness, foretell the future, control the elements, and bewitch enemies either by magical intrusion of a small object or by capture of the victim's soul in a dream. (Axtell 1985: 228) He divined the cause of illness and learned whether or not it was curable, deriving his knowledge from creatures in the form of crow, hawk, or rattlesnake. His divination techniques included casting visions, which he read as good or bad omens, direct encounters between his soul and other spirits, and insight available through the ability of his helping spirit(s) to view events in the past, future, and at a distance. The inspired role of shaman and the hereditary role of sachem (chief, headman) did not overlap generally in one individual; the few persons who combined these roles were thought to be extremely powerful. Powwows do not appear to have been full-time specialists; they fought in war, owned land, and married. The importance of the shaman continued undiminished in the colonial period. (Simmons 1976: 223, 229, 231-32, 234)

The powwows were the principal earthly adversaries in any Puritan missionary effort. (Salisbury 1982: 138) The special relationship that the shamans maintained with a great spirit called Hobbamock convinced the Puritans that they were witches; Roger Williams (c.1603-1682/83), a Puritan fugitive from the Massachusetts Bay Colony who settled in Narragansett country in 1636, declared them to be "none other than our English witches" (Cave 1992: 243-44) For his part, Hobbamock possessed many recognizable diabolical qualities. (Shuffelton 1976: 112-13) He was said to enter certain persons and to remain in their bodies as a guardian and familiar. "This Hobbamock appears in sundry forms unto them, as in the shape of a man, a deer, a fawn, an eagle etc., but most ordinarily a snake...This, as far as we can conceive, is the devil." (Winslow 1841: 356-57) Missionary John Eliot (1604-90) wrote that Chepian (Chepian or Chepi was another name for Hobbamock) appeared to the Indians in dreams as a serpent. (Shepard 1647: 21) Hobbamock also seems to have been a collective term for the disembodied souls of the dead that reappeared in the shape of humans, animals, serpents, birds, and mythical creatures. (Simmons 1981: 60; Simmons 1976: 219; Axtell 1985: 225) According to Puritan Edward Winslow, Hobbamock appeared normally to three sorts of people: one type of great shaman whose name he did not know, and of whom there were few, but who were highly esteemed and believed to be invulnerable to any weapon; the powwows, who were able to cause and cure sickness; and the *pnieses*, warriors of great courage and wisdom, whose powers were conferred on them by a powerful dream. (Shuffelton 1976: 112-13) In the Massachusett and Wampanoag areas, the strongest and most able male children were subjected to loss of sleep, fasting and drinking mixtures that altered consciousness, in order to induce visions of Hobbamock. (Simmons 1976: 220, 222) By virtue of such a vision, a man became a pniese and acquired the ability to call upon and visualize Hobbamock for protection and power on the battlefield. (Salisbury 1982: 174) "The pnieses are men of great courage and wisdom, and to those also the devil appeareth more familiarly than to others, and as we conceive, maketh covenant with them to preserve them from death by wounds with arrows, etc." (Winslow 1841: 359) The pniese also became the sachem's counselor, collected tribute annually from sachem's subjects, and participated with him in decisions about war. (Simmons 1976: 221)

Shamanism was perhaps the most difficult feature of Indian culture for Europeans to understand. Edward Winslow never made the connection between Hobbamock, the spirit, which he took for the devil, and Hobbamock, the man, the Pilgrims' friend and translator, even though he was aware that the man was a pniese and thus involved in shamanism. The Puritans' approach was to present the native religion as possessing the same structural outline as Christianity. Just as Christianity conceived two powers, God and the devil, good and evil, in conflict, so New England Indians were said to worship two primary deities, Kiehtan (or Cautantowwit, as recorded by Roger Williams) and Hobbamock. Kiehtan was the creator and sustainer of all life in this world and in that to come. Characterized as benevolent but distant, his transformation into the Christian divine father was complete. Hobbamock was identified with the devil, on account of the attributes outlined above. Yet Puritans seem to have ignored the fact that Hobbamock used his powers both to help and to harm - not only did he cause wounds and diseases but he also cured them. Hence, unlike the devil, he was morally ambiguous. In fact, the God/devil model did not fit at all since both Kiehtan and Hobbamock caused illness when they were angry with men, but it was Hobbamock who was called upon to cure. (Shuffelton 1976: 111-13; Naeher 1989: 358; Winslow 1841: 355)

Exceptionally, some Puritans perceived that native realities did not always fit Christian conceptual schemes. Roger Williams's command of Algonquian dialects allowed him to gain insight into the powwows' healing process; as he described it, it was not based on the intervention of an evil spirit comparable to, or identical with, the devil, as Edward Winslow and William Wood supposed; rather the powwow used forces or spirits within the sufferer's body. Given our present understanding of shamanism, it is clear that Williams's description and other early accounts fit not the patterns of English witchcraft, but rather the characteristics of shamanic practice. (Cave 1992: 247) But this insight was unusual. The interpretive bias that sensitized Puritans to similarities between Indian culture and devilish aspects of their own also predisposed them to misinterpret or overlook many aspects of Indian culture that were unique. For example, Indian beliefs about the soul, death and the afterlife appear to have been quite different from those held by Puritans, but nevertheless were portrayed mainly in terms of the ways in which they resembled English beliefs. In discussing native kinship data, even Roger Williams did not recognize any categories in Narragansett that differed from categories in English.

(Simmons 1981: 63) In general, English accounts of the Indians' beliefs were colored by projections of their own faith. (Shuffelton 1976: 109) Although Winslow knew the Indians saw many divine powers, he still tried to reduce this pantheon to two figures approximating the chief antagonists in the Christian scheme and thus missed a chance to understand a significant difference between Indian and English consciousness. The Indians' animistic belief was for Winslow a totally alien concept and he could only explain their powwows' shamanistic dreams and magic in the more familiar terms of European witchcraft. (Simmons 1976: 224) Puritan observers interpreted the Indian creator, and sometimes the category manitou, as mistaken, confused and desiccated vestiges of the Christian God. (Simmons 1981: 61) As Roger Williams observed, apprehending any "excellency" in living beings, the Narragansetts called out "manittoo," in other words "it is a god"; at the sight of English ships or particularly books they uttered "manittowock" or "they are gods." The manitou that Williams translated as "god" actually referred to the manifestation of any spiritual power. (Salisbury 1982: 37; Williams 1973: 191) Thus the native word 'manitou' was transposed into a Christian framework. Similarly, when an Indian told John Eliot that a humming bird came to tell him when he did right and wrong, he was obliged by the missionary to confess that by the figure of the bird he meant the sense he had of right and wrong in his own mind. Rather than try to examine the full meanings of the various native terms, missionaries more usually made them fit their own religious terminology. (Murray 1999: 17-18)

Although, in terms of fundamentals, there was little to distinguish Protestant demonology from its Catholic counterpart, the former was characterized by a greater emphasis on the extent of divine power and providence. Protestant demonology attributed affliction and misfortunes not to witches and sorcery, but rather to Man's sin, and, ultimately therefore, to God's providential design. Events apparently caused by witchcraft, like all cases of affliction, served a spiritual function, as a retribution for sin and a test of faith, and offered an opportunity for introspection and repentance. The individual, not the devil or the witch, was ultimately responsible for the misfortunes that afflicted him (in the sense that they always signified aspects of his personal relationship with the God who brought them). Hence the popularity throughout Protestant Europe of the story of Job who acknowledged no source of his ills other than divine and no remedies other than patience and faith. The devil's role (with divine permission) was to sustain the illusion of power by providing the necessary efficacy. His presence was therefore implied even in the simplest forms of magic or the most trivial superstitions. Whether God inflicted suffering himself or allowed Satan to do so, by means of a witch, was of little consequence: ultimate responsibility lay with the sufferer. However adverse events seemed to be, when Puritans believed them to be special acts of their divinity, they reinterpreted the motive as the correcting hand of divine love, the deity's edifying intervention meant to instruct erring souls and provoke repentance. Reginald Scot (neither a Puritan nor a cleric) viewed witchcraft accusations as mere delusions of impious souls who could not bear to see divine power for what it really was, and derided those who mistook the Protestant deity's providences for magic. Increase Mather's *Essay for the Recording of Illustrious Providences* (1684) embodied this understanding of the nature of affliction by including as examples of providences of the Puritan deity numerous accounts of sorcery, apparitions, demonic possession, magic, and witchcraft. Mather implicitly attributed occult power and apparently hostile acts to the Puritan deity as well as to the witch. Thus, when, in 1637, Roger Williams told the paramount Narragansett sachem that the English were not responsible for the plague but implied that the affliction was attributable to the English God through whose eyes Indians now could see themselves as sinful (Simmons 1981: 65), he expressed a view that placed emphasis on the sinfulness they believed inherent in Indian culture, rather than the sinful practices such as idolatry which the Jesuits took to be the cause of the outbreaks of sickness in New France. Although the importance of the concept of the providential origin of affliction is clearer among Protestants, it was by no means absent among Catholics and so its function as a distinguishing characteristic should not be exaggerated.

The Puritans who settled in Massachusetts, Connecticut, and Rhode Island believed that a satanic presence permeated Native American life, that the Indian inhabitants of these areas worshipped devils, that Indian religious practitioners were witches, and that the Indians themselves were bewitched. Unlike Indian beliefs about the supernatural qualities of Englishmen, which seem to have been temporary and situational, Puritan commitment to the devil-and-witchcraft theory of Indian culture intensified rather than diminished with experience. The Puritans assumed that the devil behind Indian culture was a weaker devil than their own and perhaps even a different one. This is indicated by the English fear of English witches but their low regard for the efficacy of Indian sorcery. English settlers did not fear bewitchment by Indian shamans nor did they explain their misfortunes in terms of shamanistic spells, and when behavior diagnosed as possession occurred among them, they seldom attributed it to Indians. The original settlers believed that Indian devils and witches held power over other Indians but were impotent against the English. Winslow and others remarked how Indian visions would disappear when any Christian English appeared in the vicinity of Indian ritual. Puritan missionaries attributed English immunity to shamanistic spells to the greater power of the Christian God, and offered protection from the shamans as an inducement for Indians to convert. The conversion efforts of missionaries Thomas Mayhew Jr. (ca. 1621-57) and John Eliot confirmed Puritan witchcraft theory. Both recorded testimonies in which the converts confessed their diabolical ways and told of converted shamans who confessed in detail how devils and serpents had inhabited them, and how they found themselves unable to bewitch Christians and therefore chose to convert.

Puritan witchcraft theory determined how the colonists interpreted the role of New England shamans. A number of Puritan writers acknowledged that powwows cured patients. Winslow believed that the powwows could cause the devil to appear and often successfully cured their patients, and he admired the courage and moral integrity of the pnieses. (Salisbury 1982: 174) Williams discredited their techniques, yet affirmed that they did most certainly, by the help of the devil, work great cures. (Simmons 1976: 242) "These priests and conjurers (like Simon Magus) doe bewitch the people, and not onely take their money, but doe most certainly (by the help of the Divell) worke great cures, though most certaine it is that the greatest part of their priests doe meerly abuse them, and get their money, in the times of their sicknesse." (Williams 1973: 245) Both Daniel Gookin, Indian superintendent in Massachusetts, and Thomas Mayhew (1593-1682), a missionary on Martha's Vineyard, also attributed real power to the powwows: "These are partly wizards and witches, holding familiarity with Satan, that evil one; and partly are physicians, and make use, at least in show, of herbs and roots for curing the sick and diseased. These are sent for by the sick and wounded and seem; and by their diabolical spells, mutterings, exorcisms, they seem to do wonders." (Winslow 1841: 317, n. 3) "That the Powaws by the Infernal Spirits often killed Persons, caused Lameness and Impotency, as well as shewed their Art in performing things, beyond Humane, by Diabolick Skill, such who have converted much among them have had no reason to question." (Mayhew 1694: 13)

Some Puritans believed that the best response to the shamans was the introduction of European medicine. Missionary John Eliot expressed the wish that some knowledge of "physick" could be introduced to the Indians in order to keep them from powwowing. (Shepard 1648: 25; O'Brien 1989: 41) He demonstrated human anatomy and the general principles of medicine to some of his more promising neophytes in order to lure them away from the powwows. (Axtell 1985: 228) He believed that the little that they had seen of European medicine had already had some effect: "They have no meanes of Physick at all, onely make use of Pawwawes when they be sick, which makes them loath to give it over: But I finde, by Gods blessing, in some meanes used in Physick and Chyrurgery, they are already convinced of the folly of Pawwawing, and easily perswaded to give it over utterly as a sinfull and diabolicall practice: but I much want some wholsome cordialls, and such other medicines as I have here mentioned in the inclosed." (Winslow 1649: 123) It is interesting that almost the same observation was made by Jesuit Jean de Brébeuf: "They sometimes close our mouths when we wish to undeceive them about this charlatanry, saying 'Do you cure us, then.' If some wise and upright Physician would come here, he would perform noble cures for their souls, in relieving their bodies..." (JR 10:199) Once again, Catholic and Protestant missionaries were not always as far apart as one might suppose. Eliot proposed a mutually beneficial exchange of medical knowledge between the Indians and the English, with the former sharing their knowledge of local medicinal herbs and the latter sending over money and teachers of anatomy, thus helping to undermine the Indian reliance on the magic of the powwows. (Eliot 1834: 56-57; Holstun 1983: 132) However, this openness to native medicine was exceptional. Protestant missionaries tended to shun native medicine, in stark contrast to their Catholic counterparts. New England's Puritan missionaries had so closed their minds that after nearly three decades they knew nothing of Indian medicine. A "Drug List" prepared for the use of Massachusetts troops in King Philip's War contains not a single medicinal product of American origin. In Canada, by contrast, Jesuit Father Le Mercier carefully distinguished between the Hurons' prayers to the devil and their natural remedies, in which he asked for instruction. (Jennings 1975: 57)

It is perhaps surprising to find that, despite the traditional emphasis on the stark difference in behavior between Catholic and Protestant missionaries, Protestant missionaries in New England fulfilled a comparable role in contests with native shamans. Although the greater use of ritual and ritual objects on the part of the Catholics made them seem more like shamans than their Protestant counterparts (Murray 1999: 13), Protestant missionaries did not entirely eschew the role. Thomas Mayhew Jr. prevailed over shamans in several curing situations. In one case, he prayed for an old Indian called Icogiscat, whom the powwows had given up for dead, and shortly after the man recovered. The message that the healing power of God was greater than that of powwows indicates that Mayhew was prepared to confront the shamans on their own ground. On another occasion, he prayed for and revived the son of the sachem Pakeponesso at Chappaquiddick, who thanked God for his recovery, but fell ill again and sought the aid of shamans. Mayhew sent a message, telling him that when he was with him he thought he would live since he sought God, but since he now sought witches, he thought he would perish. As predicted, the man died. On a later occasion, the powwows warned the son of Towanquattick who was feverish that if he did not seek their help he would die. He ignored their warning and sent for Mayhew who prayed for him in the Indian language and bled him a little, whereupon he recovered. (Winslow 1649: 115-16; Simmons 1979: 207-08) Mayhew sought to prove that his God could cure in a situation where the shamans had no power, and that his God could heal converts as well as the powwows could heal their followers. He stressed further that the shamans' sorcery was ineffective against Christians and thus converts were protected against a major source of physical affliction. To continue to believe in shamans, on the other hand, denied one the greater healing power of the English God and made one vulnerable to the injuries believed to be caused by shamans to which Christians were immune. Mayhew usurped the shamans' ability to cure sorcery victims, by interpreting sorcery as an expression of God's displeasure with those who continued to believe in shamans. (Simmons 1979: 208-09) Mayhew was not the only Puritan who engaged in curing. Winslow made an attempt to cure Massassoit when he was sick by administering to him "a confection of many comfortable conserves." (Winslow 1841: 319) When Uncas, sachem of the Mohegan, asked the missionary James Fitch of Norwich to pray for rain when his shamans failed to bring it, Fitch accepted, on condition that Uncas first declare publicly that if rain came, it could only be attributed to God. (Simmons 1976: 236-237)

Unlike Catholic missionaries, Puritans made little use of the compatibilities that existed between the native religion and their own. They did not emphasize common ideas or encourage Indians to use them as bridges for crossing over into Christianity. They chose rather to heighten the contrast between Indian religiosity and their own by denouncing all pre-contact activity as devil worship. (Bowden 1981: 122) The only element of continuity was the native language, which Eliot and others used to communicate their evangelical program, and which allowed Christian Indians to preserve some of their old identity. The Puritans made little use of pictorial art, dance, rituals, dreams, or private communion with spirit beings. The Algonquians had customarily utilized all these forms, and it is a measure of their inner change to see that they abandoned virtually all such practices, conforming to the Englishman's narrow definition of true religion. (Bowden 1981: 124)

28 Indian "New Birth"

Although Boston was settled in 1630, systematic attempts at conversion of the Indians were delayed for over a decade. The Bay Colony's first organized mission was launched in 1646 by John Eliot (1604-90), pastor-teacher of the first church of Roxbury (Mass.). (Holstun 1983: 131) Eliot preached his first successful sermon to an Indian audience in 1643 at the wigwam of the minor sachem and minister of justice Waban (c.1604- c.1676) at Nonantum in eastern Massachusetts Bay. (Axtell 1985: 221) By this time, the relative strength of Indians and settlers had changed considerably. In March 1644, five sachems of the Massachusetts tribe submitted their people and lands to the colony, and agreed to receive religious instruction. Subsequently, in 1646, the General Court passed a series of laws that paved the way for a missionary program: although the natives could not be compelled to the Christian faith, they were forbidden to worship their own gods or to powwow; two ministers were to be sent each year to preach to the Indians; and lands were to be purchased so that the Indians could be settled in an orderly fashion. (Salisbury 1974: 30-31) By the 1640s, the pattern of missionary activity in Massachusetts had been established, whereby evangelization was to follow settlement and pacification, not to precede it. All of the recipients of Eliot's mission program were subjugated before they were systematically evangelized.

Eliot's fame as the "apostle to the Indians" derives more than anything from the Indian reservations or "Praying Towns" that he founded, the first at Natick in 1651. These were settlements inhabited only by Indians on the mission program, isolated from the English settlers and independent Indians alike. They were intended by Eliot to be self-sufficient, self-governing, self-policing settlements. As a people in transition, partly freed from their ancestral identity, he believed that the natives had been brought to a primary, receptive state, in which they constituted an "abrasa tabula scraped board" upon which he might "write and imprint" an altogether fresh set of principles, both political and religious. (Bozeman 1988: 268) In political terms, the towns were to be administered according to biblical principles, namely the hierarchy of leaders who would govern groups of ten, fifty, and one hundred individuals, as Jethro suggested to Moses when the Hebrews made their choice of rulers in the Sinai wilderness in Exodus 18. (Bozeman 1988: 270; Maclear 1975: 247) The goal of the praying towns was to create a proper environment in which the Indians could learn to live like "civilized" men - Puritans agreed that Indians must be civilized before they could be converted - and thus progress to a condition where they, like non-Indian Puritans, could enter into social and church covenants. (Axtell 1985: 142; Kellaway 1961: 8)

By the 1640s, increasing importance was attached to the distinction between those Puritans who preferred to leave each individual church independent of outside control (Independents or Congregationalists) and those who thought that the ministers of the churches should be organized into presbyteries and synods in order to enforce orthodoxy among themselves (Presbyterians). (Morgan 1965: 12-13) Eliot belonged to the former group. All Congregationalists were required to give evidence of their "conversion," which is to say, in this context, not the process of quitting one religion for another, but the central Puritan experience of being spiritually regenerated, the "new birth" that John 3:3 made a prerequisite for salvation. This concept of "conversion," the centerpiece of Puritan spirituality, involved the explicit recognition of, and deliberate turning away from, sin. Before individuals were capable of receiving God's grace, they had to become aware of both Original Sin and their own particular sins. Preparation required two steps, contrition, and humiliation. Contrition was provoked by consideration of the truth of Christian doctrine and the guilty conscience that followed illumination of the individual's sins. Fearful of damnation, the sinner resolved to do good works, only to realize that Original Sin has tainted all the soul's faculties and vitiated their capacity to perform godly acts. False pride - deceptive self-confidence - dissolved in the terror of discovering that humans were condemned to fall short of grace on their own. Humiliation, the second step, obliterated self-sufficiency and caused unregenerates to throw themselves on Christ, who alone could save them. In this way the sinner liberated himself from Hell through subordination to God's will. In conversion's climactic moment, a person cognizant of his own complete unworthiness experienced grace as a gift inspired by the Lord's love and mercy. Infused with love, the newly redeemed saint reflected it back to God and humanity, radiating the joy of salvation and peace. Over time, a maturing saint faced down recurrent fears and doubts about his faith's authenticity, and reveled more consistently in the knowledge of God's love, and although doubt never entirely disappears, the pious faced death confident of eternal life. Thus conversion produced a predictable sequence of emotions: the fear and guilt of contrition, then terror, and holy desperation, yielding love, joy, and peace in turn. (Cohen 1993: 233, 237-38)

Any prospective church member, of whatever race, had to attend church, listen to sermons, and give a convincing account of his or her conversion experience. (Salisbury 1974: 47) This account was rendered by means of a "confession," which is to say, not merely, as in common parlance, the oral recognition of sins before a priest in order to gain absolution, as part of the sacrament of penance, but rather, as in the meaning of the original Latin *confessio*, a creed, an avowal of belief, an acknowledgment of Christ. (Rafael 1988: 87) A candidate for admission to a Congregationalist church was expected to make a narration, perhaps fifteen minutes in length, of the way in which God's saving grace came to him. If the members of the church, or a majority of them, were satisfied by the narration, the candidate went on to make a profession of faith, that is, a statement of the main doctrines of Christianity in which he believed. Then the members voted on the candidate's admission. The ruling elder then tendered to him the church covenant, and he became a member. (Morgan 1965: 88-89) Thus, Christianization of the Indians was not simply a matter of instruction and assent, but a profound spiritual experience, to which there was no short cut. Sanctity for the Puritan depended upon the concept of regeneracy, and the full experience of regeneracy involved not only an understanding of the doctrine of the Fall but a highly sophisticated conception of the way in which divine grace operated. Unlike their Catholic counterparts, the New England Congregationalists believed that conversion depended less on human effort than on the grace of God. (Axtell 1985: 222) And God's grace was given through the sermon and the sacraments, which made conversion of the Indian slow and difficult, especially with the language barrier. (Kellaway 1961: 6-7)

The process of creating the first native church community at Natick - as opposed to the simple establishment of an Indian town - took eight years (1652-60). The founding or "gathering" of a Congregationalist church began with at least seven men, who had to satisfy one another both about their knowledge of Christian doctrine and about their experience of saving grace. The ministers of some nearby churches had to be present along with some of the civil magistrates of the colony. If these experts thought the prospective founders of the church to be not properly qualified, the group was obliged to wait until suitable saints were forthcoming. Once a church was gathered, by subscription of the first members to a covenant, it elected officers: a pastor or teacher and a ruling elder or elders and deacons. Then as qualified candidates appeared, it admitted new members. (Morgan 1961: 88) The first stage at Natick took place in 1652 when the most promising converts gave personal confessions of their former sins, of their knowledge of God, and of their experience of His grace, both before the regular Indian congregations and before an assembly of visiting English churchmen, which concluded that the Indians were not yet ready to be admitted as full-fledged members of the church. The Indian confessions were published in *Tears of Repentance* in 1653 for the benefit of colleagues and benefactors in England and New England. (Axtell 1985: 238; Rooy 1965: 210) The second stage took the form, two years later, of a public examination at Roxbury, where the candidates were interrogated by a group of examiners and elders about their knowledge of Christian doctrine; an outbreak of drunkenness before the session convinced the assembly that the Indians were still not ready. It was not until five years later, and only then extremely reluctantly that they began to relent. In July 1659, the third examination was held; eight Indians read confessions of faith, which were then translated for the ministers and elders. It was decided that a few Indians would be allowed to enter communion with already existing English churches, but that they were not yet ready to form purely Indian churches among themselves. These few were admitted to membership of the church at Roxbury on trial. The following year, goaded perhaps by the Indians on Martha's Vineyard under missionary Thomas Mayhew achieving the privilege first, the Natick Indians were allowed to subscribe to a covenant of faith and form their own church, capable of calling a pastor, receiving baptism, electing officers, sharing communion, and voting in all church affairs. (Axtell 1985: 239; Kellaway 1961: 89-90) In 1669, Eliot reported that thirty or forty Indians had been accepted into church fellowship at Natick by that date.

Natick was merely the first of fourteen praying towns, each approximately twenty-five miles from Boston, established under Eliot's supervision between 1651 and 1674. The first seven, prior to 1671, were in central and eastern Massachusetts. These "old praying towns" were offshoots of Natick, which provided personnel and served as a model. Hassanamesit was the second prominent praying town and the only other of Eliot's settlements that attained church status. Indians of the second group of praying towns in the Nipmuck country of central Massachusetts, sixty or seventy miles west and southwest of Boston near the Connecticut border, on the western edge of English settlement, began to hear the gospel in 1671; Eliot and Daniel Gookin went there in 1673 and 1674, and took Natick Indians whom the Nipmucks accepted as leaders. (O'Brien 1989: 46) By 1674, one thousand one hundred Native Americans, primarily members of the Massachusetts and Nipmuck tribes, lived in the fourteen praying towns. (Cogley 1991a: 166) The Indian church in Natick had by that year between forty and fifty full members in a praying population of one hundred and forty-five. Some of these Christian Indians served as missionaries to remote peoples. (Axtell 1985: 227) Schools were set up in the praying towns in order to promote Indian literacy; by 1660, Eliot claimed that one hundred of his converts, most of whom probably lived at Natick, could read. (Van Lonkhuyzen 1990: 408) Eliot also produced for the Indians' use a number of Algonquian language devotional works. (Cogley 1990: 77) Assisted by Indian translators, he transcribed the entire Bible into the Massachusetts dialect of the Algonquian language. The first edition, consisting of one thousand five hundred copies, appeared in 1663. Eliot also translated and wrote eight to ten educational and religious tracts for the Indians, some of which went through several editions. (Salisbury 1974: 42) Of thirty-six books published in the Indian language between 1653 and 1721, Eliot was responsible for twenty. (Rooy 1965: 224) His missions produced a large body of literature: grammars, translations, catechisms, dialogues, legal codes, and The Eliot Tracts (1643-71), a series of missionary epistles by Eliot and others which solicited funding for the praying towns by describing their progress. (Holstun 1983: 130)

Despite his best efforts, Eliot was unable to prevent the outside world impinging on his praying towns. His work was interrupted by the outbreak of King Philip's War in June 1675 when Metacom (Philip), sachem of the Wampanoags of Plymouth colony, began a series of raids on exposed Puritan settlements. Within a month, the Wampanoags were joined by Nipmuck Indians from Eliot's seven "new praying towns" - not the older ones - and in December the previously neutral Narragansett entered the war, following an unprovoked attack on their chief settlement by the colonial forces. With the crucial support of New York Colony, the Puritans achieved victory in the fall of 1676, and the Wampanoags, Nipmucks and Narragansetts who were unable to escape to southern New England were placed in subjection. (Cogley 1991a: 175) At the outbreak of the conflict, the General Court of Massachusetts called for the removal of the Indians of Natick and two other praying towns to Deer Isle in Boston Harbor, in order to prevent the threat of complicity with hostile Indians (the inhabitants of three other praying towns were at one point coerced into joining a group of Indian combatants), and also to protect praying Indians from white hostility. They remained there, suffering severe deprivation, until Eliot and Gookin were allowed to transfer them back to the mainland in 1676 at their own expense; by 1677 they had resettled at Natick. By now, the fourteen praying towns had decreased to four. (O'Brien 1989: 47; Morrison 1974: 78) Eliot continued to work among these Indians until the late 1680s, when his advanced age no longer permitted him to leave Roxbury. From the mid 1680s, he passed on his work to others - Daniel Gookin Jr., minister at Sherborn, and to the Indians themselves. (Cogley 1991a: 178)

After Eliot's death in 1690, the mission communities declined. By 1698 the number of communicants fell, there was no schoolmaster, and literacy levels declined. Indians continued private and public devotions and maintained an Indian minister, but probably discontinued formal church membership. In the 1680s, the first whites moved onto the Natick reserve. (Van Lonkhuyzen 1990: 422-423) Publications in Algonquian continued to appear after 1700, but after 1720 no books in the Massachusetts tongue appeared. English was now the favored language for the Indians, as Cotton Mather indicated in 1710. It is not known when Indians abandoned their communal village, but by 1749 English and Indians both lived dispersed throughout Natick; the process probably began soon after 1700. (Van Lonkhuyzen 1990: 424) But in 1698 there were thirty congregations of praying Indians, served by thirty-seven full-time native preachers, teachers, and catechists. By the outbreak of the Revolution, at least one hundred and thirty-three Indians had ministered to their brethren in southern New England. (Axtell 1985: 225)

29   Tears of Repentance

Historians have offered widely divergent interpretations of Eliot's mission program over the years. Broadly, three schools of thought can be distinguished. One, the traditional school, advanced the view that the New England Puritans followed a humane, considerate, and just policy in their dealings with the Indians, and that Eliot exercised a largely benevolent and altruistic influence over them, enabling them to cast aside pagan ways and gain the benefits of Christian religion and civilization. (Winslow 1968: 96; Vaughan 1995: vii-viii, xlix) This school was subsequently criticized for taking the missionaries' account of themselves at face value, for concentrating exclusively on the acts and attitudes of Puritans toward the Indians, and for not trying to account for the actions and reactions of natives. Insofar as it characterized the interaction of the two societies as "the expansion of one into the areas in which the other was lacking," this school was limited by its view of Indian life as static and passive, rather than dynamic and active. (Vaughan 1995: 323) The traditional interpretation was criticized for failing to present Indians as three-dimensional, for clinging to the view of the colonists as the decision-makers, the activists who "do things to" native groups, and of the latter as the passive recipients who "have things done to them." (Brenner 1980: 135)

The second school of thought adopted a more ethnohistorical approach, which credited the Indians with "cultural integrity" and sought to offer a double-sided perspective, in which both Puritans and Indians were active participants, who exercised influence over one another. This aspect was generally seen as a step forward, and obliged the first school to revise some of its positions. However, the second school's conclusions regarding the Puritans' actions, and especially their motives, provoked great controversy. The central contention was that political and economic motives, rather than predominantly religious ones, underlay Puritan missionary activities. (Cogley 1991a: 167) The Puritans' own evaluation of their function as agents of altruism and benevolence with respect to the Indians had been

313

accepted uncritically; Eliot's primary objective was not, in fact, the conversion of the Indians, but rather the extension of Puritan power in New England by subordinating the natives to the authority of the Massachusetts General Court, by removing them from their lands (great emphasis was placed on the fact that the missions facilitated white land encroachment, by concentrating formerly scattered groups of Indians into tight units, making land available for settlers; Brenner 1980: 140) and by destroying their culture. The mission was conceived as a means to an end rather than as an end in itself. (Jennings, 1975; Jennings 1971: 207) This school of thought also proposed that the missions were successful only among Indians previously devastated by epidemic disease and victimized by Puritan aggression; that Eliot advanced the cultural values and the political goals of the white conquerors; that Indians converted to Christianity because they saw in the praying towns the only available refuge from Puritan expansion, and because in their debilitated condition they were powerless to resist Eliot's intrusions into their culture; that Indian conversions were often superficial because of the constraining circumstances under which they occurred and because of the alien and intellectually demanding nature of the culture that Eliot imposed; and that the missions were a failure because most praying Indians were never baptized or permitted to receive communion. (Cogley 1990: 78-83) Even at the highpoint of mission success in 1674, only one thousand one hundred natives lived in all of Eliot's fourteen towns, of whom no more than one hundred and nineteen were baptized. Scarcely ten percent of the mainland native population were converts, and even most of these were potential Christians residing at missionary sites but unbaptized. (Bowden 1981: 130)

The third school of thought emerged as a reaction to the second. It agreed with some of its conclusions, for example, that Eliot's missions were successful only among tribes already debilitated by Puritan aggression and by epidemic disease; that the missions operated to the political and economic advantage of Massachusetts Bay; and that they destroyed much of traditional Indian culture. These aspects are now broadly accepted by historians. Yet it also pointed out the shortcomings of the second school of thought: the questionable assumption that the missionary program entailed a repudiation of Indian identity; the inadequate evaluation of Eliot's character, motives and religious beliefs; and the underestimation of the Indians' attraction to Christianity, the success of the missions, the courage of the praying Indians, and the integrity of their conversions to Christianity. The principal exponent of this view (Axtell) argued that the cultural and political devastation that preceded and accompanied Eliot's missions presented the natives with a wholly new set of problems and imperatives, and that Eliot offered the Indians a comparatively better answer to urgent social and religious questions. Their attraction to Eliot's program was more an act of affirmation than a betrayal of their heritage. An appreciation of the intellectual and social appeal of "Christian civilization" for the Indians leads to a better ethnohistorical evaluation of the effectiveness of the missions. The proper criterion for measuring missionary success is not the number of baptized and communicant Indians but rather the sum total of persons resident in the old praying towns. The enduring attraction of the Massachusetts Indians to Eliot's program suggests that their conversions were meaningful for them. The presence of "distinctively Indian elements" in the extant confessions of faith, the elevated standards for baptism and communion in the Indian churches, and the theological learning and missionary commitment of native preachers also indicate the integrity of Indian conversions to Christianity. Finally, each culture must be treated with equal empathy, rigor, and discernment. This applies as much to seventeenth-century Puritans as it does to seventeenth- century Indians. There was a comprehensible religious motivation behind Puritan treatment of Indians. Eliot's authoritarian discipline, educational program, intolerance of blending of Christianity and native religion, perceptions of the Indians' alleged cultural deficiencies, and assurance about the rectitude of his views were products of the Puritan tradition he championed. (Cogley 1990: 83-85) Where the first school of thought empathized too much with Puritans, and the second school empathized too much with Indians, the third school argued that it should be possible for historians both to recognize the damage to Indians caused by Puritan culture and to empathize at the same time with the Puritans' thoroughgoing theocratic view of reality, which constantly dictated their economic and political behavior toward Indians. (Stineback 1978: 80-82)

The approach of the third school of thought has much to be said for it. Seeking to counterbalance the second school of thought's highly materialistic evaluation of Eliot's missionary objectives, it aims to understand Eliot and his missions within their own context. It is surely accurate that there are no reasons to doubt the sincerity of the Puritans' religious purpose in settling Massachusetts and Connecticut. What most clearly distinguished Massachusetts Bay from the Pilgrim colony at Plymouth and the Puritanism of Roger Williams in Rhode Island was its extreme sense of community election. God had made a temporal covenant with his Chosen People there as a group which complemented the covenant of works He originally made with Adam as an individual, and the Covenant of Grace He later made with all men through Christ. The fact that no Puritan leaders felt self-conscious about the fourteen year delay between the granting of their charter in 1629 and the first missionary effort to the Indians in 1643 may be attributed to the "federal covenant" concept which Massachusetts Bay espoused, and the ministerial duties it imposed on men such as Eliot, as well as to factors such as the exigencies of settlement, the language barrier and theories about Jews preceding Gentiles in the conversion process. For the Boston Puritans, a political conversion to Massachusetts Bay jurisdiction and laws had to precede religious conversion. Until the Massachusetts Indians under Cutshamekin subordinated themselves to the civil leaders of Massachusetts Bay in 1644, sustained missionary activity was premature. Furthermore, a total rejection of heathen living was a condition for true Christianization. For Eliot, as for all Puritan leaders, any Indian alliance with the English short of self-rejection was unsatisfactory. Eliot expected total capitulation to the English way of life. Puritan dominance was to be unconditional. (Stineback 1978: 82- 85) Then again, unlike the peripatetic Jesuits, a Congregational minister could not be a missionary to anyone outside his own congregation unless he did so on his own time. The remnants of the Massachusetts Indians were too far away from Eliot's Roxbury congregation to permit simultaneous involvement in their conversion. A further hindrance to the Indians' conversion in New England was the nature of the church covenant, which constructed a society in which the distinction between the elect and the unregenerate (the latter including the Indians) was the most deeply entrenched division. The pastor tended to the "saints," but obligations to those outside the covenant were extremely nebulous. (Kellaway 1961: 5-6) Eliot was something of an exception; most ministers tended only to the elect (a major criticism advanced by the Presbyterians of New England churches). This helps to explain why missionaries like Eliot were so few. Missionary activity was further delayed by the Puritan expectation that Jews would return to the Christian fold before the remaining Gentiles (including Indians) could be converted. This objection was obviated by Eliot's decision subsequently that the Indians were Hebrews, retrograde descendants of the biblical patriarchs and the Ten Lost Tribes of Israel. Speculations identifying the Indians with Jewish tradition had become common earlier in the seventeenth century. Hugh Broughton, whose writings Eliot knew, developed the theory that the American natives were the offspring of Eber, son of Shem. (Maclear 1975: 245) However bizarre this idea seems to us, it was not uncommon for Europeans in both the sixteenth and seventeenth centuries to try to locate the origins of the Indian peoples and cultures in the Old World. Rather than rejecting this view as a factor in Eliot's behavior because it makes little sense to us, it is important to appreciate that it was highly significant to Eliot and provided a genuine part of the explanation for his delay in launching missionary activity.

An empathetic approach to Eliot's missions is designed to understand, not to excuse, either his philosophy or his actions. Insofar as Eliot's philosophy viewed native peoples as instruments, principally, for the salvation of Puritans, and, only secondarily, for that of Indians themselves, it may be considered reprehensible. But the fact that we disagree with it, disapprove of it, even consider it pernicious, should not lead us to assume that Eliot's espousal of it was insincere, or that it was insignificant as a source of motivation. The historian's task is to seek to understand the past, not to like it. Nor is it necessary to impugn Eliot's character in order to lament the effects of his actions on Indian institutions and values or to show that his mission worked to the material advantage of Massachusetts Bay. Undeniably, the "Apostle" contributed to the destruction of coastal Algonquian culture and to the increase of Puritan power in New England. Furthermore, Eliot never gained a respect for the integrity of Indian culture or expressed remorse about the effect of his actions on the Indians. (Cogley 1990: 86-88; Cogley 1991b: 243-44; Cogley 1991a: 171-72, 181)

A purely materialist explanation of Eliot's objectives is difficult to accept. (Cogley 1991a: 182) The conflict of New England natives with Puritan society is best described as a religious confrontation with economic, political, and military ramifications. (Stineback 1978: 90) Only religious considerations can explain the apparent - and highly disturbing - paradox that Puritans were willing both to convert and to kill Indians. During King Philip's War, Puritans imagined the Indians to be children of Satan who were being used by God (since God ultimately controlled Satan) to chastise His Chosen People for their increasing sins as a community; for the Puritans the chastisement was an opportunity to achieve a spiritual regeneration by defending their principles and killing those same Indians. Such thinking, central to a belief in the "federal covenant," was also current at the time of the Pequot War in 1637, when, according to the second school of thought, economic and political motives were paramount. Since, by 1637, the Pequot Indians showed no willingness to submit themselves to the Christian government of Massachusetts Bay or its offshoot in Connecticut, Governor John Winthrop could conclude that God had permitted the natives, like Adam in the Garden of Eden, voluntarily to make themselves His confirmed enemies; as such, they would still be serving God's purposes by providing Puritans with the chance to defend their self-evident status as the Chosen People. In many ways, the Puritans perceived natural man - Indians as well as English sinners - as an inverted expression of their cultural ideal, and therein lies the key to the Puritans' perception of the native people in America. (Simmons 1981: 58) Indians were seen as the antithesis of all the beliefs, values, or institutions that whites most cherished in themselves. Such a negative reference group could be used to define white identity, or to prove white superiority over the worst fears of their own depravity. If the Puritans, for example, could project their own sins upon people they called savages, then the extermination of the Indians became a cleansing of those sins from their own midst, as well as the destruction of a feared enemy. (Berkhofer 1978: 27) These considerations provide a better context for understanding (but not excusing) the Puritans' readiness both to "win" and kill natives. (Stineback 1978: 86-87)

Another aspect of Eliot's approach neglected by the second school of thought is his utopianism and his millenarianism, which offer "a coherent idealistic framework for interpreting the missionary's motivation and his conduct." (Cogley 1991a: 166, 168; Cogley 1990: 78) By the 1630s, the English Puritan community had been imbued with a strong current of millenarianism, which found particularly intense, even feverish, expression in Massachusetts. The purity and faithfulness to God's word which the New England communities cultivated was taken as a sign of the approach of the millennium, and the gathering of the elect in godly communities was believed to anticipate the imminent era when the saints would reign with the Lord. (Maclear 1975: 223, 229, 230) It was in this context that Eliot sought to settle Indians into a congregational church of "visible saints." Convinced that native peoples' acceptance of Christianity contributed to the "latter-day" conversion of non-Christian peoples, Eliot came to believe that his own humble Indian flock at Natick was destined to take the first step toward the millennium. (Maclear 1975: 238) The disciplinary transformation of the Indians into regenerate saints foreshadowed the creation of a regenerate millennial community in Europe. The execution of King Charles I in 1649 conferred a new politically radical character on Eliot's millenarianism in the following decade, when the minister of Roxbury took the regicide as a sign from God that the millennial order included a non-monarchical form of political organization, and began to anticipate the destruction of the nearly universal dominion of kings. He understood the coming millennial civil polity as the restoration, internationally, of the ancient Israelite system of rulers of tens, fifties, hundreds, and thousands, found in Exodus 18. In 1652, he designed a millennial blueprint for England, *The Christian Commonwealth: The Civil Polity of the Rising Kingdom of Jesus Christ* (London, 1659), in which he turned his organization of the Indian praying towns into a "pattern" for the reformation of all civil government in England, proposing for his homeland a millennial utopia in which godly rulers were set over decimal units of people in tens, fifties, hundreds, thousands and myriads or tens of thousands. His expectation was that this sacred frame of government, established over the saints in Heaven and over the angelic hierarchy, would be replicated in God's Chosen Kingdom, England. In 1653, he even asked Oliver Cromwell to establish the millennial political order throughout the realm. His aim was nothing less than to begin the transformation of earthly governments into the universal empire of the Lord and his saints, the glorious climax to human history. Furthermore, he reckoned that the scheme, drawn from the Old Testament, would appeal to the Jews and hasten their conversion. (Maclear 1975: 254)

The restoration of the House of Stuart in 1660 brought an end to Eliot's politically radical millenarianism. In May 1661, the magistrates of the General Court of Massachusetts suppressed Eliot's book, and persons with copies were ordered to deliver them up. Eliot was obliged to recant publicly the anti-monarchical passages and confess that he had libeled the system of government by King, Lords, and Commons. (Maclear 1975: 257) Thereafter, he adopted a positive attitude toward the institution of monarchy, and he even assigned to the British Crown the primary responsibility for installing in England his version of the millennial ecclesiastical polity, *The Communion of Churches* (Cambridge, 1665). He was unable to establish this millennial church order among the Indians because he lacked a sufficient number of congregations, but he continued to assume that the Indians' conversions contributed to the latter-day harvest of souls. His commitment to a millenarian interpretation of history was diminished but not destroyed by King Philip's War, the loss of the Massachusetts charter (1684), and other events that transpired over the final portion of his life. (Cogley 1990: 85-86; Cogley 1991a: 170) Without exaggeration, Eliot's missionary endeavors have been described as "the single most ambitious utopian project within the larger Puritan utopia of New England." (Holstun 1983; Holstun 1987)

320

Eliot's conduct toward the Indians becomes more intelligible within the millenarian framework presented in his writings. It was his commitment to his millennial, utopian vision that led him to model the fourteen praying towns of Massachusetts Bay on a biblical scheme of government. The rigid program of civilizing Indians also derived from his millenarian perspective since it formed part of their preparation for efficacious grace. His politically radical millenarianism predisposed him to acts of aggression against the sachems: he elevated subordinate Indians to positions of political authority and encouraged tribesmen to withhold tribute. These were not simply naked political strategies to extend Puritan power. The restoration of the Stuarts obliged him to revise his judgment about the institution of monarchy, and as a result he altered his conduct toward the sachems. He began to encourage the Puritan leaders to respect the sachems' traditional prerogatives, and to explain to unconverted sachems that acceptance of Christianity no longer destroyed their political authority. Eliot's actions cannot be interpreted exclusively in terms of aiding Puritan land encroachment. On several occasions, he tried to defend the boundaries of the Indian settlements in disputes with Puritan towns. Furthermore, in 1649 he declined to sustain a mission among the Eastern Narragansett under Ninigret, since he was too preoccupied with Natick. Instead of turning his efforts to Rhode Island, where magistrate John Winthrop Jr. wished Eliot to proselytize as a prelude to Puritan settlement, he preferred to work among Indians already dispossessed because of their significance to his millenarian agenda. In this instance he pursued an objective consistent with his millenarianism when an alternative course of action that worked to the greater material advantage of the colonists lay at his disposal. It is probably true that Eliot's mission contributed to the militancy of the Wampanoags and the Nipmucks, whose participation in King Philip's War coincided too closely with Eliot's proselytizing activity for there to be no causal relationship. But it should also be remembered that, with few exceptions, residents of the seven old praying towns remained loyal throughout the war - some even became auxiliaries of the colonial troops. With their victory in 1676, the Puritans achieved final mastery over the native groups of southern New England, yet Eliot continued to nurture the Indians even though their subjection was complete, thus demonstrating that his motive was not simply political. (Cogley 1991a: 173-78)

The scale of Eliot's utopian, millennial vision accounts for the ambitiousness of his objectives. His goal was nothing less than to fashion a new individual, the Praying Indian, and a new collective identity in Christ for the praying town. Previously free-roaming Algonquians were to be integrated into a newly enclosed, and rationalized New England landscape. Lands were to be occupied on the basis of deed and contract, not custom and usage. The Praying Indian, a figure with a Christian conscience, was to enjoy the right to enter both the civil entity of the self-governing praying town and the church covenant. Neither the theological nor the political aspect of Eliot's utopian practice should be seen as a mere tool in the service of the other aspect, for the praying towns promised the possibility of an unprecedented experiment in the integration of religious and political life. The transformation was to be accomplished through preaching, the catechism, the encouragement of questioning, and the practice of admonition and censure. Admonition required a full publicizing and confession of private sins and doubts by the person admonished in the presence of the entire congregation. (Eliot 1834: 229-60) It seems to be the case that, by 1673, the Indians had internalized congregational self-discipline. Public confession and weeping constituted the clearest signs of regeneracy. The tearful confession by Waban (a minor Massachusetts sachem, and Eliot's first convert) of his previous sinful desires to be a sachem or a powwow were taken by the minister of Roxbury as a sign of sufficient regeneracy for him to continue as a ruler of fifty. The melancholy, which Eliot observed approvingly among the praying town Indians, probably derived from the loss of the Indians' previous collective and individual identities, but, for Eliot, this melancholy acquired a positive function in the formation of new Christian identities. Protestant procedural conversion was consciously modeled on an antithesis of instantaneous and sacramental Roman Catholic conversion. Critics of the slowness of Christianization failed to appreciate that it was not an instantaneous event, but a disciplinary procedure. The imaginative appeal of the praying towns lay not in their measurable output of Red Puritans but in the purity of their experiment in utopian discipline. (Holstun 1987 122, 129-42)

There is a great deal of truth in the second school of thought's conclusion that missionary activities were concentrated on politically fragmented and rapidly declining groups of Indians (the Massachusetts and the Nipmucks), that these groups accepted conversion as a practical means of survival (some sachems, for example, saw it as the only means of retaining authority) and that it was only the greatly weakened Indians that embraced Christianity while the stronger tribes remained independent. Generally, the Indians to whom Eliot preached had already passed through the earlier stages of English domination. They had been devastated by epidemics, sold or lost much of their land under the incessant pressure of English immigration, become economically dependent on the English, and submitted to the political authority of the colonial government. They did not freely choose "civilization" over traditional ways, for those ways were already disappearing under the impact of the English invasion. Conversely, the tribes most impervious to Christianity were those with the strongest leadership. Regardless of their political relationship with the English, each of the great sachems of the mid-seventeenth century - Massasoit (Wampanoag), Metacom (Wampanoag), Ninigret (Eastern Narragansett), Uncas (Mohegan) - consistently and successfully resisted the missionaries as threats to his tribe's survival. It was usually only minor sachems, like Waban and Weebax (a minor Mohegan sachem), who submitted to the missionaries, and even they were reluctant. (Salisbury 1974: 34-35, 50; Morrison 1974: 79-80, 87)

Far more debatable is the second school of thought's conclusion that Christianity, as presented by the missionaries, was, at best, a poor substitute for the native religions that were lost, and that the minority of Indians who did convert under the pressure of Puritan aggression never genuinely committed to what remained an alien religion. According to this view, Christianity had little to offer the aboriginal population. (Naeher 1989: 346-47) It did recognize that some aspects of Puritanism were meaningful to Indians. Once the native belief system and the community that supported it were shattered in New

England, the Puritans' notion of man's alienation from God and His universe made more sense to many Indians. And Indians' enthusiastic participation in catechizing, singing psalms, and praying reveals a group response that understood church services in terms of old familiar rituals. (Salisbury 1974: 50-51) But the main thrust of Eliot's Christianity was to undermine native culture and self-confidence yet further. The Puritans' message that all trust must be placed in God and none in the world, and that self-worth was found in isolation from others rather than in a network of kin and community relationships, ran counter to the individual and collective identity provided by tribal culture. (Salisbury 1974: 44-45; Morrison 1974: 79-80, 85) Furthermore, according to this view, Eliot's Indians' conversion narratives contain no indication that the converts understood the most basic tenets of Puritan theology, nor that the missionaries expected their saints' conversion experiences to measure up to those of the English in this respect. (Salisbury 1974: 52) In any case, the path that an Indian had to follow before converting was quite different from that of a white. Indian converts were expected to reject their ethnic and cultural identity and to adopt a new identity created for them by representatives of an entirely foreign culture. (Salisbury 1974: 47, 49-50) Yet, at the same time as Eliot required Indians to repudiate their own traditions and to emulate the English, the broader Puritan community saw little difference between them and unconverted Indians and refused to allow them to assimilate into white society. The converts were left suspended between two cultures, with their own cultural expression carefully controlled from without. (Salisbury 1974: 42, 46) The praying towns never developed any organic sense of identity and became groups of frightened, disillusioned and confused individuals searching for the community they had lost. (Morrison 1974: 88-89) In the end, Eliot's object was unattainable since he demanded that Indians no longer be Indians, but at the same time the English failed to accept "civilized" Indians as neighbors. (Morrison 1974: 83; Salisbury 1974: 54)

This interpretation is accurate in some respects. For example, no doubt there is a great deal of truth in the observation that, since most of the recorded Indian confessions were made before the appearance of even the first installment of Eliot's Algonquian Bible, the identification made by converts with specific passages (from which they were able to quote) obviously owed a great deal to the missionaries' suggestions. Eliot may have coached his Indians. It is also undeniable that the conversion of the Massachusetts and the Nipmucks was a necessary response to new conditions imposed by the English. However, this interpretation falls down in several respects. It fails to consider the integrity of Eliot's approach and of the Indian conversions. It does not adequately explain why so many Indians were willing to settle in the praying towns. It does not acknowledge that conversion forestalled the annihilation experienced by traditionalist Indian groups in New England, or that Christianity also helped to preserve the Indians' ethnic identity. (Van Lonkhuyzen 1990: 396-97) Nearly one quarter of the Indians of southeastern New England pledged themselves to Christianity in the thirty years before 1675. (O'Brien 1989: 50; Van Lonkhuyzen 1990: 396-97) They did so, not simply because they were coerced, but because Puritanism, far from being entirely alien, was relevant for Indians. (Naeher 1989: 346-47) A closer analysis of the accounts of the conversion experiences of Eliot's Indians reveals how Christianity was meaningful to natives.

Eliot's *Tears of Repentance* provides details of the conversion experiences of five individuals, all men (Eliot does not seem to have recorded confessions of any women) from the Massachusett band from Nonantum, who confessed in both 1652 and 1659. The historical development of these five persons' experiences helps to analyze their progressive apprehension of the Protestant faith. The Massachusett relations of 1652 substantially resemble those of prospective English Saints, at least in form and length, which vary from one to five minutes. The differences lie in content, for example the lack of biblical citations, which is understandable since Eliot had not printed any of his scriptural translations. In recounting their initial contact with the gospel and their awakening sense of transgression, these converts completely appropriated Christian definitions of iniquity. Confessor Ponampam recognized: "in every thing I did, I sinned." And Natick's Totherswamp acknowledged: "I break Gods Word every day. I see I deserve not pardon, for the first mans sinning; I can do no good, for I am like the Devil, nothing but evil thoughts, and words, and works...I deserve death and damnation." But recognition of sin alone was not sufficient for regeneration, and herein lies the key as to why the elders demurred at accepting these neophytes in 1652. Contrition, the first step, was evident, but they failed to display the humiliation, despondency, and "holy desperation" that had to succeed contrition. (Cohen 1993: 236, 245-48)

The relations of 1659 reveal substantial developments over the previous set. They are longer, averaging six to eight minutes to read aloud, and contain references to Genesis and Matthew. They discuss actual sins in detail, especially former polytheism and lust. They highlight the importance of the Bible's creation account in raising their consciousness of sin. They show a much keener awareness of Original Sin and express their inability to save themselves, two critical signs of humiliation lacking in their earlier narratives. Waban and Ponampam give expression to the reformed theology's emphasis on justification by faith alone, the irrelevance of human works to salvation and the inability of unregenerates to help themselves. Ponampam confessed: "nothing that I can do can save me, only Christ." These confessions evidence clear signs of humiliation; and yet they fall short of evincing its letter and spirit completely. They fail to ground the desperate search for Christ within the locus of Original Sin - the Massachusetts knew the doctrine of Original Sin and they mourned their failings, but they did not link the two systematically. Nor did the Massachusetts vilify themselves as did English Saints. Their rhetoric of abnegation pales beside the magnificent self-disgust that Puritans display. They speak far more about gaining salvation than about serving God. The themes of humiliation in Amerindian confessions differ from those in English relations in two important ways: they pay less attention to the soul's innate corruption, and they omit the association of despair and helplessness with the strength engendered by the new birth to perform God's will. (Cohen 1993: 250-52)

It is important not to underestimate Eliot's expectations of his Indians. The standards of church membership were expected to be high for Indians as well as for Englishmen. Baptism alone was not sufficient,

Indians had to engage in praying, preaching, instruction and meticulous behavior. (O'Brien 1989: 41-42) Eliot's eagerness for English ministers and elders to hear the public confessions of praying Indians demonstrated his faith in the Indians' ability not only to experience grace but to understand and articulate that experience, and was an emphatic expression of the Puritan belief in the religious aptitude of the common believer. It was at the same time an affirmation of the importance of the spoken word in expressing and defining one's inner spirituality. The central role conferred on the spoken word linked Puritanism to the most familiar aspect of Native American culture, and allowed full expression to the Indians' voice in the dialogue conducted with Eliot. Because the power of speech was respected in both cultures, Eliot was able to approach the Indians initially, and his respect for their words enabled dialogue. By their questions, the Indians directed Eliot to expand on those aspects of his message most important to them and consequently to tailor it to their new needs and traditional sensitivities. Prayer was a central element of Eliot's message to the Indians, but it was they who made it the central motif of their Christianity for it met deep human needs that the Indians shared with the New English Puritans. It was Eliot's converted Indians who first referred to themselves as "praying Indians," before the term was adopted by the English. The advantages of prayer were that it could be experienced both personally and frequently; that it was a more immediate and accessible way to communicate with divinity than the traditional vision quest, readily available to the leadership but rarely enjoyed by others; it afforded an opportunity for expressing inner anxiety; it offered a means of individual self-expression - Eliot emphasized that Indians did not learn their prayers by rote; and it provided a vehicle for self-definition within a new, alternative community. (Naeher 1989: 348, 359, 362-64, 367) A major part of every Indian service was devoted to answering listeners' questions. The missionaries welcomed queries which allowed them to impress the Indians with their book learning, to turn hostile or facetious questions to their own use, and, most important, to enable serious inquirers to understand better. Many Indians framed hard questions, including, for example, whether the devil or man was made first; why God made Hell before Adam had sinned; why man should fear God;

what the meaning was of eating Christ's flesh and drinking his blood; where little children went when they died since they had not sinned; where the soul of a man would go who had determined to convert but had died before his intent was achieved; why God made good men sick; and if God was omnipotent, why he did not give all men good hearts, and why he did not kill the devil. One Indian wanted to know why God punished in Hell for all time, when Man did not do so since people were let out of prison after a time; and why, if people repented in Hell, God would not let them out again. (Axtell 1985: 232-33; Ronda 1977: 71)

It has been suggested that the Puritan notions of sin, guilt and eternal punishment were foreign to Indian mentality, but, if so, it is not clear why so many apparently accepted the concepts so readily. In fact, in the Tracts, throughout the questions and confessions, Eliot's more difficult task is not to convince the Indians of their sin and guilt, but of the availability of pardon. The severe disruption of their social and natural worlds gave the Indians an immediate, existential understanding of the Puritan notion of alienation from God and his universe. The way in which many Indians translated that alienation into an acceptance of sin, guilt, and the need for redemption through Christ is revealed in their questions to Eliot. (Naeher 1989: 351-53) The key moment was the realization of the meaning of sin. Cutshamekin, sachem of Neponset who had repulsed Eliot's initial foray against native paganism, admitted that before he knew God he thought he was well but since he had known God and sin, he found his heart full of sin, and more sinful than it was ever before. Thomas Mayhew's convert Hiacoomes recounted a similar slow awareness of the meaning of sin. (Axtell 1985: 231) Indians were attracted to Eliot's Christianity because it offered not only a plausible explanation for their condition, but also an occasion to address their needs actively, willfully and creatively. This is not to say that Christian concepts were absorbed easily. The Creation and Fall, Passion and Resurrection seem to have been grasped more readily than the concepts of piety and divine love. Sin and God's anger made sense in the context of the morality and experiences of the old faith; almost incomprehensible was *agape*, a divine emotion pre-contact religion did not conceptualize, but Puritanism's payoff. (Cohen 1993: 242, 255-56) And there was no equivalent in native religion to the Puritan new birth.

Personal circumstances affected the response of each individual to Christianity. The conversion of one of the earliest converts, Wequash, suggests that the Christian doctrine of sin and forgiveness appealed deeply to a man who had assisted in the killing of several hundred of his own people. His efforts to convert Indians to a religion that prohibited revenge may have reflected a longing for personal acceptance among a people he had wronged. Each individual gave personal meaning to the faith by addressing it to their own problems, demonstrating that the natives accepted Puritanism on their own terms. The lives of Christian converts in the Tracts suggest a blending of Indian and Puritan ideas and experiences, whereby Native American experience gave meaning to Christian precepts, and Christianity offered a new religious perspective on familiar aspects of Native American life. (Youngs 1981-82 241, 243, 249-50, 252)

Puritanism had much to offer the Indians not only at the level of the individual, but also in social terms. Praying Church congregations were surrogates for fractured Indian kinship networks, and Praying Towns provided supportive communities for a disoriented population. They offered Indians the chance to preserve their ethnic identity on "familiar pieces of land that carried their inner history." Indians chose to enter praying towns in order to enter into such sustaining arrangements; once within them, they were increasingly drawn to Christianity as a means of giving meaning and order to their experiences. (Naeher 1989 365) The acceptance of a new religious system offered a whole set of new community relationships, complete with collective rituals to reinforce the social unit. New rituals connected with healing were created. Christ was understood to heal men's bodies as well as their souls. The confessor Anthony believed that Christ was the Son of God after hearing the words of Matthew 9: "All diseased came to Christ, the blind, halt, etc. and he healed them." Another, John Speene, believed that since "Christ healed all manner of diseases," he is "the Son of God, able to heal and pardon all." (Cohen 1993: 254) Waban, the first Indian used as a teacher by Eliot, urged his fellows to pray to God because Christians used "physick" to heal the sicknesses of the soul. (Eliot 1671: 43; Casciano 1996: 33) At a fast-day service at Natick in November 1658, two of the Indian preachers who addressed the community centered their talks on the image of Christ the physician, paralleling the shaman's traditional function of healing. But whereas shamans had typically projected social tensions onto the natural world, now each individual was being asked to look inside himself to confront an integrally evil human nature. This implied a new concept of human nature and of community, but one that was introduced within the framework of traditional concerns about health. (Van Lonkhuyzen 1990: 417) Since traditional supernatural entities no longer functioned adequately, Indians had new needs for security, order, and meaning similar to those of the Puritans - Puritanism had arisen in England during a period of economic and social ferment. (Naeher 1989: 363)

The social structure of Indian communities may provide clues to the reasons for their attraction to Christianity. Inter-band hierarchies developed around trade networks and military alliances. Subordinate bands paid tribute to a local sachem, who in turn might owe allegiance to a more powerful chief. Such alliances offered protection and access to goods, but they also burdened the community with unwanted quarrels and tribute payments. A special relationship with the English could offer a means of altogether evading or manipulating to advantage inconvenient ties. Unconverted Indians were eager to make use of European goods and technologies as a means not of abandoning, but of fulfilling their traditional way of life. Eliot was first invited to preach at Waban's wigwam at Nonantum in 1646. Previously his attempts had been rebuffed. Waban's openness to Christianity now was part of an attempt to create a powerful faction to challenge the lordship of Cutshamekin, who headed another nearby band. By 1648, John Winthrop referred to Waban as a "new sachem." The colony's efforts to protect the Natickites' land reserve and to supply them with arms, both of which required Eliot to appear before the General Court as an advocate for the Indians, spoke loudly to other natives of the band's close relationship with the powerful newcomers. The story was the same with other bands. Missionaries were sought out as a means of escaping traditional alliances, of gaining new ones with the English, or, within bands, as a means of subverting existing relationships. Thomas Mayhew convinced some sachems on Martha's Vineyard to allow him to continue proselytizing by offering them an alliance with the English as a way of escaping the influence of a tributary hierarchy on the mainland. Hiacoomes, his first convert, was catapulted to an important leadership role in the Indian community when he converted. The primary motivation for praying derived from issues of control within Indian society, which explains why conversion precipitated such exceptionally vicious factionalism among the Indians. Disputes were inflamed because the new cult created an alternate social structure, a new path to power within and among bands. Focusing on the social context of conversion helps to explain why praying to God took hold in nearly all bands in south-eastern New England, including those relatively removed from the immediate pressures of settlement. (Van Lonkhuyzen 1990: 400-04, 411)

Just as Indians most often sought out the missionaries for their own purposes, they also controlled the pace and timing of change. Eliot was not able to move Waban's band to a village of their own at Natick until 1650, when they finally overcame reluctance at the urging of Wampooas, a revered counselor and convert. Cutshamekin himself converted only in 1652, evidently in an attempt to maintain control over the band. The proliferation of many small praying towns was dictated as much by Indian demands - they wished to remain on their traditional lands - as by Eliot's grand plan. True to native tradition, the role of community leaders in encouraging conversion was significant - seven of eighteen Indians for whom confessions are available attributed their eventual conversion to either Waban or Cutshamekin, whilst nine out of eighteen state that the death of family and friends convinced them to pray. Waban was able to make a seamless transition from powwow to praying teacher. Laying claim to uncommon insight into a world that was invisible to men of lesser spiritual vision, he declared his wish to share this knowledge with other Indians. Setting his case within the context of native religious values, he exercised persuasion by arguing like a powwow. Thus, natives took an interest in Christianity for very Indian reasons. All this suggests that, at least to some extent, Indians managed to manipulate the conversion process to their own ends. Rather than being vulnerable, weak, and susceptible to control and manipulation by the English, Praying Indians were employing various strategies to adapt to the new religion on their own terms. (Van Lonkhuyzen 1990: 403-04; Brenner 1980 137; O'Brien 1989 42-45; Casciano 1996: 33)

30 God's Tribe on Martha's Vineyard

In order to put Eliot's missions into perspective, a comparison may be drawn with the activities of Richard Bourne, of Plymouth, and the Mayhews - Thomas Mayhew Sr. (1593-1682) and his son Thomas Jr. (1621-57) - of Martha's Vineyard. These regions were within present-day Massachusetts but were independent colonies in the mid-seventeenth century, and were outside the patronage and control of Massachusetts. The Indians of Plymouth colony were largely Christianized by the time of King Philip's War, and they were less disrupted by the conflict than the Indians of the Massachusetts Bay area. By 1684, there were ten communities of Christian Indians in Plymouth colony, and by 1698 the number had grown to seventeen. There were also ten communities on Martha's Vineyard and five on Nantucket. Many had Indian teachers and Indian magistrates, and there were twenty-seven Indian preachers. There had been no missions elsewhere in Massachusetts before the war, none in Rhode Island, and only a couple in Connecticut. (Trigger 1978, 15: 177) The younger Mayhew began work in 1643 one year after a handful of Puritans under his father had colonized Martha's Vineyard. One of the natives, Hiacoomes, approached the young Mayhew to request Christian instruction, after which he apparently underwent a genuine religious experience and became the community's first Indian preacher. By 1651, Mayhew's convert community in the Vineyard had grown to one hundred and ninety-nine individuals, and by 1652 more than three hundred people, as well as numerous non-converts who came for religious instruction. By 1657, there were several hundred converted people and many hundred more who attended services but whose conversion was incomplete. In 1659, after his son's death, the elder Mayhew founded the Vineyard's first Indian church. Eventually most if not all the Indians of both the Vineyard and Nantucket were converted. Neither Mayhew father nor son nor the converts themselves discussed the possibility of integrating converts within the English Christian community. Of all the Puritan missionaries in seventeenth-century New England, Mayhew Jr. was one of the most successful in the thoroughness and permanence of his conversions, and in the number of converts and the longevity of the Christian Indian communities he helped to create. (Simmons 1979: 197-98; 213-215)

The Martha's Vineyard missions differed in many significant respects from the Boston missions. No outside aid of any sort was given until eight years had passed, and the younger Mayhew continued three more years without regular salary. (Jennings 1971: 200) In numbers of Indians and English, and in relations between the peoples, Martha's Vineyard was substantially different from the mainland. When Mayhew began missionary work, the native population was at least one thousand five hundred and may have been as high as three thousand; the English numbered about sixty-five. Natives outnumbered English folk throughout the seventeenth century. On the eve of King Philip's War, there were still only one hundred and eighty English settlers while the native population was over one thousand. Whites did not become the majority until the 1720s. Thus, whereas the mainland Indians among whom Eliot worked were rapidly becoming outnumbered by the English, the Wampanoags on Martha's Vineyard remained a dominant majority and suffered much less displacement. Many of the measures Eliot considered essential such as removing Christian Indians from the influence of Englishmen were unnecessary on Martha's Vineyard. (O'Brien 1989: 49) On the mainland, the mission was part of a wider attack on Indian land and leadership mounted by a large and well-armed English population, but Mayhew had no such resources or ambitions. (Ronda 1981: 369-71) Unlike Eliot's mission, Mayhew's did not suffer from the restriction that an individual minister could not be a missionary to anyone outside his own congregation unless he did so on his own time, since in 1642 Mayhew moved, with the nucleus of a Puritan church, into the midst of the native community on Martha's Vineyard which outnumbered his parishioners, and so he could minister to both his own flock and the Indians. The Mayhews did not subscribe to the same brand of Puritan theology as Eliot. Mayhew's published reports on the Martha's Vineyard mission, which span the years from 1649 to 1653, are entirely devoid of millennial reference. (Bozeman 1988: 271)

Most important, the mission did not insist upon sudden cultural change. The Mayhews employed a more gradual approach, less immediately disruptive of existing institutions and practices, and allowed a certain amount of continuity with native religion during the transition period. Hiacoomes acknowledged before a hostile Indian assembly that traditional deities had great power, but were subservient to the god of the English. Whereas Eliot sought to undermine and isolate the shamans, on the Vineyard one shaman whose wife was a convert himself acknowledged the superiority of the Christian God, but expressed his obligation to continue serving the deity who had always treated him kindly. Mayhew could not follow Eliot and compel the Indians to adopt English civility, and political power and cultural leadership on the island remained in native hands. (Ronda 1981: 369-71) The mission was characterized by voluntarism on both sides, without either coercion or material reward. There was no equivalent on Martha's vineyard of the Massachusetts General Court's decree in 1646, forbidding denial or ridicule of the Christian God on pain of death, and proscribing the practice of Indian shamanistic ritual, backed up by heavy fines. On the island, Indian property rights were fully respected. Avoiding polarized factions, Christianity pervaded more slowly, but ultimately more successfully, than in Massachusetts Bay. (Salisbury 1975: 264) The Vineyard remained peaceful during the war of 1675-76 that desolated the rest of New England. And, by the eve of the outbreak, Martha's Vineyard had more Indian churches than any other mission. Within the territory presently occupied by the state of Massachusetts, there were, by 1674, six Indian churches - two under Eliot, one under Richard Bourne in Plymouth colony, and three under Thomas Mayhew on the islands, including at least one hundred and sixty-eight full members, and more than three hundred and fifty baptized members, in a praying population in excess of two thousand. It should be noted that of the six, only two were Eliot's whereas Mayhew had three. (Axtell 1985: 240; Naeher 1989: 346-47) By 1684, whereas there were only four praying towns in Massachusetts, there were ten Indian communities in Plymouth, ten on the Vineyard, and five in Nantucket. The Mayhews and Bourne, with their missions based on voluntarism, held a total of twenty-five Christian Indian communities, as compared with Eliot's remnant of four.

Mayhew's missions reveal that there were genuine conversions on the part of Indians searching for spiritual meaning in an increasingly hostile world, and that it was possible to become a faithful Christian while remaining no less an Indian. A substantial body of biographies of Martha's Vineyard converts exists for the period 1642-1722, preserved in Experience Mayhew's (1673-1758) *Indian Converts*, which allow the reconstruction of the process by which Indians, over four generations, transformed Christianity to suit native cultural needs. In the early 1720s, Experience Mayhew, who was the grandson of Thomas Mayhew Jr., was born on the island, and spoke Wampanoag, began to collect material for biographies of Christian Indians, of which he composed one hundred and twenty-six, touching two hundred and eight Indians in at least sixteen family lineages. His work was written neither to raise funds for the mission nor to perpetuate his family's reputation. Rather he intended to demonstrate the validity of Indian Christianity by showing that not all the gospel seeds sown among the natives had fallen on stony ground. The biographies reveal that, beginning slowly in the 1640s and gathering momentum by the 1670s, Christianity became an integral part of the lives of many Martha's Vineyard Wampanoags, but, at the same time, Indians worshipping at native churches and living in praying towns were no less Indian for their Christian beliefs. (Ronda 1981: 369-72, 389)

The biographies of Hiacoomes and his family reveal how, through conversion, an ordinary powwow, not of sachem origins, was able to acquire stature and found a powerful lineage on the island. Under Mayhew's direction, Hiacoomes exchanged the supernatural order and symbols of the powwows and traditional healing rites for equally supernatural Christian explanations. (Ronda 1981: 376) The diseases of the 1640s resisted traditional cures; loss of power of healing rites seemed a sign of deep disorder in the traditional relationship between the human and spirit worlds. In this context, Christianity seemed to offer answers. In 1643, a strange disease that afflicted the islanders left Hiacoomes untouched. Although the majority perceived the disease as a warning not to depart from tradition, the convert saw his immunity as cause for increasing his commitment to the English. (Simmons 1979: 205) Another outbreak of disease in 1645 which swept the entire island, but to which Hiacoomes and his family were immune, proved to be a turning point in the openness to Christian instruction. In contrast to the interpretation of the sickness of 1643 as a warning against departure from traditional ways, this sickness, which the powwows were powerless to counter, seemed to many a sign of the Christian God's favor to his Indian believers. (Simmons 1979: 206) Hiacoomes's belief that the Englishmen's God "did answer him" was confirmed by the fate of a sachem who, after striking the convert in the face for abandoning his people, was himself struck by lightning. (Axtell 1985: 230) Whereas Mayhew's efforts enjoyed little success before 1645, there now followed a rapid series of conversions. Hiacoomes became established as a powerful Christian preacher when he helped to convert several prominent sachems. By the 1650s, he was a respected magistrate and in 1670 was ordained as a minister. The rise of Hiacoomes's lineage suggests that conversion allowed hitherto unimportant Wampanoags to gain considerable influence as members of God's tribe. (Ronda 1981: 369-71, 375, 377)

By 1652, eight powwows on Martha's Vineyard had abandoned their craft and converted. They confessed that since the advent of God's word, they had killed more patients than they had cured and were incapable of bewitching any of their converts or their children. (Axtell 1985: 230) As the influence of powwows declined in the 1640s and 1650s, a leadership vacuum developed on the island, and Indian pastors, beginning with Hiacoomes and John Tackanash, began to fill that void. The formal ordination of these two men in 1670 by John Eliot and John Cotton Jr., put the stamp of approval on an indigenous ministerial elite. The traditional shamanistic functions were now subsumed under the larger preacher-pastor role. Indian ministers became the new holy men. Tackanash's conception of the ministerial role represented a synthesis of traditional powwow functions and English clerical practices. He served not only as a preacher and pastor but also as a healer who applied medical as well as spiritual remedies. Tackanash was succeeded as minister in Chilmark by his nephew Japheth Hannit; like his uncle, he saw himself as both a Puritan preacher and a traditional powwow healer and holy man. Pastors like Hannit were the new powwows. (Ronda 1981: 379-382)

An essential part of the Christian gospel for Indians was a new identity, one that did not deny all aspects of native culture but offered membership in God's tribe. The ideal Christian Indian embodied charity, prudence, industry, temperance, family worship, and attendance at public meetings, as well as belief in the gospel message; shaped as much by Indian cultural seeds as by English Puritan requirements, this Christian identity did not represent a radical break with the traditional past. Communal ceremonies for healing and charity were rooted in Wampanoag culture. Being part of God's tribe at once preserved and extended those ancient values, while giving them a fresh rationale. For example, the Christianity preached by Mayhew and his Indian successors tended to elevate and honor the traditional roles and tasks of Indian women, and perhaps for this reason there was a sizable group of Indian Christian women on Martha's Vineyard. The new religion provided a supportive arena for literate and articulate women - by allowing them to act as Christian healers, for example - and it extended educational opportunities for them. Lastly, it provided support and solace in the face of alcoholism and violence. Conversion most often followed family lines; as early as the 1650s, Christian Indian families were perpetuating the faith within their lineages. The example of Mittark, the sachem-turned-preacher, and others in the Mittark-Panu lineage indicates that among the first generation Christianity did not necessarily mean cultural and political disruption. Some Indians in Eliot's mainland mission rejected Christianity because they did not want to renounce family and kinship ties. Such renunciations were not necessary on Martha's Vineyard. The sense of identity was strengthened by the names used by native Christians. Some mainland missionaries attempted to persuade Indians to abandon traditional names in favor of English ones as a sign of conversion. This was not the case on Martha's Vineyard. First- and second-generation native Christians generally assumed English names while still using and being known by their Indian ones. Sometime in the second generation, Indian Christian families began to make use of the dual European given name/patronym style, but this was done with an important difference: the surname was based on the last part of the traditional Indian name. This is a good example of the blending of Indian and English ways. (Ronda 1981: 372-74, 385-87, 390-91)

There were many manifestations of the Indianization of Christianity. In the pre-contact northeast, it was common for young men to undertake solitary vision quests searching for personal identity, special powers, and a guardian spirit. By Mayhew's account, solitary prayer in isolated places was common among young Indians, and it is possible that this practice represented a kind of Christian vision quest. The persistence of traditional religious practices in the corporate life of Indian Christians was manifested in such activities as group singing and observance of a steady round of festival days. Day-to-day leadership of Indian communities was in the hands of Indians who served as ruling elders, deacons, discoursers (lay preachers who served in family worship), catechists, festival managers, counselors, and musicians. These native initiatives revealed both the strength of Christianity on the island and the Indianization of the gospel. Study of the Martha's Vineyard faithful reveals Christianity Indianized as well as Indians Christianized. (Ronda 1981: 371, 383, 384, 389)

Christianity was a survival ideology - a set of beliefs and behaviors that allowed Indians to meet English expectations while maintaining native identity. Eliot's early converts who could not read and had no access to Algonquian bibles and catechisms made professions of faith that owed a great deal to the missionaries' suggestions. Martha's Vineyard Indians who wanted to partake of the gospel had to learn to read. By the end of the first convert generation, several Indians were sufficiently literate to read both English and Indian books. Because so many were literate, Martha's Vineyard Indian faithful displayed a genuine understanding of Christian fundamentals. Exposed to sermons by Indian preachers, taught in Christian homes, and conversant with books in both English and Algonquian, native Christians demonstrated a sure grasp of ideas such as sin, grace, redemption, and reward or punishment after death. Experience Mayhew made a special point of questioning natives on matters of faith and doctrine; from his interviews emerges a consistent picture of Indians clearly comprehending and using Christian theological language. (Ronda 1981: 392-93)

It is often said that Catholic Christianity, with its ceremonies, images, processions, and symbols, was far more effective in the replacement process than was Protestantism. The experience of Martha's Vineyard converts suggests that the Puritan missionaries' version of Christianity did serve to revitalize Indian lives in a world growing more unfriendly. Their message offered a collection of beliefs about God, Humankind, and the world that made sense to a people who had always lived in a spirit-filled world. If there is little evidence for revitalization movements in New England - the mission records make no mention of Indian prophets or visionaries - it is possible that some Indians quietly embraced a kind of revitalization religion while accepting the outward forms of Christianity. Native believers on Martha's Vineyard adapted Christianity to their own needs; their culture was simultaneously Christian and Indian. That one could be a Christian and still live in a wigwam and bear a traditional name was not doubted by the Martha's Vineyard faithful. (Ronda 1977: 80; Brenner 1980: 150; Ronda 1988: 28; Ronda 1981: 394)

31 True Indian Converts

Why was missionary work on Martha's Vineyard so much more successful than in Massachusetts Bay? A shift in authority in favor of the English was a precondition for Indian populations to be open to religious persuasion, and the more implicit and less threatening this shift, the more favorably Indian subjects responded to religious assimilation. At one extreme, the powerful Narragansett reacted to the political fugitive Roger Williams by accepting that his God made Englishmen, but continuing to believe that their gods made them: "They will generally confesse that God made all; but then in speciall, although they deny not that English-mans God made English men, and the Heavens and Earth there! Yet their Gods made them, and the Heaven and Earth where they dwell." (Williams 1973: 189) Although the Narragansetts and Niantics had been exposed to Christian teaching by Roger Williams and others since the beginning of English settlement in the area, there were no converts in either group before King Philip's War. Rhode Island and Connecticut also made no headway in evangelization in the seventeenth century, in part because they had little interest in doing so. Roger Williams believed he did not have divine appointment to an apostolic, converting ministry. In a situation of relative equality, the Narragansett understood the English perspective but maintained their own. At the other extreme, a catastrophic change in power relationships also did not favor openness to the English worldview. After their devastation in King Philip's War, the Narragansetts rejected English religion for over half a century. When they did convert in the mid-eighteenth century, they selected precisely the form of Christianity - the Separate movement - that most resembled their ancestral Indian religion. Eighteenth-century accounts of itinerant preachers are remarkably reminiscent of seventeenth-century descriptions of powwows, particularly with reference to their bodily movements, singing, visions, and trance behavior. Both powwows and eighteenth-century Separate preachers were recruited to their calling by dreams, visions, and other forms of direct supernatural insight. The Narragansett converts maintained an Indian emphasis on visions, on the spoken over the written word, and on religious leadership that depended on personal experience as opposed to formal training. They redefined Christianity in their own terms, and, in converting to a faith of the broader society, they acquired a new religious basis for setting themselves apart from that society. By forming a distinctly Indian church, they also strengthened the boundary that separated them from other poor and common people. (Simmons 1983: 254, 260, 266, 267; Axtell 1985: 242)

John Eliot was more successful as a missionary than was Roger Williams but not as successful as Mayhew. He aimed his efforts at Indian populations that had not been destroyed by war but had been more explicitly weakened by disease and dominated by colonial settlement than those of Martha's Vineyard, and his program involved more coercion. Consistent with the greater coerciveness of Eliot's missionary environment, his model of the conversion process stressed behavioral obedience to Puritan social forms as a prerequisite to religious transformation; "visible civility" had to precede "visible sanctities." Mayhew's approach was the reverse of Eliot's in this regard. Conversion for him began with the implanting of English religious symbols, after which the converts voluntarily restructured their families and political institutions in the direction of English models. Without coercion, conversion appeared as a choice to Vineyard Indians who had been dominated gently at the political level, and who consequently began to doubt the efficacy of their religious powers. The Mayhews purchased land through native institutions and never threatened violence for not complying with the missionary program. On the island, deep and integrated change occurred among a people whose health, culture and institutions were relatively undisturbed at the moment of conversion. In comparison with other cases where Indian conversion occurred in seventeenth- and eighteenth-century New England, the Martha's Vineyard conversions indicate that where the traditional culture was most intact, the transference of the dominant culture was most complete. (Simmons 1979: 216-18)

There is also a relationship between how knowledgeable individual Puritans were about Indian culture, and the nature of their political relationships with Indians. Edward Winslow, Roger Williams, and Thomas Mayhew, who were among the pioneers in the areas where they settled, depended upon diplomacy, tact, and goodwill to survive. These Puritans who were most knowledgeable about Indians wrote in a context where relationships between the cultures were more equal and where English domination had yet to be established. Of all seventeenth-century writers, Winslow and Williams were the least ethnocentric (showing a tendency to regard one's own culture as the norm for all societies) in their observations. Mayhew was the most effective Puritan missionary to the Indians and, next to John Eliot, the best known. Mayhew's missionary success on Martha's Vineyard reveals a very practical understanding of Indian belief embedded in the English vocabulary of God, the devil and imps, which he used to persuade shamans and their followers to exchange one set of deities for another. Through this transfer of symbols, he initiated the most profound social conversion to occur anywhere in New England, as a result of which the Martha's Vineyard Indians became a separate English-like minority in the plural society that developed on that island. Eliot, who ministered to the most plague-weakened, subjugated, and powerless groups in southern New England, knew less about Indian culture in its own terms than did any of the above-mentioned three. Although Eliot interacted extensively with Indians, he did so from a position of greater power, and to a greater extent saw them as projections of his Christian world-view. (Simmons 1981: 68-69)

There is some evidence that Christianity was interpreted by Indians in terms of native religion. The Indians' initial recognition of manitou in the English, far from representing a move away from their own religion, was actually a confirmation of it. The Wampanoags saw the plague as a sign that they had failed to perform rituals for Cautantowwit, the supernatural being whom they considered the source of maize, and who lived in the southwest and was unseen by living men. (Shuffelton 1976: 111) As population fell, Indians took to burying European manufactured goods with their dead, as a means of reinforcing their relationship with Cautantowwit by integrating the spiritual power of the newcomers with their own. Traditionally Indians expected to take prized possessions with them at death to Cautantowwit's house where they would dwell forever; for praying Indians, Cautantowwit's house and God's Heaven were one and the same. The concept of manitou enabled its adherents to accommodate traditional religion to changing circumstances. For, as Williams put it, they attributed to manitou everything they could not comprehend. The lack of more evidence of this process of interpretation may be due to the lack of sensitivity or interest on the part of the missionaries, or to the fact that the Indians quickly realized that the Europeans' manitous were different from their own, and operated in different ways, or both. (Salisbury 1982: 37; Salisbury 1992: 502-03)

There is also evidence that native peoples adapted traditional beliefs under the impact of Christianity. Indian communities that lived in proximity to Europeans, and that were most affected by disease, trade, and shifts in the balance of power, began to question indigenous assumptions within a very short period. Shamans reported that their guardian spirits would not appear if Europeans were present, for example when Englishmen appeared in Massasoit's village before 1624. (Axtell 1985: 229) Some shamans fought back by appropriating elements of Christianity within their traditional religious framework. An early seventeenth-century shaman of Martha's Vineyard announced that he owed his powers to "a god subservient to him, that the English worshipped." (Mayhew 1694: 12) Another claimed that he acquired the ability to cure disease by journeying "in a large thing high up in the air, where he came to a great company of white people, with whom he had interceded hard to have the distemper layed." English spirits were harder to control. A Wampanoag shaman told his client that the cause of her illness was an English spirit and for that reason he could not long confine it. (Mayhew 1694: 15) Yet Indians also saw departures from tradition as one explanation for diseases and other misfortunes that afflicted them. John Winthrop of Boston and Experience Mayhew of Martha's Vineyard both noted warnings from traditional deities, such as Hobbamock, against those who departed from ancestral ways. (Simmons 1992: 321)

Some New England Indians on the threshold of Christian conversion reformulated their indigenous mythology in a way that made it appear as if their forebears had once known Christianity. Thus, while abandoning traditional symbols, they simultaneously redefined them and asserted continuity with their Indian past. A group of Puritan ministers heard testimony to this effect from Wampanoags to whom they spoke on Cape Cod: "That these very things which Mr. Eliot had taught them as the commandements of God, and concerning God, and the making of the world by one God, that they had heard some old men who were now dead, to say the same things, since whose death there hath been no remembrance or knowledge of them among Indians until now they heare of them again." Many had the idea "that their forefathers did know God, but that after this, they fell into a great sleep, and when they did awaken they quite forgot him." One Martha's Vineyard sachem told Thomas Mayhew Jr. of a similar belief held by Indians of that island. Another Martha's Vineyard legend described a woman who lost her first five children in infancy and feared losing a sixth. In despair, she came to believe that she should pray to a god, who answered her prayer, and who later proved to be the Christian God. According to her, she already knew and worshipped this God before the English introduced Christianity to her people. What seems to have been happening is that converts redefined themselves for the English Christian future, and legitimized this change in part by introducing English Christian themes into their pre-European past. (Simmons 1992: 322-23)

Conclusion: Tending the Living Organism Until it Blooms with Christian Leaves

It is misleadingly easy to assume that widely diverging national patterns of conquest and settlement (Spanish, French, English) and evaluation of the priority that was to be accorded to evangelization must have played a significant role in determining the outcome of the interaction of European and native religions. There were marked differences between the European powers. Spanish conquest of the core areas was swiftly followed by settlement and by the establishment of the institutions of government and church hierarchy. Expansion by France and England differed not so much because its beginnings were later but because, once begun, it was slow, piecemeal and disorganized. The sophisticated organs of government exported by Spain to America in the sixteenth century found no equivalent in French or English America for another hundred years; no action was taken to impose national political or ecclesiastical authority until the mid-seventeenth century in either New France or English America.

Furthermore, whereas France and England did not seriously undertake conversion of the natives until the second and fifth decades of the seventeenth century respectively, Spain began the enterprise early in the sixteenth century. If the work of evangelization was peripheral to the business of settlement and trade for France and England, conversion was an essential part of the conquest for the Iberian nations. The consequence of the *Patronato Real* was that, from the earliest days of conquest, the Castilian monarchy maintained a deep commitment to rapid evangelization of the indigenous population since it constituted an important justification for Spanish rule in America. Iberian America contrasted notably with French America in the relationship that prevailed between church and state in this field. In the former, evangelization was conducted principally as a state-backed enterprise through patronage conferred by the Pope; in the latter, by contrast, native populations remained under the direct spiritual jurisdiction of the papacy, and responsibility for conversion and Christian instruction fell on missionary orders acting independently of the state. In English America, evangelization was in the hands of lay societies and individual pastors, and so the process of conversion was even more marginal and completely separate from the state. Thus, whereas in Iberian America evangelization was from the beginning an integral part of the process of conquest and settlement, in French and English America, on the other hand, the Crown regarded the process of conversion as an ancillary part of its presence. In Spanish America, missionary policy was to a greater extent determined by the needs of the state.

With specific reference to North America, the only region where all three countries were engaged, Spain's approach to evangelization differed from that of France and England not least because, whereas the latter had no prior experience of Christianization, the Iberian kingdom had initiated missionary work in New Spain and the Andes before turning north. While early Spanish incursions led to immediate attempts at evangelization, the first recognized French missionaries were only sent to the Indians after 1610, and colonization and sustained missionary work began in earnest only after 1633. (Grant 1984: 3) The English did not even settle in North America until the end of the sixteenth century. Whereas the Spaniards were first and foremost settlers and evangelizers, the French were predominantly traders, and the English barely registered their presence. (Quinn 1988: 15, 22, 25, 30) A final important difference, related to the differential role of the state, was the substantial uniformity of religion in Catholic America (Spanish, Portuguese and French), in contrast to the (largely) Protestant diversity in seventeenth-century English America. (Codignola 1994: 36) Yet, national differences, while worthy of note, have proved of largely marginal significance in explaining the outcomes of the sacred dialogues examined here.

It is even easier to assume, and equally misleading, that European religious differences - confessional differences between Protestant and Catholic, or rival strategies of conversion among individual religious orders, such as Jesuits and Franciscans - must have played an even more significant role in determining the outcome of the interaction of European and native religions. It has traditionally been argued that

348

Catholics were the more effective missionaries, since the integral appeal of Roman Catholicism, together with the advantages of its missionaries' approach, made their brand of Christianity more attractive to native peoples. This view was reflected in the conviction of the nineteenth-century American historian Francis Parkman that the Christianity brought by the Jesuits in the seventeenth century was the only version of that religion which the Indians could have accepted. (Parkman 1997) More recently, it has been suggested that Catholic missionaries in general, and the Jesuits in particular, especially in New France, achieved much greater rates of success in conversion than their rivals, particularly the Puritans in New England. One historian contrasts "the lackluster Protestant performance among predominantly small, weakened coastal groups" with the Jesuits' "remarkable success with large, powerful, sedentary groups around the Great Lakes and with mobile hunting bands all over New France." (Axtell 1985: 276) It is true that the Jesuits baptized greater numbers of Indians, but it is no less true that the Puritans, unlike the Fathers, ordained small numbers of native ministers of religion. Estimates of success depend, in the end, on the criteria for judgment.

It should be acknowledged that the quality and training of the Jesuits, together with their sustained commitment in the field from the last quarter of the sixteenth century put them among the first rank of missionaries. In addition, they clearly enjoyed two advantages over the Puritans: their revenues and the priority that they were able to give to missionary work. Whereas the Jesuits enjoyed steady and secure finances and were free from the obligation to minister to a parish, Puritan ministers were tied to a congregation and were forced to rely on the uncertain support of lay societies of English benefactors if they wished to undertake Indian missions in their spare time. As a result, Puritan missions lacked the funding and manpower that the Jesuits could take for granted. (Axtell 1988: 86, 88, 96) But beyond this, it is not clear that Catholicism in itself possessed characteristics that made it inherently more appealing. There is no evidence that doctrinal differences between Protantism and Catholicism played a significant role in making one confession more attractive than the other. The "cultural relativism" of the Jesuits has been favorably contrasted with the "cultural absolutism" of the Puritan missionaries, but in fact the assumption that cultural transformation - "civilization" - was a necessary precondition to salvation was shared by Puritans preaching to Bay Indians, who adhered to it from the beginning, and by Jesuits seeking Huron converts, who after an initial commitment to inculturation (the insertion of the Christian message into a native context) reluctantly adhered to it in the end. (Ronda 1988: 27) Catholicism, with its colorful and affective ceremony, and imagery rich in dramatic and visual appeal, is often considered to outclass Protestantism, especially the stark Puritan variety, which, as a religion of the Book, emphasized the highly rationalistic effort to understand the inscrutable will of God, and distrusted visual images and gestures. Whereas the Protestants appealed to the mind through the power of the word embodied in the sermon, the Catholics seduced the senses with the candles, bells, vestments, incense, and chants of the mass. According to this view, when it came to attracting Indian adherents, Protestant sermons, however eloquent, competed poorly with Catholic ceremonies, which resembled native religious observances in color, drama, and participation. (Axtell 1975: 280; Axtell 1985 278) This difference may have conferred some advantage on Catholic missionaries, but it may also underestimate the intellectual interest of many Indians in Christianity of both confessions. Furthermore, the notion that native peoples responded to Catholicism mainly because the liturgy appealed to their aesthetic sense of color and sound, risks devaluing their discriminating sense of the new religion as a system of vitally effective power, a characteristic which, as we have seen, could draw adherents to the Protestant brand just as effectively. (Morrison 1981: 254) More prosaically, if there were greater numbers of converts to Catholicism than to Protestantism, the explanation is more likely to lie in the fact that in colonial America far greater numbers of Indians were exposed to the former than to the latter, and that many of those evangelized by Protestants died out or almost did so, whereas among those evangelized by Catholics there were many whose communities survived and reconstituted themselves.

At the end of two centuries of effort, both the French Catholics and the English Puritans were forced to admit they had largely failed to

CONCLUSION

convert the Indians to Christianity. (Axtell 1975: 281) This may have been a fair conclusion in the sense of reproducing Christians in the manner in which they intended. However, recognition that missionaries did not produce carbon copies of European Christians should not obscure the fact that Christianity in indigenous form did take root. Recent historiography, which has thrown into doubt the success of both Jesuits and Puritans, and questioned the quantity, quality, and longevity of their native conversions, may be too pessimistic. From this perspective, as one historian has noted, missionaries are painted "either as evil tools of imperialism or as naïve fools, and their Indian neophytes as hapless victims of clerical oppression or as cunning Br'er Rabbits of the forest." (Axtell 1988: 101) The public narrations of saving grace made by Eliot's Indian neophytes are judged to lack true understanding of Puritan theology and to fall far short of the performance expected from white English converts. The few Indians who did convert are held to be merely responding to the crisis posed by English expansion into their lands, and are considered in the end to have been left suspended between two cultures, without a spiritual home or social identity. Accounts of Catholic missions in Canada also stress the gullibility of French missionaries and the unchanging timelessness of native traditions. According to this view, neophyte Iroquois took on the protective coloration of Catholicism while going about their lives much as before contact, and the Mohawks of Caughnawaga used the Jesuits to gain advantageous trade concessions from the French while giving up little in return. There was less sincere cultural adaptation than a mere addition of Catholicism as a cultural overlay. One expert has doubted that the Jesuits managed to convey "an accurate understanding of Christianity" to early converts, since the Indians of New France were members of egalitarian societies governed by consensus whereas Christianity was a creation of hierarchical and coercive societies. He concludes that there is no evidence that the Jesuits or any other Christian group in the seventeenth century was able to make Christian doctrine comprehensible to people who lived in a self-sufficient tribal society. The crux was political and economic power since until native groups had been subordinated to European power, they stood no chance of grasping the "meaning and spirit" of Christianity. So the

351

number of Indian conversions in the northeast was small, and many, perhaps most, were not made in good faith. (Axtell 1988: 102-04)

But the assumption underlying these interpretations is that if the missionaries did not achieve exactly what they set out to do, they must be judged as complete failures. In fact, it is as untrue to suggest that both groups of missionaries entirely failed, as it is to claim that Jesuits were in every respect more successful than Puritans. Despite the enormous obstacles in the way of effective communication between Indian and missionary, there was genuine interest in the Christian message on the part of at least some natives, and by no means a tiny minority, but sufficient numbers to make the transformation of entire communities a possibility. With regard to Eliot's Indian confessions, their informed and detailed content and emotional depth belie suspicions about their quality in comparison with those of white colonial candidates. They contain distinctively Indian elements that should allay fears that the ministers were merely dictating, or that the Indians were merely parroting, a standard form of confession. The searching questions they asked during instruction drove right to the heart of Christianity's contradictions. As a result of missionary efforts, both Catholic and Protestant, many Indians - though certainly not all of them - were receptive to the solutions offered by the new religion and were capable of taking the decisive step from their old religions to the new. Some consciously chose a new faith and did as much as they could to understand it. Most significantly, they tried hard to make it coincide with their own traditional beliefs, values and behavior. It is this last fact that demonstrates that these conversions were real, even if, ironically, the missionaries took it as a sign of the corruption of their endeavors. (Codignola 1994: 43; Axtell 1988: 100, 115)

It may be that the truth has often not been acknowledged because it is uncomfortable: that, although the effects of both Jesuit and Puritan missions proved destructive for the Indians of the northeast, both types of missionaries succeeded in engaging some natives in positive dialogue. This reality has been obscured because those who have argued for the success of the evangelization (particularly historians of the orders and the church, and historians sympathetic to the Catholic or

Protestant religion, who have often found all the evil on the other side) have often preferred not to recognize the damage that came with it, for fear of denigrating or betraying the missionaries and the church; and those who have emphasized the destruction wrought by the evangelization have often proved reluctant to discern any positive outcome in such suffering, any thin silver lining on such a huge black storm-cloud, for fear of denigrating or betraying the native peoples. But real history is rarely about villains and heroes. Real missionaries do not conform to sinister two-dimensional caricatures of self-serving hypocrites, mouthing pious sentiments in order to disguise naked greed or lust for power. Economic and political considerations remained for the Jesuits means to ends rather than ends in themselves. Those who were willing to risk their own lives in order to save the Indians' souls from eternal damnation were sincerely motivated by religious convictions, even if these make us feel guilty or uncomfortable. (Trigger 1976: 845) At the same time, it should be emphasized that in some cases they engaged in religious persecution, that their actions led to cultural destruction more often than to cultural renewal, and that their right to intrude on the inner sanctums of another man's religious experience, where they were often not invited, may be challenged. The teaching of the church forbade the use of coercion to convert, but forceful methods were in reality often employed, for example in the suppression of the native priesthood, the destruction of temples, the burning of sacred texts, the prohibition of religious rites and the compulsory attendance at catechism classes. (Krippner-Martinez 2001: 189-90) This is particularly true in the case of Spanish America, where the Crown was simultaneously committed to the two contradictory goals of the salvation and the exploitation of the Indians. But starkly divergent views of the missionaries, seen alternatively as exclusively altruists or persecutors, are misleading because they fail to take account of the full range of human motivation present in groups and individuals.

Although European missionaries rarely shook off their ethnocentric worldview, they were party to the formation of an Indian Christianity which incorporated elements of native culture that were compatible with the gospel message. This approach was orthodox since it

353

followed an ancient tradition of the church. The early spread of Christianity within the Mediterranean basin had involved inculturation. The gospel could be explored and re-expressed with the terms and methods of Hellenic philosophy; pagan festivals such as the celebration of the Unconquered Sun could be assimilated by Christian feasts; pagan heroes were paralleled with the Christian cult of saints; prayers could be taken from pagan cults and used in Christian liturgical rites. (Buckley 1994 282) The Pauline maxim of *Omnibus Omnia* had urged evangelists to be "all things to all men," the Church Fathers had spoken of paganism carrying the seed of Christianity, the *logoi spermatikoi*, and Pope Gregory the Great had instructed St. Augustine of Canterbury to respect pagan shrines and make them into Christian shrines.

Squarely within this tradition, the friars in Spanish America made the new religion more attractive to the bulk of the Indian population by presenting Catholicism in terms that made sense from an indigenous perspective. Although, in principle, Christianity remained absolutely exclusive of any other religious belief, in practice, whatever did not conflict outright with it was generally admitted. Even if the friars were theoretically opposed to mixture, they did in practice allow inculturation, as demonstrated by the Corpus Christi procession in Cusco described by Inca Garcilaso. This approach was especially feasible in Hispanic America, the region that offered the greatest similarities between native religions and Christianity - including sacred doughs, worship of the cross, fasting, and oral confession of sins. Although the Jesuits were the greatest advocates of this approach, other orders such as the Franciscans pursued a similar policy, if less explicitly.

The early view that conversion was an organic process that could take place within the indigenous social and cultural framework gave way, under the pressure of prolonged familiarity with concrete circumstances, to the conclusion that native religious beliefs and practices were incapable of being transformed into Christian equivalents.(MacCormack 1985: 450) The extent and rapidity of disillusionment varied according to the native context. Missionaries in

Central Mexico nursed the most fevered expectations and therefore suffered the deepest and bitterest disappointment at the inadequacies of evangelization by the late sixteenth century; in the Andes, by contrast, where Christianization got off to a later start and more realism prevailed, the early optimism was both less intense and more short-lived. What the missionaries of the core regions of Hispanic America underwent in the sixteenth century was echoed by the experience of evangelists in New France in the seventeenth century, but here the collapse of expectations was magnified since indigenous ways were even further removed from those of Europe. The Jesuits here were forced to conclude that native culture, contrary to their earlier assumptions, would have to be entirely reformed if true Christianity was to take root. Since Puritan missionaries never adopted a policy of inculturation, they were spared the despair of their Catholic counterparts. In the end, in the Americas, the gap between European and native culture proved to be just too great for a policy of evangelization without Europeanization to work, at least in the sense of producing Christians in the mold that the missionaries intended, as opposed to producing Christians in the mold that natives chose to fashion for themselves.

Conversion is intimately related to the translation of the Christian message into the language of those to be converted. Missionaries in both American continents grappled with the complex task of introducing a concept from Western thought into native languages without altering its meaning and causing misunderstanding. It was not sufficient to declare an Indian word synonymous with a Spanish or French term, since no word of any serious philosophical or theological meaning carries with it the same background of nuance and reference as the equivalent word in a non-related language. Every Indian word had precise and complex ties with an entire cultural background. Missionaries found endless difficulty in adjusting their conceptual language to the indigenous cultural framework: to adjust too little was not to be understood; to adjust too much was to risk distorting the very essence of their message. (Bitterli 1989: 101; Ross 1994: 20) Rendering the Christian message in the native language ran the risk of mistranslation, but at the same time such "mistranslations" were the

355

only way to make the alien understandable. In reality, Christian teaching was effective only to the extent that it was compatible - or appeared in translation to be compatible - with pre-existing belief and practice. Thus, the notion that the missionary may translate in a straightforward manner is illusory; invariably he found that more (or less) was being said than was intended. Adoption of the local tongue as the instrument of evangelization was tantamount to adopting indigenous cultural criteria for the message; this was a radical indigenization wholly at odds with the standard modern portrayal of missions as Western cultural imperialism. (Sanneh 1989: 3, 5) The translation of Christianity created the opportunity for its appropriation, for its familiarization within the native terms of reference, and therefore may have consolidated rather than eliminated the indigenous religious worldview. Paradoxically, through conversion, Indians began to see the possibility of distinguishing themselves from European Christians rather than mimicking them. The encounter with the Christian message in translation entailed not so much internalizing official Catholic doctrines as creating anew an indigenized version which evaded the grip of the colonial masters and marked the difference between the native world and that of the Europeans. The evidence that we have of Indian conversion seems to suggest that it circumvented rather than coincided with Spanish intentions. (Rafael 1988: xi-xii, 211)

Indigenization was a risk that the missionaries ran in order to create the conditions for its pay-off: genuine Christianization. Wherever Christianity could be perceived as building on what was already there, it was enabled to grow, a fact illustrated by later evangelization in Africa. Almost everywhere missionaries went south of the Sahara, they used the local name for God as the name of the God of Israel and the church, when they translated biblical texts: "A new God was not being proclaimed but good news about the God whom the people already worshipped, even if, usually, only indirectly through the ancestors. This was what happened despite what many missionaries themselves believed or understood or consciously preached. Whenever they used the local name for God, then a message of continuity not discontinuity was being proclaimed, whether they consciously intended it or not. In that situation the elements of discontinuity appeared like pruning the living plant, a very different matter from uprooting it and substituting a wholly new plant." (Ross 1994: 148)

So too in the Americas, missionaries interested in practical success proclaimed good news about an old familiar god: Cabeza de Vaca and the deity Aguar; the Guarani and the Land Without Evil; the Master of the Animals in New France; the Wampanoags and Cautantowwit. More importantly, whatever missionaries themselves "believed or understood or consciously preached," the result of the interaction of the two religions was determined less by the thought and actions of Europeans than by the diverse reactions of indigenous peoples. As one historian has noted, "the Indian face of God" does not derive so much from the inculturation pursued by pastoral agents as it does from the mixture of religions promoted by the Indians, in their attempt to make the Christian God more comprehensible. (Marzal et al. 1996: 6) That the Jesuits accommodated cautiously on the whole and up to a point, without betraying the essentials of the faith, is hardly relevant. The recipients of the message could not help but interpret it in their own way, and they appear to have gone farther than their teachers would ever go. Inevitably, they worked out their own variations. (Zurcher 1994: 64)

This was possible because, contrary to the church's declared position, pre-colonial native religion was not incompatible with Christian beliefs and practices. Traditional historical interpretations have tended to take their lead from church accounts and have presented the religious history of the post-conquest world in terms of successful or unsuccessful resistance to Christianity, but in fact neither category - "true" conversion nor consistent resistance - hits the mark. Native Americans expected a conqueror to impose his god without fully displacing one's own, and their post-conquest religious life should be understood in this context. The two religions could be practiced together at different levels without explosive tension, since people may operate comfortably in more than one religious tradition at a time. Indigenous and European religious elements often reinforced one another since early modern Catholicism, as practiced by the bulk of the population, was also primarily ritual, propitiatory and corporate. Idols behind altars when the priest was away, or hidden in church walls and the bases of crosses, could just as well attest to dual worship or native expressions of Christian faith as to an underground "idolatry" that repudiated Christianity, or the utter failure of native and European worlds to communicate. Although some Indians used Christianity, especially in the early years, as a disguise or camouflage for continued secret adherence to old religion, this was not the most significant or long-lasting response. To suppose that this was how the two religions interrelated in the colonial world is to miss the true picture. One did not have to be either a true Christian or a crypto-pagan, hypocritically hiding native religion under a cloak of Christian practice. One could borrow and mix, genuinely and in good faith, from both religions. (Taylor 1996; Lockhart 1992)

A "genuine conversion" should be measured less according to European definitions of Christian orthodoxy than according to a meaningful religious experience for the recipient. Both Catholic and Protestant missionaries achieved quality conversions in the only sense that is ultimately valid: for the natives themselves who underwent the experience. The unprecedented and catastrophic events unleashed by the arrival of Europeans in the Americas created "a world turned upside down." Paradoxically, the greater the havoc wrought, the greater the need for new systems of meaning and explanation. Missionaries that held out the prospect of revitalizing native culture and religion, rather than eradicating them, stood the best chance of imbedding the Christian message. Therefore, the missionary endeavor was not simply a matter of uprooting the ancient tree of American religion, but tending the living organism until it bloomed with Christian leaves.

Notes

Introduction

1. Scholarly custom permits the use of the term "Indian." It is a misnomer, of course, resulting from Columbus' conviction that the Americas were part of the Indies. But it is too well established to abandon. I use it as a synonym for Native American, indigenous person, or native person. Its main drawback is that it disguises ethnic differences, but so does the term Native American.

Chapter 2

1. Although we talk about 'missionaries' and 'mission', these words were not used, or not used in the same sense, in sixteenth-century Spanish America. The term mission was used to refer to a group of persons sent by the Church on a work of spreading the faith; or to refer to the area in which evangelizing activities were taking place; or to refer to the residence of those sent. A mission might be for several years hardly more than an outpost providing an example for people who refused to accept the basic teachings of missionaries. Distinct from a mission was a *doctrina*, a group of native peoples who had accepted the faith, but were not fully formed in it. The term used to describe the person in charge was not missionary, but *doctrinero*, 'person dispensing instruction.' Both religious and secular clergy were able to act as doctrineros, but seculars did so with far less frequency. (Polzer 1976: 4-6) Once instruction was completed and the faithful were fully formed Christians and fully-fledged members of the church, then their unit of organization became the *parroquia*, or parish, the standard form of organization for Spaniards. Thus there was an important difference between mission, doctrina and parish.

2. In the whole of the sixteenth century, five thousand three hundred and seventy-two missionaries were sent under Crown auspices to Spanish America (two thousand seven hundred and eighty-two Franciscans, one thousand five hundred and seventy-nine Dominicans,

three hundred and forty-eight Augustinians, three hundred and twelve
Mercedarians and three hundred and fifty-one Jesuits). In the
seventeenth century, a further three thousand eight hundred and two
were sent (two thousand two hundred and seven Franciscans, one
thousand one hundred and forty-eight Jesuits, one hundred and thirty-
eight Dominicans, two hundred and five Capuchins, seventy-three
Mercedarians and thirty-one Augustinians). These numbers do not
include expeditions paid for by the religious orders themselves, so the
total number was in fact larger.

Chapter 4

1. Quetzalcoatl was god of creation, cosmic destruction and renewal,
culture, maize and the wind. Legend had it that this god became a man
and reigned as a high priest in Tula, bringing civilization to the
Toltecs, before being driven out by his enemies, and taking refuge in
the east, from where he was supposed to return one day to inaugurate a
golden age. Some Spanish chroniclers wrote that when Hernán Cortés
appeared out of the east in 1519, the Indians believed him to be
Quetzalcoatl.

Chapter 8

1. The pioneer of the historical approach based on native-language
sources was James Lockhart. Other historians who have followed in
his footsteps include Frances Berdan, Louise Burkhart, Sarah Cline,
Robert Haskett, Frances Karttunen, Susan Kellogg, Miguel León-
Portilla, Matthew Restall, Susan Schroeder, and Kevin Terraciano.

Chapter 11

1. The shrine at Coricancha (whose name, which means 'Golden
Enclosure', perhaps derives from the gold sheets that were attached to
its walls) lay at the heart of the Inca Empire, both physically and
conceptually. The principal temple of the Incas of Cusco, it stood in
the center of the city, serving as the sacred navel of the empire, and
fulfilling a role akin to the holy places of Jerusalem in Judaism,

Christianity, and Islam, or to the principal temple in Tenochtitlan. Called the Temple of the Sun by the Spaniards, the shrine in fact was not dedicated solely to the solar deity, but consisted of a series of temples to various gods, including Illapa and Viracocha, as well as Inti and Quilla. Important royal mummies were housed and venerated in the innermost sanctums. When the gods of conquered peoples were brought to Cusco as hostages and pledges for good behavior, just as they were by the Mexica, it was at Coricancha that they were received into the Inca pantheon. (Katz 1972: 299; Marzal 1993; Bauer and Stanish 2001: 1, 8; Millones 1997: 27)

2. Copacabana was the holiest site in the Andes having been a religious center for the ancient Tiahuanaco civilization, and in Inca times consisted of a temple for the sun on the island of Titicaca and a temple for the moon on the adjacent island of Coati. According to Andean traditions, the heavenly bodies first rose into the sky from these two islands. As the origin points of the universe, these sites were the destination for thousands of pilgrims from across the realm. Although there was a water deity assigned to Copacabana, worshiped as the creator of fishes in the lake, the site was much more significant for veneration of the celestial deities. The Incas appropriated the site for their religious ideology by turning a pilgrimage there by the Inca ruler into one of the principal sacred festivals of the calendar.

Chapter 12

1. Pachacamac, whose shrine lay on the coast south of where the Spaniards would found Lima, was a pan-Andean god famous for oracular pronouncements, and consulted by Andeans from far and wide, including both the humble, who desired advice on the next harvest, and mighty emperors, including Atahualpa, who sought predictions on the success of their conquests. The shrine functioned as an independent theocratic mini-state, not unlike the Vatican, run by priests who owned lands and supervised laborers for their maintenance.

2. Viracocha was an ancient culture hero, associated with creation, water, the sea, and the color white. According to myth, he emerged from Lake Titicaca, created light, and caused the sun and moon to ascend into Heaven, created mankind and taught human beings how to live, named Cusco and then disappeared into the sea.

Chapter 14

1. It is important not to exaggerate the power of European medicine; if native medicine survived contact with its European counterpart, it was because it could compete. Colonial Spanish medicine was characterized by its limitations. Its capabilities were extremely limited both in the prevention and the cure of illnesses, and it was largely impotent in the face of many diseases. The prevailing medical theories rested on the precepts of Hippocrates, as refined by Galen. Health was thought to be the result of a balance of the four principal humors: yellow bile (hot and dry), black bile (cold and dry), blood (hot and moist), and phlegm (cold and moist). Healing was a process of re-establishing the disrupted balance by the use of drugs possessing the opposite qualities. Also important were the patient's nature - sanguine (blood-dominant), phlegmatic (phlegm-dominant), melancholic (black-bile-dominant), or choleric (yellow-bile-dominant) - and the season with which each humor was associated. Diagnosis had to do not merely with determining the particular illness, which had a corresponding remedy, but with balancing the humoral disruption by the calculated introduction of correcting amounts of the contrary elements, the factors of essential personality and season being taken into account. While iron instruments and the Arab medical tradition granted the Spaniards superiority over indigenous practices in surgery, many native herbs found their way into Spanish medical writings. (Ruiz de Alarcón 1984: 31-32) As one historian of the Jesuits has observed, it was not until early in the twentieth century that a sick person had a better chance of being cured than of being harmed when he sought help from a doctor.

NOTES

Chapter 15

1. Recently doubts have been raised regarding when and where the survivors' healing rituals actually began. In other contemporary accounts, including that of the chronicler Gonzalo Fernández de Oviedo and that of the so-called Joint Report, a now lost report filed with the Audiencia of Santo Domingo and at court on behalf of the three Castilians among the four survivors of these events, Cabeza de Vaca's healing began not on the Texas coast but later, among the people they met after the Avavares. The editor of the latest edition of Cabeza de Vaca's *Relation* concludes that Oviedo and the Joint Report are more reliable with regard to the timing and first location of the healing. (Cabeza de Vaca 1999, 2:282) Even so, in the absence of a definitive answer to this question, I have chosen to conform to Cabeza de Vaca's account in his *Relation*. Since Oviedo and the Joint Report do not differ from Cabeza de Vaca's account with regard to the events themselves, but merely their timing and location, the observations about them made above remain equally valid, even if they reflect a debatable chronology.

Chapter 16

1. Jesuit expansion continued into Baja California in the late 1690s, Nayarit in the 1720s, and Alta California in the late 1760s. (Jackson 1994: 5) During the mid-eighteenth century, the Jesuit mission system also extended into northern Sonora, southern Chihuahua, and finally, southern Arizona.

2. Even so, there were some groups, such as the Tarahumara and the Yaqui, which, though much decimated, managed to survive in the longer term. The Tarahumara (or Rarámuri) Indians of Chihuahua (who live where the Mexican states of Chihuahua, Durango and Sinaloa are found today) survived by abandoning much of their homeland during the late-sixteenth and seventeenth centuries, and withdrawing to the largely inaccessible country of southwest Chihuahua. The Yaqui population declined from around sixty thousand in 1565 to approximately thirty thousand at the time of

missionization in 1617 (reminding us again of the great reductions that many groups sustained prior to regular contact), and dropped still further to around eight thousand by 1678. After reaching a nadir around 1720, the Yaqui population rebounded sharply, growing to over twenty-two thousand in 1759. (Reff 1992: 272)

3. 'Revitalization' may be defined as the process wherein a culture or a religion in danger of being supplanted reasserts itself in a modified form in order to defy its rival and to construct a more satisfying vision of reality. Revitalization movements are not unique to the Americas but have arisen across the world where indigenous religions have come into contact with Christianity. Recurring elements include ecstatic rituals, the anticipated return of ancestors, the promise of a mystical deliverance, and the imminence of both personal and tribal salvation. Examples in the modern world are the Melanesian Cargo Cults and the Ghost Dance of the North American Plains Indians, both of which stressed the imminent return of the dead and the creation of a paradise on earth. (Wallace 1956: 265, 267) The arrival of Christianity sparked in some regions, especially of Spanish America, a specific type of revitalization movement known as millenarianism. The original meaning of millenarianism was narrow and precise. It referred to the belief held by some Christians on the authority of Revelation XX 4-6 that, after his Second Coming, Christ would establish his kingdom on earth and would reign over it for one thousand years (the millennium which gives its name to the movement) before the Last Judgment. According to the Book of Revelation, the citizens of that kingdom will be Christian martyrs, who are to be resurrected for the purpose one thousand years in advance of the general resurrection of the dead. In general, Christian millenarians have interpreted that part of the prophecy in a liberal rather than literal sense: they have equated the martyrs with the suffering faithful - themselves - and have expected the Second Coming in their lifetime. But the term 'millenarian' has become detached from its Christian thousand-year etymology and has come to signify any doctrine of salvation or redemption that posits the vision of a perfect age to come, a reign of peace, justice and plenty, not as a wish or hope, but as a total certainty. To be millenarian, the vision must be collective (to be enjoyed by the faithful as a group),

imminent (to come both soon and suddenly), total (to transform life on earth so completely that the new dispensation will be no mere improvement on the present but perfection itself), and terrestrial (to be realized on this earth - in human history - rather than in a heavenly hereafter). Millenarian belief is not limited to the Judeo-Christian world; it existed before Christianity, and has been found in many societies, including those of native America. The term 'millenarian' may be applied not only to religious or quasi-religious phenomena, but also to secular phenomena that are motivated by a quest for salvation and by a deliberate effort to revitalize a society and culture, with the goal of inaugurating a golden age or accessing a paradise. Movements that emphasize the participation of a divine savior in human flesh are termed 'messianic.' Much millenarian thought is also 'apocalyptic', which is to say imbued with a certain urgency exerted by the conviction that the end of time is imminent. (Graziano 1999: 7-8; Cohn 1970: 31; Vanderwood 1992: 232)

Chapter 17

1. A *mitote* was a dance involving a large number of people, colourfully adorned, who held hands and danced in a circle around a banner, next to which there was a vessel filled with an alcoholic drink, from which they would imbibe every so often until they became intoxicated. (Pérez de Ribas 1999: 108)

Chapter 18

1. The word 'reduction' is perhaps best translated as 'community.' Jesuit Antonio Ruiz de Montoya spoke of reductions as 'gatherings of Indians and Indian villages into larger towns and into political and humane societies.' (McNaspy 1982: 8-9) "'Reductions' are what we call towns of Indians who, formerly living in their old fashion in forests, hill country, and valleys, and along hidden streams in clumps of three, four, or six dwellings situated one to three or more leagues apart, have been through the Fathers' efforts assembled into large settlements, to a civilized, human way of life." (Ruiz de Montoya 1993: 37-38) The goal was to 'lead the Indian back' from mountains

and woods into a community where he could better learn the rudiments of Christian belief and elementary forms of Spanish social and political organization. (Polzer 1976: 7)

Chapter 21

1. It has been customary to speak about North American peoples in terms of their 'tribe', which is to say, a group with mutual recognition of kinship based on a common tongue, in other words, a linguistic distinction. But, in fact, the tribe was not the most important unit for North Americans; there were different levels, both over and above the tribes (leagues and confederacies) and below and among the tribes (lineages, clans, bands). (Trigger 1978, 15:410) Whereas "tribe" refers to a unit of social identity according to use of a common language (for example, Mohawk), "league" or "confederacy" refers to a common political identity, made up of several tribes, usually on the basis of renouncing war among themselves, and for purposes of defense. The basic unit of social organization was the nuclear family, but in a society where a family was at the mercy of both the elements and enemies, this level was not the most important. More significant was the extended family (or lineage), in other words collateral kin, grandparents and their siblings, uncles, aunts and cousins. Degrees of kinship depended on whether the group was patrilineal or matrilineal (determining descent and close kin through the paternal or maternal line). Among many peoples, though not all, extended families were grouped into clans, or collections of lineages. The word "clan" does not refer to a group of relatives, friends or associates, as used in everyday conversation, but has a technical meaning: it designates a named group whose members may not marry each other, and in which membership is ascribed at birth. For those peoples who had them, clans were an important unit of social identity. Rather than residing together, members of the same clan were scattered through a number of villages within a tribe or ethnic group. Thus, clans were not neatly contained within a particular community, but their members were spread across all the different communities. (Tooker 1979: 164-65) The largest significant social group was the band, or community headed by a chief; in times of war, bands might unite against a

common enemy, thus forming a 'tribe.' Social and political organization varied from ethnic group to ethnic group, largely according to geographic location. The main differentiation was between northern hunters and southern horticulturalists. Above the Saco River (between modern New Hampshire and Maine), Indians were organized in small, semi-nomadic bands that lived by hunting and fishing in a regular territory. Essentially the band consisted of those people who normally assembled at a good fishing place during the summer. Leadership was only weakly developed and did not extend beyond the hunting group. From the Saco River southward, the native economy - the creation of semi-permanent villages located in the river valleys - was primarily, though not exclusively, based on horticulture. Both the southern horticulturalists and the northern hunters used to spend the better part of the summer along the seashore, where they gathered and smoked large amounts of fish and shellfish. The local bands of the northeast were united in tribes or confederacies, at least from the time of the earliest recorded European contacts. These alliances were brought about by the intermarriage of chiefly lineages as well as by conquest, and their duration depended upon the success achieved in stabilizing these relationships. (Trigger 1978, 15:78, 84)

2. The Micmac were known by many different names. They were called Souriquois by the early French; Tarrantines by English colonists; Toudamans by Cartier; and were also known as Gaspesians and Acadians. Some of these were subgroups - the Gaspesians lived in eastern Quebec, the Acadians in central Nova Scotia, and the Souriquois in southern Nova Scotia.

3. Other Algonquians, such as the Menominee, Sauk, Fox, Kickapoo, Potawatomi, Miami, Illinois, and Shawnee, lived in the upper Great Lakes-Ohio River area.

4. These were joined in the second decade of the eighteenth century by the Tuscaroras, a linguistically related tribe, from North Carolina, to become the 'Six Nations.' The total population of the confederacy at contact was perhaps about twenty-five thousand (other estimates say sixteen thousand). The Seneca was the largest tribe (often reported to

367

equal or exceed in size the other four Iroquois tribes combined) and, together with the Mohawk and the Oneida, politically the most important.

5. The name Huron may derive from the French nickname for Indians whose haircut reminded them of a ridge of erect bristles on the head of a boar ('hure' means boar's head, bristly head) or, more likely, from the Old French word for ruffian or unkempt person.

6. Estimates of the Huron population at the time of early French contacts vary widely. It may only be said that they numbered between twenty thousand and thirty-five thousand, with the most recent estimates tending towards the bottom end of this range (around twenty thousand). (Trigger 1978, 15:369) Like the Iroquois, the Hurons were a confederacy composed of four tribes - Attignaouantan, Attingueenougnahak, Ahrendarrhonon, and Tahontaenrat - plus the Ataronchronon, who do not seem to have been a recognized part of the confederacy and who may have been merely a division of the Attignaouantan. (Trigger 1976: 30; Trigger 1968: 109) Among these four tribes, the first two were the largest and the most senior; the third and fourth were admitted to the confederacy only shortly before the arrival of the French.

7. This association was made up of a number of allied groups, which could include any or all of the Antouaronons, Attiragenrega (also known as Atiwandaronks), Ahondihronon, Onguiaronon, Kakouagoga and Wenro. The term Neutral referred to the fact that at the time of contact with Europeans they were at peace with the Hurons, Iroquois and Algonquins.

8. There were no formal means of passing down the communities' religious knowledge save the winter narration of myths. Native Americans had no books, and very few standardized sacred texts (and commentaries on them) that were distinct from what was said and done in specific rituals or to fill practical needs, and rarely was any effort made to preserve the exact wording unchanged. They were not People of the Book. (Tooker 1979: xii)

Chapter 22

1. Some of the refugees were resettled on Christian Island in Georgian Bay, but of the six thousand people there by the end of the year, only three hundred survived the winter due to lack of food and shelter. The following year, these survivors were taken by the Jesuits to safer ground, away from the Iroquois, first to the Island of Orleans and later to Lorette, in the vicinity of Quebec. (Moore 1982: 31) This village was twice relocated, and some Christian Iroquois came to live there. (Campeau 1967: 468) Other Hurons fled to the Petuns and ultimately to the Neutrals and Eries. Yet others dispersed to, and intermarried with, the Ottawas. Many Hurons surrendered to the Iroquois and were adopted by them. Once the Neutral and the Erie were conquered as well, the greater part of the Hurons ended up being absorbed by the Iroquois. (Trigger 1978, 15:387)

Chapter 27

1. James Mooney suggested a figure between thirty-four thousand one hundred and thirty-six thousand five hundred. (Cook 1973a: 1, 22) Sherburne Cook estimated a probable native population of seventy-one thousand nine hundred for the tribes of New England and southeastern New York in 1610 (including four thousand five hundred Massachusetts and five thousand Wampanoags), though a range from sixty thousand to eighty thousand should be indicated (on the other hand, if the Indian population of this region was truly given by the counts of the late eighteenth century, and if the magnitude of decline even approximated that proposed by some recent scholars, the estimate made here is far too low). (Cook 1976: 84) Axtell gave a figure of one hundred and forty-four thousand for the Indian population of New England from the Saco River in southern Maine to the Quinnipiac in western Connecticut in 1600. (Axtell 1985: 219)

Bibliography

Unpublished Primary Sources

JL   Jesuit Annual Letter, Archivum Romanum Societatis Iesu (Roma).

Published Primary Sources

Primary sources were consulted (and hence are listed here) in their original language. However, where I have used direct quotes from sources in the text, these are listed here in English translation.

Acosta, José de. 1984-87. *De procuranda Indorum salute.* Corpus hispanorum de pace. 2 vols. Madrid: CSIC.

Benavides, Alonso de. 1954. *Memorial of 1630.* Cyprian J. Lynch (ed.). Translated by Peter P. Forrestal. Washington D.C.: Academy of American Franciscan History.

Cabeza de Vaca, Alvar Nuñez. 1999. *Alvar Nuñez Cabeza de Vaca: His Account, His Life, and the Expedition of Pánfilo de Narváez.* Rolena Adorno and Patrick Charles Pautz (eds.). 2 vols. Lincoln and London: University of Nebraska Press.

Calancha, Antonio de la. 1974-81. *Corónica moralizada del Orden de San Agustín en el Perú.* 5 vols. Lima: Ignacio Prado Pastor.

Cieza de León, Pedro.1967. *El señorio de los incas del perú. Segunda parte de la crónica del perú.* C. Aranibar (ed.). Lima: IEP.

Diaz del Castillo, Bernal. 1975. *The Conquest of New Spain.* Translated by J. M. Cohen. London: Folio Society.

Durán, Diego. 1967. *Historia de las Indias de Nueva España e Islas de la Tierra Firme.* Angel María Garibay K (ed.). 2 vols. Mexico: Porrúa.

_____. 1971. *Book of the Gods and Rites of the Ancient Calendar.* Norman: University of Oklahoma Press.

Eliot, John. 1671. *Indian Dialogues.* Cambridge, Mass.

_____. 1834. "Tracts Relating to Attempts to Convert to Christianity the Indians of New England." *Collections of the Massachusetts Historical Society.* 3rd ser. 4:1-287.

D'Evreux, Ivres. 1929. *Viagem ao norte do Brasil.* Rio de Janeiro.

Garcilaso de la Vega, El Inca. 1966. *Royal Commentaries of the Incas.* Harold V. Livermore (ed.). 2 vols. Austin and London: Univ. of Texas Press.

Hobbes, Thomas. 1946. *Leviathan.* M. Oakeshott (ed.). Oxford: Blackwell.

JR *Jesuit Relations*; see Thwaites.

Le Clercq, Christien. 1910. *New Relation of Gaspesia.* William F. Ganong (ed.). Toronto: Champlain Society.

Mayhew, Matthew. 1694. *A Brief Narrative of the Success which the Gospel hath had among the Indians of Martha's Vineyard.* Boston: Bartholomew Green.

Mendieta, Jerónimo de. 1971. *Historia eclesiástica indiana.* Mexico: Porrúa.

Molina, Cristóbal de, and Albornoz, Cristóbal de. 1988. *Fábulas y mitos de los incas.* H. Urbano and P. Duviols (eds.). Madrid: Historia 16.

Motolinía, Toribio de. 1951. *History of the Indians of New Spain.* Translated by Francis Borgia Steck. Washington D.C.: Academy of American Franciscan History.

Murúa, Martin de. 1986. *Historia general del Perú.* Manuel Ballesteros (ed.). Madrid: Historia 16.

Olmos, Fray Andrés de. 1990. *Tratado de Hechicerías y Sortilegio.* Georges Baudot (ed.). Mexico: UNAM.

Pérez de Ribas, Andres. 1999. *History of the Triumphs of Our Holy Faith Amongst the Most Barbarous and Fierce Peoples of the New World.* Translated by Daniel T. Reff, Maureen Ahern, and Richard K. Danford. Tucson: University of Arizona Press.

Polo de Ondegardo, Juan. 1916. "De los errores y supersticiones de los indios." Carlos A. Romero (ed.). *Colección de libros y documentos referentes a la historia del Perú,* 3: 1-44. Lima: Sanmartí.

Ruiz de Alarcón, Hernando. 1984. *Treatise on the Heathen Superstitions.* Translated by and eds. Ross Hassig and J. Richard Andrews. Norman: University of Oklahoma Press.

Ruiz de Montoya, Antonio. 1993. *The Spiritual Conquest.* Introduction by C.J. McNaspy. St Louis.

Sahagún, Bernardino de. 1975. *Historia General de las cosas de Nueva España.* Angel María Garibay K. (ed.). 3rd ed. Mexico: Porrúa.

San Pedro, Fray Juan de. 1992. *La persecución del demonio: crónica de los primeros agustinos en el norte del peru (1560).* Eric E. Deeds (ed.). Malaga: Algazara + CAMEI.

Serna, Jacinto de la. 1892. "Manual de ministros de indios para el conocimiento de sus idolatrías y extirpación de ellas." *Colección de documentos inéditos para la historia de España,* 104: 1-267. Madrid: José Perales y Martínez.

Shepard, Thomas. 1647. *The Day-Breaking if not the Sun-Rising of the Gospel with the Indians in New England.* London: Cotes.

_____. 1648. *The Clear Sunshine of the Gospel breaking forth upon the Indians in New England.* London: Cotes.

Thwaites, Reuben Gold, ed. 1896-1901. *The Jesuit Relations and Allied Documents: Travels and Explorations of the Jesuit missionaries in New France, 1610-1791.* 73 vols. Cleveland: Burrows Brothers.

Williams, Roger. 1973. *A Key into the Language of America.* John J. Teunissen and Evelyn Hinz (eds.). Detroit: Wayne State University Press.

Winslow, Edward. 1649. *The Glorious Progress of Gospel, amongst the Indians in New England.* London: H. Allen.

_____. "Good News From New England." 1841. *Chronicles of the Pilgrim Fathers of the Colony of Plymouth 1602-25.* Alexander Young (ed.). Boston: Charles C. Little and James Brown.

Winslow, Ola Elizabeth. 1968. *John Eliot: "Apostle to the Indians."* Boston: Houghton Mifflin.

Secondary Sources

Aburto Cotrina, Carlos Oswaldo. 1999. "Políticas y métodos de evangelización en Maynas durante el siglo XVIII: Definiendo los elementos de la cultura misionera." In Sandra Negro and Manuel M. Marzal (coord.). *Un Reino en la Frontera: las misiones jesuitas en la America colonial.* Lima: PUCP, 77-96.

Adorno, Rolena. 1991. "The Negotiation of Fear in Cabeza de Vaca's Naufragios." *Representations,* 33: 163-99.

Ahern, Maureen. 1993. "The Cross and the Gourd: The Appropriation of Ritual Signs in the Relaciones of Alvar Nuñez Cabeza de Vaca and Fray Marcos de Niza." In Jerry M. Williams and Robert E. Lewis (eds.). *Early Images of the Americas: Transfer and Invention,* 215-44. Tucson and London: University of Arizona Press.

Alberro, Solange. 1992. *Les espagnols dans le Mexique colonial. Histoire d'une acculturation.* Cahiers des annales 43. Paris: Armand Colin.

Albó, Xavier. 1966. "Jesuitas y culturas indígenas, Perú 1568-1606, su actitud, métodos y criterios de aculturación." *América Indígena,* 26(3): 249-308; 26(4): 395-445.

Arbman, Ernst. 1963. *Ecstasy or Religious Trance* 1: *Vision and Ecstasy.* Norstedts, Sweden: Svenska Bokforlaget.

Armas Medina, Fernando de. 1953. *Cristianización del Perú (1532-1600).* Seville: Escuela de Estudios Hispano-Americanos.

Axtell, James. 1982. "Some Thoughts on the Ethnohistory of Missions." *Ethnohistory,* 29(1): 35-41.

_____. 1985. *The Invasion Within: The Contest of Cultures in Colonial North America.* New York/Oxford: OUP.

_____. 1988. *After Columbus: Essays in the Ethnohistory of Colonial North America.* New York/Oxford: OUP.

_____. 1992. *Beyond 1492: Encounters in Colonial North America.* New York/Oxford: OUP.

Azoulai, Martine. 1983. "Para la Historia de la Evangelización en América: los confesionarios." *Allpanchis,* 22: 127-38.

Bailey, Alfred G. 1969. *The Conflict of European and Eastern Algonquian Cultures 1504-1700: A Study in Canadian Civilization.* 2nd ed. Toronto: University of Toronto Press.

Baker, Brenda J., and Kealhofer, Lisa. 1996. *Bioarchaeology of Native American Adaptation in the Spanish Borderlands.* Gainesville: University Press of Florida.

Bakewell, Peter. 1997. *A History of Latin America: Empires and Sequels 1450-1930.* The Blackwell History of the World. Oxford and Malden: Blackwell.

Barnes, Monica. 1992. "Catechisms and *Confessionarios*: Distorting Mirrors of Andean Societies." In Robert V.H. Dover, Katherine E. Seibold, and John H. McDowell (eds.), *Andean Cosmologies through time: persistence and emergence,* 67-94. Bloomington: Indiana University Press.

Baudot, Georges. 1995. *Utopia and History in Mexico: The First Chroniclers of Mexican Civilization (1520-1569).* Georgetown: Univ. Press of Colorado.

Bauer, Brian S., and Stanish, Charles. 2001. *Ritual and Pilgrimage in the Ancient Andes: The Islands of the Sun and the Moon.* Austin: University of Texas Press.

Berkhofer, Robert F. Jr. 1978. *The White Man's Indian: Images of the American Indian from Columbus to the Present.* New York: Alfred A. Knopf.

Biggar, H. P. (ed.). 1924. *Voyages of Jacques Cartier.* Ottawa: F. A. Acland.

Bitterli, Urs. 1989. *Cultures in Conflict: Encounters between European and Non-European Cultures, 1492-1800.* Translated by Ritchie Robertson. Cambridge: Polity.

Block, David. 1994. *Mission Culture on the Upper Amazon: Native Tradition, Jesuit enterprise and Secular Policy in Moxos, 1660-1880.* Lincoln and London: University of Nebraska Press.

Borges, Pedro. 1977. *El envío de misioneros a América durante la época española.* Salamanca: Universidad Pontificia de Salamanca.

_____. (dir). 1992. *Historia de la iglesia en hispanoamérica y filipinas (siglos XV-XIX).* 2 vols. Madrid: Biblioteca de autores cristianos.

Bowden, Henry Warner. 1981. *American Indians and Christian Missions: Studies in Cultural Conflict.* Chicago History of American Religion. Chicago and London: University of Chicago Press.

Bozeman, Theodore Dwight. 1988. *To Live Ancient Lives: The Primitivist Dimension in Puritanism.* Chapel Hill and London: University of North Carolina Press.

Brading, David. 1991. *The First America. The Spanish Monarchy, Creole Patriots, and the Liberal State 1492-1867.* Cambridge: CUP.

_____. 2001. *Mexican Phoenix. Our Lady of Guadalupe: Image and Tradition across Five Centuries.* Cambridge: CUP.

Bremer, M. 1998. "La Virgen de Caacupe. Encuentro espiritual guaraní-franciscano." In *Caazapa: las reducciones franciscanas y los Guaraní del Paraguay,* 141-53. Granada: Diputación de Granada.

Brenner, Elise M. 1980. "To Pray or to be Prey: That is the Question - Strategies for Cultural Autonomy of Massachusetts Praying Town Indians." *Ethnohistory,* 27(2): 135-52.

Buckley, Michael J. 1994. "The Suppression of the Chinese Rites: A Suggestion of Some Factors." In D. E. Mungello, *The Chinese Rites Controversy: Its History and Meaning,* 281-85. Nettetal: Steyler Verlag.

Burkhart, Louise M. 1988a. "Doctrinal Aspects of Sahagún's *Colloquios.*" In J. Jorge Klor de Alva, H. B. Nicholson, and Eloise Quiñones Keber, (eds.). *The Work of Bernardino de Sahagún: Pioneer Ethnographer of Sixteenth Century Aztec Mexico,* 65-82. Studies on Culture and Society. Vol. 2. Institute for Mesoamerican Studies, University at Albany, State University of New York. Austin: University of Texas Press.

_____. 1988b. "The Solar Christ in Nahuatl Doctrinal Texts of Early Colonial Mexico." *Ethnohistory,* 35: 234-56.

_____. 1989. *The Slippery Earth: Nahua-Christian Moral Dialogue in Sixteenth Century Mexico.* Tucson: University of Arizona Press.

_____. 1993. "The Cult of the Virgin of Guadalupe in Mexico." In Gary H. Gossen and Miguel León-Portilla (eds.), *South and*

Mesoamerican Native Spirituality: From the Cult of the Feathered Serpent to the Theology of Liberation, 198-227. New York and London: SCM Press Ltd.

_____. 1996. *Holy Wednesday: A Nahua Drama from Early Colonial Mexico,* Philadelphia: Univ. of Pennsylvania Press.

_____. 2001. *Before Guadalupe: The Virgin Mary in Early Colonial Nahuatl Literature.* Institute for Mesoamerican Studies Monograph 13. SUNY: Albany.

Campeau, Lucien. 1967. *La Première Mission D'Acadie (1602-16).* Monumenta Historica Societatis Iesu. Rome/Quebec: Université Laval.

Caraman, Philip. 1976. *The Lost Paradise: The Jesuit Republic in South America.* New York: Seabury Press.

Casciano, Jonathan. 1996. *Fear the Manitou: Continuity between the traditional native Americans and Christian Indian converts in seventeenth-century New England and New France.* Senior Honours Thesis, Brandeis University. Waltham, Mass..

Cave, Alfred A. 1992. "Indian Shamans and English Witches in Seventeenth-Century New England." *Essex Institute Historical Collections,* 128: 239-54.

Cayota, M. "Espiritualidad franciscana y cultura guaraní: un vibrar común." In *Caazapa: las reducciones franciscanas y los Guaraní del Paraguay,* 123-39. Granada: Diputación de Granada.

Celestino, Olinda, and Meyers, Albert 1981. *Las cofradías en el Perú - región central.* Frankfurt: Vervuert.

Cervantes, Fernando. 1998. "Cristianismo o sincretismo? Una reinterpretación de la conquista espiritual en la America española." In Hans-Jurgen Prien (ed.) *Religiosidad e Historiografia,* 21-33. Frankfurt: Vervuert.

Cervantes, Fernando. 1991. *The Idea of the Devil and the Problem of the Indian: the Case of Mexico in the Sixteenth Century.* University of London. Institute of Latin American Studies Research Papers. London: Institute of Latin American Studies.

Chambouleyron, R. 1999. "El manto del orden: el plan evangelizador del Padre Manuel de Nóbrega." In Sandra Negro and Manuel

M. Marzal (coord.). *Un Reino en la Frontera: las misiones jesuitas en la America colonial*, 37-47. Lima: PUCP.

Clastres, Helene. 1975. *La terre sans mal: le prophetisme tupi-guarani.* Paris: Seuil.

Clendinnen, Inga. 1982. "Disciplining the Indians: Franciscan Ideology and Missionary Violence in Sixteenth-Century Yucatán," *Past and Present*, 94: 27-48.

_____. 1987a. *Ambivalent Conquests: Maya and Spaniard in Yucatán 1517-1570.* Cambridge: CUP.

_____. 1987b. "Franciscan Missionaries in Sixteenth-Century Mexico." In J. Obelkevich, and Roper, Samuel (eds.). *Disciplines of Faith: Studies in Religion, Politics, and Patriarchy*, 229-45. London and New York: Routledge and Kegan Paul.

_____. 1990. "Ways to the Sacred: Reconstructing 'Religion' in Sixteenth-Century Mexico." *History and Anthropology*, 5: 105-41.

Codignola, Luca. 1994. "The French in Early America: Religion and Reality." In Deborah L. Madsen (ed.) *Visions of America Since 1492*, 35-56. London: Leicester University Press.

Cogley, Richard W. 1990. "John Eliot in Recent Scholarship." *American Indian Culture and Research Journal*, 14(2): 77-92.

_____. 1991a. "Idealism vs. Materialism in the Study of Puritan Missions to the Indians." *Method and Theory in the Study of Religion*, 3(2): 165-182.

_____. 1991b. "John Eliot and the Millennium." *Religion and American Culture: A Journal of Interpretation*, 1(2): 227-250.

Cohen, Charles L. 1993. "Conversion among Puritans and Amerindians: A Theological and Cultural Perspective." In Francis J. Bremer (ed.). *Puritanism: Transatlantic Perspectives on a Seventeenth-Century Anglo-American Faith*, 233-56. Boston: Massachusetts Historical Society.

Cohn, Norman. 1970. "Medieval Millenarism: Its Bearing on the Comparative Study of Millenarian Movements." In Sylvia L. Thrupp, *Millennial Dreams in Action: Studies inRevolutionary Religious Movements*, 31-43. New York: Schocken Books.

Conkling, Robert. 1974. "Legitimacy and Conversion in Social Change: The Case of French Missionaries and the Northeastern Algonkian." *Ethnohistory*, 21(1): 1-24.

Cook, Noble David. 1981. *Demographic Collapse: Indian Peru, 1520-1620*. Cambridge: CUP.

_____. 1998. *Born to Die. Disease and New World Conquest, 1492-1650*. Cambridge: CUP.

Cook, Noble David, and Lovell, W. George (eds.). 1992. *The Secret Judgments of God. NativePeoples and Old World Disease in Colonial Spanish America*. Norman: University of Oklahoma Press.

Cook, Sherburne F. 1973a. "Interracial Warfare and Population Decline among the New England Indians." *Ethnohistory*, 20: 1-24.

_____. 1973b. "Significance of Disease in the Extinction of the New England Indian." *Human Biology*, 45: 485-508.

_____. 1976. *The Indian Population of New England in the Seventeenth Century*. Berkeley and London: University of California Press.

Dean, Carolyn. 1999. *Inka Bodies and the Body of Christ: Corpus Christi in Colonial Cuzco, Peru*. Durham and London: Duke University Press.

Deeds, Susan M. 1998a "Indigenous Rebellions on the Northern Mexican Mission Frontier: From First-Generation to Later Colonial Responses." In Donna J. Guy and Thomas E. Sheridan, *Contested Ground: Comparative Frontiers on the Northern and Southern Edges of the Spanish Empire*. 32-51. Tucson: University of Arizona Press.

_____. 1998b. "First-Generation Rebellions in Seventeenth-Century Nueva Vizcaya." In Susan Schroeder (ed.) *Native Resistance and the Pax Colonial in New Spain*, 1-29. Lincoln and London: University of Nebraska Press.

_____. 2003. *Defiance and Deference in Mexico's Colonial North: Indians under Spanish Rule in Nueva Vizcaya*. Austin: University of Texas Press.

Dennis, Matthew. 1993. *Cultivating a Landscape of Peace: Iroquois-European Encounters in Seventeenth-Century America.* Ithaca and London: Cornell University Press.

Dibble, Charles E. 1974. "The Nahuatlization of Christianity." In Munro S. Edmonson, *Sixteenth Century Mexico: The Work of Sahagún,* 225-233. Albuquerque: University of New Mexico Press.

Dickason, Olive Patricia. 1984. *The Myth of the Savage: And the Beginnings of French Colonialism in the Americas.* Alberta: University of Alberta Press.

_____. 1989. "Review Article of Axtell's *The Invasion Within.*" *Ethnohistory,* 36: 89-94.

Dobyns, Henry F. 1963. "An Outline of Andean Epidemic History to 1720." *Bulletin of History of Medicine,* 37: 493-515.

Drury, Nevill. 1989. *The Elements of Shamanism.* Shaftesbury: Element.

Dunne, George H. 1962. *Generation of Giants: The Story of the Jesuits in China in the Last Decades of the Ming Dynasty.* London: Burns and Oates.

Dunne, Peter M. 1944. *Pioneer Jesuits in Northern Mexico.* Berkeley/Los Angeles: University of California Press.

Dussel, Enrique D. 1974. *Historia de la iglesia en américa latina: coloniaje y liberación (1492-1973).* 3rd ed. Barcelona: Editorial Nova Terra.

Duverger, Christian. 1993. *La Conversión de los indios de Nueva España.* Mexico: Fondo de Cultura Económica.

Farriss, Nancy M. 1984. *Maya Society under Colonial rule: The Collective Enterprise of Survival.* Princeton: Princeton University Press.

Fenton, William N. 1987. *The False Faces of the Iroquois,* Norman: University of Oklahoma Press.

Fernández García, Enrique. 2000. *Peru Cristiano.* Lima.

García Icazbalceta, Joaquin. 1954. *Bibliografía Mexicana del siglo XVI. Catálogo razonado de libros impresos en México de 1539 a 1600.* Agustín Millares Carlo (ed.). Mexico: Fondo de Cultura Económica.

Gisbert, Teresa. 1980. *Iconografía y mitos indígenas en el arte.* La Paz: Gisbert.

Gómez Canedo, Limo. 1993. *Evangelización, cultura y promoción social: ensayos y estudios críticos sobre la contribución franciscana a los orígenes cristianos de México (siglos XVI-XVIII).* Mexico: Porrúa.

Grant, John Webster. 1984. *Moon of Wintertime: Missionaries and the Indians of Canada in Encounter Since 1534.* Toronto: University of Toronto Press.

Graziano, Frank. 1999. *The Millennial New World.* Oxford: OUP.

Greenleaf, Richard. 1962. *Zumarraga and the Inquisition, 1536-1543.* Washington: Academy of American Franciscan History.

Griffiths, Nicholas. 1996. *The Cross and the Serpent. Religious Repression and Resurgence in Colonial Peru.* Norman and London: University of Oklahoma Press.

Griffiths, Nicholas and Cervantes, Fernando (eds.). 1999. *Spiritual Encounters. Interactions between Christianity and Native Religions in Colonial America.* Lincoln: University of Nebraska Press, and Birmingham: University of Birmingham Press.

Gruzinski, Serge. 1989. *Man-Gods in the Mexican Highlands: Indian Power and Colonial Society, 1520-1800.* Translated by Eileen Corrigan. Stanford: Stanford University Press.

Hamnett, Brian. 1999. *A Concise History of Mexico.* Cambridge: CUP.

Hanzeli, Victor Egon. 1969. *Missionary Linguistics in New France: A Study of Seventeenth Century and Eighteenth Century Descriptions of American Indian Languages.* Paris.

Harrison, Regina. 1994. "The Theology of Concupiscence: Spanish-Quechua Confessional Manuals in the Andes." In F.J. Cevallos-Candau et al. (eds.). *Coded Encounters: Writing, Gender, and Ethnicity in Colonial LatinAmerica,* 135-150. Amherst: University of Massachusetts Press.

Hart, William B. 1999. "' The kindness of the blessed Virgin': faith, succor, and the cult of Mary among Christian Hurons and Iroquois in seventeenth-century New France." In Nicholas Griffiths and Fernando Cervantes (eds.). 1999. *Spiritual Encounters. Interactions between Christianity and Native*

Religions in Colonial America, 65-90. Lincoln: University of Nebraska Press, and Birmingham: University of Birmingham Press.

Hassig, Ross. 2001. *Time, History and Belief in Aztec and Colonial Mexico.* Austin: University of Texas Press.

Haubert, Maxime. 1986. *La Vie Quotidienne des Indiens et des Jesuites du Paraguay au temps des missions.* Paris: Hachette.

Healy, George R. 1958. "The French Jesuits and the Idea of the Noble Savage." *William and Mary Quarterly*, Series 3 15: 143-67.

Heras, Julian. 1991. "Los franciscanos en la evangelización del Perú del siglo XVI." In P. Nguyen Thai Hop (coord.). *Evangelización y teología en el Perú: Luces y sombras en el siglo XVI*, 49-69. Lima: Instituto Bartolomé de Las Casas.

Holstun, James. 1983. "John Eliot's Empirical Millenarianism." *Representations* 4: 128-53.

_____. 1987. *A Rational Millennium: Puritan Utopias of Seventeenth-Century England and America.* Oxford: OUP.

Hu-Duhart, Evelyn. 1981. *Missionaries, Miners and Indians: Spanish Contact with the Yaqui Nation of Northwestern New Spain 1533-1820.* Tucson: University of Arizona Press.

Hultkrantz, Ake. 1979. *The Religions of the American Indians.* Translated by Monica Setterwall. Berkeley: University of California Press.

_____. 1981. *Belief and Worship in Native North America.* Syracuse: Syracuse Univ. Press.

_____. 1992. *Shamanic Healing and Ritual Drama: Health and Medicine in Native North American Religious Traditions.* New York: Crossroad.

Jackson, Robert H. 1994. *Indian Population Decline: The Missions of Northwest New Spain 1687-1840.* Albuquerque: University of New Mexico Press.

Jaenen, Cornelius J. 1974. "Amerindian Views of French Culture in the Seventeenth Century." *Canadian Historical Review*, 55(3): 261-91.

Jennings, Francis. 1971. "Goals and Functions of Puritan Missions to the Indians." *Ethnohistory*, 18: 197-212.

_____. 1975. *The Invasion of America: Indians, Colonialism, and the Cant of Conquest.* Chapel Hill: University of North Carolina Press.

Katz, Friedrich. 1972. *The Ancient American Civilizations.* London: Weidenfeld and Nicholson.

Keesing, Felix M. 1939. *The Menomini Indians of Wisconsin.* Philadelphia: American Philosophical Society.

Kellaway, William. 1961. *The New England Company 1649-1776: Missionary Society to the American Indians.* London: Longmans.

Kellogg, Louise Phelps. 1917. *Early Narratives of the Northwest 1634-99.* New York: OMEAH.

Kennedy, J.H. 1950. *Jesuit and Savage in New France.* New Haven: Yale University Press.

Kessell, John L. 1970. *Mission of Sorrows: Jesuit Guevavi and the Pimas (1691-1767).* Tucson: University of Arizona Press.

Klor de Alva, J. Jorge. 1991. "Sin and Confession Among the Colonial Nahuas: The Confessional as a Tool for Domination." In Ricardo Sanchez, Eric Van Young, and Gisela Von Wobeser (eds.). *Ciudad y campo en la historia de Mexico,* 1: 91-101. 2 vols. Mexico: UNAM.

_____. 1993. "Aztec Spirituality and Nahuatized Christianity." In Gary H. Gossen and Miguel León-Portilla (eds.). *South and Mesoamerican Native Spirituality: From the Cult of the Feathered Serpent to the Theology of Liberation,* 173-97. New York and London: SCM Press Ltd.

Kobayashi, José María. 1974. *La Educación como Conquista (empresa franciscana en México).* Mexico: El Colegio de México.

Krippner-Martinez, James. 2001. *Rereading the Conquest: Power, Politics, and the History of Early Colonial Michoacan, Mexico, 1521-1565.* Pennsylvania: Pennsylvania State University Press.

Kubler, George. 1946. "The Quechua in the Colonial World." In Julien H. Steward (ed.). *Handbook of South American Indians.* Vol. 2, *The Andean Civilizations.* Washington D.C.: Smithsonian Institution, Bureau of American Ethnology.

Kurath, Gertrude P. 1959. "Blackrobe and Shaman: The Christianization of Michigan Algonquians" *Papers of the Michigan Academy of Science, Arts and Letters* 44: 209-15.

Lafaye, Jacques. 1997. *Mesías, cruzadas, utopías: el judeo-cristianismo en las sociedades iberoamericanas.* 2nd ed. Mexico: Fondo de Cultura Económica.

_____. 1976. *Quetzalcoatl and Guadalupe: The Formation of Mexican National Consciousness, 1532-1813.* Chicago: Univ. of Chicago Press.

Langer, Erick and Jackson, Robert H. (eds.). 1995. *The New Latin American Mission History.* Lincoln and London: University of Nebraska Press.

Lapomarda, Vincent A. 1990. "The Jesuit Missions of Colonial New England." *Essex Institute Historical Collections*, 91-109.

Leland, Charles. 1884. *The Algonquin Legends of New England.* Boston: Houghton.

León-Portilla, Miguel. 1974. "Testimonios nahuas sobre la conquista espiritual." *Estudios de cultura nahuatl*, 11:1-36.

Levi Strauss, Claude. 1967. *Structural Anthropology.* New York: Basic Books.

Lewis, Robert E. 1982. "Los naufragios de Alvar Nuñez: Historia y Ficción." *Revista Iberoamericana*, 120-21: 681-94.

Lockhart, James. 1992. *The Nahuas after the Conquest: A Social and Cultural History of the Indians of Central Mexico, Sixteenth through Eighteenth Centuries.* Stanford: Stanford Univ. Press.

_____. 1999a. "Double Mistaken Identity: Some Nahua Concepts in Post-conquest Guise." In *Of Things of the Indies: Essays Old and New in Early Latin American History*, 98-119. Stanford: Stanford Univ. Press.

_____. 1999b. "Three Experiences of Culture Contact: Nahua, Maya and Quechua." In *Of Things of the Indies: Essays Old and New in Early Latin American History*, 204-28. Stanford: Stanford Univ. Press.

Lorenzen, David N. (ed.). 1981. *Religious Change and Cultural Domination.* Mexico: El Colegio de México.

Lovell, W. George. 1992. "'Heavy Shadows and Black Night': Disease and Depopulation in Colonial Spanish America."

Annals of the Association of American Geographers, 82: 426-43.

MacCormack, Sabine. 1985. "'The Heart has its Reasons': Predicaments of Missionary Christianity in Early Colonial Peru." *Hispanic American Historical Review,* 65: 443-66.

_____. 1988. "Pachacuti: Miracles, Punishments, and Last Judgment: Visionary Past and Prophetic Future in Early Colonial Peru." *American Historical Review,* 93: 960-1006.

_____. 1991. *Religion in the Andes: Vision and Imagination in Early Colonial Peru.* Princeton: Princeton University Press.

Maclear, J.F. 1975. "New England and the Fifth Monarchy: The Quest for the Millennium in Early American Puritanism." *William and Mary Quarterly,* 3rd series 32: 223-260.

McNaspy, Clement. J. 1982. *Lost Cities of Paraguay: Art and Architecture of the Jesuit Reductions 1607-1767.* Chicago: Loyola Univ. Press.

Madsen, William. 1967. "Religious Syncretism." In Robert Wauchope (ed.). *Handbook of Middle American Indians* Vol. 6 *Social Anthropology,* 369-91. Austin: Univ. of Texas Press.

Malaga Medina, Alejandro. 1992. *La evangelización del Perú siglo XVI.* Lima: PUCP.

Marzal, Manuel M. 1988. *El sincretismo iberoamericano: un estudio comparativo sobre los quechuas (Cusco), los mayas (Chiapas) y los africanos (Bahía).* 2nd ed. Lima: PUCP.

_____. 1989. *Historia de la antropología indigenista: México y Perú.* 3rd ed. Lima: PUCP.

_____. 1992. *La utopía posible: Indios y jesuitas en la América colonial (1549-1767).* 2 vols. Lima: PUCP.

_____. 1993. "Andean Religion at the Time of the Spanish Conquest." In Gary H. Gossen and Miguel León-Portilla (eds.). *South and Mesoamerican Native Spirituality: From the Cult of the Feathered Serpent to the Theology of Liberation,* 86-115. New York and London: SCM Press Ltd.

Marzal, Manuel M. (et al.). 1996. *The Indian Face of God in Latin America.* Translated by Penelope R. Hall. Maryknoll, NY: Orbis.

Maurer, Eugenio. 1983. *Los Tzeltales: paganos cristianizados o católicos mayas.* Mexico: Centro de Estudios Educativos.

Meiklejohn, Norman. 1988. *La iglesia y los lupaqas durante la colonia.* Cusco: Centro de Estudios Rurales Andinos B. de las Casas.

Melia, Bartomeu. 1996. "A experiencia religiosa guarani." In Marzal, Manuel M. (et al.). *The Indian Face of God in Latin America.* Translated by Penelope R. Hall. Maryknoll, NY: Orbis.

Merrill, William L. 1993. "Conversion and Colonialism in northern Mexico: the Tarahumara Response to the Jesuit Mission Program, 1601-1767." In Robert W. Hefner (ed.). *Conversion to Christianity: Historical and Anthropological Perspectives on a Great Transformation,* 129-63. Berkeley: University of California Press.

Miller, Arthur G. and Farriss, Nancy M. 1979. "Religious Syncretism in Colonial Yucatán: The Archaeological and Ethnohistorical Evidence from Tancah, Quintana Roo." In Norman Hammond and Gordon R. Willey (eds.), *Maya Archaeology and Ethnohistory,* 223-40. Austin: University of Texas Press.

Millones, Luis. 1997. *El rostro de la fe: doce ensayos sobre religiosidad andina.* Seville.

Mills, Kenneth. 1994. *An Evil Lost to View?: An Investigation of Post-Evangelization Andean Religion in Mid-Colonial Peru.* Liverpool: Institute of Latin American Studies, University of Liverpool.

Monteiro, John M. 1999. "The Crises and Transformations of Invaded Societies: Coastal Brazil in the Sixteenth Century." In *Cambridge History of Native Peoples of the Americas.* Vol. III *South America,* Part 1, 973-1023. Frank Salomon and Stuart Schwartz (eds.). Cambridge: CUP.

Mooney, James. 1965. *The Ghost Dance Religion and the Sioux Outbreak of 1890.* Chicago and London: University of Chicago Press.

Moore, James T. 1982. *Indian and Jesuit: A Seventeenth Century Encounter.* Chicago: Loyola University Press.

Morgan, Edmund S. 1965. *Visible Saints: The History of a Puritan Idea.* Ithaca: Cornell Univ. Press.

Morrison, Kenneth M. 1974. "'That Art of Coyning Christians': John Eliot and the Praying Indians of Massachusetts." *Ethnohistory*, 21: 77-92.

_____. 1979. "Towards a History of Intimate Encounters: Algonkian Folklore, Jesuit Missionaries, and Kiwakwe, The Cannibal Giant." *American Indian Culture and Research Journal*, 3: 51-80.

_____. 1981. "The Mythological Sources of Abenaki Catholicism: A Case Study of the Social History of Power." *Religion*, 11: 235-63.

_____. 1984. *The Embattled Northeast: The Elusive Ideal of Alliance in Abenaki-Euramerican Relations.* Berkeley: University of California Press.

_____. 1985. "Discourse and the Accommodation of Values: Toward a Revision of Mission History." *Journal of the American Academy of Religion*, 53: 365-82.

_____. 1986. "Montagnais Missionization in Early New France: The Syncretic Imperative." *American Indian Culture and Research Journal*, 10: 1-23.

_____. 1990. "Baptism and Alliance. The Symbolic Meditations of Religious Syncretism." *Ethnohistory*, 37: 416-37.

Murray, David. 1999. "Spreading the Word: missionaries, conversion and circulation in the northeast." In Nicholas Griffiths and Fernando Cervantes (eds.). *Spiritual Encounters. Interactions between Christianity and Native Religions in Colonial America*, 43-64. Lincoln: University of Nebraska Press, and Birmingham: University of Birmingham Press.

Musgrave-Portilla, L. Marie. 1982. "The Nahualli or Transforming Wizard in Pre- and Post-conquest Mesoamerica." *Journal of Latin American Lore*, 8: 3-62.

Naeher, Robert James. "Dialogue in the Wilderness: John Eliot and the Indian Exploration of Puritanism as a Source of Meaning, Comfort and Ethnic Survival." *New England Quarterly*, 62 (1989): 346-68.

Necker, Louis. 1979. *Indiens Guarani et chamanes franciscains: les premieres reductions du Paraguay (1580-1800).* Paris: editions anthropos.

Neill, Stephen et. al. (eds.). 1971. *Concise Dictionary of the Christian World Mission.* London: United Society for Christian Literature.

Nutini, Hugo G. 1988. *Todos Santos in Rural Tlaxcala: a Syncretic, Expressive, and Symbolic Analysis of the Cult of the Dead.* Princeton: Princeton University Press.

Nutini, Hugo G. and Bell, Betty. 1980. *Ritual Kinship in Rural Tlaxcala.* Princeton: Princeton University Press.

O'Brien, Jean M. 1989. "The Praying Indians of Natick, Massachusetts, 1650-1677: The Dynamics of Cultural Survival." In D.L. Fixico (ed.) *Native Views of Indian-White Historical Relations,* 39-53. Chicago: Newberry Library.

O'Neill, Sean. 1989. "French Jesuits' Motives for Baptizing Indians on the Frontier of New France." *Mid-America,* 71: 123-36.

Ortega Noriega, Sergio (coord.). 1996. *Historia General de Sonora: De la Conquista al Estado Libre y Soberano de Sonora.* Vol. 2, *Gobierno del Estado de Sonora.* 2nd ed. Hermosillo: Gobierno del estado de Sonora.

Ortiz de Montellano, Bernard. 1989. "Mesoamerican Religious Tradition and Medicine." In Lawrence E. Sullivan (ed.) *Healing and Restoring: Health and Medicine in the World's Religious Traditions,* 359-394. New York: Macmillan.

Osorio Romero, I. 1990. *La enseñanza del latin a los indios.* Mexico.

Padden, R. C. 1967. *The Hummingbird and the Hawk.* Columbus, Ohio: Ohio State Univ. Press.

Parkman Francis. 1997. *The Jesuits in North America in the Seventeenth Century.* Lincoln: University of Nebraska Press.

Pita Moreda, María Teresa. 1991. *Los Predicadores novohispanos del siglo xvi.* Salamanca: Editorial San Esteban.

Platt, Tristan. 1987. "The Andean soldiers of Christ: Confraternity Organization, The Mass of the Sun and Regenerative Warfare in rural Potosí (18th-20th Centuries)." *Journal de la Société des Américanistes,* 73: 139-92.

Polzer, Charles W. 1976. *Rules and Precepts of Jesuit Missions of Northwestern New Spain.* Arizona: University of Arizona Press.

Pomedli, Michael. 1987. "Beyond Unbelief: Early Jesuit Interpretations of Native Religions." *Studies in Religion*, 16: 275-87.

Poole, Stafford. 1995. *Our Lady of Guadalupe : the Origins and Sources of a Mexican National Symbol, 1531-1797*. Tucson: University of Arizona Press.

Powell, Philip Wayne. 1991. "Franciscans on the Silver Frontier of Old Mexico." In T. E. Sheridan et. al.(eds.). *Franciscan Missions of Northern Mexico, Spanish Borderlands*, 295-310. Sourcebooks 20. New York and London: Garland.

Pupo-Walker, Enrique. 1987. "Los naufragios de Alvar Nuñez Cabeza de Vaca: Notas sobre la relevancia antropológica del texto." *Revista de Indias*, 47: 755-776.

Quinn, David B. 1988. *Essays on the History of North American Discovery and Exploration*. Arlington: University of Texas.

Radding, Cynthia.1999. "Cultural boundaries between adaptation and defiance: the mission communities of northwestern New Spain." In Nicholas Griffiths and Fernando Cervantes (eds.). *Spiritual Encounters. Interactions between Christianity and Native Religions in Colonial America*, 116-35. Lincoln: University of Nebraska Press, and Birmingham: University of Birmingham Press.

Radin, Paul. 1972. *The Trickster: A Study in American Indian Mythology*. New York: Philosophical Library.

Rafael, Vicente L. 1988. *Contracting Colonialism: Translation and Christian Conversion in Tagalog Society under Early Spanish Rule*. Ithaca: Cornell University Press.

Reff, Daniel T. 1992. "Contact Shock in Northwestern New Spain, 1518-1764." In John W. Verano and D. H. Ubelaker (eds.). *Disease and Demography in the Americas*, 265-76. Washington D.C.: Smithsonian Institution Press.

_____. 1995. "The 'Predicament of Culture' and Spanish Missionary Accounts of the Tepehuan and Pueblo Revolts." *Ethnohistory*, 42(1): 63-90.

_____. 1998. "The Jesuit Mission Frontier in Comparative Perspective: The Reductions of the Río de la Plata and the Missions of Northwestern Mexico, 1588-1700." In Donna J.

Guy and Thomas E. Sheridan (eds.). *Contested Ground: Comparative Frontiers on the Northern and Southern Edges of the Spanish Empire*, 16-31. Tucson: University of Arizona Press.

Restall, Matthew. 1997. *The Maya World: Yucatec Culture and Society 1550-1850.* Stanford: Stanford University Press.

Ricard, Robert. 1966. *The Spiritual Conquest of Mexico. An Essay on the Apostolate and the Evangelizing Methods of the Mendicant Orders in New Spain: 1523-1572.* Translated by Lesley Byrd Simpson. Berkeley and Los Angeles: University of California Press.

Richter, Daniel K. 1985. "Iroquois versus Iroquois: Jesuit missions and Christianity in village politics 1642-1686." *Ethnohistory*, 32: 1-16.

_____. 1988. "Cultural Brokers and Intercultural Politics: New York-Iroquois Relations, 1664-1701." *Journal of American History*, 75: 40-67.

_____. 1992. *The Ordeal of the Longhouse: The Peoples of the Iroquois League in the Era of European Colonization.* Chapel Hill: University of North Carolina Press.

Ronda, James P. 1972. "The European Indian: Jesuit Civilization Planning in New France." *Church History*, 41: 385-95.

_____. 1977. "'We are Well as We are': An Indian Critique of Seventeenth-Century Christian Missions." *William and Mary Quarterly*, 3rd series 34: 66-82.

_____. 1979. "The Sillery Experiment: A Jesuit-Indian Village in New France, 1637-1663." *American Indian Culture and Research Journal*, 3: 1-18.

_____. 1981. "Generations of Faith: The Christian Indians of Martha's Vineyard." *William and Mary Quarterly*, 3rd series 38: 369-94.

_____. 1988. "Black Robes and Boston Men: Indian-White Relations in New France and New England, 1524-1701." In Philip Weeks (ed.). *The American Indian Experience: A Profile 1524 to the Present*, 3-34. Arlington Heights, Illinois: Forum Press Inc..

_____. 1996. *Revealing America: Image and Imagination in the Exploration of North America.* Lexington, Mass: Heath.

Rooy, Sidney H. 1965. *The Theology of Missions in the Puritan Tradition.* Delft: Meinema N.V.

Ross, Andrew C. 1994. *A Vision Betrayed: The Jesuits in Japan and China 1542-1742.* Edinburgh: Edinburgh University Press.

Saignes, Thierry. 1999. "The Colonial Condition in the Quechua-Aymara Heartland (1570-1780)." *Cambridge History of Native Peoples of the Americas.* Vol III *South America,* Part 2, 59-137. Frank Salomon and Stuart Schwartz (eds.). Cambridge: CUP.

Salisbury, Neal. 1974. "Red Puritans: The 'Praying Indians' of Massachusetts Bay and John Eliot." *William and Mary Quarterly,* 3rd series 31: 27-54.

_____. 1975. "Prospero in New England: The Puritan Missionary as Colonist." In William Cowan (ed.). *Papers of the Sixth Algonquian Conference,* 253-73. Ottawa: National Museum of Canada.

_____. 1982. *Manitou and Providence: Indians, Europeans and the Making of New England 1500-1643.* New York and Oxford: OUP.

_____. 1992. "Religious Encounters in a Colonial Context: New England and New France in the Seventeenth Century." *American Indian Quarterly,* 18: 501-09.

Salles-Reese, Veronica. 1992. "Apostles' Footprints in Ancient Peru: the Christian Appropriation of Andean Myths." *Journal of Hispanic Philology,* 16: 185-93.

_____. 1997. *From Viracocha to the Virgin of Copacabana: Representation of the Sacred at Lake Titicaca.* Austin: University of Texas Press.

Sallnow, Michael J. 1987. *Pilgrims of the Andes: Regional Cults in Cusco.* Washington D.C.: Smithsonian Institution Press.

_____. 1991. "Pilgrimage and cultural fracture in the Andes." In John Eade and Michael J. Sallnow (eds.). *Contesting the Sacred: the Anthropology of Christian Pilgrimage,* 137-53. Routledge: London and New York.

Salomon, Frank. 1992. *Nightmare Victory: The Meanings of Conversion among Peruvian Indians (Huarochirí, 1608?).*

Dept. of Spanish and Portuguese, University of Maryland 1992
Lecture Series, Working Papers No. 7.

Sanneh, Lamin. 1989. *Translating the message: the missionary impact on culture.* Maryknoll, N.Y.: Orbis.

Shea, John Gilmary (ed.). 1860. *A French-Onondaga Dictionary.* Vol. 1. New York: Library of American Linguistics.

Shuffelton, Frank. 1976. "Indian Devils and Pilgrim Fathers: Squanto, Hobomok, and the English Conception of Indian Religion." *New England Quarterly,* 49: 108-16.

Simmons, William S. 1976. "Southern New England Shamanism: An Ethnographic Reconstruction." In William Cowan (ed.). *Papers of the Seventh Algonquian Conference 1975,* 218-55. Ottawa: Carleton University.

_____. 1979. "Conversion from Indian to Puritan." *New England Quarterly,* 52: 197-218.

_____. 1981. "Cultural Bias in the New England Puritans' Perception of Indians." *William and Mary Quarterly,* 3rd series 38: 56-72.

_____. 1983. "Red Yankees: Narragansett Conversion in the Great Awakening." *American Ethnologist,* 10: 253-71.

_____. 1992. "Of Large Things Remembered: Southern New England Indian Legends of Colonial Encounters." In Anne Elizabeth Yentsch and Mary C. Beaudry (eds.). *The Art and Mystery of Historical Archaeology: Essays in Honour of James Deetz,* 317-29. Boca Raton: CRC Press.

Smith, Dwight L. 1988. "Mutual Dependency and Mutual Distrust: Indian-White Relations in British America 1701-1763." In Philip Weeks (ed.). *The American Indian Experience: A Profile 1524 to the Present,* 49-65. Arlington Heights, Illinois: Forum Press Inc..

Snow, Dean R., and Lanphear, Kim M. 1988. "European Contact and Indian Depopulation in the Northeast: The Timing of the First Epidemics." *Ethnohistory,* 35: 15-33.

Spalding, Karen. 1999. "The Crises and Transformations of Invaded Societies: Andean Area (1500-1580)." *Cambridge History of Native Peoples of the Americas.* Vol III *South America,* Part 1, 904-72. Frank Salomon and Stuart Schwartz (eds.). Cambridge: CUP.

Speck, Frank G. 1919. "Penobscot Shamanism." *Memoirs of the American Anthropological Association,* 6: 239-88.

Spicer, Edward H. 1961. *Perspectives in American Indian Culture Change.* Chicago: Univ. of Chicago Press.

_____. 1980. *The Yaquis: A Cultural History.* Tucson: University of Arizona Press.

Spores, Ronald. 1984. *The Mixtecs in ancient and colonial times.* Norman: University of Oklahoma Press.

Stern, Steve J. 1982. *Peru's Indian Peoples and the Challenge of Spanish Conquest: Huamanga to 1640.* Madison: University of Wisconsin Press.

Stineback, David C. 1978. "The Status of Puritan-Indian Scholarship." *New England Quarterly,* 51: 80-90.

Sweet, David. 1995. "The Ibero-American Frontier Mission in Native American History." In Erick Langer and Robert H. Jackson (eds.). *The New Latin American Mission History,* 1-48. Lincoln and London: University of Nebraska Press.

Taylor, William B. 1987. "The Virgin of Guadalupe in New Spain: an Inquiry into the Social History of Marian Devotion." *American Ethnologist,* 14: 9-33.

_____. 1994. "Colonial Religion and Quincentennial Metaphors: Mexican Santiagos and Cristos de Caña." In Robert C. Dash (ed.). *Mesoamerican and Chicano Art, Culture and Identity,* 27-49. Williamette Journal of the Liberal Arts, Supplemental Series 6.

_____. 1996. *Magistrates of the Sacred: Priests and Parishioners in Eighteenth-Century Mexico.* Stanford: Stanford University Press.

Terraciano, Kevin. 1998. "Native Expressions of Piety in Mixtec Testaments." In Susan Kellogg and Matthew Restal (eds.). *Dead Giveaways: Indigenous Testaments of Colonial Mesoamerica and the Andes,* 115-40. Salt Lake City: University of Utah Press.

_____. 2001. *The Mixtecs of Colonial Oaxaca: Ñudzahui History, Sixteenth through Eighteenth Centuries,* Stanford Univ. Press: Stanford.

Thornton, Russell. 1987. *American Indian Holocaust and Survival: A Population History Since 1492.* Norman and London: University of Oklahoma Press.

Tooker, Elisabeth (ed.). 1979. *Native North American Spirituality of the Eastern Woodlands: Sacred Myths, Dreams, Visions, Speeches, Healing Formulas, Rituals and Ceremonials.* London: SPCK.

Trexler, Richard C. 1982. "From the Mouths of Babes: Christianization by Children in Sixteenth-Century New Spain." In J. Davis (ed.). *Religious Organization and Religious Experience,* 115-35. Association of Social Anthropologists Monograph 21. London: Academic Press.

Trigger, Bruce G. 1965. "The Jesuits and the Fur Trade." *Ethnohistory,* 12: 30-53.

_____. 1968. "The French Presence in Huronia: The Structure of Franco-Huron Relations in the First Half of the Seventeenth Century." *The Canadian Historical Review,* 49: 107-41.

_____. 1976. *The Children of Aataentsic: A History of the Huron People to 1660.* 2 vols. Montreal: McGill-Queen's University Press.

_____. (ed.) 1978. *Handbook of North American Indians* Vol. 15: *Northeast.* Washington D.C.: Smithsonian Institution.

_____. 1985. *Natives and Newcomers: Canada's "Heroic Age" Reconsidered.* Kingston and Montreal: McGill-Queen's University Press, and Manchester: Manchester University Press.

Underhill, Ruth M. 1965. *Red Man's Religion: Beliefs and Practices of the Indians North of Mexico.* Chicago: University of Chicago Press.

Vanderwood, Paul J. 1992. "'None but the Justice of God': Tomochic, 1891-1892." In Jaime E. Rodríguez O. *Patterns of Contention in Mexican History,* 227-41. Wilmington, Delaware: Scholarly Resources.

Van Lonkhuyzen, Harold W. 1990. "A Reappraisal of the Praying Indians: Acculturation, Conversion, and Identity at Natick, Mass., 1643-1732." *New England Quarterly,* 63: 396-428.

Vaughan, Alden T. 1995. *New England Frontier: Puritans and Indians 1620-75.* 3rd ed. Norman and London: University of Oklahoma Press.

Vecsey, Christopher. 1983. *Traditional Ojibwa Religion and its Historical Changes.* Philadelphia: American Philosophical Society.

_____. 1990. *Religion in Native North America.* Moscow: University of Idaho Press.

_____. 1996. *On the Padres' Trail.* Notre Dame, Ind.: Univ. of Notre Dame Press.

Verastique, Bernardino. 2000. *Michoacan and Eden: Vasco de Quiroga and the Evangelization of Western Mexico.* Austin: University of Texas Press.

Wachtel, Nathan. 1977. *The Vision of the Vanquished: The Spanish Conquest of Peru through Indian Eyes, 1530-1570.* Translated by Ben and Sian Reynolds. Hassocks: Harvester Press.

Wallace, Anthony F. C. 1956. "Revitalization Movements." *American Anthropologist,* 58: 264-81.

_____. 1958. "Dreams and the Wishes of the Soul: A Type of Psychoanalytic Theory among the Seventeenth-Century Iroquois." *American Anthropologist,* 60: 234-48.

_____. 1966. *Religion: An Anthropological View.* New York: Random House.

_____. 1970. *Death and Rebirth of the Seneca.* New York: Alfred A. Knopf.

Weber, David J. 1989. "Blood of Martyrs, Blood of Indians: Toward a More Balanced View of Spanish Missions in Seventeenth-Century North America." In David Hurst Thomas (ed.). *Columbian Consequences,* 1: 429-48. 2 vols. Washington and London: Smithsonian Institution Press.

_____. *The Spanish Frontier in North America.* 1992. New Haven and London: Yale University Press.

White, Richard. 1991. *The Middle Ground: Indians, Empires, and Republics in the Great Lakes Region 1650-1815.* Cambridge: CUP.

Williamson, Edwin. 1992. *The Penguin History of Latin America.* Harmondsworth: Penguin.

Youngs, J. William T., Jr. 1981-82. "The Indian Saints of Early New England." *Early American Literature*, 16: 241-56.

Zurcher, Erik. "Jesuit Accommodation and the Chinese Cultural Imperative." In D. E. Mungello, *The Chinese Rites Controversy: Its History and Meaning*, 31-64. Nettetal: Steyler Verlag

New English Bible OUP/CUP 1970.

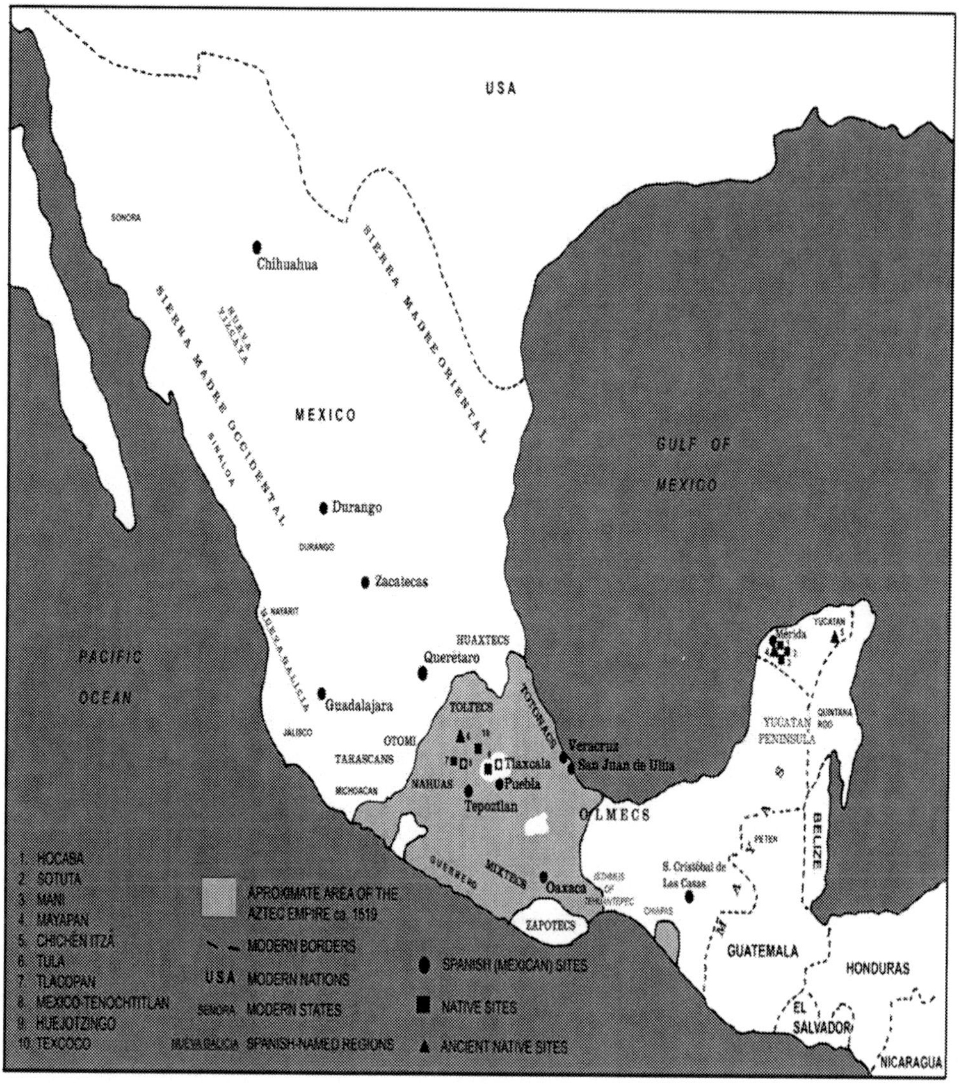
USA
GULF OF MEXICO
PACIFIC OCEAN
MEXICO
SIERRA MADRE OCCIDENTAL
SIERRA MADRE ORIENTAL
Chihuahua
Durango
Zacatecas
Queretaro
Guadalajara
HUAXTECS
TOLTECS
OTOMI
TARASCANS
NAHUAS
Tlaxcala
Puebla
Tepoztlan
Veracruz
San Juan de Ulúa
OLMECS
MIXTECS
Oaxaca
ZAPOTECS
S. Cristóbal de Las Casas
Mérida
YUCATAN PENINSULA
BELIZE
GUATEMALA
HONDURAS
EL SALVADOR
NICARAGUA
1. HOCABA
2. SOTUTA
3. MANI
4. MAYAPAN
5. CHICHÉN ITZÁ
6. TULA
7. TLACOPAN
8. MEXICO-TENOCHTITLAN
9. HUEJOTZINGO
10. TEXCOCO
APROXIMATE AREA OF THE AZTEC EMPIRE ca. 1519
MODERN BORDERS
USA MODERN NATIONS
SENORA MODERN STATES
NUEVA GALICIA SPANISH-NAMED REGIONS
SPANISH (MEXICAN) SITES
NATIVE SITES
ANCIENT NATIVE SITES

Mexico

APACHE
NAVAJO
TOWA
TIWA
Taos
TEWA
Picuris
ZUNI
NEVADA
HOPI
Santa Fe
TIWA
Pecos
Zuni
Acoma
Laguna
APACHE
TOMPIRO
Rio Grande
ARIZONA
PIRO
NEW
MEXICO
ALTA
CALIFORNIA
APACHE
APACHE
USA
El Paso
R. Pecos
GULF OF CALIFORNIA
SERI
TEXAS
PIMA ALTO
OPATA
R. Sonora
PIMA BAJO
SIERRA MADRE OCCIDENTAL
R. Conchos
Rio Grande
Chihuahua
YAQUI
BAJA CALIFORNIA
R. Yaqui
TARAHUMARA
SIERRA MADRE ORIENTAL
MAYO
R. Mayo
ZUAQUE
R. Fuerte
ACAXEE
TEPEHUAN
XIXIME
Durango
MEXICO
SPANISH SETTLEMENTS
NATIVE SETTLEMENTS
Zacatecas

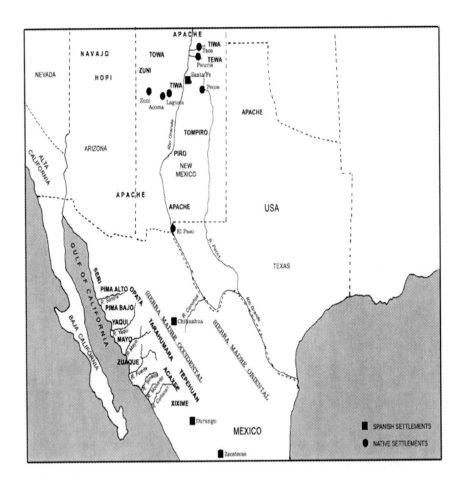

Northwest Mexico

Quito
ECUADOR
BRAZIL
CHACHAPOYAS
PERU
Huamachuco
Trujillo
HUANCAS
San
Pedro de Hacas
San Damián
Lima
Huarochirí
Pachacamac
Yauyos
INCA
Anta
Huamanga
Cusco
Lake
Titicaca
Chucuito
BOLIVIA
PACIFIC
OCEAN
Julí
Copacabana
Tiwanaku
LUPACA
Lake
Poopó
Chuquisaca/
Sucre
Potosí
MODERN COUNTRIES
INCA EMPIRE
SPANISH ORIGIN SITES
NATIVE SITES
ANCIENT NATIVE SITES
CHILE
ARGENTINA
San Miguel de
Tucumán

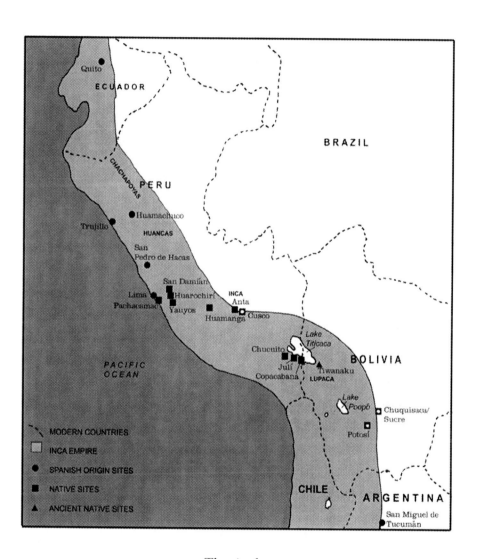

The Andes

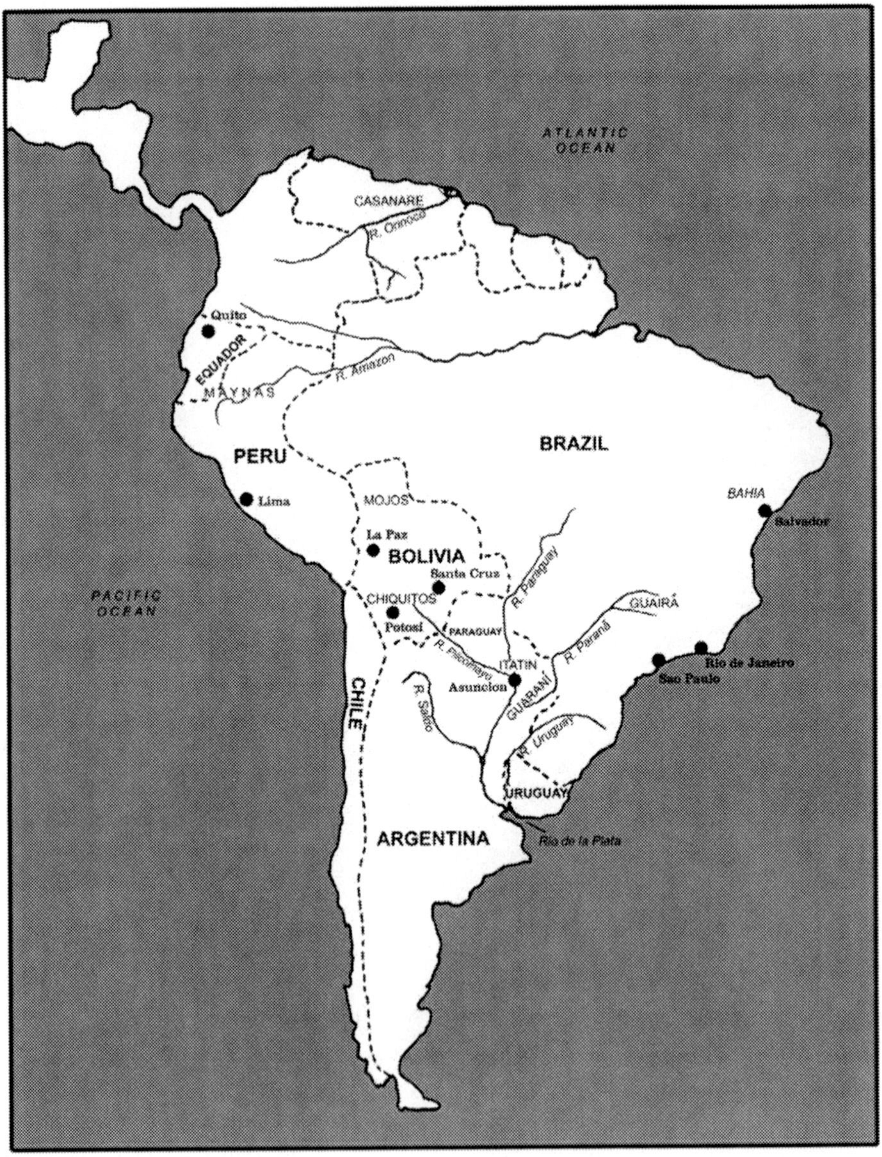
ATLANTIC OCEAN
CASANARE
R. Orinoco
Quito
EQUADOR
MAYNAS
R. Amazon
PERU
BRAZIL
Lima
MOJOS
La Paz
BOLIVIA
Santa Cruz
CHIQUITOS
Potosí
PARAGUAY
R. Paraguay
GUAIRÁ
R. Paraná
R. Pilcomayo
ITATIN
Asuncion
GUARANÍ
R. Salto
R. Uruguay
URUGUAY
Rio de la Plata
BAHIA
Salvador
Rio de Janeiro
Sao Paulo
PACIFIC OCEAN
CHILE
ARGENTINA

South America

Northeast North America

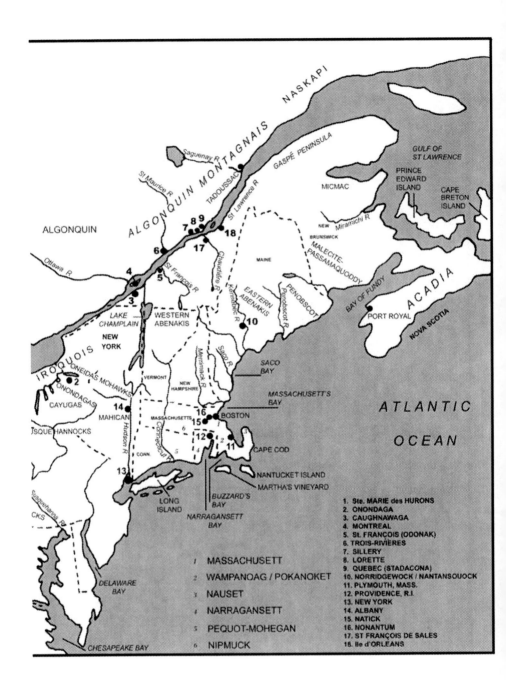

ALGONQUIN MONTAGNAIS

NASKAPI

Saguenay R.

St. Maurice R.

TADOUSSAC

St. Lawrence R.

GULF OF
ST LAWRENCE

PRINCE
EDWARD
ISLAND

CAPE
BRETON
ISLAND

MICMAC

GASPÉ PENINSULA

Miramichi R.

NEW
BRUNSWICK

MALECITE-
PASSAMAQUODDY

ALGONQUIN

Ottawa R.

7 8 9

18

6

17

4

5

St. François R.

Chaudière R.

Kennebec R.

MAINE

EASTERN
ABENAKIS

PENOBSCOT

Penobscot R.

BAY OF FUNDY

PORT ROYAL

ACADIA

NOVA SCOTIA

3

LAKE
CHAMPLAIN

WESTERN
ABENAKIS

10

NEW
YORK

SACO
BAY

Saco R.

IROQUOIS

ONEIDAS

MOHAWKS

2

ONONDAGAS

CAYUGAS

VERMONT

NEW
HAMPSHIRE

Merrimack R.

MASSACHUSETT'S
BAY

ATLANTIC

SUSQUEHANNOCKS

MAHICAN

14

MASSACHUSETTS

16

15

BOSTON

OCEAN

Hudson R.

Connecticut R.

6

12

11

2

CAPE COD

CONN.

5

3

13

NANTUCKET ISLAND

MARTHA'S VINEYARD

Susquehanna R.

CKS

LONG
ISLAND

BUZZARD'S
BAY

NARRAGANSETT
BAY

1. Ste. MARIE des HURONS
2. ONONDAGA
3. CAUGHNAWAGA
4. MONTREAL
5. St. FRANÇOIS (ODONAK)
6. TROIS-RIVIÈRES
7. SILLERY
8. LORETTE
9. QUEBEC (STADACONA)
10. NORRIDGEWOCK / NANTANSOUOCK
11. PLYMOUTH, MASS.
12. PROVIDENCE, R.I.
13. NEW YORK
14. ALBANY
15. NATICK
16. NONANTUM
17. ST FRANÇOIS DE SALES
18. Ile d'ORLEANS

DELAWARE
BAY

CHESAPEAKE BAY

1   MASSACHUSETT

2   WAMPANOAG / POKANOKET

3   NAUSET

4   NARRAGANSETT

5   PEQUOT-MOHEGAN

6   NIPMUCK

Index

Lightning Source UK Ltd.
Milton Keynes UK
26 August 2009

143102UK00001B/8/A

9 781847 531711